SO-AHD-566

Praise for Jim Sterne's *World Wide Web Marketing, Third Edition*

"Jim Sterne is one of the cleverest thinkers around. He understands the ins and outs of Internet marketing. Buy his books and listen up!"

—Seth Godin, author, *Permission Marketing*

"A classic in an industry where classics are rare. This is the most well-rounded tutorial on Web marketing ever written."

—Kristin Zhivago, Editor of *Marketing Technology,*
Columnist for *Marketing Computers,* and President
of Zhivago Marketing Partners, Inc.

"Jim Sterne has an invaluable *feel* for what works on the Web. Take his advice and avoid needless blunders."

—Christopher Locke, co-author, *The Cluetrain Manifesto,*
and author, *Gonzo Marketing: Winning Through Worst Practices*

"Web marketing can be such an intimidating mystery that many companies end up paying millions to an army of analysts. Luckily Jim Sterne has the ability to explain everything in plain language. Read this book and get enough action items to save the said millions. Your customers will be much happier than if you spent the money chasing the latest fads and buzzwords."

—Jakob Nielsen, Ph.D., author, *Designing Web
Usability: The Practice of Simplicity*

"Jim was explaining electronic customer relationship management back in 1994. Jim has stayed on target and ahead of the game."

—Patricia Seybold, author, *Customers.com*

World Wide Web Marketing

Integrating the Web into Your Marketing Strategy

Third Edition

Jim Sterne

WARNER MEMORIAL LIBRARY
EASTERN UNIVERSITY
ST. DAVIDS, 19087-3696

Wiley Computer Publishing

John Wiley & Sons, Inc.

NEW YORK · CHICHESTER · WEINHEIM · BRISBANE · SINGAPORE · TORONTO

10 - 18 - 02

HF 5415.1265 .S742 2001
Sterne, Jim, 1955-
World Wide Web marketing

Publisher: Robert Ipsen
Editor: Cary Sullivan
Developmental Editor: Christina Ber
Managing Editor: Marnie Wielage
Associate New Media Editor: Brian Snapp
Text Design & Composition: Publishers' Design and Production Services

Designations used by companies to distinguish their products are often claimed as trademarks. In all instances where John Wiley & Sons, Inc., is aware of a claim, the product names appear in initial capital or ALL CAPITAL LETTERS. Readers, however, should contact the appropriate companies for more complete information regarding trademarks and registration.

This book is printed on acid-free paper. ∞

Copyright © 2001 by Jim Sterne. All rights reserved.

Published by John Wiley & Sons, Inc.

Published simultaneously in Canada.

No part of this publication may be reproduced, stored in a retrieval system or transmitted in any form or by any means, electronic, mechanical, photocopying, recording, scanning or otherwise, except as permitted under Sections 107 or 108 of the 1976 United States Copyright Act, without either the prior written permission of the Publisher, or authorization through payment of the appropriate per-copy fee to the Copyright Clearance Center, 222 Rosewood Drive, Danvers, MA 01923, (978) 750-8400, fax (978) 750-4744. Requests to the Publisher for permission should be addressed to the Permissions Department, John Wiley & Sons, Inc., 605 Third Avenue, New York, NY 10158-0012, (212) 850-6011, fax (212) 850-6008, E-Mail: PERMREQ @ WILEY.COM.

This publication is designed to provide accurate and authoritative information in regard to the subject matter covered. It is sold with the understanding that the publisher is not engaged in professional services. If professional advice or other expert assistance is required, the services of a competent professional person should be sought.

Library of Congress Cataloging-in-Publication Data:

Sterne, Jim, 1955–
    World Wide Web marketing / Jim Sterne.—3rd ed.
        p. cm.
    "Wiley computer publishing."
    Includes index.
    ISBN 0-471-41621-5 (pbk. : alk. paper)
    1. Internet marketing. 2. World Wide Web. 3. Intenet. I. Title.

HF5415.1265.S742 2001
658.8'4—dc21   2001033011

Printed in the United States of America.

10 9 8 7 6 5 4 3 2 1

This book is dedicated to Colleen.

CONTENTS

I'd like to thank:

Alanna Coyne for her untiring assistance

Bill English of English Associates for his research skills

Derrith Lambka from Insights for Action for her willingness to share

Doug Newell at Genalytics for his ability to clearly explain complex ideas

Jakob Neilson at Useit.com for doing what he does so I don't have to

Jenn Barr and Jim Shanks from CDW for their geniality and candor

Karl Sterne, my father, for his encouragement and editorial skills

Kristin Zhivago for her insight and friendship

Matt Culter of NetGenesis for his laser-like focus and sense of humor

Mark Gibbs for his wit, intelligence, and writing flair

Mellanie Hills for her shining example

Mark Weaver for his technical skills

Sandra Schuerer at Jupiter Communications for her generosity

And those wonderful people at Southwest Airlines who refuse to accept e-mail, proving that there will be a need for consultants for some time to come.

In 1994, Jim Sterne co-founded a regional Internet access provider and produced the world's first "Marketing on the Internet" seminar series. Since then, he has been an Internet marketing strategy consultant, offering advice to Fortune 500 companies and to Web-based start-ups. He focuses on helping his clients grapple with the brave new world of online advertising, marketing, sales, and customer service, by using these new tools to best advantage.

Mr. Sterne has written three other books, *What Makes People Click: Advertising on the Web* (Que, 1997), *Customer Service on the Internet, Second Edition* (John Wiley & Sons, 2000), and *Email Marketing: Using Email to Reach Your Target Audience* (John Wiley & Sons, 2000). He has been a columnist for *CIO Magazine, Network World, Business 2.0, Customer Service Management, Inc. Technology,* and on numerous Web sites. He is an internationally recognized speaker who has earned "best of show" for a half a dozen years running at Internet World. He has been introduced to audiences in Germany as a Web-Meister and to audiences in India as a Web-Guru. While Mr. Sterne admits to being enthralled by technology, his main interest is divining how the Internet can best be used to achieve business objectives. With a special focus on Web metrics, he is dedicated to helping companies understand the possibilities and manage the realities of conducting business online.

I f you were lucky enough (or alive at the time) to get to Flushing Meadows for the 1964 World's Fair in New York as I was, then you were infused with great expectations. Nuclear power would give us electricity "too cheap to meter." We would have picturephones, daily recycled dinner plates, self-navigating cars, undersea cities, lunar cities, and our history classes would all be taught by audio-animatronic Abe Lincolns.

Needless to say, even the best prognosticators have a bit of trouble when looking too far into the future. Nobody told me to expect the World Wide Web. I had to trip over it by accident and try to make sense of FTP, Gopher, and newsreaders and become friends with that good old Unix prompt. I had to venture far and wide to find people who could speak intelligently about the possibilities because nobody had any practical experience.

I've spent all of my attention on how business can make the most of the Internet. I've watched closely since 1994 when I produced the first series of "World Wide Web Marketing" seminars across the country. I clearly remember the session in the heart of Silicon Valley. One hundred people showed up, and by their hands they disclosed that only half had e-mail addresses and only 15 had seen the World Wide Web in action. Times have changed.

We've learned a lot about the Web in the meantime, and it's changed a lot since then. That means there's a great deal that needn't be belabored. This book examines marketing on the Internet without going over old ground. In other words, I will *not* be wasting your time explaining the following ideas.

We Hold These Truths to Be Self-Evident

The Internet is growing fast with 17 gazillion more people, more Web sites, and more spam every day.

It works. It works well. It can be trusted to continue working.

The customer has assumed control of the playing field, and businesses of all kinds better listen up. We have to build and deliver what people want, rather than what we think they should want.

Customer service is a competitive-edge issue, not a cost center that should be minimized as much as possible.

We can remember everything about every customer, but it's not always valuable to do so.

People like playing with technology, but when push comes to shove, people need to talk to people to answer questions, solve problems, and just feel better about the decisions they're making.

Spam sucks.

These are the basic premises on which this book rests. If you're not sure that customer service is important, read Patricia Seybold's books (www.psgroup.com). If you doubt the veracity with which the Internet is taking over the world, spend an hour or so wandering around www.internetstats.com and www.nua.com. If you're not sure whether the customers have escaped their cages and are now running the zoo, you clearly haven't been exposed to The Clue Train Manifesto (www.cluetrain.com) (appropriate head protection and skin recommended). And, finally, if you don't understand the pain of spam (unsolicited e-mail), you are hereby ordered to reread Seth Godin's book, *Permission Marketing* (www.permission.com). What do you mean you haven't read it already?

So why a *third* edition of *World Wide Web Marketing*? Why rehash all of this all over again? Because times change, and on the Internet, they change so fast that I consider the previous two editions to be fine period pieces—something a history professor will be delighted to discover holding up an uneven conference room table in the halls of academe some years hence. They are instructive for those who want to know how we got here and what on earth we were thinking at the time.

As for the rest of us, there's a job to do.

We have to make the most out of this Internet stuff and use it to improve the bottom line. Full stop. We are no longer reveling in the wonder of a changing world. We have stopped shifting paradigms. We have moved into a world where there are a new set of tools to grease the wheels of commerce along the path of the sales cycle and the customer retention process:

Advertising. Raising awareness about our brand and our offer.

Marketing. Educating the masses on why they should buy, buy now, and buy from us.

Sales. Consummating the deal by taking their money.

Customer service. Answering questions and solving problems.

Customer retention. Using customer information to upsell, cross-sell, and keep them coming back.

The value you get out of working on Internet projects is the same as with any other project: It depends. What are your current corporate goals? Some firms will benefit more by using this new communication tool for direct sales. Others will see an immediate reduction in the cost of customer service. Still others will view the Web as an opportunity to create and sell new services altogether.

We know the major corporations are all jumping on the band wagon, but smaller firms are benefiting as well. Professor Rosabeth Moss Kanter's E-Culture project at Harvard Business School looked at 785 companies across the size spectrum and came up with a review of the most popular ways to exploit the Internet at the beginning of 2001 (see Table I.1).

Table I.1   Percentage of Companies Use Applications Online

APPLICATION	FEWER THAN 100 EMPLOYEES	100–500 EMPLOYEES	500–5,000 EMPLOYEES	MORE THAN 5,000 EMPLOYEES
Attracting new kinds of customers	41%	42%	52%	50%
Selling to traditional customers	45	43	41	50
Working with customers	38	46	54	54
Working with suppliers	38	47	50	50
Purchasing	32	40	32	43
Conducting meetings, doing work	41	47	36	32
Getting employee feedback	40	39	38	36
Training	37	36	39	36
Telecommuting	44	35	36	24
Getting news and information	43	46	69	67
Advertising	39	53	53	54
Kanter E-Culture Project at Harvard Business School				

As you can see, the Internet is a tool of diverse uses. Think of this book as your guide to the customer side of the equation.

How This Book Is Organized

I'll spend a fair amount of time in the first chapter revealing how I conduct my on-site consulting. How do you identify goals? How do you brainstorm? How do you convince the top brass that your new Web-based project is a good idea? How do you prioritize?

Chapter 2, "Customer Service First," nails down the must-dos and outlines the nice-to-haves while hinting at the knock-their-socks-off kinds of advantages you can create online. Chapters 3 and 4 explain why Web navigation and interaction are important to your customers and to your brand.

Chapter 5, "Selling Services," is for those who sell more than boxes of stuff. Chapters 6 and 7 delve into the fine art of listening to your customers in order to give them the best. Chapter 8 takes a look at the Web's most interesting capability, personalization, and Chapter 9 looks at extranets and divulges the realities of customer relationship management. Chapter 10 looks at the world of online channel conflict and online channel convergence—working with your resellers instead of against them. Having worked out all of this, you'll have put together a pretty decent Web strategy—that's when it's time to blow your horn and try to get as many people to your site as possible. That's where Chapter 11 comes in.

Chapter 12 goes into the details of E-Metrics—how do you know you're doing a good job? What do you count? How do you make it all add up? Finally, Chapter 13 looks over the political landscape of running a Web site from the business side of the picture. Running servers is one thing; running well-oiled teams is quite another.

Then, for dessert, Chapter 14 takes a gander into the old crystal ball to give you a clue about what's coming. Forewarned being fore-armed and all that.

Taken together, this book is one part philosophy, two parts strategy, and three parts feet-on-the-ground, actionable tips for Web success. This is a practical guide for those who are responsible for getting the job done.

I'll not only explain what thought leaders are up to with lots of examples, but I'll help you figure out how to come up with some of those leading thoughts yourself.

What's On the Web Site

On the companion Web site (www.wiley.com/compbooks/sterne), you'll find a complete listing of all the URL's in this book. That means you'll be able to see the examples for yourself—live. Because they are live, they are subject to change, so don't expect the pictures to match the sites as they exist today. In fact, you should keep your eyes open to the changes that have been made and determine if you think they are for the better.

The Web is a powerful new tool that lets people do the same old stuff a bit faster and a bit further afield, with the occasional surprise thrown in to keep you awake. It's true that regular companies built on blood, sweat, and profits still have a lot to learn about using this new medium for competitive advantage, but the hoopla of the last millennium is behind us. It's time to get to work.

CHAPTER 1

Using the World Wide Web for Marketing—What Are You Trying to Accomplish?

Marketing on the World Wide Web finds us stepping off the highway of 500 cable channels and into a quiet field of 500 million channels. These aren't broadcast channels. They don't spew reruns, sitcoms, and talk shows sprinkled with infomercials and 30 attention-getters. These are informative messages patiently waiting for us to interact with them.

The Web offers information to people who might be willing to reach in and pull it out. Kristin Zhivago, publisher of the *Marketing Technology* newsletter (www.zhivago.com), understood this difference and clearly illustrated it in her February 1994 issue:

> If your delivery medium was water, broadcasting would be like using a big hose to spray a crowd of prospects, hoping some of them will enjoy getting wet. Narrowcasting, a term used by producers of specialized cable TV programs, is like using a smaller hose and only aiming it at people who have already expressed an interest in getting wet. Cybercasting (marketing online) is the act of creating a pond of water in cyberspace, telling people that you now have a pond, and inviting them to come for a swim. Prospects can visit your pond anytime they want, stay as long as they want, and dive in as deeply as they want. The extent to which they immerse themselves in your pond is determined completely by their own personal interest.

Some people may come just to look around. Some may take a dip. Some may swim, and some may stay submerged for days at a time. The faster, better looking, easier to navigate, more fun, and more informative your Web site is, the more likely it is that people will want to come back—and even bring their friends. But let's get these in priority order, shall we? Here's what's crucial:

- Fast
- Interesting
- Useful

A slow Web site will work against you, and I'll dig into that subject in Chapter 3, "The Usable Web—Be Kind to Your Users." An interesting site will draw people in and keep them coming back. But a useful site really takes advantage of what the Web is best at: getting things done.

The whole point is to engage your target audience right up front and give them something of value, something that holds their attention, something they find useful, something they'll tell their friends about.

The World Wide Web allows an organization to create a library of materials anybody with an Internet connection can access. The ability to allow prospects and customers to get things done by entering data, looking things up, configuring product solutions, and so forth, means the possibilities are more restricted by the limits of imagination and available resources than by technology. Therefore, the first step toward marketing on the Web is to get a handle on realistic goals.

Each establishment, be it corporate, not-for-profit, entrepreneurial, or "other," must determine what it hopes to gain by implementing a global, electronic presence. You undoubtedly spend a great deal of time and effort on every magazine ad or direct mail project. Maintaining this level of effort is even more critical on the Web. Your message is available to millions, so special care is required to create a Web site that will elicit the desired response. Knowing what you want out of your site in the first place is the only way to ensure you might get there and have a chance at measuring your success.

Knowing the possibilities doesn't help much because there are so many:

- Improve corporate image
- Improve customer service
- Find and test new prospects
- Increase visibility and awareness
- Perform transactions
- Discover and enter new markets
- Improve customer retention
- Reduce costs

How do you best determine goal prioritization? That depends on your corporate goals, your personal goals, and your customers' goals. In order to know your goals, you need to know what's possible.

The Leading-Edge Image

In the mid-1990s, deciding between an empty storefront and a delayed storefront was a tough choice. If you took the time to build a robust Web site, your competitor might steal your thunder. Put up a site too quickly, and you take the chance your public will be disappointed by hasty efforts. News of a new, exciting, intriguing Web site traveled only slightly faster on the Internet than the latest e-mailed joke.

Today, having a site at all is a foregone conclusion. Well, almost. An article published on September 19, 2000 in *USA Today* pointed out a few laggards. "More than 99 percent of Fortune 1000 companies have corporate Web sites, setting up an awkward race for being last to the Web. The competitors: Adams Resources & Energy (1999 revenue of $4 billion), Jacobs Engineering Group ($2.9 billion), Grand Union ($2.3 billion), Stater Bros. ($1.8 billion), and Charming Shoppes ($1.2 billion)."

Not having a site whatsoever seems like trying to do business without a phone or a fax machine. Having a site that's cool and looks sharp is fine if that's all your target market is really after. The game, though, will go to those who come up with unique services. If you have to choose between fun, interesting, or useful, *useful* wins. Every time. Hands down.

In order to create the impression of being a leading-edge company, you have to create the image of a company that cares about its customers. Create the image that your company cares enough to explore new technologies and master them for the benefit of your clients. A leading-edge image also informs your clients that your company is financially strong. It is willing to take on new projects that seem merely service-related, rather than revenue-driven.

While superior service will bring superior profit, inferior service will certainly have a negative effect on the balance sheet. If your competitors have robust fax-back systems, sophisticated voice mail, and efficient Web sites and you don't, the marketplace will assume you are not profitable. You must not have enough resources to support your clients in the manner to which they have become accustomed. Or you simply don't care.

Nowadays, a leading-edge image is hard earned through the successful hosting of information and services that make life easier for customers. That means some serious investment in your Web site rather than mild experimentation funded by curiosity and spare time.

A company with a leading-edge image becomes a magnet for leading-edge employees. Don't forget to post your job openings on your Web site to attract talented staff members. It may seem that this task belongs more to the human resources department than the marketing department, but job postings give your prospects the impression of a vital, growing, successful organization.

When all is said and done, the only sure-fire way to create a leading-edge image is to create new services that weren't possible in 1993 (the Pre-Mosaic Era). More on this—a lot more—in Chapter 4, "Interactivity Goes with the Flow."

Prospect Qualification

It is possible to make a profit through all selling and no marketing. It is possible to make a profit through all marketing and no selling. A salesperson can walk door to door with a case of samples and sell them without spending a dime on marketing. A pizza company can bake and deliver truckloads of pizzas through ads in newspapers, the Yellow Pages, and direct mail without any salespeople. Most businesses, though, fit between these two extremes and will greatly benefit from a site designed to lead the prospect through the persuasion process.

The cost of an hour of a salesperson's time differs for each firm and for each product. Without a doubt, a major part of the marketing function is to find the largest number of the most qualified buyers, so it falls to the marketing department to keep the salesperson selling instead of prospecting. For a company involved in the sale of a sophisticated product with a long lead time, the most attractive goal of an Internet Web site is to shorten the sales cycle. A prospect may require a good deal of education before understanding and appreciating the product and making a reasonable buying decision. If so, the World Wide Web is a wonderful place for promotion.

Photographs, technical detail, and the answers to the most frequently asked questions are all available at any time of day or night. Every time somebody understands the electronic answer to a pressing question, he or she has saved your salesperson cumulative minutes of telephone time and who knows how much time tracking down the answer. As a result, the salesperson spends more time with prospects toward the end of the sale's cycle, instead of at the beginning, in the education phase.

Because the Web site has become the electronic prospect qualifier and tutor, your salespeople can concentrate on making more sales.

Product Sales

Technical companies were successfully using the Internet for marketing long before the World Wide Web arrived. Their fax-back systems, Gopher sites, and file transfer protocol (FTP) sites were information vending machines. If information is made available, people will fetch it as long as it has value. Depending on the product, the results can be surprising.

Your Web site might be able to close the deal without the help of a salesperson. Your Web site might allow prospects to select colors, styles, configurations, shipping methods, and payment terms. Your system can then print pick lists, shipping labels, and invoices without human intervention.

InterCon Systems Corporation in Herndon, Virginia, made networking software for Macintosh and Windows platforms. Granted, it had a built-in audience on the Internet, but its experience is still interesting. Several years ago, Jeff Osborn, then vice president of sales at InterCon, decided to try putting up an FTP server. He populated the directories with descriptive documents and trial versions of InterCon's software. The software would run for 30 days and then quit unless the keycode was provided via e-mail.

Jeff set the system up on a Friday afternoon and went home for the weekend. He accessed his server several times over the next two days to test it and to marvel in the ability to publish his promotional materials worldwide. On Monday he checked the logs to make sure his transactions were recorded. He discovered that 500 people had logged onto this unannounced, unpublicized machine and had taken a look at the software.

Two weeks later, InterCon received a wire transfer from the Republic of Kazakhstan for more than $10,000 for software that had been downloaded via FTP. InterCon e-mailed the customer the 20-digit code to unlock the software. Jeff still laughs at how they might try to calculate the cost of goods sold.

Customer Service

One of the best uses for a new communications medium is customer contact. The customer service department should always be the first to receive new methods of information exchange. The telephone, the telex, the fax, and voice mail all began as curiosities, then found their way into more and more companies. Before long, they became a requirement for helping and keeping customers. The World Wide Web belongs on this list as well.

Customer service desks and help desks have already discovered the value of the database. With telephone headset in place and hands on the keyboard, the freshest recruit can provide the most detailed explanation and answer the toughest question. The bottleneck has been information delivery. The World Wide Web offers a method that is faster and more direct than fax-back. This meaty subject is covered in more detail in the next chapter, "Customer Service First."

Customer Interaction and Feedback

Web sites can contain forms to fill out, including long text blocks for lengthy comments. In this way, they are like e-mail. A Web site can also contain areas where visitors can post comments to be read by all. In this way, they share attributes with newsgroups. Web sites can include questions that can be answered with a click of the mouse. In this way, they are like surveys.

Online, interactive communication with your customers and prospects allows more direct feedback than ever. Each phase of product development, positioning, and promotion can include the most intelligent, experienced, and expert resource on earth—your customers. They become part of your team. That's what Chapter 6, "Feedback," is all about.

Internal Communications

The marketing task is not directed entirely outward. A great deal of time is spent communicating within the walls of a corporation. Getting everybody to understand product positioning or corporate vision can be daunting. Keeping the sales force aware of product line changes and pricing updates is a monumental task. Just as the Web offers better communications to prospects and customers, it can offer better communications internally. Every data capture event, every report, every scheduling task can be managed with an intranet.

There are many good books on creating intranets for your company; this one is about marketing. It's worth a moment, though, to think about how an intranet can benefit the marketing department. If you're not using Web services inside your company for internal communications, your competitor is about to eat your lunch.

Web Site Traffic as Its Own Reward

The billboard philosophy tells us to place our names in front of people as often as possible. The more product impressions people see, the more likely they are to remember, trust, and buy the product. Some Web sites are designed with foot traffic in mind. Internet shopping malls and periodical e-zines (electronic magazines) are trying to sell advertising space based on the number of people who visit their sites.

Causing people to make a habit of visiting a particular Web site is a unique challenge. If your purpose for a public Web site is to disseminate technical information, the number of new visitors may not be important. If your goal is a high degree of awareness and a change in your branding, you can use techniques that encourage repeat visits. Or you can simply buy ad space or sponsorship at other sites.

But we'll assume that your goal is to find new prospects, turn them into customers, and keep them buying from you for as long as you have products and services to sell and they have the means to buy. This brings us to the single, most important question to ask when determining what your highest Web site development priorities should be: What do your *customers* want?

What Do Customers Want?

If this question seems like an afterthought, you need to get out of the 1950s and join the rest of the world. After World War II, the United States was deep into the production era. It all started back in the 1920s when Henry Ford hit on this wild idea of the assembly line.

Instead of having craftsmen working all over the place, he brought together all the people and materials in one location and got them working sequentially. Cars came rolling off the line and onto waiting trains that carried them all over the country. The philosophy was this: Build things cheaper and faster and get them out there and people will buy them.

It's not like that any more. People discovered mass-customization and started wanting to have things custom made to their specifications. "Have it your way at Burger King" was not a blast of brilliance by a burger boss; it was the recognition that people were becoming more and more demanding. In modern times, this means moving from asking customers for their opinion to making their ideas a central part of your planning process. How do you do that? First, figure out who the audience is.

Who Comes to Your Site?

Make a list of all the different kinds of people who come to your site, focusing on the noncustomers to start with. Here's a sample list:

- Press
- Students
- Investors
- Potential employees
- Potential vendors
- Marketing partners
- Channel sales partners

Clearly, they are all looking for something different. The media want the history and the background and the texture of the company. They want the anecdotes and the personalities. More about that in Chapter 11, "Attracting Attention."

Students are looking for the big picture, the trends, the technologies, and the shifts in the marketplace on which they can hang a thesis. Investors want the financials and the assurances. Potential employees want to know about corporate culture and job opportunities. Vendors want to know what you sell to determine if you're a prospect for their goods and services. Marketing partners and channel partners want the latest marketing materials and product information. Everybody's after something different. Catering to them pays off. They're going to pester you for information anyway, so you might as well put it online and make it easier on them and on yourself.

Then it's time to see what you have in the way of customers. In the next chapter, I'll get into the customer life cycle and the lifetime value of a customer. For now, let's look at the different shapes and sizes customers come in.

What's My Line?

Chances are excellent that you sell to more than one vertical industry. Thermedics, Inc. (www.thermedicsinc.com) sells plastic tubing to the medical world, the industrial world, and the world of optical applications (see Figure 1.1).

The medical visitors can learn about Thermedics' plastics in terms of biostability, reaction to radiation sterilization, and solubility in organic solvents. Visitors from the industrial side of the fence learn about stone guard applications for automotive use,

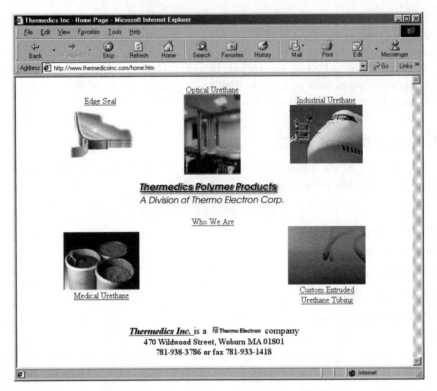

Figure 1.1 Thermedics describes the same products in different ways to different industries.

computer privacy screens, leading-edge protection for aircraft wings and rotor blades, breathable fabrics, and UV resistant fabric coatings (air blimps, protective coverings for aircraft, etc.).

Those interested in the optical uses of these products discover that they "are designed to adhere to dissimilar materials such as glass, polycarbonate, acrylic, and CAB (Cellulose Acetate Butyrate). These laminating films can be used for Architectural or Transportational Glazings. Architectural resins can be formulated to resist repeated physical attacks, bullets, and explosive blasts. These products are widely used in prisons, jails, mental hospitals, and service station kiosks, banks, and ATM machines. Transportation applications are armored vehicles, limousines, money transports, and military vehicles."

You may be selling the same product, but you're selling it into different markets, and those markets are inspired by different features and benefits.

Role Playing

It seems obvious that people who do different jobs would have different interests when it comes to your products and services. The person who uses the product will be motivated by ease of use or size and shape. The person with her finger on the figures is interested in financing or return on investment. The company buyer is more interested in availability. The logistics coordinator wants to know how many are shipped at once, what size tractor-trailer will fit which loading dock, and whether you can drop-ship them to their clients.

National Semiconductor (www.national.com) asked its customers what they wanted on the site, and the answer was pretty much what it expected. Electronics design engineers wanted every single specification about every single component National offers. The company was more than happy to replace its Manhattan-phonebook-sized catalog with no-charge-to-ship Web pages.

But Phil Gibson, the change agent responsible for National's Web efforts, saw that the company was leaving out a big chunk of its customers. Buyers have one job and one job only: Get the stuff the engineers want, when they want it, at the best price possible. They don't care about speeds, feeds, sizes, temperature, or form-factors. Price and availability are all they have on their minds.

Price information crosses over multiple organizations. If a buyer has an approved requisition on her desk for a large number of parts, she wants to be able to comparison shop. The parts are identified by a very specific National Semiconductor part number, but the price and availability might change from distributor to distributor. The solution? Access.

National's My Bill of Materials (see Figure 1.2) lets buyers look at the inventory levels of 50 distributors and source the buy. Some distributors have enough stock; others do not. The price may be higher at the distributor in Taiwan, but because the customer factory is in Malaysia, the difference in shipping is significant. The time and money it saves the purchase agent are remarkable.

Although it's fairly easy to identify who does what based on their job titles, it is not easy to determine who influences a corporate decision. If you're selling directly to consumers, the story is really only a little different. In the business world, salespeople all over have been trained in the mysteries of *Strategic Selling: The Unique Sales System Proven Successful by America's Best Companies* by Robert B. Miller, Stephen E. Heiman, and Tad Tuleja (Warner Books, 1998).

Strategic Selling identified four kinds of people involved in the buying process: economic, user, technical, and advocate. The economic influencer is looking for the ROI and the best deal. The user wants to make sure the purchase is going to actually help him or her reach his or her goals, rather than inflict more overhead that will stifle productivity. The technical buyer is there to try and find the unspoken limitations before the product reaches the door and causes more trouble than it's worth. Finally, the advocate has been presold on the idea and is the salesperson's best ally in the struggle to make the sale.

Strategic Selling walks through how to deal with each of these individuals. It will be well worth your while to read this cornerstone of American selling and think about what sort of information might appeal to which sort of influencer in your marketplace—even if the economic influencer is Mom, the advocate is Dad, the technical side is represented by the teenage son, and the user is the grade-school daughter.

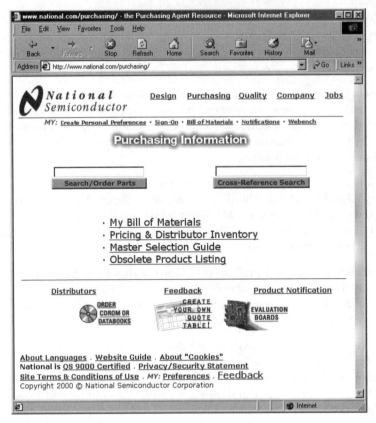

Figure 1.2 National Semiconductor created the Purchasing Web section to cater to purchasing agents. Smart.

Size Matters

Chances are excellent that you sell into businesses of various sizes. Companies pulling in less than $10 million per year make decisions differently from those raking in billions. It's not necessarily easier for one over the other; they just have different concerns.

So now we have a growing matrix of customer classifications. If you add them all up, you might find hundreds of possible combinations. Technical influencers in the medical industry who work for small companies are going to be swayed by different types of persuasion on your site than administrative assistants working for large industrial corporations.

Identifying all of them is not the aim of this exercise. You're trying to identify those who are the most likely to buy. The only way you can determine that is to find those with attributes most like your current customers. Stop for a moment and make a list of the three to five most important business sectors, the two or three most important influencers, and the size of company most likely to become a customer. For each cross-section you come up with, it's time to figure out what motivates them.

Figuring Out What Customers Want

Check out your competitors' sites. Read the trade magazines in your industry. Talk to your customers directly. What might each group want from you?

When you have some real, live feedback from your actual marketplace, it's time to put on your thinking cap and see what else you can invent. Brainstorming is the most fun I have in my consulting practice. I do it for companies large and small and enjoy doing it on the fly at conferences.

I was recently at an eMarketing conference and sat in on a Q&A session with Patricia Seybold after she had given one of the keynote presentations in her usual informative and example-filled style. The marketing manager from a natural gas company asked for help understanding the results of a promotional program on his site. With the intention of making the site sticky (getting people to stick around longer) and getting them to come back more often, they instigated a "frequent-clicker" program. The more articles you read, the more pages you viewed, and the more times you came back, the more points you could earn. The points were redeemable for tee-shirts, hats, golf balls, you name it, with the company logo on them. Fiasco. He asked Patricia and the collected discussion group why it had failed so miserably.

"Why would I want a baseball cap with your logo on it?" came the first question from the assembly.

"Well," he defended himself, "it's working for Pepsi."

"Yeah, but Pepsi is a brand that says I'm part of the hip, younger generation. I'm associating with the brand and borrowing brand attributes for myself. What will my friends think of me if I proudly put a gas company logo on my head? No thanks."

"So what would be the right thing for my site?"

Patricia asked the zinger, "What does a gas company customer want from the gas company?"

The answers came quickly and stopped coming just as fast, "Lower bills." "Service if there's a problem." That was it. A room full of natural gas users couldn't think of anything else they might want. And then it was time to brainstorm:

- An energy audit of my small business to save me money
- Discounts on products and services that'll improve my insulation
- Emergency numbers to call and a manned chat session to click on if I smell gas
- A calculator that shows the impact of an annual level-payment plan
- A calculator that shows the cost savings of a gas stove over an electric stove
- A directory of local plumbers who are certified by the gas company

Lower my bills. Help me out in an emergency. Keep your hats to yourself.

For each of the cross-sections of buyers on your list, there will be things they want, things they need, and things that you can give them to help them get the job done. This last one is an important idea and worth thinking about for a moment.

The old saw says that nobody wants a ¼-inch drill bit, they want a ¼-inch hole. That's good as far as it goes, but it doesn't go far enough. Nobody really wants a ¼-inch hole; they want a chair or a dresser or a new shelf. When figuring out what customers want, first figure out what they are trying to accomplish. Are they building a dog house? Are they implementing a new database? Are they looking for a prime location for a seminar?

Once you have a firm picture in your mind of a particular type of customer with a typical set of goals to accomplish, then you can really start dreaming up and researching what would help those customers be successful.

Talk to your customers and find out who they are and what they want. We'll take a closer look at how in Chapter 6, "Feedback." For now, it's time to turn up the juice on how you can help your customers reach *their* goals.

How Innovative Can You Be?

The most valuable virtues of the Internet are the most important to keep in mind at this stage. They are the qualities you are going to bend to your will. They revolve around the ability to communicate. They deal with the ability to make information available to people around the globe at any time of day or night. They are wrapped up in the fact that there is a computer on either end and customers and prospective customers can access your database of aggregate information, or run a program you've written especially for them, or engage in asynchronous conversations with like-minded people without cost.

This is where a good brainstorming session can put you on the map as a leader in your industry and a formidable competitor. This is where you foster the ideas that will earn you public attention, critical acclaim, and loyal customers. There's only one drawback—you can't do it all. You have to prioritize.

What Your Budget Allows

Even if you did have more money than Bill Gates, Larry Ellison, and the Sultan of Brunei combined, there aren't enough hours in the day to accomplish all the great things you'll come up with in the focused brainstorming session. You have to choose. Fortunately, this isn't nearly as hard as it seems. Just ask yourself (and a team of your most creative people) the following questions:

- Which of your ideas are the easiest to implement?
- Which are the least expensive to implement?
- Which will most efficiently take you in the direction you want to go in the long run?
- Which will provide the most value to your customers?

Time to head back to the white board and make a handful of snap decisions on each of these questions for each of the ideas you've spawned. Lay out a grid like the one in Table 1.1.

Then quickly assign a value from 1 to 5 for each attribute of each idea. On a scale of 1 to 5, how much time will it take? Will it take a lot of time? Give it a 5. Will it be pretty easy? Give it a 1. Expensive? 5. Cheap? 1. Add the values up, and the results will be your priority order. The one with the lowest scores are always the winners, right?

Table 1.1   Prioritizing Your Brightest Web Ideas

	EASY	CHEAP	DIRECTION	VALUE TO CUSTOMER
Idea One				
Idea Two				
Idea Three				
Etc. . . .				
Totals				

Almost.

You have one more critical element to consider before you green-light any of these wonderful projects.

What Your Management Wants

What do the executives with their hands on the corporate wallet want?

Corporate goals change from time to time so it's important to scope out the current direction in which your chief executives are headed. Are they out to open new territories? Cut costs? Beat the competition?

Read over the speeches they've recently given in public, and then look over the internal memos they've penned and the pronouncements they've made inside the company. Yes, they'll be slightly contradictory, but your purpose is to select those projects that move the company toward those internal objectives *and* allow the CEO to point to your project to the outside world as proof that the firm is living up to previously made public promises.

Before creating the killer PowerPoint presentation that proves to upper management you have measurable metrics in mind to prove the return on investment, you have one last task ahead of you. Verify your brainy ideas with your customers. Remember them?

Yes, you went to them at the beginning of this process, but now that you've proven your astonishing powers of creativity by concocting more than a few brilliant ideas, you really should go find out if your customers think you're as brilliant as you and your mother do. *Then* it's time to go to the executive board, not just with killer PowerPoint slides and ROI calculations, but with a big thumbs-up from your best customers.

Go out into the world with a video camera, and come back to the boardroom with actual customers in their native habitats telling the budget-masters what customers really want for Christmas. There's nothing like hearing something from the horse's mouth. When the desire for a new Web service or better online information comes directly from customers, top executives will try to take credit for the idea. Let them—it's one sure way of getting project funding.

So what do customers want? First and foremost, better customer service. Think customer service, think Chapter 2 . . .

Customer Service First

Although I've written two editions of *Customer Service on the Internet* (John Wiley & Sons, 1996 and 2000) since *World Wide Web Marketing* was first published in 1995, this chapter is very important to marketers for three reasons:

- A customer in the hand is worth between 5 and 10 in the bush.
- Great customer service might just be the most important competitive edge in the coming years.
- Customer services are the last factor in calculating the profitability of a customer.

Customers Are Where the Money Is

How much more does it cost to find a new customer than to sell to an existing one? That depends on whom you listen to. Common figures range from 5 to 10 times more. That means you can spend $10 finding a new customer or spend $10 to sell something to 10 customers. It doesn't take a mental giant, or an HP 19bii business calculator, to figure this out.

Yet most of the sales compensation plans out there pay off big when new customers are signed. Most marketing plans are geared toward bringing fresh blood to the table.

Your Best Marketing Is Great Customer Service

If this comes as a surprise, you simply haven't been wearing your customer-colored glasses enough. Think about it: You visit two different Web sites that have the same products. At about the same price. At about the same availability. With about the same warranty. Which do you choose? All that's left is to look at the label and pick the brand you trust the most.

But what if one of the sites has lots of information on how to use the product? Has lots of information on how to fix problems? Has lots of ways you can contact the company and talk to somebody? Now the scales of value are clearly tipped. You buy from the company that offers more value for the same product.

Therefore, every marketer should understand what the electronic customer is all about. Every marketer should be actively interested in the level of service the customer service department provides. Every marketer should be thinking of customer service in terms of branding.

We'll start off simply—with e-mail.

Using E-Mail for Customer Service

E-mail provides a wonderfully frictionless way to communicate. A message comes to the desktop. The reply is written on the same screen, and out it goes at the speed of light. No paper trays to fill, no fax machine to run out of paper, and the response is delivered directly instead of sitting in interoffice mail. An e-mail can contain more detailed, specific information than can be written on a "while you were out" note or left in voice mail. Answers to questions that come up again and again can be stored for quick retrieval.

More sociable people like speaking on the phone. More formal people prefer writing letters or sending faxes. Some prefer e-mail. With so many people using e-mail in their homes and offices, it behooves you to cater to them.

You wouldn't consider running your company without a fax machine. Customers won't consider doing business with a company without an e-mail address—and the skills to use it wisely.

Basic Training

Responding to a customer comment, question, or complaint via e-mail requires the same care used when responding over the phone or in writing. Inflection and attitude are critical to maintaining a happy and healthy customer/vendor relationship over the phone. The correct answer, spoken in the wrong manner, can have a negative effect. On paper, the wrong words can return to haunt the well-meaning customer service representative over and over again. Those words may even show up in court.

E-mail falls between the spoken word and the written word. It is fast; it is spontaneous. When an e-mail beeps onto your desk, you get a feeling of instant communication—somebody wants to tell you something right now. The natural reaction is to respond at once, with the same informal manner used when passed a note in school. This casual regard for the written (but e-mailed) word is creating a middle layer of communications. Companies will have to protect themselves from employees' being overly informal.

Let's Be Careful Out There

I recently consulted at a large software company in Chicago, which will remain nameless because it doesn't want to appear in next Sunday's Dilbert strip. This company pulled off one of those classic e-mail goofs.

I was working with one gentleman—let's call him Mike. We were sending e-mail back and forth, and he was copying some others on the project to keep them in the loop. True to proper netiquette, I made sure they were all included in my reply. Mike inquired if I could come out right away, within the next couple of weeks. I replied that I had only one day open and it would mean taking a red-eye to get there. "In order to be non-comatose, I'm going to have to request business-class travel." Within a couple of hours, I got a response from somebody I'd not come across before, nor even heard of before. We'll call her Michelle. Michelle's message was a copy of my message with the following at the top:

```
Wow. what a woosiekins. Can't believe he's requesting business class
travel. Funny stuff. Let's put his email on the Web and see what it does
for his career...
```

I was nonplussed. I reacted the way I have trained myself to do whenever a particularly upsetting message hits my screen: I sat on it for 24 hours. My wife got an earful. My brother got an earful. I was livid. But I sat on my hands.

The next day, as I carefully started constructing an additional 10-minute seminar segment for my consulting trip that would include e-mail do's and don'ts, Mike called. Understand, this was the first time I'd ever spoken with the man on the telephone.

"Uh, Jim?"

"Yes."

"This is Mike."

"Hi, Mike," in slightly frosty tones, "How are you?"

"Great, great. Thanks. Uh, Jim, did you get an e-mail from my boss?"

"I'm not sure. Who's your boss?"

"Michelle."

"Yes."

"Uh, well, uhm. Heh-heh. You see, uhm. She's got a really wry sense of humor and, uh, well, heh-heh, you know, and uh, so I just wanted to, sort of, well...We'll be seeing you on the 6th, right?"

"Yes, Mike. I'll be there."

"Oh, great! That's real good. OK! Well, I'm glad we got that cleared up. Thanks, and, uh, see you on the 6th!"

I looked at the dead receiver in my hand. Whatever happened to "I'm sorry"? What the heck happened to Michelle? That 10-minute segment was now going to be a half hour. Not only did she send it to me, but she took away the element of surprise—I was going to flash her name up on the big screen in front of their whole marketing department.

It wasn't until five days later that I received the following:

```
Date: Tue, 26 Nov
From: Michelle Xxxxxx <xxxxxx@xxxxxx.com>
To: jsterne@targeting.com
Subject: So, what have I learned pre-seminar?
I posed my obviously beyond stupid self-imposed dilemma to my former
sixth grade teacher, who suggested the following retribution:
(in lieu of chalkboard)
I will never thoughtlessly hit the send key
I will never thoughtlessly hit the send key
I will never thoughtlessly hit the send key
I will never thoughtlessly hit the send key
I will never thoughtlessly hit the send key

. . .
```

[Yes—there were 100 of them.]

```
. . .
I will never thoughtlessly hit the send key
I will never thoughtlessly hit the send key
I will never thoughtlessly hit the send key
Please fly out here first class on us. We will also provide limo
service. All this is paid for under a grant called the Michelle's-An-
Idiot Fund (it's not a big fund, but an incredibly worthy cause).
```

I decided they didn't need to have an extra e-mail seminar after all.

Protect Yourself

Create a company policy for using e-mail. Emphasize clarity and professionalism. Help employees understand how the casual nature of e-mail can be misleading. Apply the same rules to the company's e-mail capability as you do to the phone, the fax, and the copy machine. If an employee cannot live without daily postings about bicycle racing, make it clear that he or she should get a private e-mail address. The office account, especially with @company.com attached to the user's name, should be used for business only.

Besides protecting the company from embarrassment and deeply unhappy customers, an e-mail policy can protect the company from litigious ones as well. An e-mail is a legal document. It is words on paper. If somebody is going to send the wrong thing to a customer, it's much better to be able to say it was the individual's failing. He or she was going against policy.

Doing It Right

Every now and then, you get great customer service via e-mail. I received a spam for a public relations service that was surreptitiously sent through the mail servers of Charles Schwab. Knowing that a company as deeply ingrained in the Internet as it is would be appalled that its good name might be besmirched, I forwarded the offending message to abuse.schwab.com. I was confident that the company would be interested enough to use the industry standard address and would wish to take action.

I expected one of three responses. The most likely would be a bounced e-mail, if the company had not created such an address. The next most likely would have been the auto-responder thanking me for my time and wishing me well. Next? No response at all. This would have told me that the company did indeed have such an address, but that nobody bothered to read/reply to the messages. But what I got was not expected at all.

In less than 24 hours, a response from a human came back:

```
Dear Mr. Sterne:
Thank you for your email. We regret that you have received any unwelcome
email.
Despite the return address that has the domain of @cc8eb001.schwab.com,
we wish to assure you that the message you received was not from Schwab.
We have received other reports, in addition to yours, with the same
address: bwnews@gte.net. Only the domain is changed from email to email.
We are currently researching this matter with our Email Policy
Department.
We want to thank you for taking the time to write us about your
concerns. We are afraid that the Spam you have received is all too
common for all Internet users, including myself. We assure you that
Schwab is very much opposed to Spam and email sent to individuals who
have not granted prior permission to the sender to do so. We appreciate
your patience in this matter while we conduct our investigation.
Mr. Sterne, we hope that we have completely addressed your concern about
receiving the unwelcome email. Please contact us if you have any further
questions or concerns. Thank you for using Schwab's Email Customer
Service.
Sincerely,
Andrew Bishton
Schwab Email Customer Service
```

Addressed my concern? Schwab smashed my concern. A real live human responding with information and empathy in a timely manner makes me feel *very* good about the Charles Schwab brand. Maybe I'll add a little SCH to my portfolio.

Using the World Wide Web for Customer Service

Quality customer service is critical to happy customers, repeat customers, and word-of-mouth referrals. Having the right answers to customers' questions and solutions to customers' problems is central to excellent service. Getting those answers and solutions to customers in a timely fashion is the deciding factor; a Web site can automate this function and improve satisfaction significantly.

The Frequently Asked Questions Solution

Your customer service people hear most of these questions daily:

- How much will it shrink if I wash it in hot water?
- How long is the warranty?
- How long does it take to paint and ship a custom-colored version?
- Where can I get it fixed?
- Has it been reviewed by *Consumer Reports*?
- Is it compatible with the other equipment in my office?

The answers to these questions are ingrained in the customer service department's collective memory and have become a fixed part of their speech patterns. These are the questions and answers taught to new employees on the first day. Each time a customer learns one of those answers without calling your toll-free 800 number, you save the price of a call and the service representative's time.

The most helpful resource on a Web site is often the Frequently Asked Questions (FAQ) page, a practice borrowed from newsgroups and FTP sites. The most common questions and their answers are collected and made available for electronic retrieval. At any time of the day or night, from anywhere around the world, customers and would-be customers can find solutions to the problems they face at that very moment.

If the answers are plentiful and cogent, you have reduced the customer frustration factor. You have electronically turned an annoying problem into a pleasant experience. Compare that to a customer waiting for the proper time of day, waiting on hold, explaining the problem two or three times to two or three different people, and then waiting for an answer.

But pay close attention to how those questions are asked and answered. Customers don't really ask questions the way that customer service managers think they do.

Sometimes you catch yourself asking "Do I need to draw them a picture?" Sometimes the answer is "Yes." Such was the case at First Republic Bank (www.firstrepubliconline.com). In answer to the question "How does bill payment work?" it figured the best answer was a figure. "To help you understand the process, we have provided a diagram" (see Figure 2.1).

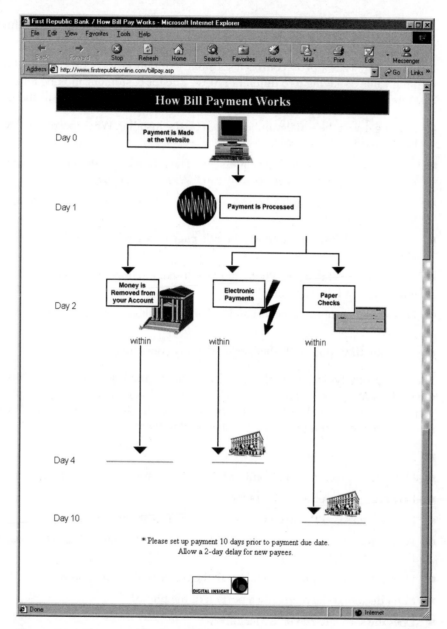

Figure 2.1 First Republic realized that a picture is worth a thousand words, 113 phone calls, or 86 e-mails.

And don't forget to post Frequently Asked Questions for prospects as well. There's no better way to hasten the education portion of the sales cycle. But there's an even bigger upside. If you track which questions people are reading, you might learn that you need to change your marketing materials to better describe your products in the first place.

At the very least, you'll find out what's important to people—and that is the first step to decent marketing.

Pixid Software (www.pixid.com) is a subsidiary of PolyVision Corporation. It discovered the value of having two different FAQs—one for customers and one for potential customers. Its technical support FAQ asks and answers questions such as these:

- I can't get past the serial number screen on the installer. Why doesn't the "Next" button work?

- As I install the software, I get a message "The following system files have been replaced by a program you recently ran." What happened?

- When I load your sample photos they load really fast, but my photos take forever to load. How come?

- When I start Whiteboard Photo, the title page appears but then nothing happens. How come?

- I've installed Whiteboard Photo, but I can't seem to import images from my camera. What am I doing wrong?

- I colored areas of my flipchart and they don't look very good when I convert the photos.

- There are tiny spots in the background of my converted photo.

These are pretty typical examples of software users running into problems. But at the top of this FAQ page, Pixid offers an alternative. "If you are considering a purchase, you might want to read these <u>frequently asked questions</u>". The prospective customer is looking for something else, and Pixid gives it to them:

- Do I need to own a camera?

- How many pixels (what resolution) should my camera have (be)?

- Do I need any special adapters for my camera?

- Does Whiteboard Photo convert multiple photos at once?

- Why couldn't I just use my image editing software? What makes Whiteboard Photo different?

- Does it take a lot of my time to tweak the conversion of my photos?

- Can I decide to clean up only a portion of the photo?

- Does the software run on a Macintosh?

- What kind of printer do I need to have?

The Special Question Opportunity

When a solution or answer isn't immediately apparent, the FAQ-seeking customer should be invited to contact the company via a fill-in form on the Web page or to send an e-mail. This option doesn't provide the same immediate gratification as finding the answer, but it offers two aspects that may make the transaction an even more positive experience for the customer.

Asking a difficult question may provide its own source of pleasure. This customer may feel that he or she knows more than the others, has more insight than the others, and therefore is able to ask better questions than the others. This is the pride found in knowing that your question isn't frequently asked. A special question posed to an automated Web page also may receive a really good answer. This is the second opportunity to turn this problem into a positive experience for the customer.

The Right Customer Service Information

If you sell technology, chances are your customers are going to want to see product specifications, compatibility charts, product release schedules, and pricing. If you sell tickets to local events, your customers are going to want to see performance schedules, ticket pricing, theater seating charts, and driving directions. What goes up on your customer service Web site depends on your product.

A customer service Web site can answer technical questions before they are asked and solve technical problems before they occur. Hours of telephone time can be saved simply by posting known problems, solutions, and suggestions.

Instead of arming an 800 operator with a database of solutions, the company makes the database available to the customer. The savings in personnel costs can be dramatic. FedEx (yes, it's the law—if you write about the Internet you have to talk about www .fedex.com somewhere) learned the value of having customer information available online.

When FedEx started giving customers access to its package tracking system over the Internet (see Figure 2.2), the Web team, the press, and the public were very pleased. But what about upper management? When they heard that hundreds of people a day were tracking packages online, they said, "So what?" The Web team responded, "So, it's really cool." Upper management shrugged.

Several months later, thousands of people were tracking their packages online. Upper management said, "So what?"

"So," said the Web team, "It costs us $7 every time a customer calls 1-800-GoFedEx, and it costs $0.07 every time a customer does it on the Web, and we've put a big dent in the number of calls we're getting."

"Cool!"

For a very serious look at a very serious customer service Web site, check out how Cisco (www.cisco.com) uses the Web on its support site (see Figure 2.3).

Cisco is automating as much of the process as it can: the shopping process, the buying process, the support process, all of it. It has implemented Configuration Agents that allow you to search for and create a product configuration. Pricing Agent allows you to access Cisco's online price list, Status Agent provides status reports on open orders, and RMA/Service Order Agent lets you get status on a service order.

Figure 2.2 FedEx is often credited for being the first to give customers access to live data, in this case package tracking.

The Software Image Library provides downloadable software updates for all Cisco products, with interactive upgrade planners to help you choose the right software for your environment. The Bug Toolkit contains a variety of popular bug searching tools. You can also set up a network profile so that Cisco can alert you to new bugs via e-mail or fax. The Open Forum provides database searches for quick answers to technical questions. The Troubleshooting Engine helps customers resolve a variety of common internetworking problems using an intuitive Web interface.

If that's not enough, Cisco also has both customer service engineers who wear beepers that notify them of high-level e-mails and online training to become a Cisco Certified Internetwork Expert. Why bother? Because a customer in the hand is worth 5 or 10 in the bush, and paying close attention to the customer experience on your Web site can lead to public relations exposure you cannot buy. In 1999 alone, Cisco took top honors in no less than 12 industry awards events:

Top 25 Web sites—Peppers and Rogers

Top 100 E-businesses sites—*Information Week*

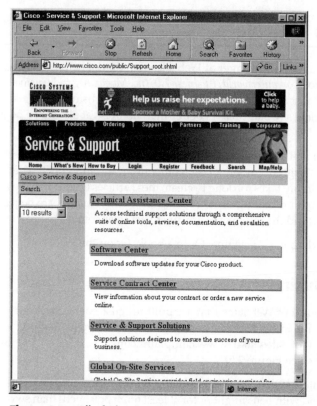

Figure 2.3 All of Cisco's customers are online, and Cisco spends a lot of effort supporting them there.

Semi-Finalist in the Commerce category—The Fourth Annual Global Information Infrastructure (GII) Awards

Service Marketing Excellence—Information Technology Services Marketing Association

Award for Excellence—Press Release Network

Seal of Excellence Award—Majon Web Select

200 Best Business to Business Web Sites—NetMarketing

Top Ten Support Sites—The Association of Support Professionals

WebBusiness 50/50 Award—*CIO Magazine*

Number One Leading Company of the Net Economy—*Business 2.0 Magazine*

Award of Excellence—Awebpage.com

Mark of Excellence—Holt WorldWide

The flip side should be obvious. If people and organizations are going to hold you up as a paragon of Web wizardry when you do well, they are most certainly going to hold you to ridicule if you can't make the grade.

Being Held Up to Ridicule

I have a wonderful outlet for my anger at Web sites that do not help me in my hour of need: I write articles for *Computerworld*, *Business 2.0*, *Inc. Magazine*, and *Customer Service Management*, to name just a few. It's one thing to upset your customers; it's another to be vilified in print. Some say bad press is better than no press at all. Those people live in Hollywood.

The *Industry Standard* and *Information Week* magazines both published articles entitled "Customer Disservice" within a month of each other (May and June 1999). They weren't playing copy-cat—it simply takes too long to create these articles for one to have followed the other. They were both reporting on a common theme: Customers are being treated rather shabbily online, and the miscreants are due to get their comeuppance in print.

You don't want to end up in a magazine. Or in a book. Or on the Web.

Web Ridicule as a Business

Now, there are a handful of Web sites that are built for customer complaints. Besides the good old Better Business Bureau (www.bbbonline.org), you really don't want to become the target of sites like www.complaint.com (see Figure 2.4) or www.EllensPoisonPen.com (see Figure 2.5).

These sites are the Internet-version of consumer advocates. They'll take on your customers' complaints, and with pens mightier (or at least more poisoned) than swords, they will charge after you until the wronged party gets satisfaction. These are professional complainers—people who have made an art of telling you just how lowly your level of service is and why you should grovel to get back into your customers' good graces.

Some customers are going direct. What does it do to your image as a leading-edge, customer-caring, right-minded company if there are Web sites up that target your firm as incompetent? It's not hard to come across people with a grudge and a Web server:

- Microsoft-sucks.com
- eToys-sucks.com
- Delta-sucks.com
- Sony-Sucks.com
- AllstateInsurancesucks.com
- Lucenttechniologiessucks.com
- Cineplex-sucks.com
- AOLsucks.com
- HomeDepotsucks.com
- ChaseBanksucks.com

and many, many more.

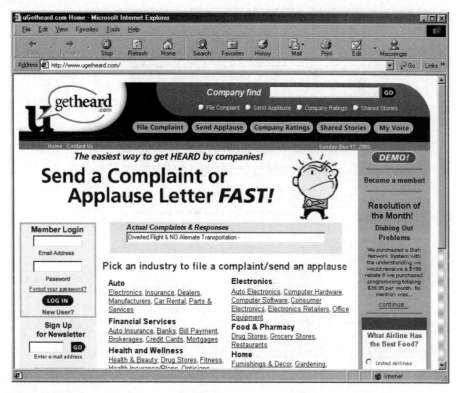

Figure 2.4 Complaint.com aggregates complaints to shame the offenders into remunerative action.

Live and in Person

If you want to—really want to—get up close and personal with your customers, be there for them 24 × 7 in real time. Text chat, VOIP (voice over Internet Protocol, or voice over IP), and streaming video allow you to communicate one-to-one online.

Customer service is not just about answering the questions and solving the problems of *current* customers. It's also about helping out *potential* customers. People who are on the cusp of clicking that "Submit Your Order" button might have one last question, one little datum that will push them over the edge of resistance. They hang on to that one missing bit like a security blanket, and if you could just show them how their concern is misplaced, they would open their electronic wallets in a heart beat. But e-mail takes too many heart beats. They want answers now.

Customer service becomes an important part of a marketer's life as soon as that marketer understands the difference between advertising, marketing, and sales. Advertising is the art of acquiring new prospects. Marketing is the art of education and persuasion. Sales is the art of closing the deal. The most important question is whether your advertising, marketing, and sales efforts are bringing in profitable customers.

Figure 2.5 Ellen's Poison Pen is a little gentler in its approach, but along the same vein.

People Who Need People

From *Inc. Magazine*, September 15, 2000
By Jim Sterne

Remember when you thought the Internet would let you get away with ignoring your customers? Self-service was one of the great early promises of the Web: people could read your Frequently Asked Questions, check out your troubleshooting page, peruse your online manual, and dig up the As to all their Qs. Relieved of interruptions, you, the company owner, could get some real work done.

But man does not live by customer self-service alone. Even on the best Web sites, people get disconnected. They get confused. They get frustrated. Then they get in touch. They e-mail, fax, and call, assaulting you with queries that are specific and challenging and that cry out for immediate attention. Someone has to answer them.

Yes, there are database-managed conversation applications out there, like eGain Assistant, offered by eGain Communications Corp. (www.egain.com); see Figures 2.6 through 2.8. But software alone won't cut it. You need operators standing by. Sympathetic hand-holders. Human beings.

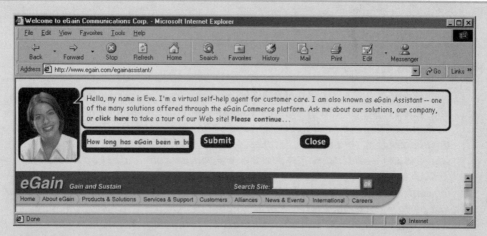

Figure 2.6   eGain's Eve will do "her" best to answer your questions . . .

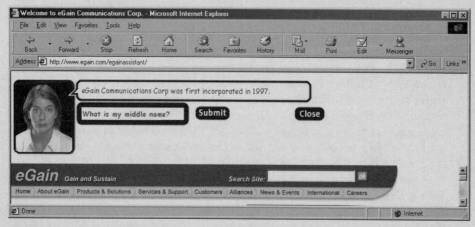

Figure 2.7   . . . as long as they are questions she understands . . .

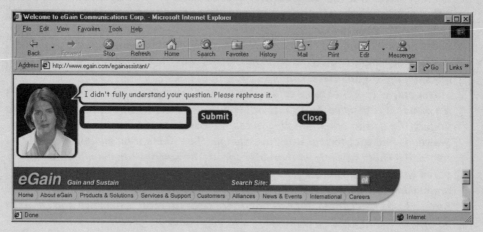

Figure 2.8   . . . otherwise, she gets confused.

continues

People Who Need People (Continued)

Fortunately, a passel of technologies promise to connect customers with flesh-and-blood representatives right on your site. Internet telephony is one: these days most PCs have built-in microphones, allowing customers to speak through their computers. And companies like HearMe offer free Internet phone calls anywhere in the world. Users just surf to www.hearme.com and set up a session.

Such services are perfect for college kids phoning home or for anyone who makes frequent calls to the folks back in the old country. But they lack the speed and performance required by a professional customer-service environment. While companies wait for voice-compression technology to jell, many are finding an acceptable alternative in text chat.

PETAL PUSHERS

I came across one example of using text chat both wisely and well while ordering a Valentine bouquet at 1-800-Flowers.com last winter. Since I can no more visit a Web site without evaluating its offerings than Roger Ebert can see a movie without raising or lowering a thumb, I checked out the company's customer-service page. Like all virtuous Web sites, this one supplied directions for sending e-mail and phoning. But it presented a third option as well: visitors could connect to the company's eQ&A Chat. Curious, I typed in a message for the rep I assumed must be out there, asking what life was like on the other side of the screen. "Busy!" her response came back.

Before I could type an apology for bothering her, she had transferred me to her supervisor, Marc Noel, who graciously answered all my questions about the fine art of managing e-chatters. Noel told me that his company's customers feel that buying flowers should take just minutes. When questions arise, they don't want to disconnect the modem, pick up the phone, and wither away on hold. Using software from eShare Technologies Inc. (www.eshare.com), the company's reps answer questions instantly; customers never leave the site. And like master chess players in the park, reps can juggle as many as six sessions simultaneously. They simply read a question, answer it, and then move rapidly to the next question before the first customer's reply appears.

Not only is text chat more efficient than other communication mechanisms, but it's also less expensive. In a study of 1-800-Flowers.com, Don Peppers and Martha Rogers, the one-to-one marketing gurus, concluded that answering customers' questions in a chat format was 30% cheaper than doing it by e-mail, because reps using chat can reply with greater speed. The savings are even greater compared with service over the phone. And chat isn't just for posy purchasers who are making low-cost decisions in a hurry. Hewlett-Packard, Gateway, and Mail Boxes Etc. all use chat in the sales and service of far more expensive and complex products, working with a demanding and often knowledgeable constituency.

There's an interesting anthropological angle to text chat, however. The questions you get tend to be either much smarter or much dumber than the stuff that comes through an average call center. Maybe customers are more comfortable asking the obvious when they know they won't be answered in a voice dripping with scorn. Whatever the reason, expect a steady stream of queries from folks with less than optimum technical proficiency. (Q: How do I print out your page if I don't have a printer?) Needless to say, your human reps must resist the very human urge to imply a groan in their typed responses. (Software, to give it its due, is rarely sarcastic.)

On the flip side, customers who frequent sites that are highly technical may possess unprecedented amounts of information. "Our customers are better informed and are asking a higher tier of question," says Peter Corless, product manager at Cisco Systems' IOS technology division (www.cisco.com). That means customer-service reps must be better informed—or better connected to the people and systems that are better informed—than ever. Cisco reps need to find out how customers obtain self-service so that they can understand the mechanism from the customer's point of view, says Corless. "They do not need to be breathing encyclopedias but rather reference librarians," he says.

SHOW AND TELL

Sites manned by live people can draw on more than the power of the written word. Tools like Hipbone (www.hipbone.com), for example, enable a rep to share a browser with a customer so that they can co-navigate. The rep types, "If you click here and then on this specifications button, you'll find the table with the relevant technical specs," while the customer watches the cursor slide across the page. The two can then fill out the form together.

Of course, there are always customers for whom you must literally draw a map—and others who prefer to draw one for you. Companies that want their reps to get a little graphic can try Groupboard (www.groupboard.com), a kind of electronic whiteboard on which dispersed users work simultaneously.

Tools like Groupboard not only allow your reps to diagram their instructions; they also let customers draw circles around the parts that confuse them or underline those passages they find perplexing. By combining such simultaneous sketching with a few product shots, reps can easily show customers what fits where and how.

Moving your customers' cursors and drawing pretty pictures in their browser windows is one thing. Taking control of their computers is another. It's an action that requires perfect trust, the kind that a patient has in a surgeon. It is also the deepest connection your human reps can make with your customers and is con-sequently, when managed well, the most powerful testament to your company's capabilities.

I learned to trust recently when my e-mail software turned on me. E-mail is critical to my well-being; its failure sends me into paroxysms of disconnected-ness. Desperate, I sought relief at Expertcity.com, a Web-based provider of per-son-to-person technical help.

continues

People Who Need People (*Continued*)

On the Expertcity site (www.expertcity.com) I typed a description of my problem into a text box, and a few moments later a list of Eudora experts popped up together with their proposed fees for saving my bacon. I read some of the experts' bios and a few reviews provided by earlier users. Then, after correlating the depth of my need with the contents of my wallet, I made a selection.

A chat session materialized, and Chet, my very own personal expert, started asking me questions. Since I had already tried several corrective courses to no avail, he asked if he could take over my machine. Have your way with it, I replied, withdrawing my fingers from the keyboard. Immediately, my cursor started wandering in Ouija-board fashion across the screen. Chet checked my settings and opened a new browser window. Next he clicked to the Eudora Web site, found an updated version of the software, and downloaded it into the proper directory. Then he advised me to install the new version, restart my machine, and call if the problems persisted. Finally, he gave me his home number and thanked me for the five bucks. If you sell or service technical products, this is your future.

But as wonderful as text chat and related applications are, sometimes your customers will insist on talking to you. With their mouths. So until Internet telephony is ready for prime time, please don't forget to include your company's telephone number on each and every page of your Web site. And don't get angry when a customer's call interrupts that real work. Instead, remember what your real work is.

The Life-Time Value of a Customer

The One to One Future (Bantam Doubleday, 1997), *Enterprise One to One* (Doubleday, 1999), *The One to One Fieldbook* (Bantam Books, 1999), and *The One to One Manager* (Doubleday, 1999) are all by Don Peppers and Martha Rogers with some help from Bob Dorf (www.1to1.com). These are books that drive home one lesson: Because it's less expensive to sell something to a current customer that to drum up a new one, spend your time and effort getting as close as possible to your current customers.

This is a slap-on-the-forehead, D'oh!, tell-me-something-I-didn't-know sort of pronouncement. What makes these books must-reads is that you know it, but you're not doing anything about it. Even more important, today's technology lets us get closer to our customers than ever before. The competitive advantage to treating customers on a one-to-one basis is enormous.

It boils down to recognizing that customers mean more than momentary profitability. Momentary profitability means spending as little time with customers as possible. Call management systems are being sold as call avoidance systems. Phone representatives are measured on how many calls they can take a day.

There's something so obviously insincere about a customer service rep who finishes a call with, "Thank you for calling Acme Rent-A-Pencil. Have a nice..." and then hits the disconnect button before the word "day" is uttered.

Instead, Don and Martha beg us to see how a little more care with each customer can turn each customer into a life-long customer.

The *life time value* (LTV) of a customer is based on the premise that the most expensive part of the relationship is starting it in the first place. Field sales reps in the business-to-business world, advertising in the consumer marketplace, direct mail, print and broad-cast advertising all abound—it adds up. It can cost hundreds to thousands of dollars to find a suspect, qualify the suspect as a prospect, and close the prospect as a customer.

Measuring LTV

The first step is thinking of your customers as assets. Just as you would want to spend more of your energy on maintaining a building rather than buying a new one every year, you want to focus on customer relationships as something of value that need to be preserved. You want to calculate the net present value of the profit a single customer will generate over time.

This is the sort of thinking that allows stores to sell loss-leaders. If they can get the customer into the shop and show him or her what a nice store they have, that customer will become a return customer. The questions that need numerical answers are easy to ask, but not easy to answer. Some creative accounting may be in order to give you some idea of the LTV of your customers:

- New customers per year (or month or quarter)
- Customer loss per year
- Revenue per customer per year
- Cost per customer per year (acquisition)
- Cost per customer per year (service)
- Cost per customer per year (production and distribution)
- Cost per customer per year (G&A)

A net present value calculation is thrown in as a discount you apply based on the time value of money and a rate you apply for risk. If 2 percent of your receivables end up as bad debt, that needs to be part of the equation.

In an ideal spreadsheet, the numbers apply to a specific market segment. If it costs three times as much to sell something to a teenager in the Northeast who is five times more likely to leave the fold within months, then advertising on MTV is not your best move.

You're going to use the resulting LTV to give you a compass. Should you spend more on customer retention such as a frequent buyer program? More on upselling and cross-selling? Changes in distribution channels? Changes in customer complaint management systems?

Let's say you run the calculations on a loyalty program and determine that you can increase retention by X if you spend Y. Once through the spreadsheet might show that the cost of the program will be recovered in three years, but you've only extended the average customer life by two years and eight months. Not a wise move.

The Real Bottom Line

Rather than focus on the profitability of each product, look at the profitability of each customer. This is not an obtainable, specific number, but a rolling average for each individual. If customers go through a period of calling in with problems, their profitability declines. If they buy twice as much of your highest-margin goods and services, their profitability increases.

If you've listened to both Peppers and Rogers *and* Tom Peters, you'll have figured out that you want to find your most profitable customers and cater to them. Then you want to find your least profitable customers and fire them. Wouldn't you like to take the most costly 10 percent of your customers, wrap them in a pretty package, and send them over to your competitors?

If this seems like a light-handed treatment, worry not. We'll revisit the whole E-Metrics thing in Chapter 12, "Measure by Measure." First, there are some ground-rules to cover, starting with how well you treat your customers online at the moment and how much better you could.

The Web used to be about cool graphics and astonishing design, stretching the envelope and inventing wild, new ways to bend HTML to your will, but now it's about usability. That, plus giving the best to your prospects and customers while learning the most about them, is worthy of a whole new chapter.

The Usable Web—
Be Kind to Your Users

With your goals firmly prioritized and the idea that great customer service really is a marketing maneuver, it's time to create the electronic persona of your company—the Web-based version of a visit to your office. You've spent a fair amount of time, money, and interior design effort to make a professional statement with your office, and you should do the same with your Web site.

Designing a Web site is as simple as creating a combination magazine ad, brochure, trade show exhibit, demo diskette, CD-ROM, crystal ball, and Ouija board. You can do it in your sleep. You just can't do it in your sleep *well*. That's why it's so important to understand what a Web site is not.

Your Web Site Is Not a Brochure

A brochure has a cover. A brochure has an opening statement. It has a progressive flow from front to back. Experiencing a brochure is a very predictable thing. But a visit to a Web site is anything but predictable.

If you look at your server logs, it *looks* as if everybody came to your Web site through the home page. So many more people looked at the home page than any other page. A scenario closer to the truth is that lots and lots of people came to your home page but decided it was not the place for them so they took off and never came back.

The people who came to your site, hung out for a while, and drilled down into the pages they found valuable may not have seen your home page at all. Chances are excellent that they found you through a search engine or had a URL e-mailed to them by a friend or colleague.

Because your site is not a brochure, you need to be aware of two things:

- There is no need for a brochure cover or splash page.
- Every page should be well branded and easily navigated.

Trash the Splash

Kristin Zhivago (whom you'll remember from Chapter 1) refers to the graphic artists who make your life difficult as the "short-haired pony-tails." These are the guys who dress all in black, sport a little goatee, wear sunglasses indoors (excuse me, shades), and grew up on Madison Avenue. Their goal in life is to win awards for design. They want to establish a new paradigm of design. They want to create a permanent impression with their design. Brand? They're all over it. Sell stuff? Only under duress.

Short-haired pony-tails feel your home page should constitute the front cover of your electronic brochure. It should fix the image of your organization firmly in the visitor's mind. Hey, I'm all for branding, but these guys simply do not understand the need for navigation. And face it, some of them have never heard of it. Case in point? SupraNet (www.supranet.com) (see Figure 3.1).

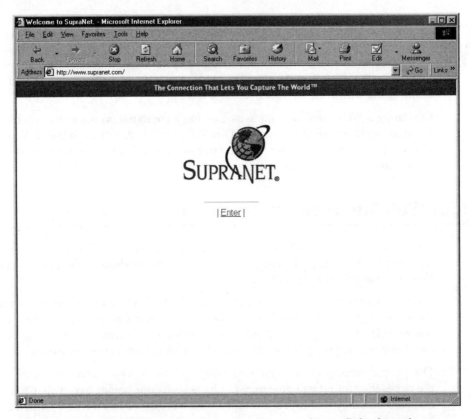

Figure 3.1   The SupraNet home page succeeds in revealing as little about the company as possible.

There is no clue about what the company does unless you can intuit that "The Connection That Lets You Capture The World" means it is an Internet access provider. There is no navigational support at all. Not a single button.

Question: How do you double the hits on your Web site?

Answer: Force people to click through a splash page to get to the other side.

One of the surprising things about the infinite design possibilities on the Web is that no matter how bad somebody's site is, there are dozens of ways to make it worse. How could this site be worse? It could be animated. You could force the visitor to wait for the animation to download in order to not understand what your company does for a living and make it impossible to figure out what to click on. Happens all the time. Proof? Glad you asked.

Trash the Flash Splash

You have to experience ZeeNet.com to really understand how painful it can be, but I'll try to give you a feel for it (see Figure 3.2).

The first insult comes when this Web site takes over your screen. Browser? Not needed. Desktop? Pardon us while we make it disappear. A Macromedia Flash animation is launched that immediately covers up everything on your monitor. So ZeeNet not only makes its site hard to use, it makes it impossible to navigate your own desktop. The browser you were using is still alive and running in another active window, but it is completely black. Zip, zero, nada on it.

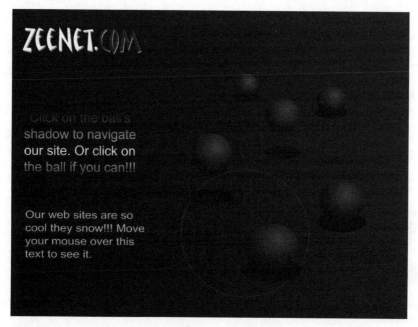

Figure 3.2 Navigate the ZeeNet site . . . *if you can.*

On top of that, there is a daughter window, the size and shape of a banner ad, that hovers on top of the Flash animation inviting you to sign up for the company's newsletter (see Figure 3.3).

The big spheres are constantly bouncing, and there's a musical soundtrack playing in the background. That's bad enough, but then it goads you into *trying* to click on the spheres. Why should you? What will you get when you do? Hovering your mouse over each bouncing ball reveals a label for each one, but only as long as the mouse hovers:

- shop ZeeNet
- FLASH design
- HTML design
- free CD ROM
- contact us
- free web e-mail

A click on the FLASH design button plays another animation that assembles the next screen (see Figure 3.4).

There's no clue as to what page you're on. There's no clue about why you should be motivated to click on any of the options. The "design" button walks you through three paragraphs of text on how wonderful animation on a Web site can be.

The next question is this: How do I make this screen-grabber go away? I can Alt-Tab from window to window, but I cannot gain access to the Status Bar at the bottom of my desktop. The Escape key has no effect. Left-clicking on the screen brings up a Flash menu that offers me these choices:

- Zoom In
- Quality
- Play
- Loop
- Rewind
- Forward
- Back
- Print
- About Macromedia Flash Player 5 . . .

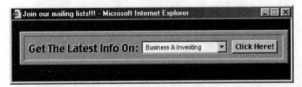

Figure 3.3   You have to close this window before you can even try to navigate the ZeeNet site.

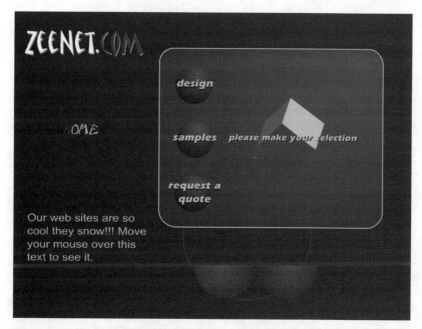

Figure 3.4 Quick: Which ZeeNet page are you on?

Alt-F-C doesn't file-close the window. There's no Stop button to click. No Click Here To Quit. No way out! And that music is *definitely* getting on my nerves. There's only one thing left to try: Atl-Ctrl-Del and End Task.

All in all, the impression is that these people are good at graphics that are way too cool for normal humans. ("If you don't *get* it, dog, you should simply sidle on back to your midtown condo and interface with your GameBoy.") They can make an animation run smoothly. They're cool. They're hip. They have no idea whatsoever about Web site navigation or common courtesy.

Help old people across the street.
Love thy neighbor as thyself.
Wear your seatbelt.
Make it as easy as possible to find things on your Web site.

With that said, ZeeNet does have one redeemable feature on its site: an example of its work, a Flash animation for Intermountain Building Panels (www.intermountainpanels .com).

This animation explores the construction of the company's stressed skin insulating core panel system consisting of 4- to 10-inch core panels of expanded polystyrene laminated between two layers of oriented strand board (see Figure 3.5). And ZeeNet manages to make it interesting. Honest, it does.

OK, so maybe it's a guy thing.

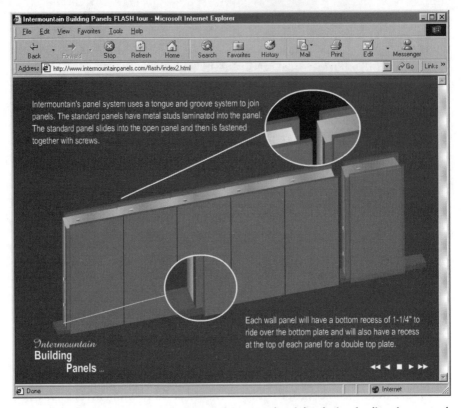

Figure 3.5 Intermountain Panels found ZeeNet the right choice for livening up a dry (wall) subject.

Where did ZeeNet go wrong and Intermountain Panels go right? Style over substance. ZeeNet wanted to impress you with its visual graphics abilities to the point of overwhelming you. Intermountain Panels offered up a Flash animation in order to educate, rather than entertain. The Intermountain Panel home page (see Figure 3.6) is a paragon of simplicity and functionality.

The Intermountain USP (unique sales proposition) is right up front for all to see. "Approximately 15 percent more energy efficient, and 40 percent less on-site labor. Unique Patented Designs." The menu is the main focus. There's an e-mail contact link on the home page. It *warns* you in advance that a Flash animation is just a click away. Its products are not simplistic, nor is its Web site. But they are both simple.

Starting in the Middle

You've created your Web site to be easy to understand—from the beginning. But what happens if somebody walks into the middle of your site? Does this happen? You bet. Some friend sends you an e-mail that says:

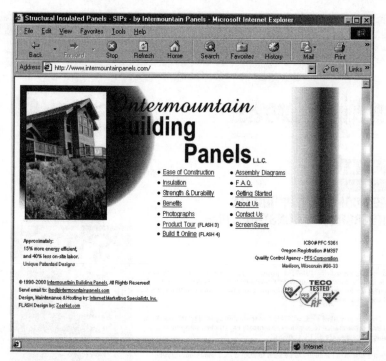

Figure 3.6   Intermountain Panels shows that simple—almost boring—is better.

```
Hey, I just found this new stuff that looks like it'll do the job
housing our underground of fiber optic cable. Check it out:
http://www.strongwell.com/CONCRETE/quazite.HTM
```

So you click and you read about the product (see Figure 3.7). But who makes it?

Is "Precast Polymer Concrete" the name of the company? Nope. How about Quazite? Sorry, that's the product name. The hint comes in the second sentence, "With manufacturing/distribution centers in Lenoir City, Tennessee and San Jose, California, Strongwell can provide nationwide service and prompt delivery."

OK, now we know the company name, but how do we find out more about it? There's no navigation to speak of. No Home Page button, not even an enigmatic Back button. It takes a good deal of hunting to find a link that leads to a link that leads to a button that'll take you to the home page. The only sure way to get there is by looking up at the Address field at the top of Internet Explorer and deleting "/CONCRETE/quazite .HTM" from the rest of the URL. When you realize that, at the end of the year 2000, half the people on the Web had been on the Web for less than one year, you understand that people need all the help they can get in the navigation department.

Coming up out of a subway station is horribly disorienting. You can spot the street signs, so you know what corner you're on, but in what direction are you facing? Which

Figure 3.7 The Strongwell Corporation didn't count on people walking into the middle of its site and forgot about branding.

way is your destination? Why aren't there arrows pointing north at subway station exits all over the world? And while we're at it, why isn't there a standard approach to Web site navigation?

Navigating in a virtual world is an acquired skill. Navigating a ski slope, a crowded freeway system, or a computer game filled with danger and surprise all require agility. Practice can help a lot. When people come to your Web site for the first time, they will react like novice skiers and student drivers. Be considerate of them. Give them lots of visual clues, and make your site as intuitive as possible.

When I arrive on your electronic doorstep, I have a fairly good idea of where I am. Your corporate logo is prominent, and there's a short description of what your company does for a living. But as soon as I step off the home page and into the traffic of your pages, it's easy to get lost. The challenge for Web site designers, therefore, is to make navigation information as comprehensible as possible.

Think about the first time you installed a new piece of software on your computer. Aside from the commands we've all grown to know and love (File: New, Open, Close, Save), the different features of a new program are hard to pick up. Once they're explained, they seem obvious. But if the documentation or Help screens aren't in place or are so full of help you can't find what you're looking for, you struggle to find your way around. It seems hard to fathom that this software will make you more productive in the long run.

Consider first-time Web site users and reach out to them. Give them guidance without being overly protective. Give them encouragement without hindering their progress. At the same time, consider users who may be coming back again and again. Give them shortcuts to the information they want. Make it easy for them to use your site as a resource.

What have we learned so far? You have to experience your Web site through customer-colored glasses. If it is difficult to maneuver through your site, you are hurting your brand. Make it as simple as possible. Make it downright boring if you have to.

We'll spend a good deal of time on navigation because it's critical. First, we pause for a word about slow Web sites.

Large Graphics

When I started admonishing Web developers back in 1994, the first thing I begged them to do was to take pity on all of us who dialed up with 14.4 Kbps modems.

"Stop the insanity!" I cried. "We don't want to wait forever for a picture of your CEO and a picture of the new corporate headquarters. We don't care!"

I knew that, in time, technology would give us faster connections. We went from 14.4 to 28.8 in a matter of months. I've heard that there are people who were in the market for a modem during the 37 minutes when 36.6 modems were all the rage. Then, of course, vendors started shipping the 56.6 variety.

More and more people are logging on via DSL and cable, and when a company hits that sweet spot of a certain number of employees, it's time to get a fixed T1 line. But a great many are still on the old dial-up line.

You may hear people in your company say that *your* customers are more sophisticated than the rest, that *your* customers are connecting at the office over high-speed T1 lines. Don't fall for it. Are you connected at the office over a T1 line? Isn't it great? It's great at 7:00 A.M. Eastern, before anybody else is there, but as soon as the other 200 people you share it with start checking stock prices, football scores, and the latest industry gossip, things tend to slow down, don't they?

The more data you put on your Web site, the longer people have to wait to receive it. The longer people have to wait, the more likely they are to leave the store, hang up the phone, or go look at some other Web site that's more responsive. Many Web sites use large pictures to offer a pleasant visual experience. The drawback to this approach is the time it takes a picture to reach the user's computer.

If graphics are critical to your customers and prospects, or if all your customers and prospects have superior Internet connections, then you might think a graphics-heavy approach is a requirement. But please offer visitors a choice, rather than inflicting your fine arts background on them.

The Web allows for multimedia. Multimedia is good. A picture is worth a thousand words. But a picture takes a thousand times more data than a word, and that means people go away before you've even had a chance to tell them what you sell for a living.

Multimedia Must Add Value

I thought that as compression techniques improved and bandwidth grew, this issue would fade. My father proved me wrong. He called to ask if I thought he should install a cable modem and sign up for @Home. I said, "Absolutely. You'll love it. It's *so* much faster!" I was deeply annoyed that they were wiring his neighborhood before they wandered up the hill into my neck of the woods. It would be another 16 months before cable came to my humble abode, so I was all in favor of Dad getting broadbandedly wired.

A month later, he called to tell me that there were two men in his attic, one outside drilling a hole through the wall, and two underneath his desk arguing about protocols. Was I *sure*, he wanted to know, that this was a good idea? I said, "Absolutely! You're gonna love it! You'll be able to see videos and get music and not have to wait for Web sites anymore!"

He said, "We have a television for videos."

Three days later, he called again to say that somebody was coming out again to try to configure the modem and he was going to bring a couple of spares along just in case and did I still think this was worth the pain and suffering I had encouraged him to bring into his home?

I said, "Absolutely! Call me tomorrow."

He called the next day—ecstatic. "It's so fast! I'm watching the news on CNN. I'm getting pages to show up within seconds instead of minutes. This is great!" I breathed a very large sigh of relief.

I called him a couple of days later. "How's the new cable connection working out?"

"It's OK."

"Just OK?"

"Yeah."

"Isn't it faster? Can't you get a bunch more stuff without waiting?"

"Yeah. I guess."

"Isn't it way better than that 56K modem?"

"Yeah, I suppose." His voice clearly included phrases like, "But it was a royal pain to install and isn't nearly as interesting as "West Wing" on TV." I threw in the towel.

"Well," I said, "for what you'll be paying per month, you might want to cancel it when the free period runs out and go back to the modem."

"Oh, no! I'd never do *that*!"

And thus I learned that like computers themselves, there's no such thing as an Internet connection that's fast enough. If I have my own T1 line, it means only that I'll be waiting on the Web servers and the backbone traffic, instead of my dinky phone line. It will never be fast enough.

For now, be aware that many people on slower connections might be interested in your products and services. Don't create hurdles that will keep them out. Regardless of bandwidth, remember the three reasons to use multimedia:

Decoration. Decorative pictures and interesting videos make the site look nice.

Navigation. Navigational elements keep the user from getting lost.

Information. Informative components communicate information that the user otherwise could not glean or could not glean as fast from text.

Pictures that belong to the decorative category should be kept as small as possible (datawise), without losing their artistic appeal. Larger graphics for aesthetic use are likely to offend, due to the time it takes to download them. Once downloaded, these images do nothing to help users locate, retrieve, or understand the information they want. If you're trying to explain what makes Intermountain Panels so great, Flash away!

Navigation in All Things

A Web site designer's job is to help people find their way around. Strong visual clues can help users access desired information—including the information you want them to see.

Computer design has traditionally been in the hands of engineers, with some help from human factors researchers. Engineering frequently comes first in design due to economic constraints. When Xerox rolled out its 860 word processor, it had an $8\frac{1}{2}$ x 11-inch screen to mimic paper and used dark letters on a white background. These were very unusual features at the time. But the marketplace voted with its feet and demanded less expensive machines, which meant smaller screens—something we've lived with ever since. Now that laptops are ubiquitous, the small screen is here to stay. Therefore, we must design with this format in mind.

There are an infinite number of ways to navigate through electronic space. We've seen enough good and bad examples to get a handle on what works and what doesn't. When Amazon.com opened its servers in 1995, the pages were long, the backgrounds were gray, and the navigation was primitive (see Figure 3.8).

Amazon has always placed an emphasis on navigation. It takes usability very seriously. "I am a firm believer that all sustained growth is the result of sustained improvements in customer experience," opined Amazon founder Jeff Bezos. "We want to be earth's most customer-centric company," he explained. "And by doing so, we want other companies to copy us. And so the big mission, the mission that's bigger than us, is to uplift the entire worldwide standard for customer service and customer experience."

Bezos went further in an interview in the *Red Herring* in March 1999 (www.redherring .com/mag/issue64/news-angler.html):

Figure 3.8 Amazon.com's first home page could only improve.

Our goal is to make it possible for customers to find and discover anything they want to buy online at the lowest prices with the highest-quality service level. This does not mean we will directly sell these products ourselves, but we will do it in partnership with other merchants. One metric of our success in the long-term, I think, will be the degree to which we can defy easy analogy. We want to be something completely new.

Whatever that new thing is, the vision is not to create the world's biggest store. The driving concept is to create the world's best place to find things (see Figure 3.9).

The Basics of Navigation

If you're interested in design and you want to create the very best Web site navigation possible, you need to absorb the thoughts and writings of one Jakob Nielsen. Holder of 28 patents, alumnus of Sun Microsystems, IBM, and the Technical University of Denmark, Jakob has been the champion of the user of the Web site since the early days of the Web. Read his book, *Designing Web Usability: The Practice of Simplicity* (New Riders Publishing, 2000). Head over to his Web site (www.useit.com), which is probably the least decorated site online (see Figure 3.10).

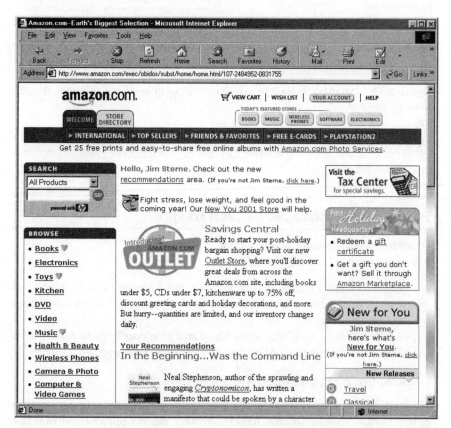

Figure 3.9   Now that Amazon sells more than 18 million items, the site has to be easier to use.

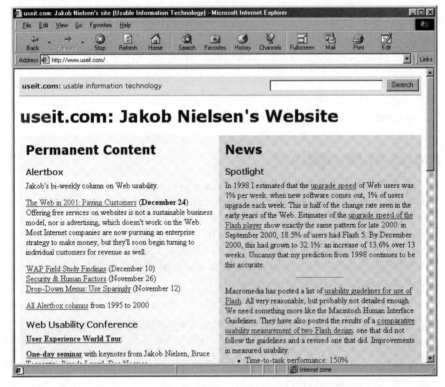

Figure 3.10 What Jakob Nielsen's useit.com lacks in aesthetic splendor, it makes up in valuable content.

If you are managing a team of designers or a Web development service and it is your job to critique and approve the work of others, the following sidebars cover the basics from the master.

The Top Ten *New* Mistakes of Web Design

Jakob Nielsen's Alertbox, May 30, 1999
(www.useit.com/alertbox/990530.html)

The "top ten" design mistakes I identified in 1996 are still bad for Web usability and are still found on many websites. So in that sense, not much has changed over the last three years.

But unfortunately new Web technology and new applications for the Web have introduced an entirely new class of mistakes. Here are the ten worst.

1. BREAKING OR SLOWING DOWN THE *BACK* BUTTON

The Back *button is the lifeline of the Web user and the second-most used navigation feature (following after hypertext links). Users happily know that they can try anything on the Web and* always *be saved by a click or two on Back to return them to familiar territory.*

Except, of course, for those sites that break Back by committing one of these design sins:

- *Opening a new browser window (see mistake #2).*
- *Using an immediate redirect: every time the user clicks Back, the browser returns to a page that bounces the user forward to the undesired location.*
- *Preventing caching such that the Back navigation requires a fresh trip to the server; all hypertext navigation should be sub-second and this goes double for backtracking.*

2. OPENING NEW BROWSER WINDOWS

Opening up new browser windows is like a vacuum cleaner sales person who starts a visit by emptying an ash tray on the customer's carpet. Don't pollute my screen with any more windows, thanks (particularly since current operating systems have miserable window management). If I want a new window, I will open it myself!

Designers open new browser windows on the theory that it keeps users on their site. But even disregarding the user-hostile message implied in taking over the user's machine, the strategy is self-defeating since it disables the Back button which is the normal way users return to previous sites. Users often don't notice that a new window has opened, especially if they are using a small monitor where the windows are maximized to fill up the screen. So a user who tries to return to the origin will be confused by a grayed out Back button.

3. NON-STANDARD USE OF GUI WIDGETS

Consistency is one of the most powerful usability principles: when things always behave the same, users don't have to worry about what will happen. Instead, they know what will happen based on earlier experience. Every time you release an apple over Sir Isaac Newton, it will drop on his head. That's good.

The more users' expectations prove right, the more they will feel in control of the system and the more they will like it. And the more the system breaks users' expectations, the more they will feel insecure. Oops, maybe if I let go of this apple, it will turn into a tomato and jump a mile into the sky.

Interaction consistency is an additional reason it's wrong to open new browser windows: the standard result of clicking a link is that the destination page replaces the origination page in the same browser window. Anything else is a violation of the users' expectations and makes them feel insecure in their mastery of the Web.

Currently, the worst consistency violations on the Web are found in the use of GUI widgets such as radio buttons and checkboxes. The appropriate behavior of

continues

The Top Ten *New* Mistakes of Web Design   (*Continued*)

these design elements is defined in the Windows UI standard, the Macintosh UI standard, and the Java UI standard. Which of these standards to follow depends on the platform used by the majority of your users (good bet: Windows), but it hardly matters for the most basic widgets since all the standards have close-to-identical rules.

For example, the rules for radio buttons state that they are used to select one among a set of options but that the choice of options does not take effect until the user has confirmed the choice by clicking an OK button. Unfortunately, I have seen many websites where radio buttons are used as action buttons that have an immediate result when clicked. Such wanton deviations from accepted interface standards make the Web harder to use.

4. LACK OF BIOGRAPHIES

My first Web studies in 1994 showed that users want to know the people behind information on the Web. In particular, biographies and photographs of the authors help make the Web a less impersonal place and increase trust. Personality and point-of-view often win over anonymous bits coming over the wire.

Yet many sites still don't use columnists and avoid by-lines on their articles. Even sites with by-lines often forget the link to the author's biography and a way for the user to find other articles by the same author.

It is particularly bad when a by-line is made into a mailto: *link instead of a link to the author's biography. Two reasons:*

It is much more common for a reader to want to know more about an author (including finding the writer's other articles) than it is for the reader to want to contact the author—sure, contact info is often a good part of the biography, but it should not be the primary or only piece of data about the author.

It breaks the conventions of the Web when clicking on blue underlined text spawns an email message instead of activating a hypertext link to a new page; such inconsistency reduces usability by making the Web less predictable.

5. LACK OF ARCHIVES

Old information is often good information and can be useful to readers. Even when new information is more valuable than old information, there is almost always some value to the old stuff, and it is very cheap to keep it online. I estimate that having archives may add about 10% to the cost of running a site but increase its usefulness by about 50%.

Archives are also necessary as the only way to eliminate linkrot and thus encourage other sites to link to you.

6. MOVING PAGES TO NEW URLS

Anytime a page moves, you break any incoming links from other sites. Why hurt the people who send you free customer referrals?

7. HEADLINES THAT MAKE NO SENSE OUT OF CONTEXT

Headlines and other microcontent must be written very differently for the Web than for old media: they are actionable items that serve as UI elements and should help users navigate.

Headlines are often removed from the context of the full page and used in tables of content (e.g., home pages or category pages) and in search engine results. In either case the writing needs to be very plain and meet two goals: tell users what's at the other end of the link with no guesswork required and protect users from following the link if they would not be interested in the destination page (so no teasers—they may work once or twice to drive up traffic, but in the long run they will make users abandon the site and reduce its credibility).

8. JUMPING AT THE LATEST INTERNET BUZZWORD

The Web is awash in money and people who proclaim to have found the way to salvation for all the sites that continue to lose money.

Push, community, chat, free email, 3D sitemaps, auctions—you know the drill.

But there is no magic bullet. Most Internet buzzwords have some substance and might bring small benefits to those few websites that can use them appropriately. Most of the time, most websites will be hurt by implementing the latest buzzword. The opportunity cost is high from focusing attention on a fad instead of spending the time, money, and management bandwidth on improving basic customer service and usability.

There will be a new buzzword next month. Count on it. But don't jump at it just because Jupiter writes a report about it.

9. SLOW SERVER RESPONSE TIMES

Slow response times are the worst offender against Web usability: in my survey of the original "top-ten" mistakes, major sites had a truly horrifying 84% violation score with respect to the response time rule.

Bloated graphic design was the original offender in the response time area. Some sites still have too many graphics or too big graphics; or they use applets where plain or Dynamic HTML would have done the trick. So I am not giving up my crusade to minimize download times.

The growth in web-based applications, e-commerce, and personalization often means that each page view must be computed on the fly. As a result, the experienced delay in loading the page is determined not simply by the download delay (bad as it is) but also by the server performance. Sometimes building a page also involves connections to back-end mainframes or database servers, slowing down the process even further.

Users don't care why response times are slow. All they know is that the site doesn't offer good service: slow response times often translate directly into a

continues

The Top Ten *New* Mistakes of Web Design (Continued)

reduced level of trust and they always cause a loss of traffic as users take their business elsewhere. So invest in a fast server and get a performance expert to review your system architecture and code quality to optimize response times.

10. ANYTHING THAT LOOKS LIKE ADVERTISING

Selective attention is very powerful, and Web users have learned to stop paying attention to any ads that get in the way of their goal-driven navigation. That's why click-through rates are being cut in half every year and why Web advertisements don't work.

Unfortunately, users also ignore legitimate design elements that look like prevalent forms of advertising. After all, when you ignore something, you don't study it in detail to find out what it is.

Therefore, it is best to avoid any designs that look like advertisements. The exact implications of this guideline will vary with new forms of ads; currently follow these rules:

- *Banner blindness means that users never fixate their eyes on anything that looks like a banner ad due to shape or position on the page*

- *Animation avoidance makes users ignore areas with blinking or flashing text or other aggressive animations*

- *Pop-up purges mean that users close pop-up windoids before they have even fully rendered; sometimes with great viciousness (a sort of getting-back-at-GeoCities triumph). I don't want to ban pop-ups completely since they can sometimes be a productive part of an interface, but I advise making sure that there is an alternative way of using the site for users who never see the pop-ups.*

Ten Good Deeds in Web Design

Jakob Nielsen's Alertbox, October 3, 1999
(www.useit.com/alertbox/991003.html)

It is much harder to say what good things to do since I have never seen a website that was truly stellar with respect to usability. The best major site was probably amazon.com as of late 1998, but during 1999 Amazon declined in usability due to the strategy of blurring the site's focus.

Of course, articles that list 30 mistakes can be seen as constructive criticism and a prescription for 30 things to do in a Web project: design to avoid each of the mistakes!

Here's a list of ten additional design elements that will increase the usability of virtually all sites:

- *Place your* name and logo *on every page and make the logo a link to the home page (except on the home page itself, where the logo should not be a link: never have a link that points right back to the current page).*

- *Provide search if the site has more than 100 pages.*

- *Write straightforward and simple headlines and page titles that clearly explain what the page is about and that will make sense when read out-of-context in a search engine results listing.*

- *Structure the page to facilitate scanning and help users ignore large chunks of the page in a single glance: for example, use grouping and subheadings to break a long list into several smaller units.*

- *Instead of cramming everything about a product or topic into a single, infinite page, use hypertext to structure the content space into a starting page that provides an overview and several secondary pages that each focus on a specific topic. The goal is to allow users to avoid wasting time on those subtopics that don't concern them.*

- *Use product photos, but avoid cluttered and bloated product family pages with lots of photos. Instead have a small photo on each of the individual product pages and link the photo to one or more bigger ones that show as much detail as users need. This varies depending on type of product. Some products may even need zoomable or rotatable photos, but reserve all such advanced features for the secondary pages. The primary product page must be fast and should be limited to a thumbnail shot.*

- *Use relevance-enhanced image reduction when preparing small photos and images: instead of simply resizing the original image to a tiny and unreadable thumbnail, zoom in on the most relevant detail and use a combination of cropping and resizing.*

- *Use link titles to provide users with a preview of where each link will take them, before they have clicked on it.*

- *Ensure that all important pages are accessible for users with disabilities, especially blind users.*

- *Do the same as everybody else: if most big websites do something in a certain way, then follow along since users will expect things to work the same on your site. Remember Jakob's Law of the Web User Experience: users spend most of their time on other sites, so that's where they form their expectations for how the Web works.*

Finally, always test your design with real users as a reality check. People do things in odd and unexpected ways, so even the most carefully planned project will learn from usability testing.

Show Me Where to Click

In the UI Design Update Newsletter for October 2000 from Human Factors International (www.humanfactors.com/library/oct00.asp), Bob Bailey offers up some do's and don'ts to help visitors figure out if an area on a page was "clickable":

Text-Based Links

Do use blue underlined text for most links

Do use underlined headers as links

Do use words in a left-justified list as individual links

Do use bullets, arrows or some other indicator in front of certain text links

Do use "mouse-overs" appropriately and with care

Do use page location to help communicate that an item is clickable

– Left or right margins

– Top or bottom of the page

Do use the term "click here" when appropriate

Do specifically refer to nearby graphical links in the text ("click on the Lion")

Graphical Links

Do use meaningful words inside graphical links

– Target locations (Home, Back to Top, Next)

– Common actions (Go, Login, Submit, Register)

Do use graphical "tabs" that look like real-world tabs

Do use graphical buttons that look like real-world pushbuttons

Do use clear, descriptive labels inside tabs and pushbuttons

Do put clickable graphics close to descriptive, blue underlined text

Do use a frame (border) around certain graphical links

Do make all company logos clickable (to the home page)

Don't require users to do "mine sweeping" to find links

Don't use stand-alone graphics that are not close to, or do not contain, text as links

Don't Make Me Think

One of the wonderful things about writing the third edition of this book is that I am no longer on the hook for *all* of it. I can quote Jakob Nielsen. I can also point you to other sources of information, such as Steve Krug and his book, *Don't Make Me Think* (Que, 2000) (see Figure 3.11).

Jakob Nielsen is a scientist and a researcher. Steve Krug has spent 10 years in the trenches as a consultant and has written a book on usability that employs large doses of humor to make the whole thing palatable. Jakob's writings are a must-read for the practitioner, while Steve's are for anybody with an hour on his or her hands.

Read Steve's book for one reason only: So you completely incorporate the title into your entire Web design and development strategy. Do *not* make people think about what

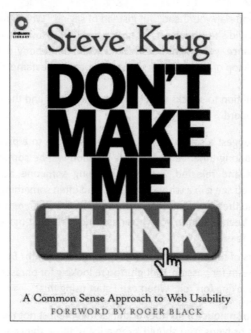

Figure 3.11   Steve Krug takes a slightly different approach, with the same results.

they see on your site. Bend over backward to make it as dead-bang simple to use as possible. And then grab five people off the street to test it and show you where you've made your mistakes.

Not people you know, not people who know anything about the company or the products it sells, just random people with some Web experience. How much? You get great results from all kinds. Long-time Web users will try some short cuts you haven't built in, and neophytes will bang their heads up against walls you didn't know you built. Here's Steve's take on usability testing:

What to Do If You're Observing
Being an observer at a usability test is a cushy job. All you have to do is listen, watch closely, keep an open mind, and take notes.

Here are the types of things you're looking for:

Do they get it? Without any help, can the users figure out what the site or the page is, what it does, and where to start?

Can they find their way around? Do they notice and understand the site's navigation? Does your hierarchy—and the names you're using for things—make sense to them?

Head slappers. You'll know these when you see them: the user will do something, or *not* do something, and suddenly everyone who's observing the session will slap his or her forehead and say, "Why didn't we think of that?" or, "Why didn't we ever notice that?" These are *very* valuable insights.

Shocks. These will also make you slap your head, but instead of saying, "Why didn't *we* notice that?" you'll say, "How could she (the user) *not* notice that?" or, "How could she not understand that?" For instance, you might be shocked when somebody doesn't notice there is a menu bar at the top of each page or doesn't recognize the name of one of your company's products.

Unlike head slappers, the solution to shocks won't always be obvious and they may send you back to the drawing board.

Inspiration. Users will often suggest a solution or a germ of a solution to a problem that you've struggled with for a long time. Very often, the solution will be something you've already thought about and rejected, but just watching someone actually encounter the problem will let you see it in a whole new light. And often something else about the project has changed in the meantime (you've decided to use a different technology, for instance, or there's been a shift in your business priorities) that makes an abandoned approach suddenly feasible.

Passion. What are the elements of the site that the users really connect with? Be careful not to mistake mere enthusiasm for passion, though. You're looking for phrases like, "This is exactly what I've been looking for!" or, "When can I start using this?"

In the course of any test, you'll also notice a number of things that are just not working like missing graphics, broken links or typos. You should keep a list of these things so you can pass it on to whomever will fix them, but they're not what you're there to find, and you shouldn't let them distract you.

Here are some things to keep in mind when you're observing:

Brace yourself. You may be disappointed by the users' reactions. Some people just won't get it. Some just won't like it. Some will get lost and confused, apparently with no reason. It can be emotionally wrenching to watch someone have a negative reaction to something you've poured your soul into. The mantra you want to have in your head is not "It's not working!" but rather, "What will it take to fix it?"

This emotional reaction is why I decline to review brand new Web site designs. People e-mail me asking for my opinion on their latest achievement. "How long has the site been live?" I like to ask. If it's been online for less than three months, the birthing pains are still too fresh. Telling somebody that their baby is ugly is OK if they are on their way to the plastic surgeon and want some advice. But within a few minutes of birth is cruel and unusual punishment. Back to Steve Krug:

Don't panic. Try to resist the temptation to jump to *any* conclusion until you've seen at least two users, preferably three.

Be quiet. There's nothing more disconcerting for a test participant than the sound of laughter—or groans—coming from the adjoining room when she's having trouble using the site.

Remember you're grading on a curve. When a participant who uses the Web two hours a day doesn't know how to type a URL, don't think "Sheesh! What a dolt." Think, "How many people are just like that out there? Can we afford to lose all of them as users?"

Remember you're seeing their best behavior. When you are watching a test you need to remember that people will tend to read Web pages much more thoroughly and put more effort into figuring things out in a test situation than they will in real life. After all, they're not under any time pressure, they're being paid to figure it out, and—most importantly—they don't want to look stupid. So when they can't figure something out, you have to realize that they're trying much harder than most people will and they *still* can't get it.

Pay more attention to actions and explanations than opinions. Opinions expressed during user tests are notoriously unreliable. People will often exaggerate their opinions— because they think you *want* them to express strong opinions.

There is no substitution for having real, live humans giving your Web site the once-over—or is there?

Navigation Investigation Automation

There's a company up in Portland, Oregon, that's come up with a systematic approach to letting you know if your site is suitable for human consumption. It's called WebCriteria (www.webcriteria.com), and it has several software packages that act like humans. Here's how it describes what it offers:

> Task Analysis is based on WebCriteria's proprietary Max technology and provides answers— task-by-task and page-by-page—to exactly where and why users will experience frustration because of the time and effort required to complete their objectives.
>
> WebCriteria's Task Analysis navigates your and your competitors' sites the same way customers do when searching for information or buying products. The time and effort required to complete each transaction on each site is reported on-line, including a diagnostic summary, easy-to-understand graphical comparisons, and supporting page view detail.
>
> Task Analysis can help you answer the following questions:
>
> Can visitors complete tasks in a timely fashion?
>
> How easily can customers complete tasks on my site compared to my competitors' sites?
>
> Which actions, pages, and elements are keeping customers from getting to their end goal?
>
> How can I streamline the transaction flow to optimize for speed?
>
> Are the tasks on my site consistent with current "Best in Class" sites?
>
> How do the transactions on my site differ for first-time versus repeat visitors?

Skeptical? I certainly was, so I called and asked the company to explain itself. Max surfs your Web site as a human might. Max counts the cognitive and motor cycles it takes to get to a certain point or accomplish a specific task. Using human factors techniques, WebCriteria has determined how long it takes to choose between two different choices—not long. How about between four choices? A little longer. How about seven choices? A *lot* longer. Motor cycles are not grown-up Vespas but mouse movements. If the choice is simple, but the location of the button is far removed from the previous click or the button is unusually small, that can add to the time it takes to position the mouse and click.

Max assumes that humans read only the first line of each paragraph. It counts the number of paragraphs on a specific page, accounts for the fact that embedded text links are not given more than a cursory glance, and reviews how many choices there are on the page to render a factor in the navigability quotient.

Given a specific task (buy this book), Max starts from the goal and works back to the beginning. It determines the shortest number of clicks from the goal, back to the home page, and then calculates forward to determine how many clicks and how much time would elapse if a human did it. The initial results are a benchmark that can be used to improve your navigation or to compare your site to others.

Buying a Razor Scooter for Christmas 2000 was a significantly different experience at Amazon.com (see Figure 3.12) than it was at FAO Schwartz (www.faoschwartz.com) (see Figure 3.13).

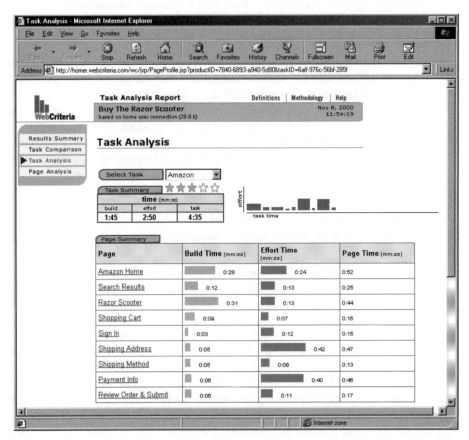

Figure 3.12   Amazon aced out FAO Schwartz on *build* but required a little more *effort*.

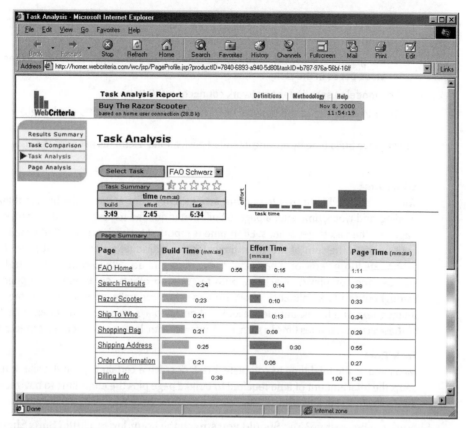

Figure 3.13   FAO Schwartz pages loaded so slowly that the overall *task* scores were painful.

Here's how Webcriteria, the makers of Max, describe the difference between *build time* and *effort time*:

Build Time

The time required to load enough of the visible page needed by a user to make the first interactive choice in the specified sequence for the page. Note that this is typically smaller than the load time for the entire page. Build time is contrasted with page load time, which is a measure of how long it takes to load an entire page (visible and scrolled region). The build time specifically measures what is visible and needed for a user to select the first navigational element in the task segment under evaluation. Many web sites employ a design that optimizes for this first choice. Build time is influenced by the speed of the network connection, the weight of the page view, and where on the page first task interaction or navigation point is positioned. WebCriteria Task Analysis uses a network model to factor out Internet delay variations and vantage points to give an objective measure of web site and task design. A simulated 28.8Kbps modem connection is used. Build time is influenced by:

The target position of the first action on the page.

Size and placement of graphical elements on the page.

Which graphical elements were cached (already loaded in the course of building previous pages in the task).

The modeled speed of the network connection (28.8Kbps).

The modeled size of the browser window (800 pixels wide x 600 pixels high).

Tip: Improve build time by moving intended navigational elements earlier in the visual page view.

Effort Time

The time required for a user to perform actions. Effort time includes the human thinking, reading, and typing time after a page is built that is needed to navigate and interact with a page and the task target actions. Effort time is reported for each action; effort time for the entire page is the sum of the effort times for the individual actions on that page. Target actions are those items on a page that a user must interact with to complete the task. The number and complexity of actions, both targets and others, on an individual page and throughout the task, influence effort. Human effort generally increases with more links, images, text, and forms, but their layout and design plays an equally important role. Each of these actions requires time to scan, read, interact with, learn and remember across pages.

Task Time

Measured as the total time to complete a task or reach a certain page in the site. It represents the total amount of time required to build a page plus the effort time to navigate and interact with the page.

Should you be creative? Yes. Should you stretch the boundaries a little? Sure. Should you do your very, *very* best to make it as easy on your visitor as possible? Yes. In doing so, don't forget to take advantage of the knowledge they already have. Refer back to #3 (Non-Standard Use of GUI Widgets) in Jakob Nielsen's *The Top Ten* New *Mistakes of Web Design*.

Nonstandards

A navigational tool that can find things on your site quickly and elegantly might also be able to find things on the Web quickly and elegantly. The creator of such a tool will eventually be able to compare houses with Bill Gates. It's a monster problem, and millions of us are anxious for a solution.

Interesting efforts are underway as we speak. Inxight (www.inxight.com) has come up with several alternatives, including the hyperbolic tree (see Figure 3.14).

Intuitive? No. Easy to grasp? Not really. A fabulous way to surf once you've got the hang of it? I'll have to get back to you on that one. Let's just say that the examples Inxight has on its site are generic, in-house creations, and its list of active customers for this software is not in evidence.

Inxight's Summary Server, on the other hand, has been put to good use at a couple of sites, such as the CNN Industry Watch pages (cnniw.yellowbrix.com/pages/cnniw/

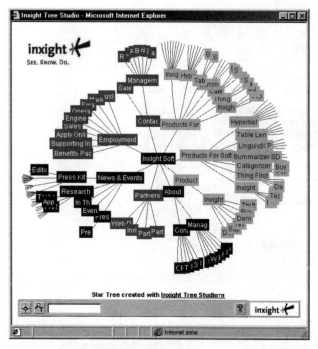

Figure 3.14 Inxight has imagined your Web site as a multidimensional globe.

Headlines.nsp?category=Business+and+Finance&ID=cnniw&scategory=Computers) (see Figures 3.15 through 3.17).

This sort of interface gives visitors a better idea of what's to come if they click. But is all that technology better than simply writing the description on the same page? Wouldn't it be better to remove the Executive Summary box and widen the Headlines column? By the time I got down to the Inxight "Thing Finder Server" package, I was thinking hard about the title of Steve Krug's book.

If you are inclined to pursue the odd ways people have come up with to navigate around sites, you'll enjoy wandering the links at www.parc.xerox.com/istl/projects/uir/projects/InformationVisualization.html. In the meantime, keep in mind that simplicity is next to deity and that boring is often best.

Search as Navigation Tools

The first time somebody comes to your site, he or she is wandering from page to page to get a feel for what you have to offer. Thereafter, the visitor wants to quickly zero in on the informational object of his or her desire. If visitors can't remember how they found it the first time, they are going to be on the look out for a search box.

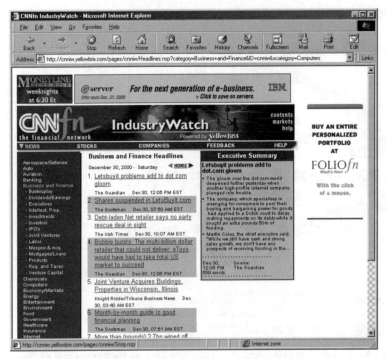

Figure 3.15   Roll the mouse over the article on the left . . .

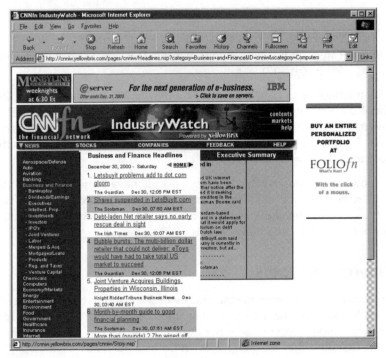

Figure 3.16   . . . and the summary animates its way into . . .

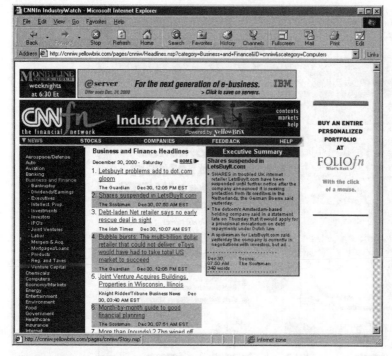

Figure 3.17   . . . the box on the right.

Good Search

We've all experienced bad on-site searches, so I'll spare you those examples. Instead, here's a good one: Sun Microsystems (www.sun.com). It's good for a number of reasons. First of all, you don't have to hunt for it. There is no "Click here to search" on the Sun home page. Oh, there *used* to be (see Figure 3.18), but Sun got rid of it (see Figure 3.19). It decided to allow visitors direct access to the search pages. One click less.

But Sun didn't stop there. It decided to make the results of the visitor's search meaningful to the visitor, instead of just to the computer or the programmers (see Figure 3.20).

To begin with, Sun maintains the main menu bars at the top of the page. Should the visitor decide he or she was hunting up the wrong tree, he or she can change direction at a click. A search tip shows at the upper left, while instructions on how to get the most out of the search engine (Help and Advanced) are found right where the visitor needs them—by the search box. If the results aren't to the user's liking, he or she may wish to give it another try. A little help would be in order. Next, the statistics for the results are shown. This gives a feel for how well the user is narrowing the inquiry:

Results for: web site usability

Document count: web (12500) site (24063) usability (364) web site . . . (3820)

27417 results found

Figure 3.18 The Sun Microsystems magnifying glass in the upper right led to the search page.

We can switch the sorting from "by relevance" to "by date," and we can hide the summaries if we choose. Then come the results themselves. Not a file name and the number of bytes, but document titles, degree of relevancy, date, location (URL), size, and the first 30 to 35 words *on the page*, rather than lines of HTML code. In other words, this page of results was designed for a human user.

Then Sun made use of a very valuable tool, the Find Similar button. "Users can easily find information related to their original search by clicking the Find Similar link in the search results." Did Sun write this search engine itself? No. It licensed it from Inktomi (www.inktomi.com). That means you can, too.

But does that mean you should? Not necessarily.

Bad Search

My Web site (www.targeting.com) is a case in point. In fact, it was the subject of an article in the Backspin column in *Network World* magazine on October 9, 2000 by my good friend Mark Gibbs (www.nwfusion.com/columnists/2000/1009gibbs.html):

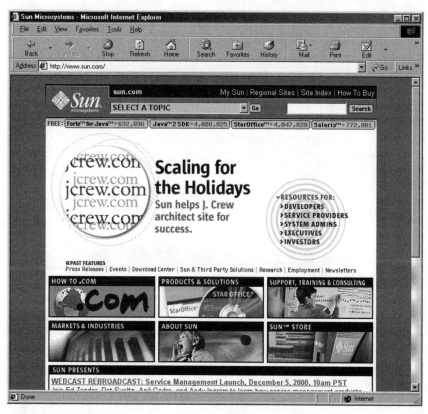

Figure 3.19 Today's Sun customer is saved a click. The magnifying glass is replaced by a search field.

How often do you use search engines? Most of you will do so at least once per day, and some will be lucky enough to do so perhaps dozens of times before morning coffee.

Some of the search engines you use will be the 800-pound gorillas of the searching market, such as Yahoo, Google and AltaVista, while others will be site-specific.

It's the site-specific ones I want to talk about. First, let me ask if you have one on your Web site? You do? Great. What for?

Now you might say something like, "So people can find stuff." If you appended "duh" to your answer, you can leave this column straightaway and go stand in the corner until you think you can act politely.

Really, readers these days: no restraint and far too much back talk . . . saying things like, "Look at me, I know my ARP from my MBONE" . . . I don't know . . .

Anyway, where was I? Oh, yes . . .

So my good friend who shall remain nameless and we shall call Mr. X but is, in reality, Jim Sterne of Target Marketing, told me he had a problem with getting a search engine to work on his site. This was an ASP service that had previously worked, but for some reason on this day wasn't working properly for a trivial reason not worth going into. After looking at the problem and concluding that his HTML coding was correct and that his trouble was with the ASP, the issue repaired itself within an hour.

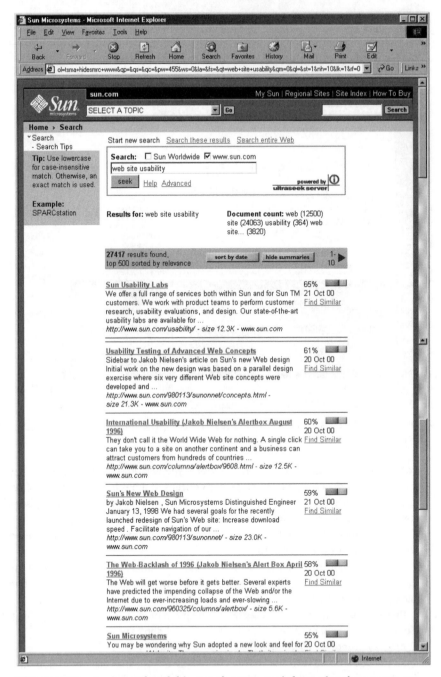

Figure 3.20 Sun's results of this search are more informative than most.

I then asked Jim, er, sorry, Mr. X, why he wanted to have a search engine. He was nice enough to not reply "duh," and said he wanted people to be able to find stuff on his site. Now Mr. X has quite a bit of stuff on his site about online marketing and related topics, but my question was, what was it the site visitors wanted to find?

He checked, and this is the list of queries starting with the least popular: marketing; target marketing; targeting; sport; Net-based stock trading; ABCs of marketing; target affinity; marketing segmentation; Web marketing; cigarette advertising; soccer; total available market; Nike; track and field; clear message; business plan; Club Med; response cards; marketing magazines; and advertising technique.

The obvious searches such as "marketing" would yield far too generic results to be really useful, while the people who were looking for "sport," "Net-based stock trading," "soccer" and "Club Med" were obviously on a different planet.

I contend that these peculiar searches are symptomatic of visitor behavior on most Web sites that offer local searching because the majority of people don't know what they want to know about and where they should look for it.

Sure, where you have a ton of varied content local searching may make sense, but usually there's a more important objective: You want to transfer your sales and marketing messages to the person looking at your site. You want to give them access to something that supports your view of the world, and a well-indexed site is, in my opinion, better than a search tool.

If you think visitors might be looking for "green, left-handed widgets" on your site, then give them an index that makes those terms findable. For example, a hierarchical index that included "widgets:color:green" and "widgets:handedness:left" would be far more useful than a search engine that returns 256 hits, none of which is relevant because your visitor misspelled "widget."

And if there's one thing that overwhelms people on the Internet, it's too much data. How often have you heard people say that the 'Net is too big, and it is too hard to find what they are looking for?

Don't make your Web site just another data swamp if you want to get your message across. Mr. X has since done away with his search engine.

Careful Search

If your site is large enough to warrant a search engine, then by all means implement one but pay close attention to it. You'll find that people aren't necessarily finding what they're after on your site.

One Web manager told Forrester Research (www.forrester.com), "Last month we had an intern look at the most common search queries and then see which results were displayed. It turned out that the right answer for the top query wasn't showing up until item 47." Time for some search engine tuning.

The same Forrester report ("Must Search Stink?", June 2000) cited one Web virtuoso who placed a "Buy" button next to each line of search results. That link now generates 30 percent of its orders. Not everybody is looking for the latest, in-depth information. Some just want to give you money.

Don't Lose Them to Another Site

Many are the times it makes sense to offer a promotional plug to a business ally. A Web site should be a resource to your customers. That may mean telling them where to get additional information on specific subjects. These types of links are valuable to people, and they will come back to your Web site again and again if they see it as a useful source of pointers to other information. But first, consider a couple of ideas to ensure that you haven't spent a lot of time encouraging your users to see P. T. Barnum's Grand Egress.

You want to be sure that the links to the outside world are properly positioned so that it is abundantly clear that the user is now leaving your site. The underground interconnections between the buildings around New York's World Trade Center are very useful all year round, but it's quite easy for visitors to lose track of which building they're under at any given time.

Tell users that they may find more information at these sites, but be sure to let them know why they need to come back again and again.

Are you sending customers to your distributors' sites? We'll talk about that more in Chapter 10, "Partner Relationship Management." For now, let's keep the focus on the user experience on *your* site.

Controlling the Action

A brochure is a linear medium. You expect people to read it from front to back. People expect you to have written it to be read from front to back. Knowing that some people will want to jump right to the information that's important to them, you can offer an index or table of contents. A Web site is not a linear medium. By its nature, people are free to hyperjump wherever they choose. It is incumbent on the Web designer to create a site that encourages people to select the right links.

Many dollars are spent studying what people look at when they see an ad, a store shelf, or the inside of a department store. The graphic artist spends hours arriving at just the right layout to draw the prospect's attention to the salient components. The department store designer works feverishly to ensure that the sight lines from every entrance lead shoppers to the most profitable departments, aisles, and shelves. Consumer goods packaging is a science. Shelf positioning is a hard-fought contest steeped in the knowledge of how the eye roves over competing brands. These activities are a mere game of checkers when compared to the three-dimensional chess of an interactive Web site. CD-ROM designers have been sweating the details over the management of game players, and now you are tasked with helping the online shopper.

You are going to create an electronic environment for people to explore. What do you want them to find? Where do you want them to look first? What do you want them to learn? What do you want them to do? Whether you're selling a toy, a car, a service, or a political perspective, you must determine what outcome you want. In fact, you have competing desires: You must support multiple products with multiple product managers—the political issues are not entertaining.

But, above all, keep in mind the most important question: What does the visitor want to learn/see/do/accomplish? You must also cater to the casually curious, the seriously prospective, and the current customer with a problem to solve. Therefore, with your goals firmly in mind, look to your home page to set the standard style and begin the process of moving the user toward his or her objective.

The Home Page

There are as many choices for the look and feel of a home page as there are artists, programmers, and marketing managers. No matter what corporate personality you are trying to project, some basics apply. The first is to make it a nice place to visit.

Learning from the Past

The Microsoft home page (www.microsoft.com) (see Figure 3.21) used to be hideous. There. Now I've done it. Somewhere in the world is a programmer who created this vision of a home page in 1994, and I have offended him or her deeply. Maybe some of you reading this book like this graphic. Maybe I've offended more than just one.

You may or may not like the picture, but it's devoid of meaning. Is it a landscape? Half a nova exploding? A diskette partially eaten by screensavers? A sunrise? I can assure you that Microsoft would *never* put something on its home page that even slightly referred to its competitors in Palo Alto, California.

This home page doesn't communicate Microsoft at all. The only brand awareness on this page was the Microsoft typeface. Where's the Windows logo? Is this really Microsoft? This flat, low-resolution image did nothing to instill confidence in the company.

Keep It Simple

The basic rule Microsoft seems to have ignored is the KISS principle (keep it simple, stupid). Keep it crystal clear. The KISS principle is in effect on the Web like nowhere else. People want instant gratification from their computers and from you. They want to get where they're going. Unfortunately, this home page was cumbersome. Too many choices were scattered across the sky. It took a few minutes to determine which category to select to find out about a bug.

A handful of usual suspects are found on most home pages:

- What's new
- What's been added since (date)
- Press releases
- Company and industry events
- About the company
- History

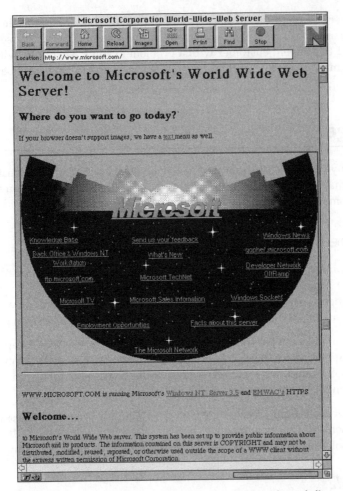

Figure 3.21 The Microsoft home page of old—ugly and disorganized.

- Current accomplishments
- Financials (for public companies)
- Upper management Who's Who
- About the industry
- White papers
- Special knowledge we have that you want
- About our products
- Product line A
- Product line B
- Product line C
- Customer service

- Frequently asked questions
- Order processing support
- Product support
- How to contact us
- Employment opportunities

Having more choices than these quickly becomes confusing in any setting. In studies of the human mind, it has been determined that people can simultaneously remember seven items plus or minus two. That is, a list of five to nine items is just about right. Less than that doesn't make use of the potential; more than that tends to confuse and impair one's ability to retain the information. That's why menus in Chinese restaurants are always daunting.

Information Mapping (www.infomap.com) has made a business of helping companies put information, instructions, and procedures online. It started years ago on mainframes back when it was determined that, on a computer screen, people can remember only five items, plus or minus one.

The reasons for this are still being argued. Perhaps because the page is smaller, there are fewer spatial clues than on paper. Perhaps people expect the screen to scroll away or present new data any second, so they are speed reading instead of concentrating for retention. Maybe they have been trained by television to believe something on the screen is ephemeral, momentary, and of dubious authenticity. Mostly, it seems that due to the lower resolution on a screen (72 dots per inch, rather than 600+), it's simply harder to read.

For whatever reason, the people at Information Mapping have verified the need to keep choices to a minimum; the art lies in balancing that limit with the need to remove the layers between the user and the data.

Today's version of the Microsoft Web site (see Figure 3.22) uses the concept of information chunking quite well. Rather than an overwhelming number of choices, you can readily see that there are three main topic areas, along with two main menus. The first menu is the button bar that lives at the top of every page on the site: All Products | Support | Search | microsoft.com Guide. The next button bar changes from section to section on the site and is context sensitive.

Then Microsoft chunks the content into three areas. On the right are the news and the downloads. In the middle are Microsoft's major products (Exchange 2000, e-commerce solutions, Windows 2000, and Office 2000). On the left, in the spot reserved for menus, Microsoft engages in subchunking. After seven years of Web site development, the de facto standard seems to have fallen to the left side for the site guide, and, in keeping with the times, Microsoft chunks this menu once again. There are four choices, none of which contains more than six options:

Product Family Sites

Windows	Servers
Office	Developer Tools

Figure 3.22 Microsoft counts on chunking to help the neophyte visitor decipher this home page.

Web Services

Office eServices	MSN
Windows Update	bCentral

Customer Sites

Home & Personal	Developer
Business	Partner/Reseller
IT Professional	Education

Resources

Shop	Microsoft Jobs
Microsoft Press Books	Privacy Statement
Newsletters	DOJ vs. Innovation

Within each of these categories, there are no more than six choices, which stays within the five-plus-or-minus-one rule. The net effect of subchunking is that the user determines which of three page areas to look at, is then presented with four menu choices, and finally ends up with a decision among six options. There may be 51 choices on the screen, but they don't overwhelm the visitor.

Microsoft also offers a text-only option (www.microsoft.com/default_text.htm) (see Figure 3.23), which stays true to its word. No logo, no special font, no background—just text.

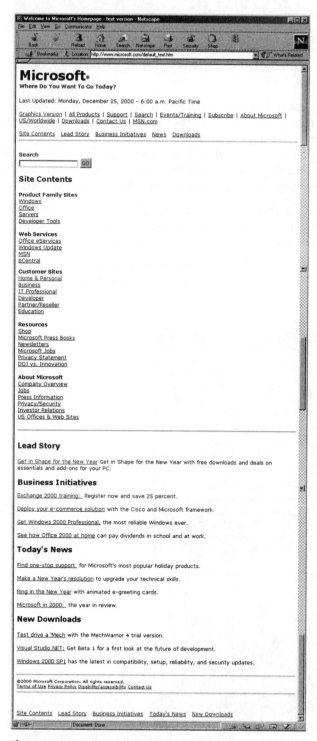

Figure 3.23   Microsoft understands that there are those who don't want the fancy pictures of pull-downs, just the information.

Keep It Flat

Looking for information is hard enough if you don't know where to look. Pursuing data requires patience and fortitude. Using a Web browser means honing your skills at following a train of thought.

If you are offering a service to the user, make it easy to use. If you are providing valuable data to the user, make it easy to find. You must not give too many choices on each menu, but you must not require too many clicks to get to the information. So, you're damned if you do and damned if you don't. After all, each click is an opportunity for users to choose the wrong path, forget what they wanted in the first place, and become frustrated that this marvelous medium (and therefore your company) isn't delivering on its promise.

FedEx (www.fedex.com) learned this the hard way. When the Web was young, the FedEx home page was, well, boring (see Figure 3.24). But that was OK because you could find the one thing you were looking for: Track a FedEx Package.

FedEx got it right the first time for two reasons: technical limitations and lack of imagination. Back in the dark ages, the background of your Web site could be any color you

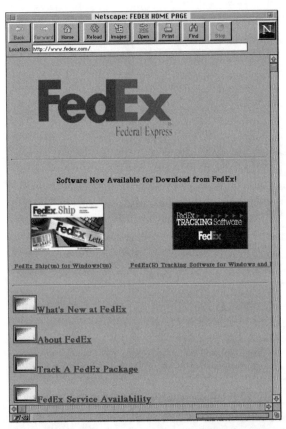

Figure 3.24 FedEx also started Web life as an ugly duckling.

wanted as long as it was gray. Everybody's Web site was gray; that's what there was. For navigation, it was a breeze. The third item got all the attention: Track a FedEx Package. That's what we all wanted to do.

Over the course of time, FedEx altered its design. It had more technical choices in how its pages looked. It had more graphic artists designing the site, instead of leaving the task to the engineers who built it. The result was absolutely frustrating (see Figure 3.25).

FedEx significantly increased the time it took to track a package. Consider the steps required. From the home page (which did not load in a jiffy), you had to identify which country you're in. Or was that which country you're shipping to? If you're visiting Mexico, did you pick Mexico or "your" country?

Then, there was an interminable wait for the next page to show up (see Figure 3.26). Even if you knew where the "Tracking" button was going to pop up, it took a lifetime to do so. Finally, after identifying the destination country, you could enter the airbill number (see Figure 3.27).

Maybe FedEx did a study, reviewed its server logs, and stopped people on the street for interviews. Maybe it discovered that most of the people who come to www.fedex.com are there for the Employment Opportunities. But even if the vast majority are not there to track a package, the people who are tend to be a bit anxious. Why put them through the torture of multiple pages? Why not let people enter their airbill numbers as soon as possible and more than one at a time?

Figure 3.25 FedEx took one step forward and three back with its new design.

Figure 3.26 FedEx, take two. You're getting closer . . .

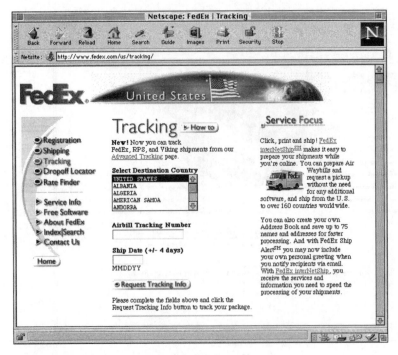

Figure 3.27 . . . to entering your airbill number.

That decision changed the site design again. Once the visitor identifies his or her country on the home page, he or she can enter up to 25 airbills at a time (see Figure 3.28).

Think like a customer.

Study How the User Uses—The Sun Story

In their paper "SunWeb: User Interface Design for Sun Microsystems' Internal Web" (www.sun.com/sun-on-net/uidesign/usabilitytest.html), Jakob Nielsen and Darrell Sano described four different usability studies to help them determine the navigational tools for the Sun Microsystems internal Web site:

- Card sorting to discover categories
- Icon intuitiveness testing
- Card distribution to icons
- Thinking-aloud walkthrough of page mock-up

The team wrote up 51 types of information that might be found on the internal Web site. They wrote each on note cards and scattered them across a table. The experiment subjects were asked to sort these cards into piles based on similarity. As a result, they created proper groupings for information categories for the home page.

The resulting categories required icons or pictograms to represent them on the home page. Once the first draft of these icons was created, they were submitted to the icon

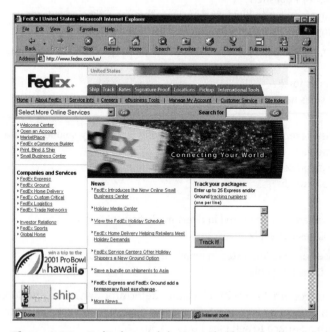

Figure 3.28 FedEx learned that people like to look up a lot of airbills at once, so it made it easier.

intuitiveness test. Subjects were asked to interpret each unlabeled icon to see how understandable it was. Most were good or excellent, but several had to be substantially altered.

The two tests were then combined. The new icons were printed and handed to subjects, who then had to place them in the proper categories on the table. This test ensured that users would associate the correct concepts with each of the general groups previously defined. The "thinking aloud" study simply asked subjects what sort of information they would expect to find behind each of the icons.

The conclusions from this project are that a uniform user interface structure can make a Web significantly easier to use and that "discount usability engineering" can be employed to base the design on user studies even when project schedules are very tight.

Today, the Sun Web site is the starting point for thousands of internal Web servers.

Stepping into the Future

How about letting your customers control what they see on your site? Online advertising network DoubleClick (www.doubleclick.com) does just that. On its home page is a "Streamline This Site" button that leads to a series of questions:

> In order to provide you with the DoubleClick information most relevant to your company's needs, please fill out the form below. The results will be used to streamline our site, enabling you to quickly and easily find information about DoubleClick products and services.
>
> Are you an Advertiser or Publisher?
> > Advertiser: Looking for ways to build your business through online advertising
> > Publisher: Looking for sales representation or ad management solutions
>
> If you're a publisher, do you have your own sales force or are you looking for a sales representative?
> > I have my own sales force
> > I am looking for sales representation
> > Does not apply
>
> If you're an advertiser, are you looking for an ad serving technology solution or are you looking to buy media?
> > I am looking for an ad serving media technology solution
> > I am looking to buy media
> > Does not apply
>
> If you're an advertiser, are you interested in direct marketing solutions?
> > Yes   No   Does not apply
>
> If you're an advertiser, are you interested in email marketing solutions?
> > Yes   No   Does not apply

Your answers will, in conjunction with a cookie, determine what the site looks like when you return. An advertiser is presented with a different menu set (see Figure 3.29) than a publisher with ad space to sell (see Figure 3.30).

When in doubt, let your customers figure it out.

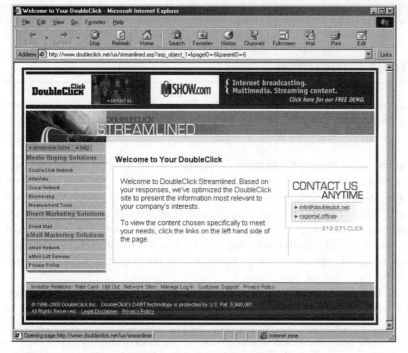

Figure 3.29 Advertisers are shown a menu that includes Media Buying Solutions, Direct Marketing Solutions, and eMail Marketing Solutions . . .

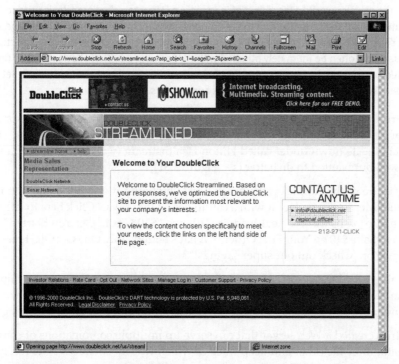

Figure 3.30 . . . while publishers are offered information on how DoubleClick can sell their available inventory.

Watch Your Language

Ron Richards of ResultsLab (www.resultslab.com) has a great deal of experience fine-tuning new-media materials for his clients. In an article on his site, Ron points out ways you can multiply response severalfold by making even the slightest changes in copy:

> To get big gains for a Web advertiser, the first task is to rewrite the words you want people to click on (the jump points)—turning them into compelling grabbers, with lots of genuine curiosity. For example, one of an Internet (travel store) bookseller's jump points reads, "Different Trips, Different Styles," which is an attempt at creating blind curiosity, which usually fails to get users to jump because it only makes sense after the jump. By rewriting it to read "Which Guides Are Best For Which Interests, Destinations, and Budgets?", the grabber becomes a clear offer of valuable learning and creates benefit-oriented curiosity.
>
> The key is to realize that about 95 percent of all persuasion tools are riddled with poison language and poison graphics—often dozens of hidden elements, any one of which can kill the response. Even the best sites could multiply their response if they found their missed bets. The trick is to look for the subtle ways in which you've built in confusion, triggered a qualm, suboptimized the argument sequence, lost eye-control, or failed to find language psychologically grabbing enough to stop and fascinate the fast-browsing mind.
>
> In the most powerful sites, a "gift of learning"—a "How to . . ." approach—is used to "decommercialize" the message and make it appreciated. And the advertiser's message isn't kept separated under a "click-here-for-commercial-message" icon. Instead, the advertiser's message can often be intimately bundled with the learning gift. That allows stronger, undefended persuasion. In fact, it's amazing how often this approach can virtually reset the product/service standard and disqualify all competitors.

Memetrics (www.memetrics.com) is an Australian company dedicated to measuring the effect of the changes a master like Ron Richards might make. One of its clients, a health and vitamin site down under called Hilton Healthstream (www.lifestream.co.au), was doing well but wanted to do better (see Figure 3.31).

Is the picture of the couple on the beach best? Or should it go with a family portrait? Or should Memetrics replace it with a call-to-action that says, "Click here to talk to one of our naturopaths for free health advice"? Is the "$10 Gift to Get You Started" better than, say, "Save $10 on Your First Order"? What's better: "Buy One Get One Free—Limited Time" or "Check out our super savings!"?

We've all worked these sorts of promotions out in our heads. Oh, yes, you think, I'm sure the health-conscious public is more apt to respond to "Half Off" rather than "Save 50%." But how do you *know*? You know by measuring, and that takes technology.

Memetrics created a Web server that can serve up multiple combinations of content to one visitor after the other and keep track of which was most effective. Its recommendations after running 20 different versions of the home page?

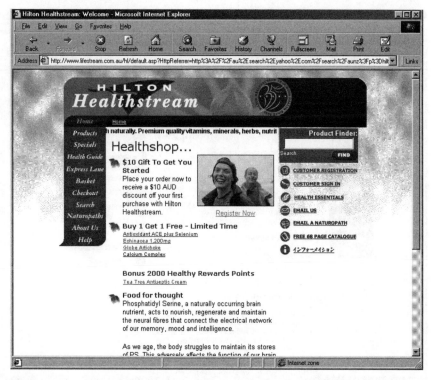

Figure 3.31 Memetrics discovered that small changes make big differences.

- Replace the picture with a button that says, "Click here for a complete list of this month's savings."
- Keep the "$10 Gift to Get You Started" (nothing else was as effective).
- Replace "Buy 1 Get 1 Free" with "Save up to 50%!"

Its results? Hilton Healthstream's whopping 13 percent conversion rate almost doubled to 25 percent (see Figure 3.32).

Just Make It as Easy as Possible

As strangers in a strange land, your Web users need all the help they can get. As more and more sites populate the Web, more and more navigational methods, models, and tools will be created and tested on the public. Over time, some will win favor, and some will be looked on as old-fashioned and clumsy. Some will appeal to different market segments, and some will be rendered useless by the changes in technology. Insist that the goals for your Web site be well established before heading out to create road signs, maps, and online suggestion-toting databases.

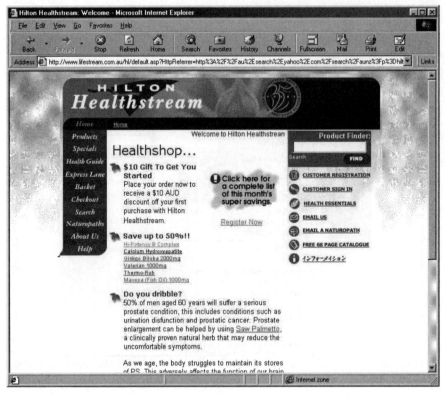

Figure 3.32 Memetrics produced a more effective homepage.

Want to make sure you're doing the bare minimum? Avoid showing up in the next Giga Information Group (www.gigaweb.com) Web Site Score-Card study. In October 2000, Giga found the following errors in its study of 200 major Web sites:

No action links on the home page (e.g., how to buy)	66%
No privacy policy link from home page	60%
No link to site map on home page	50%
No text links, navigation bars, back to home page links	43%
No link to site search tool	39%
No link to employment opportunities	35%
No link to corporate profile	16%

On the bright side, things can only get better.

Multiple Screen Sizes

And please don't forget that you are going to have to ensure that your Web content is readable by a variety of screens. It used to be enough that you created your content so that it would run properly in various versions of Netscape and Internet Explorer. Now, you have to be on the lookout for visitors using PDAs (Palm Pilots, Handspring Visors, etc.) as well as cell phones and wrist watches. Human Factors International (www.humanfactors.com) keeps an eye on such things (see Figure 3.33).

Think Like a Customer

You have to forget that you know everything there is to know about your products and services. You have to try to understand what it's like being a customer who tries to slog through your massive Web site in search of that one bit of information that will help him or her decide which of your offerings is right.

No matter what you sell, people want access to information about your product. Your job is twofold. On one hand, give them so much information that they will not go wanting. Everybody will be able to find that scrap of information he or she is after. On the other hand, use all the tools, techniques, tricks, and ingenuity you can muster to help users find that information as quickly and painlessly as possible. Make sure they can get to it and make a buying decision before they click away to the next vendor down the list at Yahoo!.

If you keep your customers' needs and desires clearly in mind at all times, it will be much easier to help users find what they're looking for.

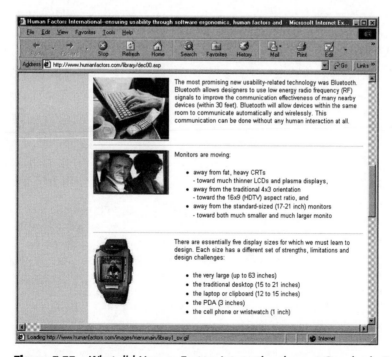

Figure 3.33 What did Human Factors International see at Comdex in December 2000? More user interface complexity ahead.

Congratulations. You've managed to put together a Web site that offers people what they want, and they can get at it without waiting a lifetime or getting lost along the way. Now you have to find a way to hold their attention. Fortunately, you have three things you can put together to do so: a computer, some data, and a programmer or two to create true interactivity.

Interactivity Goes
with the Flow

*A Web site is not something people
read, it's something people do.*

A brochure is a linear, passive medium. As the reader peruses your prose she lets the information wash over her. Television is a linear, passive, time-constrained medium. While the viewer is glued to your wildly expensive 30-second extravaganza he lets the image and sound wash over him. A brochure is not time constrained. The reader can pick it up and put it down any time. Television is time constrained, unless your viewer has carefully videotaped or Tivo-ed your commercials for playback at a more convenient time. Accessing the World Wide Web can be done at any time, but it is time constrained nonetheless.

Your Web site is always available for "picking up" like the brochure. Once ensconced in a Bookmark file, your home page can be retrieved as easily as if it were stored on a local disk. But people don't usually treat it that way. Usually, they set aside a period of time for an online session. During that session, they are looking for something that provides value. You can create value by offering in-depth knowledge. You'll see examples of that in Chapter 7, "Value-Added Marketing—It's Personal." That chapter is about providing real value. This chapter is about providing the perception of value in order to hold readers' attention.

On television you can provide the impression of authority by placing an older actor in an expensive suit behind a large desk and shooting from a lower angle. You can create the impression of value with classical music, rich colors, and repetition, repetition, repetition. (If they can afford to buy all this TV time, they must be doing well. "As seen on TV.") On the Web, graphics are important, but the central mechanism to improve the impression of value is interaction.

Interaction means convincing users they are getting information instead of its being given to them. It means users feel they are actively pulling information rather than having data pushed at them. To do this, you need to make them work for it.

Wait a minute, Jim. You just got finished telling me that I have to make it as easy as possible for visitors to get information and now you say I should make them "work for it." Which is it?

It's the fine balance between effort and reward that makes a major difference in the perceived value of your Web site. Make it too easy, and you give the impression that it's not that important. Make it too hard, and you give the impression that it's not worth the effort. Let's try an example.

Robin, a student, picks up a book from John, her classmate, looks at the marked page, and copies the paragraph into her report in progress. John spent two hours looking through the library to find that book and that paragraph in that book. John perceives the information to be of higher value due to the ratio of content to effort.

Robin takes John's word that the information is good. John *knows* that this is the right information and that it's the *best* information because he made the determination himself.

The Flow Construct

This balance of effort and reward as it pertains to the World Wide Web is explored in "Marketing in Hypermedia Computer-Mediated Environments: Conceptual Foundations" (www2000.ogsm.vanderbilt.edu, December 15, 1994), by Donna L. Hoffman and Thomas P. Novak of the Owen Graduate School of Management at Vanderbilt University. They first define the psychological term "flow":

> Flow has been characterized as a "peculiar dynamic state—the holistic sensation that people feel when they act with total involvement." Flow involves a merging of actions and awareness, with concentration so intense there is little attention left over to consider anything else. A consumer's action in the flow state is experienced "as a unified flowing from one moment to the next, in which he or she is in control of his or her actions, and in which there is little distinction between self and environment, between stimulus and response, or between past, present, and future" (*Beyond Boredom and Anxiety*, Csikszentmihalyi, Jossey Bass, 1977, p. 36). Self-consciousness disappears, the consumer's sense of time becomes distorted, and the resulting state of mind is extremely gratifying.

This conjures up pictures of small children at play, athletes in the heat of competition, and any teenager glued to a video game. It also conjures up a picture of the Internet junkie at 2:00 in the morning, unable to extricate himself or herself from the screen. Hoffman and Novak explain why the experience is so addicting:

> Only when consumers perceive that the hypermedia CME [Computer-Mediated Environment] contains high enough opportunities for action (or challenges), which are matched with their own capacities for action (or skills), will flow potentially occur. This congruence between the control characteristics of the consumer's skills and the challenges of network

navigation enables the consumer in flow to feel "in control of his actions and of the environment. He has no active awareness of control but is simply not worried by the possibility of lack of control" (Csikszentmihalyi, 1977, p. 44). In such cases, consumers have a sense that their skills are adequate to cope with the challenges presented by navigating the environment. When flow occurs, the moment itself is enjoyed and consumers' capabilities are stretched with the likelihood of learning new skills and increasing self-esteem and personal complexity. However, . . . if network navigation does not provide for this, then consumers will become either bored (skills exceed challenges) or anxious (challenges exceed skills) and either exit the CME or select a more or less challenging activity within the CME.

eLab

eLab is a corporate-sponsored research center at the Owen Graduate School of Management, Vanderbilt University. Directed by professors Donna Hoffman and Tom Novak, eLab was founded as Project 2000 in 1994 to study the marketing implications of commercializing the World Wide Web. In the years since, this pioneering scholarly effort has emerged as one of the premiere research centers in the world for the study of Electronic Commerce. eLab can now be reached at eLabWeb.com or ecommerce.vanderbilt.edu.

Why is a hypertext environment like the World Wide Web absolutely captivating to newcomers? Because they come to the Web with some skills in place: computer keyboard familiarity and mouse control, and a desire to see what's out there on the Net. The first thrill of astonishment comes when they grasp the portent of being able to view files from a computer in Spain one moment and from one in Finland the next. The second rush comes as they find Web sites with information of personal interest. "Gee— I could use this Web thing for school or work!" Now, the new Internaut is off on the never-ending surf, clicking freely to see what else there might be.

The Web as Time Sink

It's no wonder corporate executives dread giving Web access to employees. Once hooked, the new Web surfer can spend hours and hours online. The fascination comes from the balance between skills and challenges.

In the past managers were terrified of the telephone. "Give one to each employee? What on earth for? Do you know what that would cost? Do you know how much time would be wasted? People would spend all day talking to each other instead of getting their work done!"

When Microsoft decided to put a solitaire card game into Windows, managers were aghast. "I'll have hundreds of people playing games all day long!" In fact, it was an excellent way to train users on the hand-eye coordination required to use point-and-click functionality.

Over time, the novelty wore off. People stopped making calls just because they could and used the phone to help them do their jobs. (Except for a brief relapse a few years back. Remember those calls? "Hey! I'm on a cell phone! That's right—I'm calling from my car!") Solitaire quickly lost its excitement except as a sanity-maintaining device on long conference calls, and the computer once again became a tool for efficiency.

Yes, people will spend an inordinate amount of time on the Web looking at insignificant rubbish—at first. In doing so, they will hone the skills they need to make it a truly useful tool. If individuals don't curtail their personal surfing habits, you have a management problem, not a technology problem.

Now that you understand the power of *flow*, it's time to take advantage of it.

Putting Flow to Work

You don't send the owner's manual to everybody who calls for a brochure. You don't offer a tour of the factory to somebody who circles an item and returns a bingo card found in a trade journal. You don't fly the president of the company out to meet somebody who just bought a box of your breakfast cereal. You want to provide the right amount of information to the right individual at the right time.

You want prospects to learn about your products at a speed appropriate to the product and appropriate for them. You want them to understand each step. You don't want to overwhelm them with information. Instead, you want to calibrate their reaction at every turn so that you can determine what the proper next step might be. Now you can let your computer participate in that decision-making process and let it "distribute product literature" for you.

You're selling yo-yos? Show a picture or two and a video clip. Explain how consumers can amaze their friends with the skills they'll learn on your Web site. Only then should you announce the price. Selling sophisticated network management and security software? Walk prospects through the learning process slowly. Make sure users feel they are getting the information they want, rather than the information you want them to get. Be sure to engage the users in the activity of learning about your products. Make them participate instead of being passive spectators. Demand action from them. Force them to make decisions. Keep them actively involved.

Interaction Holds Your Attention

What's a noosh? In its own words, "The noosh.com service makes it easier and less expensive for companies to procure and manage Enterprise Communication projects such as print, digital media, packaging, creative services and direct mail." Aren't you glad you asked?

Why is noosh.com worth knowing about? Because it has found a way to use Macromedia's Flash in a way that is neither annoying nor passive. It uses Flash animation to give a software demo (see Figures 4.1 through 4.3).

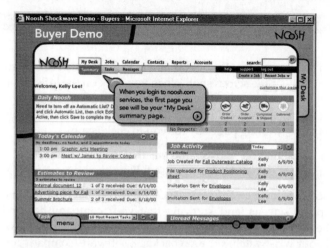

Figure 4.1 Noosh uses Flash . . .

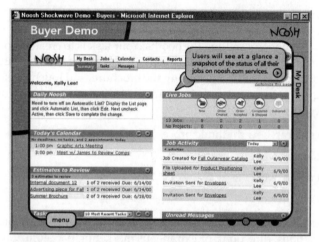

Figure 4.2 . . . to walk you through a software demo . . .

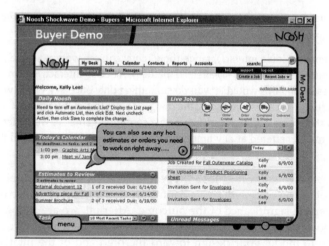

Figure 4.3 . . . that would otherwise be stultifyingly boring.

What you can't tell on this page is that the bubble of dialog that floats over the software screen shot actually floats over the screen shot. When you click on the little right-arrow icon, the whole text bubble glides over to its next spot and displays the proper text. It draws your attention across the screen, instead of just popping up somewhere new. Then, the box just sits there, waiting patiently for you to click again.

It's this combination of animation and interaction that keeps you focused on the screen, mildly entertained, and completely engrossed. Flow.

Knowing that *flow* increases the learning experience, knowing that people can be captivated at their computer screens, and knowing that your company has or knows something that can be useful to your prospects and customers—how do you tie these ideas together to sell your wristwatch, vacation package, software, company image, or political perspective?

It is up to you to provide information as an interesting, engaging activity. Your Web site should be fun, interesting, or useful—or all three. Picture a trade show with no marketing or salespeople and nobody staffing the booths. Your task is to create a booth that is attractive in the purest sense: It must attract people. It must hold their attention sufficiently for them to step inside the booth, pick up the brochure, and touch the samples. We'll address getting them to your booth in Chapter 11, "Attracting Attention." For now, let's focus on holding their interest.

Interacting on a Web site can be a rhythmic process:

Make a selection; get an answer . . .

Make a selection; get an answer . . .

Make a selection; get an answer . . .

Use that rhythm to your advantage. Don't force your users to stop what they're doing in order to read instructions, directions, or extraneous marketing pabulum. Give them choices, but not too many. Give them interactivity, but not too much.

In *Computers as Theatre* (Addison-Wesley, 1993), Brenda Laurel describes the continuum of computer game interactivity as being composed of three variables:

> Frequency (how often you could interact), range (how many choices were available), and significance (how much the choices really affected matters). A not-so-interactive computer game judged by these standards would let you do something only once in a while, would give you only a few things to choose from, and the things you could choose wouldn't make much difference to the whole action. A very interactive computer game . . . would let you do something that really mattered at any time, and it could be anything you could think of—just like real life.

The World Wide Web as we know it is not a "very interactive" place by Laurel's standards. Too many choices too often will create confusion, and as marketers, we wish to maintain control over the significance of the outcome. After all, we are trying to sell something. If your goal is to attract foot traffic in order to sell advertising on your Web site, you might wish to model your design toward the high end of the interactivity scale. But if you are merely trying to promote your company, product, and/or service, you need to guide users instead of handing the controls over to them.

In designing your site, strive to keep visitors engaged. A long block of text will make their eyes glaze over. Too many clicks will frustrate them. The philosophy here is to put your customer in charge of the relationship.

When my dry-cleaning shop closed down, I had to find a new one. There were three nearby, and I went to the closest one first. "Your shirts will be ready by Friday," the clerk said and gave me the ticket.

The next Monday I picked up my shirts and went to the next one to drop off the next load. "Your shirts will be ready on Friday. Is that OK?" I liked that. They were actually concerned about what *I* wanted.

The *next* Monday I went to get my shirts and dropped off the next batch at the third store. "When would you like your shirts back?" Bingo! I was in control; I was in charge. I was bringing my trade to them, and they knew it. Friday would have been fine, but Monday was just as good to me. Not only do I get my shirts when I want them, the laundry has an extra day to get them done. They are less stressed, and I am a happier customer.

There are three kinds of navigation on your site. The first is: Where the heck is the site? We'll cover that later in Chapter 11, "Attracting Attention." The second is: Where the heck is the information I'm looking for? The third type of navigation is different: Which of your products is right for me?

Remember, you don't want to hand the prospective customer the answer too quickly.

Lend Them a Hand

If you walk into a store and tell them what you want, a savvy clerk will ask a few more questions, even if there is only one model available that meets your needs. It's the difference between "You want a broom? Here," and "So, you need a broom that you can use in the kitchen but won't harm the finish on your hardwood floors? I think this one will be right for you." Customers feel they're getting the right thing.

If you have a large variety of items, choices, or configurations, asking site visitors to check the boxes and fill in the blanks is the only way to go. If your back-end technology is sophisticated enough (and these days most Web servers are robust enough to handle it), the resulting "datasheet" can be assembled from content pieces stored in a database.

Just give your visitors the opportunity to navigate your site by clicking on things about them. They'll feel like they're getting closer and closer to the right answer. At the same time, you'll amass a wealth of knowledge about the people who come to your site just by watching where they click.

Help Me Choose

Time was, if you went looking for a printer on the Hewlett-Packard site (www.hp.com), you would begin by scanning the home page for the "Products" button. The Products page (see Figure 4.4) was a test to see how much of a nerd you were. Did you know enough to click on "Peripherals," as opposed to "Computing" or "Components"? "Peripherals" led to a page that included the "Printers" button, in all its glory. Not exactly the shortest distance between two points.

HP took a look at its logs and discovered that quite a few people were interested in printers. In fact, almost half of those who came to the home page were seeking printer information. So, HP took a bold step: It changed its home page. HP made the very first button on the home page "Printing & Imaging" (see Figure 4.5). With so many people looking for so many things online these days, HP currently (a very relative term) offers the four major food groups on its home page: products, help, printer drivers, and shopping.

HP offered up a long list of product model numbers, and there were a lot of them. The customer had to choose between the LaserJet 5MP, the OfficeJet300, the CopyJet M, or one of the 30 other printers listed—all before knowing anything about them but their names. Today, HP continues to evolve a feature it added years ago called "Help Me Choose" (see Figure 4.6):

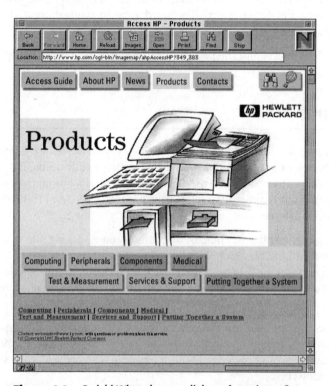

Figure 4.4   Quick! What do you click on for printers?

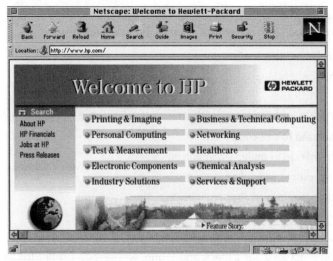

Figure 4.5 HP realized that popularity was a good way to set button priority on its home page.

Find the hp printing and digital imaging products you need fast with our interactive product advisor! Simply follow the guided questions and product advisor will quickly provide you with a detailed list of the products that most closely match your criteria.

If you already know which hp product type you are looking for, select hp quickpick for detailed hp product comparisons and price information.

Figure 4.6 After selecting "printer" for "business," Help Me Choose walks you through choosing among HP's 39 products.

The questions are simple, and the choices are few. The interactivity is high, and the result is like talking to a clerk in a printer store who knows what to ask:

Do you require color, or black & white output?

    Black and White

    Color

Will you require an HP printer for your workgroup, your personal use, or for portable use?

    Personal (connected to one computer)

    Workgroup (connected to multiple computers)

Will you need print output wider than letter size?

    Letter size only

    Wide format

At each step, the number of printers to choose from dwindles to a manageable size. After telling HP that you're looking for a black and white, workgroup printer for letter-sized documents, you're down to 11. Choosing 8 to 16 pages per minute over 17 to 32 brings the total down to 6, and a chart shows the price range for different features (see Figure 4.7).

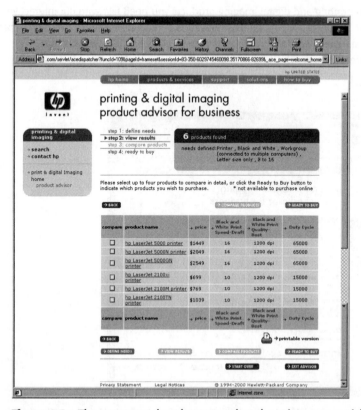

Figure 4.7 The summary chart lets you select the printers you wish to see compared head to head.

The resulting chart shows the specifications of the selected printers for the following features:

Print Speed Black Draft Quality

Print Quality Black Best

Input Capacity Std

Input Capacity Max

Connectivity Std

Connectivity Optional

Duty Cycle

Memory Std

Memory Max

Print Languages Std

Print Languages Optional

Dimensions

Weight

Now you can clearly tell the differences between the machines and choose the one that's right for you. Unfortunately, the e-commerce promise ball gets dropped between one HP department and the next.

Don't Drop the Ball

HP's product comparison chart provides the information you need to choose and then offers the call to action to help you purchase. A "READY TO BUY" button takes you back to the summary chart. On the summary chart, there are two buttons: "BUY ONLINE FROM HP" and "OTHER WAYS TO BUY." Want to buy direct? Great, that button will take you to the HP Business Store (see Figure 4.8).

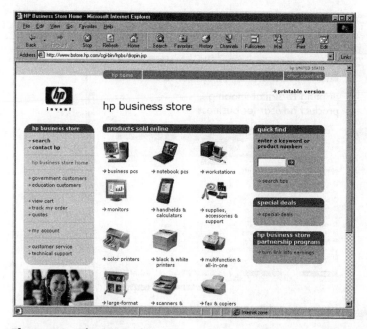

Figure 4.8 The HP Business Store acts like a brand new salesperson who has no clue about your interests.

Now that you have taken the time and effort to identify the printer that would be just right for you and you have *indicated a desire to buy it*, you're shown into a whole new store. There, the ever-attentive shopkeeper asks, "What can I do for you? Are you interested in a business pcs? (whatever that is) a notebook pcs? a workstation?" The eighth choice happens to be black-and-white printers.

Did you remember the model number of the printer you finally selected? Did you write it down? No? Well, no problem . . . just hit the back button and . . . Ooops (see Figure 4.9).

Due to the rocky nature of cookies and Javascripts and handing a session off from one server to another, a click on the Back button from the HP Business Store takes you to the beginning of the Help Me Choose process. Forget taking a quick peek at the model number of the printer *you wanted to buy*, and forget trying out the other ways to buy. Unless you have the patience of Job, this Web site just experienced another abandoned session.

Aside from this poor hand-off, the Help Me Choose or Product Advisor model is a winner. The Web site asks a few questions to steer you in the right direction. This approach works because it engages the visitor in an electronic conversation about the visitor. This isn't about HP. It's not about HP products. As a potential customer, it's about me and what I want. I *want* to click on the next button and tell the machine more about my needs.

Figure 4.9 HP has ignored Jakob Nielsen's number 1 top mistake of Web design—it broke the Back button.

Don't Underestimate Your Clients

Leading people by the hand is great, unless they don't need it. HP offers "Quick Find" that lets you drill down by category or just type in a part number. But what if you live in that difficult market where you have very savvy clients, but very complex products? What if just one of your products had enough options that there could be as many as 1,866,240 permutations? Consider parametric search.

Zilog, Inc. (www.zilog.com) is a purveyor of microcontrollers and microprocessors. Its clients are design engineers. They are not students. They are not mom-and-pop grocery stores. They know what they want, but they want it just so. That's why Zilog turned to Saqqara (www.saqqara.com) and its Step Search data delivery product.

Once you've chosen TV Controllers from its main menu, Zilog lets you know that it has 33 different controllers to choose from and offers a bewildering assortment of options (see Figure 4.10).

If the design engineer selects the SDIP package, 8KW of read-only memory, and 640KW of random access memory, the search engine replies that there are 6 products that meet his needs, but that he'll have to choose between 24 and 32KW of ROM because there are no products that have the other features he wants *and* only 8KW of ROM (see Figure 4.11).

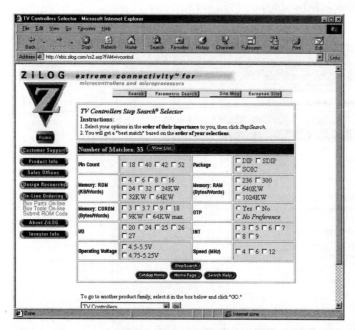

Figure 4.10 Parametric search works by getting the searcher to focus on the *most important* features first.

Figure 4.11 Six products match the first round of choices, and more choices are offered.

Making one more choice narrows the field from 33 products to 3. That's when the "Compare" button comes in. With only 3 products to choose from, Step Search lets the engineer see them side by side (see Figure 4.12).

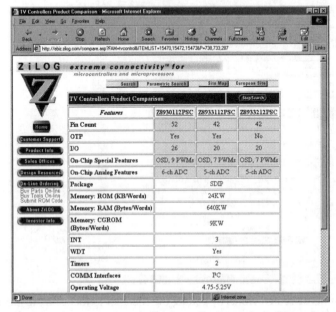

Figure 4.12 Step Search displays Zilog's product differences at the top and all of the similarities at the bottom.

This type of comparison focuses on the distinctions between products, making it that much easier to tell them apart.

Configure It Out

This seems to work well for printers and microprocessors, Jim, but what about my products?

With only a little imagination, you can dream up ways to let people configure your goods. This is the brainstorming side of strategy consulting that I enjoy so much. Come up with a dozen different ways to deliver information to people, then ask them which they'd like best. To prime the pump, here are a handful of examples.

Dell Lets You Decide

Dell Computers has sales of more than $40 million per day as I write this. This is a little time capsule nugget that is sure to explode in my face. The second edition of this book listed the daily sales at $5 million. By the time you get to this page, Dell's sales are sure to have changed again.

One of the things Dell has done very well is allowing people to customize standard product offerings. Instead of just buying a Dell Dimension 4100 as is, you can tweak it here and there. First, Dell makes it easy: as is. Then it lets you make some choices (see Figure 4.13).

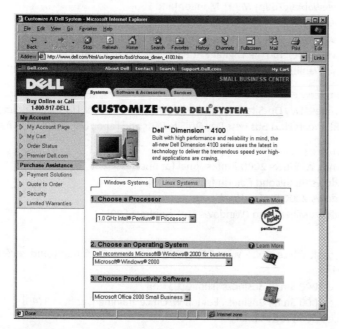

Figure 4.13 Dell lets you choose the processor speed, the operating system, the application software, and the multimedia package.

Then it gets down to business:

The Dimension 4100 offers high performance at a great value. For Dell's fastest performing desktop, you can customize a Dimension 8100.

Dimension 4100 Series, Pentium III Processor at 1GHz [add $80]
Dimension 4100 Series, Pentium III Processor at 933MHz

Hard Drive
20GB Ultra ATA-100 Hard Drive (7200 RPM)
20GB Ultra ATA-100 Hard Drive (5400 RPM) [subtract $30]
40GB Ultra ATA-100 Hard Drive (7200 RPM) [add $60]
60GB Ultra ATA-100 Hard Drive (7200 RPM) [add $120]
80GB Ultra ATA-100 Hard Drive (5400 RPM) [add $170]

Memory
64MB 133MHz SDRAM [subtract $60]
128MB 133MHz SDRAM
256MB 133MHz SDRAM [add $130]
384MB 133MHz SDRAM, 2 DIMMs [add $250]
512MB 133MHz SDRAM, 2 DIMMs [add $370]

Monitor
Video Ready w/o Monitor [subtract $210]
15 in (13.8 in viewable) E551 [subtract $110]
17 in (16.0 in viewable, .26DP) M781 Monitor
17 in (16.0 in viewable, .24-.25AG) P780 FD Trinitron Monitor [add $90]
19 in (18.0 in viewable, .26dp) M991 Monitor [add $90]
19 in (17.9 in viewable, .24 -.25AG) P991 FD Trinitron Monitor [add $240]
21 in (19.8 in viewable, .24AG) P1110 FD Trinitron Monitor [add $550]
15 in (15.0 in viewable) 1501FP Digital Flat Panel Display [add $660]
17 in (17.0 in viewable) 1701FP Flat Panel Display with Digital Support [add $1090]

Hardware Support Services
1 Year Next Business Day On-Site Parts and Labor, Yrs 2 and 3 Parts, Unisys [subtract $79]
PROMO OFFER! 3 Years Next Business Day On-Site Parts and Labor, Unisys SAVE UP TO $20

Operating System
Dell recommends Windows 2000 Professional for business
Microsoft Windows 98 Second Edition [subtract $99]
Microsoft Windows 2000 Professional
Microsoft Windows Millennium (Windows Me) [subtract $99]

Bundled Software
Purchase Microsoft Office 2000 with Office 2000 Training Curriculum and receive a Great Value!
Microsoft Office 2000 Small Business [subtract $199]
Microsoft Office 2000 Small Business Edition w/Office Training [subtract $149]
Microsoft Office 2000 Professional

Video Card
- NEW 32MB NVIDIA TNT2 M64 AGP Graphics Card
- 32MB DDR ATI Radeon 4X AGP Graphics [add $90]
- NEW 32MB DDR NVIDIA GeForce2 GTS 4X AGP Graphics Card [add $180]
- NEW 64 MB DDR NVIDIA GeForce2 GTS [add $310]
- NEW 64MB DDR NVIDIA GeForce2 ULTRA GTS w/DVI Graphics [add $360]
- DVD-ROM or CD-ROM Drive
- 48X Max Variable CD-ROM Drive
- 12X DVD ROM Drive w/ Software Decoding for 32MB TNT M64/16MB ATI Graphics [add $70]
- 12X Max Variable DVD ROM w/ Software Decoding for 32MB/64MB DDR NVIDIA N15 [add $70]
- 12X DVD ROM Drive for 32MB DDR ATI Radeon Graphics [add $70]
- 12XDVD ROM Drive with Software Decoding for Windows ME [add $70]
- 8X/4X/32X CD-RW Drive [add $99]

CD-RW DRIVE FOR 2nd Bay
- None
- 8X/4X/32X CD-RW, 2nd Bay [add $199]

Floppy Drive
- 3.5" Floppy Drive

Zip Drives
- None
- 250MB Iomega Zip Built-inDrive w/ one disk for 3rd bay [add $149]
- 100MB Zip Drive with One Disk [add $79]

Iomega Zip Disk Packs
- None
- 3-Pak of Iomega 100MB Zip Disks [add $29]
- 2-Pak of Iomega 250MB Zip Disks [add $49]

Sound Card
- ADI SoundMax 2.0 Integrated Audio

Speakers
- Harman/Kardon Speakers
- Altec Lansing ACS-340 Speakers with Subwoofer [add $30]
- NEW Harman Kardon HK-695 Surround Sound [add $80]
- Altec Lansing THX Certified ADA885 Dolby Digital Speakers with Subwoofer [add $180]
- No Speakers Requested [subtract $30]

And that's not even the half of it. But at any point, you can hit the "Update Price" link and see how much trouble you've gotten yourself into. As broadband comes in, Michael Dell has promised that visitors will be able to enter their Zip code and have the site tell them whether their neighborhood supports DSL, cable, or merely dial-up.

Cobbler's Clients

Been to Nike.com lately? You can make your own shoes. This was one category, right after food, that I felt could *never* work online. Wrong on both counts.

Mary Kate Buckley, Vice President of Nike.com, knew better. "Over the years we've gotten letters from so many people whose dream job is to be a Nike designer." The "Build your own Nike products" process doesn't quite give you complete creative freedom, but it does start out on the right foot, by having you print out a foot chart (see Figure 4.14).

It's a little surprising to see that your feet really aren't the same size, but the feeling of accuracy is very satisfying. Nike even goes so far as to ask if the measurements were taken in the morning or the afternoon. Next, you choose the shoe that comes in your size, you choose your colors, and you tell them what you'd like stitched on the back (name, rank, serial number). At the end, you're one click away from a purchase (see Figure 4.15).

Nike was careful, though. It started selling customized shoes in the United States only and limited orders to 400 per day. Maybe it's time I had a professional measure my feet.

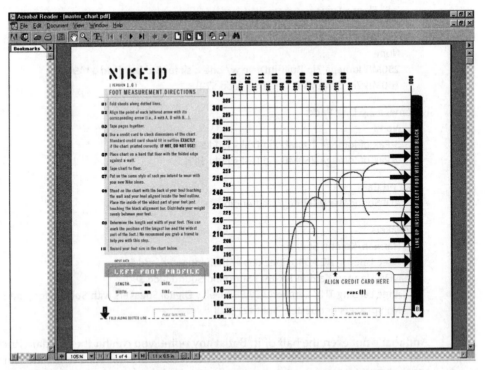

Figure 4.14 To be absolutely sure you do it right, Nike's Foot Chart shows you where to place the Scotch tape and how to check your print accuracy with a credit card.

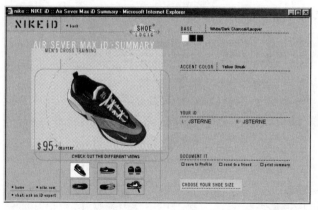

Figure 4.15 The Nikes I designed look great, but they recommended a size 12 and a half and I've never bought anything larger than an 11. Hmmmm. . .

Paper or Plastic?

In July 2000, Meridith Levinson wrote about a Web application on the GE Plastics Web site in *CIO Magazine* (www.cio.com/archive/071500_destructive.html):

> The new tools let product engineers get a sense of which materials they should use and how much they will cost. For example, a product engineer at a cell phone manufacturer plugs the dimensions of his product into GE Plastics' system and selects four different materials he's interested in using. GE's system then helps him determine how many molds he has to build to make a part. "When he's done in a few hours," says (Gerry) Podesta (general manager for e-commerce at GE Plastics), "he has a fairly extensive matrix of what products would work and a ballpark figure on costs. It gives him an enormous head start on the process of designing the product."

Lotion or Cream?

In December 1999, Procter & Gamble launched a site that was the opposite of what P&G had stood for for so many years. Instead of major-brand, on-the-shelf, trust-us-we-know-about-these-products, those good folks in Cincinnati came up with a product that didn't exist—and wouldn't exist until the customer ordered it. At Reflect.com, you get to design your own cosmetics. In its own words:

> If every woman is an individual, then how can she be satisfied with products which are not made uniquely for her?
>
> Now, you can voice your specific beauty needs and desires with a precision that has never been available before. At Reflect.com, we interact with you through specific questions composed by our top beauty experts and research scientists, to mirror your needs creating one-of-a-kind products just for you.

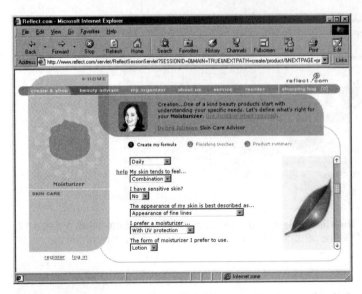

Figure 4.16 Reflect wants to know about you and your skin before formulating a moisturizer.

Of course Reflect.com wants to know what color your skin is (ethnic background, age, how much sun do you get?). It wants you to tell it if you want your moisturizer scented or not. It also needs to know whether you prefer lotion or cream (see Figure 4.16). But then the questions get a little, well, personal.

Some you expect. Do you have sensitive skin? Dry skin? Blemishes? How long is your hair? Is it damaged? Dry? Colored? In order to produce shampoos, cosmetics, and lipsticks with you in mind, Reflect.com wants to get the benefit of your own, special perspective on the world. Do you still live with your parents? Have kids? If you were a bird, would you be a peacock or a dove? A swan or a hawk?

And when it comes to fragrances, it gets deeply personal. When will you wear this perfume? What mood are you trying to create? For which occasion would you like to wear it, casual or special? Do you feel more like the picture of the dinner table overlooking the sun setting into the Pacific, the picture of the Japanese maple, or the Scottish Highlands? Are you creating a feeling of winter, spring, summer, or fall? You then choose the name of your fragrance—25 characters, engraved on the bottle.

Make Them Draw You a Picture

What if you had 130,000 different products to choose from? What if your customers have a good idea of what they want, but no idea if you have a match? Or even a near match? Make them draw you a picture.

Sigma-Aldrich Corporation (www.sigma-aldrich.com) in St. Louis, Missouri, does just that (see Figure 4.17).

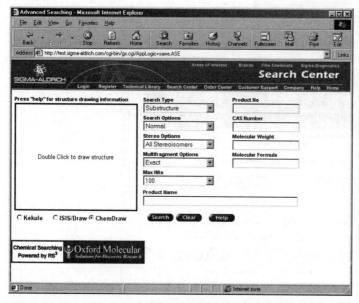

Figure 4.17　Well, it's got *these* molecules and *these* molecules and the hair's darker and the eyes are closer together . . .

"The integration of our chemical database with Oxford Molecular's RS[3] Discovery (software) represents a significant advance in convenience for our customers," boasts Michael Reinhard, Marketing Manager of Sigma-Aldrich. "Chemists have long recognized the value of utilizing structure-based product searching to facilitate their R&D programs."

The joint Sigma-Aldrich/Oxford Molecular February 8, 2000 press release put it this way:

> A user simply draws a structure, substructure or compound fragment using one of three popular chemical structure drawing tools, ChemDraw, ISIS/Draw or Kekulé, and then submits it against the Sigma-Aldrich database. Users can also choose to input the name, partial name, molecular formula or weight of the compound of interest. RS[3] Discovery allows users to modify their search along the way, adjusting their queries as often as necessary. A search will then instantly yield all available Sigma-Aldrich products that fall within the stated criteria, allowing the user to then place orders directly from his or her desktop. And for those without one of the drawing tools listed above, the site offers free use of Oxford Molecular's Kekulé.

How do your customers search for the solutions you offer? What's the thought process? Do they think in terms of materials? Applications? Style? Weight? Color?

Calculators for Hire

You are not necessarily going to have to write a lot of sophisticated software yourself. Consider buying or leasing some smart tools from firms that make them for a living. If, for example, you are a member in good standing in the financial industry, chances are

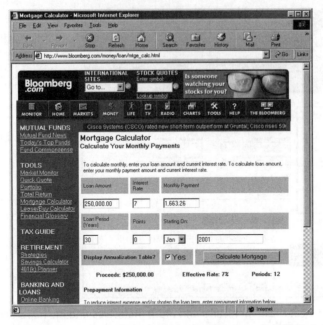

Figure 4.18   Bloomberg could have written its own calculators, but it was more cost-effective to lease them from FinanCenter.

excellent that your clients want to run a few numbers to help them decide how to avail themselves of your services. In that case, take a look at FinanCenter.

Sherri Neasham has been building and selling financial calculators since 1995. The look and feel are yours, the database connectivity grabs your data (average rates, average prices, etc.), and the hard work is theirs (see Figure 4.18).

From account aggregation to asset allocation, FinanCenter's TransMetric Tools help consumers learn about critical issues, calculate costs, and compare products and services. They also report consumer behavior metrics so that you can maximize marketing, product planning, and cross-selling.

FinanCenter offers tools to calculate and understand financial options, education tools that teach key concepts and product features, comparison tools to sort and weigh product features, selection tools to identify appropriate options given preferences or circumstances, and optimization tools to evaluate replacement options and calculate the benefits of switching.

Chances are excellent that you can find tools out there for cataloging, configuring, and calculating just about anything.

Yes, Jim, that's all well and good if you're selling products, but I sell services. How on earth do you configure services online?

Glad you asked. Many people do. That's why it's worth a whole new chapter: Chapter 5, "Selling Services."

Selling Services

S o much attention is paid to selling things online. What if you don't sell things? What if you sell advice? Or opinions? Or recommendations? Then this chapter is for you.

Here's What I'll Do For You

From *Inc Technology Magazine*, November 15, 2000
By Jim Sterne

SERVICE COMPANIES NEED A TOUCH OF INGENUITY TO MAKE THE WEB WORK FOR THEM

Explicators of the digital economy generally break e-commerce into four handy categories. First there are purveyors of stuff—be it puppy chow and mascara to consumers, or generators and ball bearings to industry. Next come the purveyors of content, such as The Wall Street Journal, Dun & Bradstreet, and Steven King. Purveyors of eyeballs include sites like Yahoo! that make money selling banner ads—chiefly to purveyors of stuff and content. Finally, there are the purveyors of Web-based services, the so-called ASPs that transform the Internet into just one more company department.

But that stratification leaves people like me up a creek without an online revenue model. I'm a Web marketing consultant—a service provider whose expertise

Here's What I'll Do For You *(Continued)*

(aside from the occasional Web site review) can't be confined to a digital stream. In that sense I'm like the tens of thousands of other companies that dry clean clothes, repair cars, massage aching muscles, read palms, and do other stuff for which the Web holds little apparent advantage beyond that offered by a flyer on a windshield. Service companies—particularly small, local businesses—have lagged in the new economy not for lack of opportunity but for lack of imagination. Think your two-location day spa gains nothing by going online? Think again.

Think, for example, about Nick's Auto Repair (www.nicksautorepair.com) (see Figure 5.1), which has been at the same location in Boulder, Colo., for over 20 years. But its proprietors understand that mere longevity doesn't necessarily translate into familiarity or trust. So they've built a Web site designed to inspire those sentiments in customers old and new.

First the familiar: a visit to Nick's Web site is a warm introduction to the company's past and present. There you learn the names and backgrounds of all six employees and are treated to reassuring photos of technicians up to their elbows in car engines. There's also a company history extending back before 1977, when Nick's was a Sinclair Gasoline Station. Such background may or may not testify to how well a company performs, but history adds ballast, and local history anchors the company in its community, which to some customers may matter a great deal.

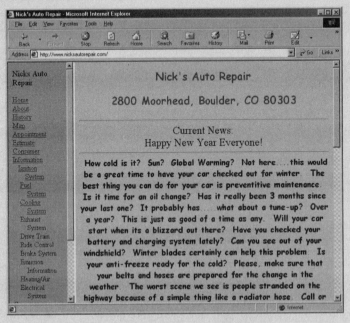

Figure 5.1 Nick's Auto Repair does not have the prettiest site on the Web, but it knows how to gain customer trust.

When it comes to choosing an auto mechanic, however, familiarity runs second to trust. Nick's site engenders trust both through its helpful presentation and its straightforwardness about the company's limitations: "The work we are not able to do is because of a lack of space," Nick's informs its customers. "We have three technicians with three bays. As a result, we are not able to do any major overhauls. However, if you need this type of work done, we will be more than happy to point you to a reliable specialist."

Then Nick's does something really smart: it provides three pages of detailed information about an engine's ignition, fuel, and cooling systems, handsomely illustrated with pictures of an ignition coil and distributor cap. This material clearly serves to demonstrate the company's expertise. But it also suggests that Nick's doesn't use intentional obfuscation as a sales tactic, which is enormously reassuring to those of us who don't know the difference between a fan belt and a Sansabelt and who feel vulnerable in the presence of those who do. When Nick's sends you an e-mail warning that your pickup coil needs replacing, you can visit the site for an English translation. You then e-mail the company requesting an estimate and an appointment.

A FULL-COURT PRESS

Dry cleaners have traditionally made hay of their brick and mortar status: the "Plant on Premises" claim is considered a major selling point. The people at Dry Cleaning Depot (www.drycleaningdepot.com) in Fort Lauderdale, Fla., know their customers will never be able to get rid of gravy stains by hitting the delete button, but they've figured out another way to make those customers' lives easier. "Got a minute?" ask the company's site. "Probably not. Let Dry Cleaning Depot be your corporate partner. We will pick up and drop off your dry cleaning right where you work."

A nice service, but not exactly Web-centric, right? But how about this: "Sign up for our convenient office pick up and delivery service on-line and receive an additional 10% off your first bill." The online form also lets you indicate your starch preferences and, better still, the site accepts credit-card payments. That means you don't have to write checks every week or shamefacedly reimburse the receptionist who shelled out $25 to redeem your silk blouse and crushed-velvet trousers. If you're uncomfortable committing your card number to the Web, Dry Cleaning Depot also has a monthly billing option.

In addition, Dry Cleaning Depot aggressively pursues new customers using that proven online tactic: word of e-mail. Customers are invited to e-mail the Depot with the name and location of prospective corporate accounts, together with some contact information. If three or more people from the targeted company sign up for the Depot's services, the referring customer receives $25 worth of free cleaning. By advertising the offer on its site and giving customers an easier-than-easy way to make a referral, Dry Cleaning Depot greatly increases the chance of being taken up on its offer.

continues

Here's What I'll Do For You *(Continued)*

DOCTOR, LAWYER, INDIAN CHIEF, CONSULTANT. . . .

But what about those of us in the professional service professions? I'm no snob, but offering 25% off my consultation fee for customers tendering an online coupon is a bit declassé for a business such as mine. And if you need to consult a glossary to understand my recommendations, then I'm not doing my job. So what can consultants—not to mention doctors, lawyers, and accountants—do online besides boasting about their skills, posting a list of clients, and hosting an archive of articles?

We can get interactive, for a start. That's what Don Peppers and Martha Rogers do, and it's only what you'd expect given the Web's pride of place in their celebrated one-to-one marketing philosophy. On its site (www.1to1.com), the consulting firm has posted some interactive tools that inform, entertain, and— best of all—explain why you need their help. For example, a program called Checkpoint (see Figure 5.2) poses a series of questions about your company: what proportion of customers account for the bulk of profits, how different customers are from one another and the like. It then produces a chart, based on your responses, that shows how valuable a 1-to-1 program would be for your organization. And no, the results aren't always really really valuable.

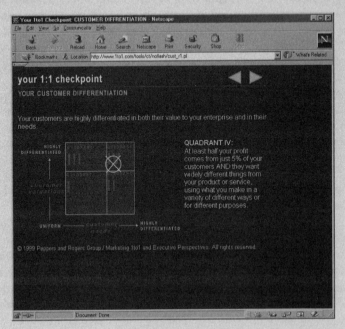

Figure 5.2   Peppers and Rogers' 1-to-1 Checkpoint walks you through the value proposition.

Peppers' and Rogers' Web application is smart. But Eric Ward's is inspired. Eric's company, Netpost (www.netpost.com), has been helping clients raise their hands on the Internet since 1994. His knowledge and understanding of Web-site publicity are unsurpassed, and—not surprisingly—his public Web site is grand. But it's his secret, password-protected site that exemplifies service-company marketing at its finest.

Want the password? First, you have to attend one of his presentations.

In vivid detail, Eric lays out before his audience the glorious gestalt of marketing Web sites. He explains how to make your presence felt on search engines. And in directories. And on What's New sites. And in e-zines, and newsletters, and newsgroups, and discussion lists and on and on and on. . . . Invariably he talks a mile a minute and still never finishes in time.

At the end of his speech, Eric gives the audience a gift: the password to a section on his site where all of his resources and tools and ideas are listed, ripe for the plucking. Anyone with the time and inclination can follow the bouncing browser and perform by themselves the services for which Eric charges. It sounds like he's giving away the store. But here's what actually happens: Those who are willing to invest the time to follow Eric's exhaustive program on their own tend to be the people who couldn't afford him in the first place. Those who value time over money and who want the job done right by the best in the business flock to Eric and count themselves lucky that he's not booked until the next millennium.

Service companies are purveyors of expertise, skills, and knowledge, which in the end will always be tougher to sell online than content, ad banners and stuff. The trick, perhaps, is to be like the Wizard of Oz. Use your public face in whatever way possible to impress the hell out of people. And always be sure that the man behind the curtain fulfills his promises.

Do You Sell Services?

More and more, it's getting harder and harder to tell the difference between products and services. Snap-on Inc. (www.snapon.com) sells tools. Everybody knows that. It is a manufacturer. It deals in atoms, not bits, and not labor. The company is easy to identify, isn't it?

Don't be too sure. The top left corner of its home page (see Figure 5.3) talks about Snap-on's army of dealers. Those are the guys who drive the big white trucks all over the place, delivering tools to professional mechanics. Under "What Your Dealer Does For You," there's a side of Snap-on you're not so familiar with.

That big white truck carries more than just tools. It has to because the tools themselves are getting more sophisticated every day. The dealers can demonstrate the features of a

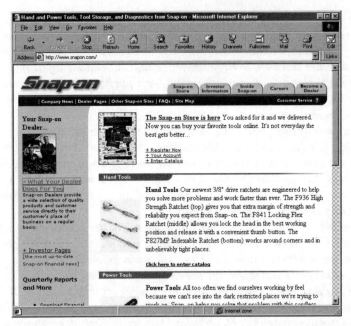

Figure 5.3 Snap-on is much more than a manufacturer of automotive tools.

range of diagnostic equipment, shop equipment, and software that Snap-on offers. They can also provide first-aid warranty repairs and replacements. They know how the tools work well enough to help shop owners plan what services they can offer the driving public, based on the steady acquisition of the right tools. But that's not the end of it:

> Using extended credit accounts, open accounts and equipment leases, your Snap-on Dealer offers the financing that fits your tool and equipment purchase needs. In addition, your Snap-on Dealer collects revolving account payments from customers each week.

Like Snap-on, anybody in the business of making and selling stuff is also in the business of offering services around that stuff. They are also in the business of disseminating information about that stuff and those services. Moral of the story? Everybody is in the services business.

But some of us sell services exclusively. Dentistry instead of drill bits. Car insurance rather than automobiles. Bookkeeping rather than computers. Systems integration rather than routers, hubs, and switches.

Are Services Really So Different?

In some ways, there are no differences. Regardless of what you sell, you need to worry about branding your company, positioning it against competitors, finding prospects, persuading them to consider your offer, and getting them to buy. But services are seen in a different light, and things take on a different hue.

Describing your service is not as straightforward as showing a datasheet filled with specifications and mean-time-between-failure numbers. You can't compare your services to your competitors' by saying your services weigh less, lift more, and have a 15 percent larger carrying capacity. Unless you sell discrete services (one shirt laundered and folded for $1.05), it's hard to show a list price. Rather than focus on proof-of-quality (withstands 2,000 pounds per square inch), you have to evoke trust by touting awards and testimonials. Therefore, branding is your first step.

Branding a Service

Bristol-Myers Squibb manufactures Excedrin, but it wouldn't occur to you to go to www.bms.com when you need pain relievers. You'd never go to www.bms.com to get hair coloring, even though the company owns Clairol. But services are rarely branded. Even though you may never create an entire Web site for each of your services, you can imbue your offerings with additional brand attributes, just by giving them a specific brand name.

Label your services. Give them distinctive names. It makes them easier to remember and clearly identifiable from those of your peers. You might also push the point that you're not just offering a service, you're providing a report, a review, an implementation, or a spotless shirt.

Sun Microsystems understands the power of adding labels to its services. Sun will come in and analyze your data center. It will hand you a "comprehensive report that includes details on the proposed production environment, recommended and required tools, and a roadmap to production." In other words, it takes a look at what you've got and tells you how to improve it. So what does Sun call this service?

Data Center Upgrade Plan Analysis?

Business Continuity Transition Plan?

Resource Evaluation and Recommendation Study?

Nope. While those names are all somewhat accurate and descriptive in their own obfuscating way, Sun decided to call this offering the "Sunready Production Design Service" (see Figure 5.4).

IBM calls its version "Infrastructure & systems management services." HP refers to it as "Mission critical infrastructure services." Compaq calls it "Data Center Availability Assessment." "Sunready" tells prospects that Sun is ready to make your data center ready. The word "ready" adds an air of preparedness, a feeling of anticipation, as in ready, set, go.

Sun doesn't just have support for its hardware and software; it also has "SunSpectrum Support." In one turn of phrase, Sun lets you know it offers a wide range of services, and it ties it in nicely with the sun theme.

For more on branding and positioning services, I recommend Harry Beckwith's *Selling the Invisible, A Field Guide to Modern Marketing* (Warner Books, 1977).

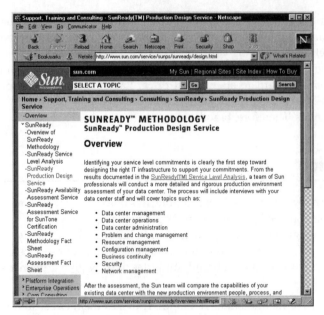

Figure 5.4 The name "Sunready" adds significance to a service that could have been called Computer Performance Evaluation.

Full Disclosure

Because trust is the goal, rely on full disclosure to carry the day for you. Make sure you provide enough information for people to feel truly comfortable buying from you. Set the proper level of expectation. If you can clean the whole house and everything that's in it, great! Say so. But if you don't do windows, let them know. Will you lose prospects who were interested in getting their windows cleaned? Yes. Might they have purchased other services from you? Maybe. Are they worth it? Nope. Stick to your knitting.

Don't promise the moon to people, but don't be too nebulous. It's OK to claim to be a star—just as long as you don't imply you're the whole universe.

As with all things on the Web, you're trying to create a learning experience for your site visitors. That means you have to reveal the details about your services in a staged manner, from the customers' perspective and in the customers' language. You're not going to sell anything over the Internet unless you understand your customers' needs and prove to them that you do. Put on your customer-colored glasses and start asking customer-style questions:

- What do you do?
- What's the benefit?
- How do you do it?
- How long will it take?

- How do you report progress?
- What will it cost?
- What can I expect?

HP describes its consulting services by offering specific benefits. "Provides a higher potential of cost savings" is a little vague. But HP follows that up with "typically 20% savings or greater." That's setting some pretty specific expectations.

If you want a real lesson in putting your cards on the table, you could learn a thing or two from Dell Computer (www.dell.com). Dell goes way out of its way to set expectations when it comes to installation services by publishing a complete statement of work (see Figure 5.5).

Dell describes everything it is going to do in detail, including the following:

Meet with the designated customer contact to verify that:

The ordered Dell installation services match the customer's expectations (i.e., services will install what the customer expects).

The ordered configuration matches the customer requirements.

The customer has documented any specific information required to perform the installation (e.g., Domain name(s), IP Address(es), Host Computer types).

The customer has reviewed the Site Checklist and understands environmental requirements for installation of the specific product(s).

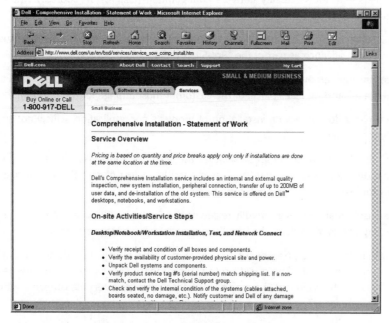

Figure 5.5 Dell believes in the WYSIWYG school of service description, down to the finest detail and price.

Physically inspect the area where the equipment is to be installed and verify that:

The appropriate power outlets are available (as documented in Dell's Site Checklist).

Physical space and airflow are adequate for the products to be installed.

The equipment to be installed is available.

Document any issues that require resolution, and note any problems that may cause a delay or re-schedule of the installation service(s):

Work with the customer to resolve, or gain commitment to resolve, any physical site issues that will inhibit installation or configuration.

If rescheduling is required, work with the customer to satisfy any scheduling needs.

Notify the Dell Installation Management Team of any schedule changes or additions associated with the installation service(s).

Then Dell goes a step further. It outlines the customer responsibilities:

The customer must place the Dell products in the immediate area in which the products are to be installed.

The area in which the server is to be installed must be sufficiently large, well-lit, and properly ventilated to accommodate the server and its installation.

The customer must ensure that the required power outlets have been installed and other environmental/technical prerequisites specified in Dell's Site Checklist have been met.

If the system to be installed will be connected to your network, you must provide the installers with the necessary network configuration (i.e., TCP/IP address) when they arrive onsite.

If the installation is for complex systems (clusters or storage), this information must be provided in advance as part of the "Pre-Site Configuration" Survey.

Services include removal of packaging to a customer-designated area within the building that the installation takes place, or the customer must arrange for the removal.

These services do not include installation of products nor application activity not specifically mentioned.

Prior to the delivery of any upgrade services, the customer must take normal precautions to backup systems to safeguard against any accidental loss of data. Dell will have no liability for loss of data or computer programs.

Please ensure that you have carefully reviewed the Customer Responsibilities specified in the Statements of Work for the installation services you have purchased.

By the time they're done, prospective customers know every step along the path from signing up to signing off. The question that remains for most service purveyors is this: Do I really want to spell out my entire business plan and service offering where my competitors can see it?

Let me put your mind at ease: Your competitors already know what your business model looks like, how you deliver your services, and what you charge for them. How?

Standard operating procedure. They have your administrative assistant make copies of everything for her boyfriend's uncle who works in your rival's customer service department. Simple.

If you withhold information from the your Web site, the only people you are making life hard on are your prospects and your customers.

Now that you've got all that information online, make use of interactivity to help prospects and customers decide that all-important question: Do your services match their needs?

The Qualification Process

Are those prospects wandering your site worthy of your attention? Maybe. Are you worthy of theirs? The qualification process has to be considered from both sides. They are scrutinizing you, while you're trying to decide how much to invest in them.

Even more with services than with products, the process of awareness, understanding, confidence, and trust is essential before the purchase can take place. I want to see references before I let a contractor tear my old roof off. I want to see a detailed proposal before I commission a software project.

So, just like picking a printer, give me decision support tools. Give me some guidance. Give me a hand. Give me a clue. Help me choose.

Self Identification

Just as you'd want to watch which type of computer people were configuring, you'll want to watch which configuration of your services interests most people. The same, classic decision-tree approach can be used for, say, a home remodeling company.

Are customers interested in indoors or outdoors? Outdoors? Good. Now then, landscaping, tree trimming, or garden maintenance? Landscaping? Got it. Landscape or hardscape? (See Figure 5.6.)

When they get down to choosing between the sandstone wall, the bench, or the fountain, then your site is serving up information about privacy, seating, or decoration. Along the way, you continue to show examples of other clients who have benefited beyond their wildest dreams. If you make the path your prospects follow long enough, their journey will reveal their desires.

More Complex Services

But what if you sell something a bit more complicated than tree-trimming services? What if your offering requires an elaborate harmonization between server and serviced?

Buying an airline ticket has relatively few choices when you get down to it: departure city and time, arrival city, coach, business, or first class, and how much you're willing

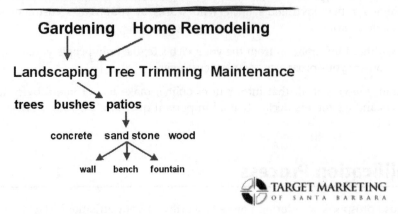

Figure 5.6 The classic decision tree helps customers choose your services and helps you get to know them.

to pay. But when you start booking an entire vacation, think of all those choices about airlines, rental cars, hotels, theater tickets, restaurants, and more.

If you're selling highly complex networking services, you're not hunched over your Web server online reporting screens to see how many network administrators are plunking down their Mastercards for a half a million dollars' worth of implementation support experts. So how is the Web going to help you help your customers write large checks to you for your talents? By using the Web's talent for self-qualification.

Get your customers to reveal themselves to you by leading them down the same sort of decision tree. Lead them down that path by sprinkling it with something enticing, something that will encourage them to take the next step. If you trade information for information, you'll find that people are rather forthcoming.

Talking to a sales rep on the phone includes the concern that this individual is going to do everything in his or her power to close the sale. Can the rep be trusted? It's too soon to tell, so the prospect is wary. But the perception is that a Web site, a computer, is there only to lead the prospect to the proper solution. That means prospects are inclined to be a bit more free with intelligence about their needs. Besides, this sort of self-service allows them to experiment. They can answer a question one way to see what the results might be, and they can click the Back button to try something else.

Here's a hypothetical example to make this whole thing as clear as possible. Let's say you're selling networking services. You can help medium-sized companies and large companies. Your expertise does not come cheap, and everybody in the world seems to want your help. That's good. But you can't help everybody. That's bad. That means your sales and presales technical support teams are wasting a lot of phone time and face time talking to the unqualified. The trick is to figure out which Web site visitors are worth calling on.

Here's how to do it:

> We can give you a clear picture of how our networking services can save you time and money while improving communication, speed, and reliability. Please answer the following questions:
>
> How big is your network?
>
> > 10-25 Routers, Hubs & Switches
> >
> > 25-100 Routers, Hubs & Switches
> >
> > >100 Routers, Hubs & Switches

These choices are not check boxes or radio buttons. We're keeping it *much* easier than that. This approach is much easier to implement because you're simply creating pages with links that point to other pages. No forms. No databases.

This method makes it easier for you to segment your prospective customers because only people that meet certain criteria will reach certain pages. This is also the easiest for your prospects to navigate. All they have to do is click one of the three choices.

Notice that there is no option for fewer than 10 network devices. If prospects don't have at least 10 network devices, they are instantly disqualified. If they click on the first one (10–25 Routers, Hubs & Switches), the next page asks them about in-house support. Do they have anybody on staff who manages this sort of equipment? Do they have more than one? Do they outsource that work to local consultants?

If they identified themselves in the 25–100 range, that link takes them to a page that asks them about the automated systems they have in place to help them manage. Do they have any? Are they considering getting some? More than 25 networking devices is a lot to handle by hand.

If (we hope) they selected the greater-than 100 Routers, Hubs & Switches category, the next page asks them about the third-party support they are currently using. Either they have a large in-house networking crew, or they are teamed up with somebody who can provide the expertise.

After the prospect has clicked three or four times, you already know he or she has:

- Between 250 and 500 routers, hubs, and switches
- Network management tools from X & Y
- 1,500 clients and 250 wireless devices
- 25 outage complaints per month
- 4 people dedicated to network administration

At each step, you pace the prospects by feeding back what they told you. You want to do this in such a way that they could print out the results and use them as a description of their facilities when talking to anybody.

> Based on your situation: (recap of what they said) . . . we can help with X, Y, and Z. For an idea of the potential improvements in the speed and reliability of your network that we can help you realize, please answer the following 3 questions:

Lead them through the process with promises of more and better information.

> Based on your situation: (recap of what they said) . . . we can improve the speed of your network between 15% and 35% and decrease outages by 10% to 15%.
>
> To get a feel for the time it might take to achieve these improvements, please answer the following 4 questions:

Keep dropping those breadcrumbs for them to follow.

> Based on your situation:
> (recap of what they said)
> . . . we can help make your network faster and more reliable in 45–60 days from the moment we start working with you.
>
> At this point, we only need to know a few more things in order to present you with an out-line of how we might work together . . .

You've delivered a good return on their clicking investment so far, and now they're hooked.

> Here is an outline of the potential services we have in mind and a timeline for getting the job done.
> (outline)
> Obviously, this is only a rough estimate of your needs and our services. There's just one more step before we are able to present a complete proposal . . .

The final step gets them to tell you things they would never tell a cold-calling sales rep. Here there might even be some open-ended questions to be answered in a text box.

> Because of your unique situation, and in thanks for taking the time to explore these possibilities with us, we'd like to set up a conference call between a senior networking project manager, several of our key implementation engineers, and several of your key networking managers.
>
> To help determine the best time for this telephonic meeting, please enter the e-mail addresses of your key people, and the above outline will be forwarded to them for their review and your internal discussion.

The prospect has done all the work for you. He or she has told you everything you need to know. Imagine how long it might take for a sales rep to glean that information from a company with all of the usual politics and delays.

You now have the information you need for a conference call. You're calling on only the most well-qualified of prospects, and you get to hand pick the engineers and experts on your end who have the right skills to match this customer's requirements. You've just reduced the sales cycle down to weeks from the months you're accustomed to.

Read the sidebar titled *I Wanna Hold Your Hand* to see how I describe this kind of approach.

I Wanna Hold Your Hand

From *Inc Technology Magazine,* **March 15, 2001**
By Jim Sterne

The right Web site can walk customers through even the most complex selling process.

If only we'd seen this whole e-commerce thing coming. We would have done things so differently. We would have sold something simple (teacups/pork). We would have offered minimal options (bone china/boneless loin). We would have targeted customers with few requirements (no chips/no gristle). And, as a result, we would have sat back and watched traffic clock in and out of our site with 12-items-or-less-lane speed.

Alas, our business isn't simple. Here at Jim's Factory Floor Automation Boutique we sell seriously complex products at nothing-to-sneeze-at prices to companies whose operations are riding on our performance. These folks are not going to look us up on a search engine, click a few items into their shopping carts, and proceed to checkout. They need us to spend time with them. They need to know that we understand their exact circumstances before we start telling them what to buy. And they need to trust in our technical abilities and interpersonal skills because our equipment is only half of the battle and one-third of their cost. (We provide consulting, installation, and training as well.)

Having recently graduated from the initial "pleased-to-meetcha-here's-our-stuff" iteration of our site, we've been spending a lot of time brainstorming about how to do things better. And because we're a beneficent bunch (not to mention reliable, competitively priced, and did I mention our new 10-year service contracts?) we've decided to let other companies learn from our example. If you are a high-end, high-customization, high-service-level business, then something like this could work for you.

TELL ME MORE, TELL ME MORE

At first glance our home page looks pretty much like everyone else's. We have all the usual buttons: About Our Services, Contact Us, What's New, Win An Armadillo. But we've added a special button: Walk Me Through It. Once prospects click there, the sales process is off and running.

Walk Me Through It leads to a questionnaire. People hate questionnaires, right? We worried about that, too. So we realized we would have to sell the thing—to convince people that filling it out was a good use of their time. Here's what we came up with:

"In order to provide you with the best information about our products and services we need a little background data. If you answer the following questions,

continues

I Wanna Hold Your Hand *(Continued)*

we'll be able to give you a very clear idea of how our factory automation systems can save you time and money while producing more grommets and dribs than your fondest dreams deemed possible."

You see the psychology there? Prospects now know they're going to get something in return for their time. They also know we're not going to stick them with some off-the-rack solution. Next we set about designing the survey. It's always best to start with a softball question:

"How many grommets and dribs do you make per day?

> *<5000*
> *5001-10,000*
> *10,001-100,000*
> *100,000-250,000*
> *>250,000"*

Notice that we didn't ask them to fill out a form or check a box, merely to click on a link. That's easy for them, and technically trivial for us. It also allows us to commence the customer segmentation process. Here's how it works. Businesses that manufacture fewer than 5000 units per day have about as much reason to buy our products as Upper Volta has to launch a space station. So the <5000 link leads visitors to a page that congratulates them on their chutzpah and suggests they try the Web site for Bobby's Grommet Toolhouse and Teacakes. Prospects who click on the 5001-10,000 link arrive at a page that asks:

"How soon do you plan on making an investment in your physical plant that will help you compete with significant players in the grommet and drib arena?

> *1–3 Months*
> *4–12 Months*
> *>12 Months"*

The >12 Monthers are nudged toward Bobby's. The 4–12 Monthers are sent to a page with questions about their business plans and financing options meant to elicit just how serious they really are. Those whose answers show sufficient promise are deposited on the Current Equipment Page. Also sent directly to that page are prospects who clicked on 10,001-100,000 in response to the first question. The Current Equipment Page asks prospects what gear they already have:

"In your factory, you currently use:

> *A grommet and drib splammer*
> *A grommet and drib splammer and a blodget*
> *More than one splammer*
> *More than one splammer and a blodget*
> *More than one splammer, a blodget, and a flanger*
> *More than one splammer, a blodget, a flanger, and a clompfenster*
> *Multiple grommet and drib splammers, blodgets, flangers, and clompfensters"*

Each response links to a page of questions tailored to that response. If, for example, prospects have more than one splammer but only one blodget, we have to know how much pin-closter training their workers have had. If they have a flanger but no clompfenster, we need to assess their consumption of plitmer gel. (Obviously if you're not in our industry you'll want to compose questions pertinent to your own business. Simply imitating ours may cause some confusion.)

This process continues through several layers, with each response linking to a new page of questions. Ultimately, we are able to form an extremely good picture of our Web visitors' companies. And this is where we ice the cake. At the terminus of each of these paths live pages bearing summaries of prospects' circumstances. This lets them know that we've been listening to them and that we remember what they've told us. It also gives them an opportunity to correct any mistakes that may have cropped up along the journey.

WE'RE HERE. WE'RE WAITING.

At the bottom of each summary page is the kicker and an invitation:

"Obviously you are doing well in your field with the limited equipment you have. Based on everything you've told us, we are confident we can improve your output and lower your costs.

As you probably know, your situation is unique. In order for us to design the best of all possible solutions for your company, our highly skilled technicians will need just a little more background information. Please select a date and time from the Conference Call Calendar below. We will make Clem Glustermann from engineering, Horace Ploint from our energy conservation team, Winifred Dripple from logistics, and Waldo Wigman from materials planning available for a 25-minute review of your needs and our capabilities."

It's one thing for a vendor to threaten you with an imminent call from some faceless account manager. It's quite another to offer you the opportunity to arrange, at your convenience, a conversation with a team of flesh-and-blood human beings.

What happens next? Clem, Horace, Winifred, and Waldo pour over the Web site output and familiarize themselves with prospects' circumstances. Having dazzled on the conference call, they then offer to make a personal visit and dazzle further with customized PowerPoint presentations proposing the exact amount of consulting and training the prospect needs. And they offer congratulations on being this month's winner of their very own, house-trained armadillo.

And what about those people who said they produced >250,000 grommets and dribs per day? We send them straight to the End of the Internet (www.mythologic.net/end) because they're lying. It's impossible to produce that many grommets and dribs without more clompfensters than you can buy at Amazon.

The whole thing is cheap. It's easy. And we're hiring blodget installers as fast as we can.

Customer Interaction Leads to Customer Satisfaction

The one subject everybody likes to talk about most is themselves. Make your Web site a mirror of the individual users. Do not tell them what you want to tell them. Tell them what they want to hear.

Syndicated columnist and MIT research associate Michael Schrage says, "The real value is in the interaction. . . . Real interactivity isn't about giving people more content to choose from, it's about letting people create their own content. The new media challenge, then, is how do you create content that creates content?"

The tools are available to capture information about users and use it to help them. The more you help them, the more they value you. The tools are out there for making individual users the center of the universe on your Web site. That's why getting their feedback is so important. In fact, it's worth a whole new chapter.

Feedback

I t used to go without saying that a company had to manufacture demand when manufacturing a product. A better mousetrap would languish unless people were made
aware of their deep-seated desire for a mousetrap and why a better one was absolutely
necessary to their well-being.

Television blossomed into an ideal way to mold public opinion and acquisitiveness.
The medium changed the way corporate America communicated with its customers.
In *Sponsor* (Oxford University Press, 1979), Erik Barnouw pointed out that the move
from the 60-second spot to the 30-second spot on television changed the tenor of messages broadcast into our homes:

> Everyone knows what the job is: instant drama, posing threat and promise. An important
> corollary is that the promise should be an undeliverable promise. There is scarcely time
> now for technical persuasions, documentation, "reason-why" advertising. Everyone knows
> that soap will clean hands, a razor remove hair, and a car transport you from one place to
> another. To promise such things means little or nothing. But there is no sure formula for
> being irresistible, for winning and holding those you love, or for rising to the top of the
> business or social circle. These are the promises worth dangling.

The goal was clearly defined as figuring out new and better ways to make people want
the products we were making. If they couldn't understand the value of brighter teeth
and fresher breath, you simply had to convince them that they would find a life partner within minutes of brushing with your paste. Creating demand equaled survival.

In the next dozen or so years, focus shifted. "Create Demand" became "Find a Need
and Fill It." It was the task of the marketing professional to scour the country (global

marketing belonged only to the few) for a product that people wanted but couldn't find on their store shelves—yet. In addition, the public was no longer a mass audience. They were being segmented through database marketing. Soft-drink companies created a flavor and a campaign for each market segment. Cars were made to captivate different age groups. Products took on personalities to appeal to more and more diverse audiences.

The Demassification of the Market

Then we were hit with mass customization. Henry Ford's "You can have any color you want as long as it's black" has become "You can have any color you want." The assembly line producing pagers at Motorola was designed to create any of 250 configurations based on customer orders. Mrs. Fields Cookies and Benetton Clothing jumped on the power of a computer in every store to shoot sales information straight to the factory floor. Each day's production was tied directly to the previous day's sales. What flavor are they buying *today?* What color are they buying *today?* Clothing is manufactured white, awaiting electronic news of whether powder blue is selling better than baby blue or light gray melange.

Product development and production have become service industries. If you find a product that has universal appeal, you had better exploit it faster than the knock-off shop down the street because holding a lead in this fast-moving world depends on dexterity.

Sitting in an ivory tower and prophesying the future is a risky business. Sitting in a corporate laboratory and counting on a scientist to invent the next Post-It Notes is more magical thinking than marketing. Today's marketer is out in the street asking people what they want to buy. The era of the engineer creating the better mousetrap is over. Welcome to the era of creating what the customer wants.

How do you like our current product? How would you improve it? How can we change our services to better accommodate your needs? I always felt that it was not the vice president of marketing's job to know what customers want. It is the VP's job to *ask* customers what they want. Constantly.

The Survey Finds a New Form

A hefty envelope arrived at my desk one day from a company I enjoyed doing business with. Perhaps it was a new product update or another special discount for good customers. Maybe it was the company's annual report on the state of the industry. It usually sent me items worth reading, so the envelope went into my in-basket until I could get to it. When I opened the envelope several weeks later, I found a three-page survey in eight-point type and a five dollar bill. I was surprised and wondered how many five dollar bills had wafted their way through the U.S. Postal Service.

I wanted to help this company and was very pleased they thought my opinion was worth buying me lunch. I was happy to gift them with the benefit of my wisdom in return. I carefully placed the survey back in my in-basket until I could get to it. I carefully placed the five dollar bill in my pocket. The survey stayed in the basket for weeks; the five dollars lasted until noon.

When I finally dug down into my in-basket far enough to find the survey, I saw that I had missed the deadline. Good intentions or not, five dollars or not, that company did not find out how much I liked their services or what ideas I had for improvement. They would never know that I would buy significantly more from them if only they would change a few things.

When logging on to America Online in the middle of March 1995, I was stopped short by the question:

Do you own a CD-ROM?

   [Yes]   [No]   [I don't know]

In my momentary frustration and my desire to get my work done I answered with the truth. After all, it was the first answer that popped into my head. It took all of about three seconds to read and answer the question. I immediately forgot about it and went on my way. The next time I logged in, the question was nowhere in sight.

Since then, AOL has peppered its customers with advertising. In that short window of time, it learned a critical piece of information about its customers. Since then, AOL has been mailing out CDs instead of floppy diskettes.

Surveys, focus groups, and market research are the glass-bottom boats we use to guess what the fish are thinking. We are able to ask only a handful for their opinion, and we try to scientifically extrapolate the answers out into a sea of consumers. A Web site gives us the ability to ask each individual. A Web site gives us the tools to accurately record every answer.

The survey has gone online. Everybody who dialed in to America Online that day had to answer that question. Scientific? No. Controlled? No. Valid enough for clinical trials of FDA-approved drugs? No. Valid enough and valuable for America Online? Infinitely. Instead of asking a few people, we now can ask everybody. Instead of watching a couple of people watch TV, we can watch all of them surf. Can we ask everybody on the planet? No. Can we ask everybody who buys our product? Only if we are America Online. Can we learn about the needs and wants of those people who visit our Web sites? Absolutely.

You've put a lot of time and energy into providing an accommodating, interesting Web site for your users. Now, it's time to get something from them in return—demographics and psychographics. Who are they? What are they interested in? What do they like about your products? Your company? Your competition? Your Web site? Probe them, and respond quickly with thanks and praise for their participation and good ideas. This will help create the bond that keeps an individual a customer for life. You might want to start off easy.

Poll Position

Polls on your home page are fun. They're not scientific. They're not representative. The questions are not carefully crafted, conscientiously considered, or flawlessly answered. But they are a reason to come back, and if you do it right, they might just give you that one extra bit of insight you didn't have before. Make them fast and painless, and you can learn about your visitors' general attitudes about things.

The Time Digital supplement to Time Magazine sports a poll of its site (www.time.com/time/digital) asking about the future (see Figure 6.1).

There are several reasons people like to answer poll questions online. First, they're anonymous. At least, they should be. If you are using cookies to track people's opinions without telling them, you'll need to study the section on privacy in Chapter 7, "Value Added Marketing—It's Personal."

The second reason people like polls is that they get to see the results immediately. Everybody wants to know if they fit in. Everybody wants to see if they are in the majority. Parentweb (www.parentweb.com) has a poll every week or so to keep people coming back. Parents are *very* interested to see if they fit in with their peers. It's interesting to see what people out there think when it comes to questions like these:

What is the appropriate age for girls to begin wearing makeup?
When should you tell your employer you are pregnant?
What is an appropriate allowance amount to give a preteen?
What do you and your partner fight about most?
At what age would you allow your children to stay home alone?
Should libraries and schools use Internet filtering software?

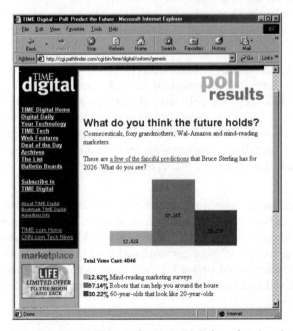

Figure 6.1 Confidence by Time Digital readers in mind-reading marketing surveys is low.

The Wine Spectator (www.winespectator.com) wants to know what are the up and coming wine regions in the United States. Just how much time and space does wine take up in your life? Are bargain-basement bottlings part of your wine world? And, of course, what would you like to see on the Web site?

Which, if any, of the following would you be interested in seeing on the site?

Puzzles 4.0%	Wine trivia 41.3%
Cartoons 8.0%	I like it just as it is 16.0%
More contests 20.2%	Other 10.5%

Valuable information. Cheap.

Polls have their downside, of course. The most common one is self-selection. You face this with any poll, survey, interview, or questionnaire you try. You get the opinions of only those people who are willing to answer your questions. You're not getting a true picture of "public opinion" or "customer opinion," only the opinion of those who had the time for that particular question at that particular time of day and day of the week.

And, of course, people lie.

I'm sorry, but it's true. People will tell you what they think you want to hear if it will get them access to that great white paper you've been touting. They will tell you what they think you want them to hear so you'll like them. They'll tell you what they want to think of themselves. None of these conditions may accurately reflect the truth. You'll have to take all of that into consideration when you start conducting surveys.

You can pop a poll on your home page in 10 minutes at no charge by heading over to Global Guest Poll (www.globalguestpoll.com) (see Figure 6.2). Fill out the form, choose

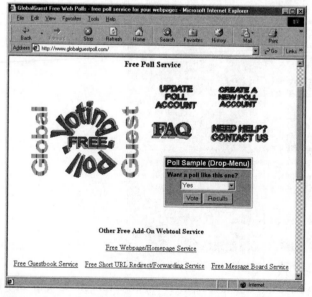

Figure 6.2 If you don't mind the ads, Global Guest Poll is a free service.

the colors and the fonts, and you're in business. Of course, you'll have to endure the advertising on the results pages, seeing as how there's no such thing as a free lunch.

Foolproof and accurate? No. But results can be indicative. Just don't forget to use cookies to prevent pollees from stuffing the ballot box.

Keeping It Simple

When the DealerNet site first went up in 1994 (www.dealernet.com), it wanted to know a few things about the people visiting its Web pages, so DealerNet gave away a car (see Figure 6.3).

DealerNet's approach to getting visitors to reveal something about themselves was a wonderful example of simplicity. It asked for the usual information: name, e-mail address, street address, and so on. Then, when it had the user salivating over the prospects of acquiring a new car, it asked a few more questions.

Figure 6.3 Giveaways like this one at DealerNet are great for collecting information.

Rather than ask for blood type, shoe size, and eating habits, DealerNet went right for the smallest bits with the biggest bang. It wanted to know the year, make, and model of the visitor's current car. Why didn't it go whole hog? Why not age, income, family size, miles driven per year, plans for next purchase? Didn't it understand about *flow*? Didn't it realize that the bigger the prize, the more willing people would be to disclose personal data? DealerNet's philosophy was clear: The fewer the questions, the larger the response.

These few answers gave DealerNet the information it needed to carry out its marketing strategy. People were encouraged to answer the questions because they were so short and easy to answer. Then DealerNet asked a key question, "Would you like to subscribe to DealerNet's upcoming monthly e-mail newsletter, *dealerNet Report*—Yes/No."

You can be sure the person who claimed to drive a 1968 Volkswagen Microbus got a very different *dealerNet Report* than the person who drives a late-model Mercedes convertible. The latter was filled with trade-in value reports and leasing options; the former described how to get oil stains out of the driveway.

How Are We Doing?

In 1998, the good people at Leon Leonwood Bean (www.llbean.com) wanted to know what you thought, and they got right to it in their survey (see Figure 6.4).

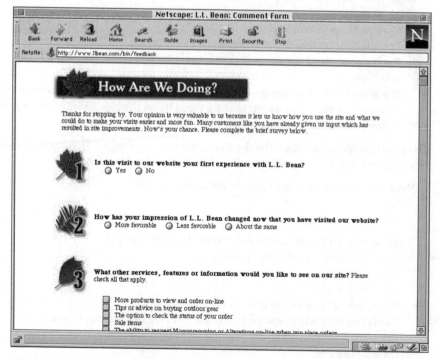

Figure 6.4 L.L. Bean was dead-set on making its Web site the best it could be.

L.L. Bean received more than 14 million phone calls in 1996. That represented 80 percent of contacts, the rest coming in the mail and over the Net. If you account for the growth of the Internet over the past few years, it's quite reasonable to say that it gets 20 percent of its orders online (about 2.8 million orders/e-mails/surveys on its Web site).

If you had that much traffic on your site, you'd want to make it better, too, right?

Is this visit to our website your first experience with L.L. Bean?
  Yes
  No

How has your impression of L.L. Bean changed now that you have visited our website?
  More favorable
  Less favorable
  About the same

I just love it when it's obvious that the people in marketing have participated in the design and development of a Web site. The previous question wasn't about sales. It wasn't about merchandising. It wasn't about advertising. It was about brand. L.L. Bean wanted to know if it was helping or hurting its image and its reputation in the real world.

The next question was a direct shot at "How can we make it better?" and "Here are some ideas we like, but we want to know what *you'd* like." Bravo.

What other services, features or information would you like to see on our site? Please check all that apply.
  More products to view and order on-line
  Tips or advice on buying outdoor gear
  The option to check the status of your order
  Sale items
  The ability to request Monogramming or Alterations on-line when you place orders
  Chat/on-line discussion forums to share thoughts on outdoor adventures: the gear, the
    destinations, the great experiences

The next questions plumbed the depths of buyer misgivings. "This Web stuff might be fun and cool, but is it helping us sell you stuff. If not, why not?"

Have you purchased L.L. Bean gear or clothing on our site?
  Yes
  No

If you haven't, please tell us why not. Please check all that apply.
  I couldn't find the product(s) I wanted.
  It takes too long.
  I'd rather just call.
  It's too difficult to navigate through the ordering process.
  I don't feel comfortable sending my credit card number over the Internet.
  This is my first time visiting the site.
  I'm still browsing.

How would you prefer to place your orders using the L.L. Bean website? Please check all that apply.

View and order items from the On-Line Product Guide.

Place L.L. Bean catalog orders on-line using Catalog Quickshop.

View information and products on-line and place orders by telephone.

At the turn of the century (this one—today) L.L. Bean has stopped asking. Oh, you can still get in touch. The Contact Us page is easy enough to find:

Contact Us

Do you have a question about one of our products or services? The links below will help you find the information you're searching for—or put you in touch with one of our customer service representatives.

Shopping FAQs	Quick answers to common questions
Email	Reach a customer service representative by email
L.L.Bean Live Help	Chat with a customer service representative online
Phone, Fax or Mail	Our phone and fax numbers, plus mailing addresses

But for some reason, the powers that be at the Bean have decided they've heard enough. What a shame. It's not the company's job to know what customers want. It's the company's job to *ask* customers what they want.

What Could We Be Doing Better?

You're reading this book because you want a better Web site, right? So ask your customers! My all-time favorite question when soliciting feedback from customers requires just enough spin on the old "How do you like it?" to elicit thoughtful answers:

If you had a magic wand and could make one or two improvements with a wave of the wand, what would they be?

This is such an easier question to answer than "What's wrong?" or "How can we improve it?" This question empowers the visitor to think of all the disappointments, all the impositions, and all the drawbacks in a positive light. You haven't asked visitors to complain, you've asked them to help. They are now free to say, "The best thing would be to get rid of that awful music it plays" instead of being forced to say, "Your music sucks."

The Wine Spectator (www.winespectator.com) did more than just ask people what they wanted to see on the site and rank the responses by percentages. It went digging for gold.

Tell us what you think we could be doing better.

More vintage breakdowns by region and type of wine * wine shop ratings? * maybe a weekly wine and food matching with a receipe (sic) for the dish * theme tastings - i.e. verticals or horizontals * Current wine ratings for what is being sold NOW * more reference lists, like cross-indexing varietals to french vintages, listing vintage year ratings, enhanced ratings search (searching for a varietal doesn't always find hits in countries where it should) * A place where we could make questions (e-mail) to the experts * the science of wine—brief but technical explanations of winemaking techniques, etc. * a pronunciation guide (for example so we know the famous stemware is pronounced ree'-dle as opposed to rye'-dell) * label images * Surprise me * KEEP SEASONAL WINE-RELATED ARTICLES AVAILABLE LONGER . . .

Invaluable information. Cheap.

A Survey That Hits Close to Home

Mama's Cucina (Van den Bergh Foods, Ragú Sauce) (www.eat.com) (see Figure 6.5) was the first site on the Web for packaged goods. Not technology, not books, but canned pizza sauce. In 1994. It is still a brilliant piece of Web marketing and a fine example of playful brand building by providing a service to customers. Users are invited to participate; write stories, list restaurants, share recipes. Go. Enjoy. Mangia! as Mama herself might say. If you spend half an hour there, you'll learn to not take yourself too seriously. Then you should admire, with tears of admiration in your eyes, the questionnaire with almost 50 detailed shopping, eating, and consuming questions.

The questionnaire at Mama's Cucina is nothing if not complete. Its length may have an effect on the quantity of the responses, but the depth is nothing to sneeze at. Fifty questions. How could they expect people to bother?

"The response has been overwhelming," Alicia Rockmore, Ragú's Associate Brand Manager told me. Tom Cunniff, of the Cunniff Consulting Group in New York who worked with Ms. Rockmore, is "still amazed at the number of people who take the time to fill in the form. After working 16 years in traditional mass advertising, it's gratifying to learn that if you charm people and show a little respect, you can begin to build real relationships between a brand and its customers."

Alicia told me they were shocked at the responses they received. Oh, sure, I thought, anybody who would spend 20 minutes outlining their shopping and eating habits in

Figure 6.5 The Ragú Sauce people bring you a whimsical touch of Italy.

detail was only there to get their hands on a Ragú "Surfing Team" t-shirt. I know that's why I did it, and that t-shirt is one of my prized historical Internet possessions.

But Alicia said that even after Ragú stopped offering the shirts, they got many more responses than expected. Perhaps the tone of this delightful Web site was enough to encourage people to fill out a form that includes so many questions:

What is your overall opinion of the site?

How did you find out about Mama's Cucina?

How often do you think you will return to our site?

The phrases listed below may or may not apply to the Mama's Cucina Web Site. On a scale of one to five (1 = Strongly Disagree: 5 = Strongly Agree), indicate how much you agree with each of these phrases: Mama's Cucina . . .

Is enjoyable
Improved your image of Ragú
Is very innovative
Is relevant to you
Told you something important
Is something you would like to visit again
Is informative
Is different from other web sites
Told you something new

For those phrases that you selected "4" or "5," please explain why:

How often do you eat pasta for dinner?

Which of the following products have you used in the past year? (check all that apply)

Are you:
Male - Female

Age:
Married - Non-Married

How many people in your household (yourself included) are (enter numbers below):
Under 3 years old
3–6 years old
6–12 years old
13–17 years old
Over 17 years old

Do you work:
Full Time
Part Time
Homemaker/Do Not Work Outside the Home

What is your level of education?
High School or Less
Some College or More
Graduate Education or More

> Mama, write to me when Ragú (check all that apply):
> Offers coupons in the newspaper?
> Features new items on the Web site?
> Introduces a new flavor? Introduces a new product?

When so many of the first Web sites went up because it was possible, the technical crowd carried the most weight. Page design, graphics, and questionnaires were the responsibility of the software and systems people while the marketing departments stood by in awe. Sites like Mama's Cucina show that marketing departments caught on pretty quickly in some companies and had an important impact on how the company is represented online.

Rethinking the Survey Process

The World Wide Web gives us a lot more latitude than we've enjoyed in the past. We no longer need a number 2 pencil—we have a mouse and all of cyberspace in which to play. We also get to take advantage of the fact that people prefer online surveys to phone, direct mail, or being accosted in the mall by the clip-board-toting grad student.

Digital Marketing Services (www.dmsdallas.com) asked AOL users a few questions about answering questions. Of those surveyed, 32 percent said they will *only* answer surveys online, and 94 percent said online surveys are more convenient. While 91 percent will answer another online survey within 6 months, only 68 percent said they'd answer a direct mail survey, 38 percent would answer a phone survey, and only 36 percent would stop to talk to somebody at the mall. Digital Marketing got the same answers when it asked online, over the phone, through the mail, or at the mall.

A couple of the surveys described earlier are fairly complete, but they're lengthy. As a consumer, you have to *really* want them to know what you think to spend so much time answering questions. Given the level of interactivity available on the Web, you can create surveys that do not resemble their paper progenitors whatsoever.

The Conversational Survey

If you want to run a long survey, build it out of multiple pages. Each page should contain several questions that all fit on one screen. When the questions are answered, the user can click on the Continue button and the next set of questions pops up.

This model of feeding users a few questions at a time has a very positive effect on the experience. Instead of receiving one long page that scrolls and scrolls to the end of time, the user is asked to answer only a couple of questions at once. This method makes the user feel as if he or she is participating in the survey instead of just being an input device—being interviewed instead of being shown to a desk monitored by a proctor with a stopwatch and a suspicious disposition. This is the kind of action/interaction that keeps the user involved.

If it seems like a stretch to head over to the Center for Methodology and Informatics at the University of Ljubljana in Slovenia (www.ris.org) then you've forgotten that the

Internet is a global place. Two projects conducted by the Research on Internet in Slovenia in 1996 and 1998 reveal that screen-to-screen is better, but why is not obvious at first.

The completion rate for the long scrolling survey was better—85.4 percent versus 83.5 percent—and the scrolling survey took less time: 368 seconds versus 466 seconds. Why is screen-to-screen better? Because the scrollers left 16.3 percent of their questions unanswered while the screeners left only 12.8 percent without so much as a pregnant chad. In addition, only 67.5 percent of scrollers were willing to include their e-mail addresses as compared to 70.4 percent of the screeners. This same group also discovered that decorating your survey is a no-no (see Figure 6.6).

Abandonment rates also went up when too much information was offered (see Figure 6.7).

It's always nice to have hard data to back up common sense, but you can't measure everything so it's good that common sense exists. Common sense tells us that you have to set the proper level of expectation. A screen-by-screen survey with two or three questions per screen is great—as long as I know how long it's going to take.

Tell me up front that it's a 5-, 10-, or 15-minute process. Then I can decide if I want to participate. We love to watch the little progress bar on our computers when downloading or copying files. The same holds true for surveys. Show me the "Page 2 of 6" indicator. And remember to keep your questions to a minimum because every additional page of questions loses another 5 percent of your respondents.

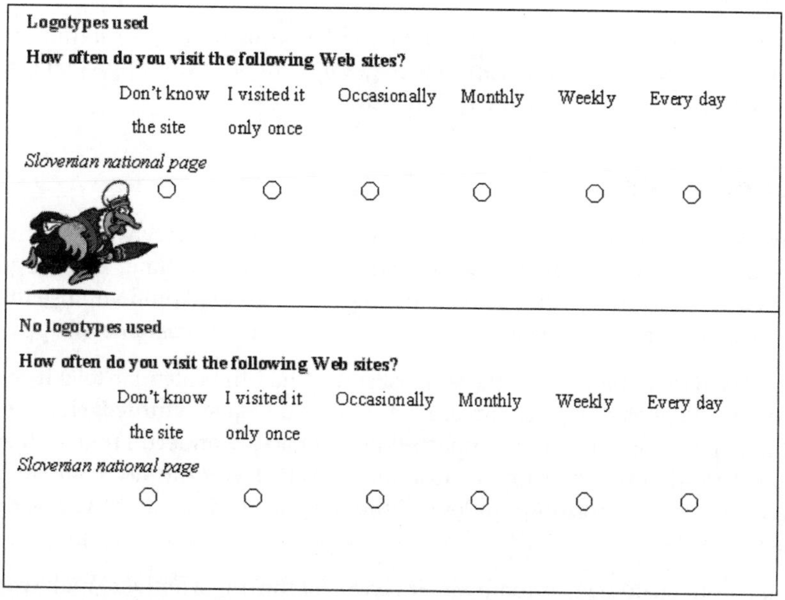

Figure 6.6 The University of Ljubljana found that more than 4 percent abandoned the survey with pictures, compared to less than 1.2 percent without.

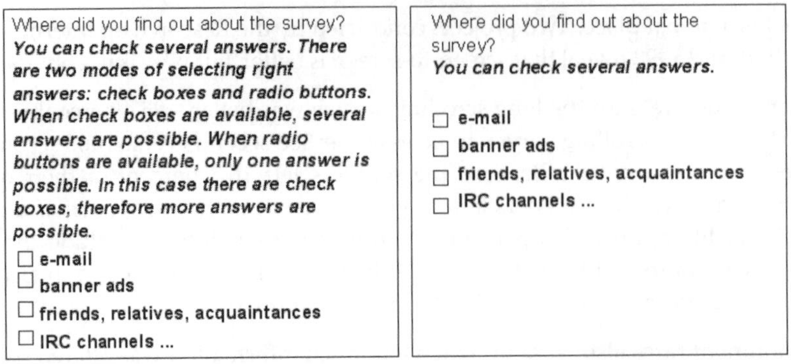

Figure 6.7 The university also found that giving people explicit instructions on how to answer your survey was a detriment to completion.

The Intermittent Survey

There is no need to make users sit through a survey session per se. Why not ask on-point questions as they traverse the Web site? A user surfs over and clicks on the mini-van selection. At the top of the minivan page is a question box—"Are you looking for a minivan for work or for family use?" A quick click, and the user has given you an important data point.

The Hewlett-Packard "Help Me Choose" a printer is a fine example. Hewlett-Packard will help you find the right printer for your needs. At the same time, Hewlett-Packard collects a good deal of information about who is visiting its Web sites.

Another method for collecting information about your user's proclivities is tracking the number of people who visit specific pages in your site. This approach is discussed in detail in Chapter 12, "Measure for Measure."

The Personal Survey

If you take a vacation that you booked through Travelocity (www.travelocity.com), it wants to know how the vacation went. Did you have a good time? Did the accommodations meet your expectations? Were the flights on time? Would you use this service again? Travelocity really needs to know in order to keep its customers happy.

Travelocity uses e-mail to ask these questions. When the calendar tells it that you're back home, off goes the questionnaire. Because you've just returned, chances are very good you're willing to tell the company that you had a wonderful time—all except for that hotel in Montreal that lost your laundry. And if you did not have a wonderful time, it's a grand opportunity to let the site have it. And having it is exactly what a company wants.

You *want* your customers to complain. It gives you the opportunity to make corrections, make amends, and keep a customer. The alternative is to lose a customer and a potential reference or even advocate, all because you didn't know there was something wrong.

Ask the Right Questions

E-Satisfy (www.e-satisfy.co.uk) describes itself as "a Customer Relationship Management company that measures the customer experience for click and mortar companies. We help you improve customer loyalty by measuring how effectively you deliver goods and services across all of your enterprise channels."

Translation? It runs pop-up questionnaires on your site for you. What is interesting are the questions it asks (see Figure 6.8).

Tell us about YourWebSite.com

What is your primary reason for visiting YourWebSite.com today?

To see what has changed since my last visit	To make my regular visit to this site
To search for specific information	Other
To browse the content	

How often do you visit this Web site?

Daily	One to three times a month
Several times a week	Less than once a month
Once a week	This is my first visit

How did you first hear about YourWebSite.com?

In a print ad (newspaper, magazine, etc.)	From a news story
	From a family member, friend or colleague
In a radio ad	Through an on-line ad/promotion
In a television ad	Other

How did you arrive at this Web site today?

Bookmark	Banner ad
Typed in URL	Search engine (Yahoo, Excite, etc.)
Link or recommendation from another site	Other

Figure 6.8   The E-Satisfy screens are small, but the questions are detailed.

Tell us more about YourWebSite.com

How likely would you be to recommend YourWebSite.com to a friend or colleague?

Definitely would not   Probably would

Probably would not   Definitely would

Might or might not

How satisfied are you with the content of YourWebSite.com?

Extremely Dissatisfied   Satisfied

Dissatisfied   Extremely Satisfied

Neutral

How satisfied are you with the "ease of use" of YourWebSite.com?

Extremely Dissatisfied   Satisfied

Dissatisfied   Extremely Satisfied

Neutral

How satisfied are you with the design of YourWebSite.com?

Extremely Dissatisfied   Satisfied

Dissatisfied   Extremely Satisfied

Neutral

Overall, how satisfied are you with this site?

Extremely Dissatisfied   Satisfied

Dissatisfied   Extremely Satisfied

Neutral

And that's only the beginning. Further questions cover demographics, technographics, the check-out process, delivery options, and the return policy, and a query asks what the surfer is likely to do on leaving the site. There's a spot for comments. There's even an opportunity to sign up for a prize drawing.

Ask the Right Kinds of Questions

To achieve statistical validity, you have to ask lots of different types of questions. This list is described in detail and with excellent examples at Bus Design (www.bus.net):

- Open ended
- Forced response
- Multiple choice randomized
- Filtered list, ranking
- Scaled rating, randomized
- Multiple choice
- Numeric ranking
- Single choice, skip pattern

The one thing the Internet gives us that brings joy to the hearts of survey statisticians everywhere is the ability to randomize. The concept is simple; the implementation offline is very expensive. The idea is that the order of the questions has a significant effect on the answers.

If you ask, "Do you like pizza?" before you ask, "What kind of restaurants do you like to go to?" the second question has been contaminated by the first. Online, you can have the server create the page on the fly, changing the order of the questions for each visitor, yielding statistical validity that would make any statistic wonk proud.

For a detailed look at what it takes to enthrall a wonk, take a look at Naresh K. Malhotra's *Marketing Research: An Applied Orientation* (Prentice Hall, 1999).

Convincing Customers to Cooperate

Avoiding what Organic Online research director Christian Alfonsi calls "online focus-group junkies" requires some planning and some psychology, but mostly it requires offering the right incentive.

If you want every business card from every visitor to the trade show, you give away candy, ice cream, popcorn, and cappuccinos at your booth. That should cover everybody, and nobody will turn you down. But you end up with more business cards than are useful. So offer something easy to start with, just as Mama did at www.eat.com. Offer appreciation.

Tone Down the Blue Suit

Thank them for taking the time to help you make the Web site better for them. Make them feel welcome. Make them feel like part of the family. Put a little personality into it.

Sun Microsystems realized that people didn't feel comfortable telling one of the first sites on the Web how it should run things. So Sun decided to go right to the heart of the matter with a large button at the bottom of its home page that said, "Click here to criticize Sun's website" (see Figure 6.9).

Offer an Incentive

Give something away. I was delighted to receive my coveted Ragú Surfing Team shirt, so I was delighted to answer 50 questions. But I'm not the one who shops for pizza sauce in my house, so I was not necessarily the best one to take the survey. The secret is offering an incentive that will be of value only to those who are the right sort for your inquiry. You might offer free shipping. Only those serious about buying would care. You might offer 10 percent off their next purchase. You might sign them up to win a free training course. A membership can be just the ticket.

Memberships offer a number of incentives for customers. The first is that feeling of exclusivity, that sense of belonging. You can pile discounts and deals on top of that, but what people are really after here is inside information.

If you tell TravelSpots (www.travelspots.com) how old you are, how many vacations or business trips you plan to take this year, and whether you prefer deluxe, superior,

Figure 6.9 Sun Microsystems understands the value of humor when engaging people to give feedback.

moderate, or budget accommodation on your trips, it will give you what it considers significant compensation:

> As a preferred member, you will receive first notification of travel specials and discounts. Of course, you will also receive our e-mail newspaper comprising the latest travel trends, information, and handy ideas. Plus, there are contests you will be entered in and prizes to win!

Case Corporation (www.casecorp.com), manufacturers of those big tractors and harvesters, wants to know all about you, so it offers a variety of insider information in return for your registration. Case wants to know all about the gear you have on your ranch or farm as well (see Figure 6.10).

What do you get in return?

- Product Support Article Library History Archives
- Product Support Navigator
- Machine Specific Information
- Online Access to your machinery inventory

You might offer to list your members in a directory, allow them to chat with each other, or let them download special information.

Figure 6.10 Telling Case Corporation the whole story about your equipment entitles you to access special areas on its site.

The Wine Spectator provides the following:

Exclusive Access!

Only signed-in users get to enjoy our Personal Wine List service, which lets you select specific wines from our database of tasting notes and copy them effortlessly to your own private list. The next time you sign in, your list will be waiting for you.

WS Forums

Registered users of Wine Spectator Online can post messages on WS Forums, our online wine community. Whether you want to join a tasting group, learn more about Chianti or just hobnob with fellow wine lovers, you'll have to register to join the conversation.

Finding Out Who They Are

There are a number of reasons to collect an individual's specific identity—the e-mail address. The first is to be sure one individual is answering one question, one time only. An Auto Emporium user could easily indicate a need for a family minivan 5 or 10 times before getting bored. Somebody with a competitive desire to throw your numbers off wouldn't get bored so easily.

Once you have people's e-mail addresses, you can entice them to put themselves on your e-mailing list for future contact. This is such a good formula that you should offer something in return: "Each month our e-Newsletter contains hundreds of dollars in discount coupons you can use online or in our stores" or "Once each month we give away a free widget to one lucky subscriber." You'll find more details on this in Chapter 11, "Attracting Attention."

A more subtle reason for collecting an e-mail address has to do with the validity of the answers received. After people have identified themselves, they are much more likely to give their answers a little more thought than the individual just surfing through. Asking for an e-mail address is not a simple step; there must be something in it for the user. This is where the buying-and-selling, give-and-take dance begins.

Just like a trade show booth, you want people to come up and finger the literature on your site. You want them to examine the product. You want them to ask questions. But many exhibit hall habitues are repelled from a booth by an eager salesperson intent on getting name, title, company, address, phone and fax numbers, and shoe size.

Trading Knowledge for Information and Money

Offer information about the company, the products, and the industry. Give users something of value. Prove to them that you are worth their time, and then offer them something better. Begin by dividing your valuable information into three progressively interesting categories. The first category is of general interest, will attract people to your site, and will show them that you are to be taken seriously as a vendor. This first class of information belongs on your Web site, prominently displayed and available to all.

The second category is a bit more interesting, a bit more precious, and worth a little effort to obtain. For example:

> This White Paper is the first of its kind and is yours if you answer the following 12 quick questions.
> We've collected a wide variety of copyright-free images regarding the widget industry. You can download them after helping us improve our Web site.
> We've created a database of useful tips and tricks.

The third category is absolutely fascinating and should literally be worth its weight in gold—so charge for it. If you're in a knowledge business, this is your stock-in-trade. If not, this is the intelligence that you've carefully gathered and that is truly unique. A Web site is a fine place for the sale and distribution of your unique monographs, images, and videos.

At each progressive stage of information sharing, be sure you are on the receiving end of data that is just as valuable. Munificence is a wonderful corporate image builder, but it can be a drain on the budget when carried too far.

The people who visit your office can tell you if the waiting-room chairs are comfortable. They can give you their impressions about the physical plant, the way they are treated at the reception desk, and how far they had to walk through the snow to reach the front door. People who call your company can open your eyes to what it's like being on hold, how frustrating your voice-mail system is, and whether your customer service department is worthy of the name. Therefore, you should look to the people who visit your Web site as the source of information about how your company represents itself online. What impression does your Web site give of the company? Does it look like a Fortune 500 corporation? A nimble start-up? Or a couple of grad students with their own Web server?

Make Them a Coconspirator

When Eastman Kodak (www.kodak.com) had a new home page design that it wanted to test, it asked site visitors for their opinions. It linked its then current home page to the new design and invited people to take a look and vote. The voters had comments about what they saw, which prompted changes. When the voters registered their approval by more than 90 percent, the new page was put online.

Now and then you can find what Yahoo! is thinking about for their next rendition of their home page by going to beta.yahoo.com. You'll notice predominant "What Do You Think?" and "Please Give Us Feedback" links at the top of the proposed page. These people are serious about catering to their public.

Closing the Feedback Loop

If you are brave, you publish the results of the surveys you take. The managers at net.com (www.net.com) are brave (see Figure 6.11).

> net.com performs service transactions in a Remedial capacity, such as incidents opened with our Technical Assistance Center facilities. net.com also performs scheduled service transactions in a Project capacity, such as network upgrades and expansions. net.com has a host of other service offerings, but those have yet to be monitored by internet mechanisms.
>
> The survey innovations enable net.com managers to promptly discover and take the actions needed to turn customers into loyal advocates. They also involve net.com's own employees in the process, thereby enforcing the awareness that they are a crucial part of the relationship between customers' satisfaction and net.com success.

That's one way of closing the loop. The more expected approach is via e-mail. If you advertise an 800 telephone number on TV, you'd better have operators standing by. If you send a direct mail offer to a list of 500,000, you'd best be prepared for a round of business reply cards. If you put up a Web site, you most certainly ought to be prepared to respond to your e-mail.

This is where free-form feedback comes in. Maybe they couldn't find it in the FAQ. Maybe they couldn't find it in the knowledge base. Maybe they didn't even look. Doesn't matter. E-mail is the customer's way of reaching out to you.

It absolutely amazes me that today, as I write this at the start of 2001, there are still companies like Southwest Airlines (www.southwest.com). For all the flashy colors and

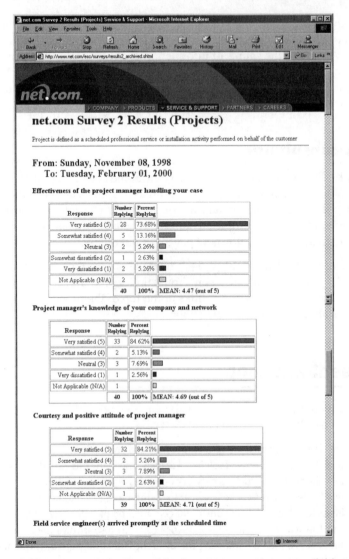

Figure 6.11 Customer satisfaction survey results are available to the public on net.com's site.

online ordering on its site, it simply does not want your e-mail. If you want to send them an e-mail you might start at the home page (see Figure 6.12).

Given the choices, the most obvious approach might be to click on "Help." E-Mail Updates will get you only a list of the e-mails the company wants to *send* you. At the bottom of the menu, there's a link to "How to contact Southwest Airlines." That takes you to the bottom of the same page where the link is repeated. Why? No quality control, I suppose.

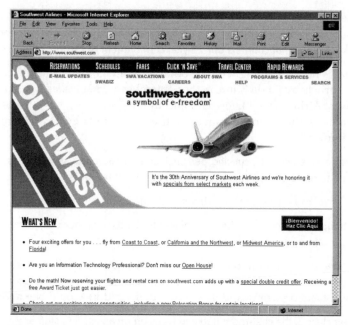

Figure 6.12   Southwest Airlines says look, but don't talk.

There are 16 telephone opportunities spelled out and one paragraph:

Why we don't accept e-mail

At Southwest Airlines, we want to provide you with the best possible Customer Service by responding to your concerns and questions in a timely manner. At the moment, our ability to support e-mail in a manner consistent with our service expectations is not fully in place. Please feel free to drop us a line at the above address.

After being dumbstruck, I am amused by that corker in the middle: "At the moment, our ability to support e-mail in a manner consistent with our service expectations is not fully in place." How long did it take you to get your e-mail support in place enough to at least offer an address to your customers? This paragraph, unchanged, word for word, has been on this Web site for at least four and a half years.

Want another giggle? The Southwest Mission Statement reads as follows:

The mission of Southwest Airlines is dedication to the highest quality of Customer Service delivered with a sense of warmth, friendliness, individual pride, and Company Spirit.

In June 2000, a colleague faxed me an article by Colleen Barrett, executive vice president for customers at Southwest Airlines, published in some magazine. The magazine itself is a mystery to me. But I have the fax, and the article has been replicated on the Dinlan Web site (www.dinanbmw.com) as an apologia for their own fear of e-mail.

The article reads in part as follows (www.dinanbmw.com/html/e-mail.htm):

> Southwest does not solicit or respond to e-mail. We just don't feel it allows us to "do the right thing" for our valued Customers. Call us traditional, but the chat-style, respond-on-demand, quick-casual format counters our 29-year commitment to Customer Service.

Quick and casual is not in keeping with the Southwest image? Isn't this the company that boasts of the article by Linda Burke in the September 4, 1991 *Dallas Times Herald* by saying, "Southwest Airlines, long known for encouraging zaniness, has attracted some creative job pleadings after launching an advertisement campaign to find employees with a sense of humor."

> Our Customers deserve accurate, specific, personal, and professionally written "answers," and it takes time to research, investigate, and compose a real business letter.

Clearly, the rest of us must be e-mailing dross and slag to our customers.

> We also track trends and provide useful internal feedback based on our mail. E-mail does not give us these capabilities or opportunities.

Somebody's not paying attention to the technology out there. Kana (www.kana.com), eGain (www.egain.com), Mindwave Software (www.mindwavesoftware.com), Tacit Knowledge (www.tacitcorp.com), and dozens of other vendors would beg to differ.

> We elect to steer clear of the chat-room trap and focus on meaningful Customer dialogue.

The chat room trap? Oh, I see, only people who want to waste your time and spoil your day would dream of looking for a "Chat" button on your Web site. Real humans use the phone.

> A reasonably sized staff couldn't do this if, say, a quarter of the 1.5 million monthly visits to our website resulted in e-mail.

Heaven forbid you might learn something from them.

> Some years ago, we experimented with comment cards and quickly learned a valuable lesson: If you build it, they will come. The majority of respondents felt compelled to complete them because they were there and offered suggestions or questions about full-service meals, open seating, pricing, new destinations, etc. These are basic business strategies that underwrite our lower fares. Still, we believed that everyone who took time to comment deserved a response. The volume left us with clear, but not very good, choices: Ignore those Customers, triple our staff, or send "form letters." One was rude; one was costly; the other (we learned the hard way), ineffective and displeasing. From e-mail correspondence that has found its way into our organization, or others we've studied, most are modern equivalents of comment cards—e-surveys, if you will. So, this time, we opt to ignore.

We screwed up using this old paper-and-pencil technology, and it scared the bejeepers out of us. So we're going to go sit in the corner with our eyes closed, our fingers in our ears, humming loudly.

> This is not because we don't care. We jump through hoops to make general information available on our website and through our telephone Reservations Service. We answer every letter we receive in the order it arrives, and we streamline in order to keep our costs low, our People productive, our operating efficiency high, and our responses warm and personal.

Figure 6.13   Scott Adams seems to hit the nail on the head consistently with Dilbert.
DILBERT reprinted by permission of United Features Syndicate, INC.

We just can't for the life of us figure out the difference between Reply and Reply-All.

> We pass the savings along to you.

See Figure 6.13.

> So, if you want information about Southwest Airlines, visit our website at www.iflyswa. com. Or call us at 1-800-I FLY SWA. Letters are welcome in Customer Relations, P.O. Box 36647, Dallas, Texas 75235-1647. We'll get back to you—in writing or by phone!

I think I'll pass, Colleen, but thanks, anyway.

Respond Quickly

The general expectation on the Internet has always been 24-hour turnaround. This is due in part to crossed time zones, late-night e-mail sessions, and automated Mailbots. It is also due to the informality of the Internet. Responses don't have to be channeled through six layers of management; they just get written and sent. Therefore, have responders at the ready, with ready responses.

Build a staff of people to handle the incoming mail from your Web site. Draw on the team that handles the 800 phone lines. They already know most of the questions and have the answers on hand. Bolster this group with a few people who know their way around the Internet, people who know a good idea when it comes in and can acknowledge it appropriately. This is the public relations side of things (where the "public" has become the audience of one).

Go the Extra Mile

It is necessary to give people every means possible to get in touch with you. Accept their e-mail, post your phone number, list your postal addresses, and take phone calls.

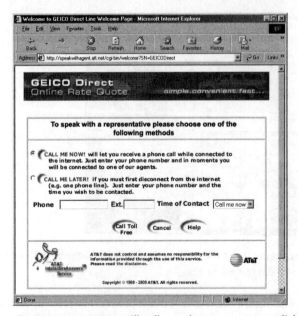

Figure 6.14 GEICO will call you the moment you click.

For the moment, that means training your phone operators in the fine points of your Web site. You want them to be able to say "Yes, I can help with that!" rather than "Oh? We have a Web site?"

The folks at GEICO Direct Insurance (www.geico.com) definitely want to talk to you, and they've hooked up their phones to their Web site to do it (see Figure 6.14). Click the mouse; your phone rings.

This is a momentary workaround solution to a problem that's going to go away soon. There's no mystery to sending voice packets over the Internet. It's just a matter of time before you'll simply be able to talk through your computer. That time may even have been between my writing and your reading. Then "Can I help you?" comes with complete knowledge of what page you're on and an idea of how to help you.

Get Them to Talk to Each Other

This topic was brought up in a previous chapter, but it bears repeating here. If you want to know what your customers are thinking, get them talking. I devoted an entire chapter about this subject in *Customer Service on the Internet, Second Edition* (John Wiley & Sons, 2000) and with good reason:

> Besides posting purified, disinfected data for the masses, and beyond answering e-mail from individuals, there is tremendous value in getting your clients to talk to each other on your site. Getting them to talk about you and your products can be a very powerful tool for building loyalty. It can also expose you in unpleasant ways.

Marketers have always used testimonials. Now there is a way to get people to express their on-going love affair with your products and services in their own words; online and in real time.

On the other hand, they will also air their dirty laundry. They will be only too happy to espouse your shortcomings. They will be delighted to take their frustrations out on you in public. Kept them waiting on hold for more than they could tolerate? Didn't offer a refund? Didn't even say "I'm sorry"? Now your customers can tell the world in an instant. Is this really such a good idea?

It's a very good idea. Managed properly, these complaints become a wealth of information for product and service improvement. They become the spring board to people helping each other and forming a community of customers. They prove to your customers that you value their contribution. It also shows your company is embracing this new technology in order to open the doors between you and your clientele instead of using it to simply disseminate the company line.

Getting clients to talk is one thing (and a good thing), but building a community is another thing entirely (and a great thing).

Awareness in marketing leads to branding. Community on the Internet leads to bonding. Bonding occurs when customers are so closely connected to your products that they don't just use them and repurchase them; they also recommend them and are happy to make public pronouncements about how your products changed their lives.

One way to move customers toward bondage is to create a place for them to congregate. They'll get to know each other. Then they'll complain. Then they'll gang up on you. Then they'll start helping each other.

If You Build It, They Will Bond

Cisco Systems did more than create automated methods of helping its customers; it created a way for its customers to help themselves. Open Forum was one of Cisco's first customer-only and customer-specific features. A private newsgroup managed by the customer service staff, Open Forum was created for posing less straightforward technical support questions.

Open Forum provides a timely, online mechanism for Cisco customers to receive answers to common technical questions. Customers submit their questions using the Open Forum tool and choose the priority level of their query. It's a quick and easy way for customers to get answers without having to open a case with Cisco's TAC.

CCIE professionals are invited to participate in Open Forum by answering customer questions about Cisco technology. Only CCIE professionals are allowed to post answers to questions posed in the Forum. Participating in Open Forum is a great way to stay in touch with Cisco customers and to stay current with internetworking technologies

Here's the process: A customer asks a particularly troublesome question, and the system scours a Cisco knowledgebase for the answer. Potential answers are shown to the customer; if the answers don't fit or aren't sufficient to solve the problem, the customer can ask again, or the customer can send the question to the engineers. Cisco engineers are tasked with finding the answer. If they do, great. The question and the answer are fed into the knowledgebase for next time. If they don't find the answer, the question goes to the Open Forum, where all customers can take a crack at it.

If the customer sees an answer he or she likes, it and the question are sent to a team of technical writers and senior engineers to check the veracity of the information, as well as to review grammar and style. Once they clean it up, the question and answer go into the knowledgebase.

As a result of this system, 75 percent of questions are answered before they hit the Open Forum. The bonding happens because of the interesting mix of camaraderie and competition in the Open Forum. Celebrities are created and honored for being willing and able to help their fellow customers.

The reason this customer service application shows up in a marketing book is simple. If you add more value to your products through customer service, your products are more valuable to your prospective customers. And besides, you had better give them a place to talk to each other about your products for one good reason . . .

If You Don't Build It, They Will

Imagine the surprise over at Corel Corporation (www.corel.com) when, in 1995, it heard that people were talking about the company. Lots of people. In fact, there was a whole Web site set up by Corel customers just to talk about Corel products. In fact, this Web site was so popular and so populated, it was able to sell advertising (see Figure 6.15).

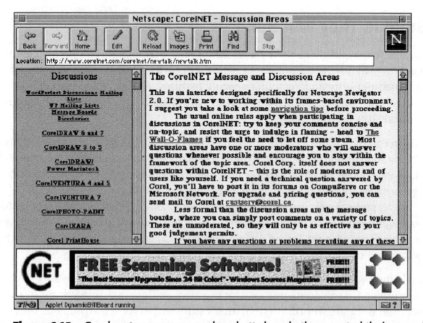

Figure 6.15 Corel customers were such a chatty bunch, they created their own clubhouse.

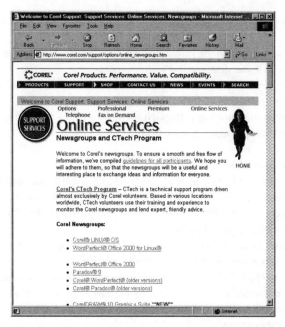

Figure 6.16 Corel wanted to open the discussion to all while keeping a close eye on it.

When Corel got wind of this site, it rushed right out and bought up the advertising before its competitors could. But that didn't quite make Corel feel comfortable enough.

Its lawyers advised that advertising on a discussion site that could contain questionable information might be construed as endorsement of that information by association. So Corel bought the site—lock, stock, and server. This move was far easier in the long run. Now, Corel has the Corel newsgroup page (see Figure 6.16).

> CTech is a technical support program driven almost exclusively by Corel volunteers. Based in various locations worldwide, CTech volunteers use their training and experience to monitor the Corel newsgroups and lend expert, friendly advice.

Corel understands the power of letting customers talk to each other and understands the power of being the focal point, the starting place, the portal to that discussion. Corel also understands that some rules are valuable and that some moderation is necessary.

Guidelines for Corel Newsgroups

Please stay on topic. It's normal for some of the message topics to drift from the stated subject; however, for maximum benefit for all involved, please keep your messages close to the newsgroup's subject.

While we recognize and welcome the international scope of Corel's newsgroups, English is the predominant language of these discussion forums. If your message is in a language other than English, responses may be quicker and you may reach more people who might be able to help you if you post in the international areas or if you include an English translation with your message.

Personal attacks or slurs ("flaming") and any use of profanity in your messages is not permitted.

Please do not disrupt or interfere with the running of the newsgroups. Everyone is entitled to his or her opinion, even if you disagree.

If you find you have a problem with another user that you can't resolve on your own, please e-mail us at ctechmgr@corel.com.

The preferred method of communication is through these forums, as other users can benefit from the answers to your questions as well. Do not contact users by e-mail unless specifically asked to do so.

Do not post copyrighted material without permission of the author.

Generally speaking, if a message is easy to read, more people will actually read it. To that end, if you post your message as ASCII text which is 76 characters wide, it will appear neatly laid out in virtually every news reader. To do this when posting from a Web browser, you should set it to NOT post messages with HTML tags.

Do not post messages with large attachments as large files fill up our servers quickly and annoy people who download and read the newsgroups off-line.

If you have a component or application that you wish to share, post a message describing it and offer to mail it to interested parties or make the item available on the Web.

Posting advertisements or solicitations that do not pertain to the intended use and purpose of the newsgroups is not permitted.

Please post your question in the most appropriate newsgroup. If you don't know which group is the best, put this in your post and ask for suggestions.

Corel does not offer any formal support in the public newsgroups. Instead, Corel staff and CTech volunteers monitor and moderate the newsgroups to ensure the smooth flow of information and messaging guidelines are maintained.

Users are free to exchange advice among one another but should use discretion when relying upon technical information contained in newsgroup messages. Information contained in one message may apply only in the context of a set of facts contained in an earlier message which is no longer visible, or which your newsgroup reader may have mis-threaded, or may be based upon inaccurate information provided by the person asking the original question. Corel staff and CTech volunteers make every reasonable effort to provide accurate technical information in these message areas. Although it is impossible for Corel staff or CTechs to read all user to user messages, whenever inaccurate technical information is observed in such messages an effort is made to provide correct information. Because of these and other limitations inherent in this medium, Corel, including CTechs, can assume no responsibility for, and must disclaim all liability with respect to, information contained in newsgroup messages.

Do not use the Corel.com newsgroups to encourage conduct that would constitute a criminal offense, give rise to civil liability or otherwise violate any local, state, national or international law or regulation.

Corel reserves the right to remove, without warning, any messaging that does not fall within the outlined criteria for message postings within these areas.

Even with all those disclaimers, you have to hand it to them for being brave enough to ride herd on more than 100 different discussions covering all the different versions of all their products and another 5 discussions in each of 6 languages.

Letting people gripe and grumble as a group empowers them to be more vociferous. It's the mob-mentality thing: "Yeah! Me, too!" You certainly don't want that to get out of hand, but you do want your customers to feel that you *want* to hear from them and that their opinion is *important*. And what you hear in discussions between customers can go a long way toward helping you make your products and services better and more fungible.

Marshall McLuhan said, "The medium is the message." Less well known, however, is his farsighted "The audience is the content." Little did he know . . .

Building Community

I'd say that 1998 was the Year of the Community. Every Web site had to be a community center in order to be valuable to all and sundry. Every site manager was bombarded with offers of community-building tools that were merely chat, threaded discussion groups, and e-mail enhancements.

But if you make your customers part of your site, they will come back for more. Amazon gives readers a place to write reviews. Digital Origin (www.digitalorigin.com) develops digital video camcorder owners' needs: still capture, motion capture, nonlinear editing, and postproduction:

> The "wishlist" list is a way to communicate your ideas and suggestions to Digital Origin's Product Management team. The posts to this list are read and reviewed monthly. If your question requires an immediate response then please contact our Sales department.

Talking to your customers is great. Letting them talk to each other is good, too. But the significant rewards (market share, customer loyalty, positive public relations) are going to go to those companies that walk the walk.

Make Customers a Part of Your Team

Level 1 companies take surveys and look at the results. Level 2 companies make customer input a fundamental part of the product development process. Level 3 companies don't make a move unless their customers are by their sides, feeding them fresh insights and clear direction.

Your Web site is an opportunity to bond with your customers through enthralling information, entertaining activities, and exceptional service. If you concentrate on getting feedback from them, you will know how to cater to them. If you acknowledge them individually and in public for their participation, they will cling to the relationship.

Consider creating an electronic advisory council that can help your company by offering up an outside perspective from your most trusted customers.

Make customer satisfaction one of your most important metrics.

Create a culture of customer focus, and do it soon because the Web has brought you and your customers closer together than ever before. The tactics you've used in the past to keep customers at arm's length are too transparent at this range.

Siebel Systems (www.siebel.com) and Cisco Systems (www.cisco.com) pay bonuses based on customer satisfaction rather than simply on sales. That motivates everybody from the sales team to the administrative assistants to be there for their customers. Your Web site should give the same impression.

Some companies' clients are looking for communication; others are looking for more. SupplyForce.com is a construction industry marketplace. Senior VP of Marketing David Cohen was quoted in the July 17, 2000 edition of *B2B* (netb2b.com) saying that his customers "are not looking for community in the sense of dialogue with each other, but they do want tools and mechanisms to make their purchasing decisions better, more efficient and faster."

That's why Chapter 7 focuses on what you can do to help your customers succeed at whatever they're trying to accomplish. That's why it's called "Value Added Marketing—It's Personal."

Value-Added Marketing—
It's Personal

D o you want to win the game? Then you must take the next step in winning the hearts and minds of consumers in your marketplace—you must offer proof. Not money-back guarantees (although those are good). Not celebrity testimonials (although those can help). Not even free trials (although they are a good start, with a happy track record online) are enough.

You need to offer proof to your prospects that you understand their needs and desires, understand the industry you're in, and understand your competition. You have to prove that you are a worthy vendor. You must prove you have price, value, status, quality, and convenience sewn up before you make the offer to your prospects.

The most precious commodity on this planet is time. If you expect a prospect to expend any amount of this unrenewable resource, this priceless asset, thinking about your products and services, you had better offer something of value in return. You are going to have to pay people to consider your products.

It used to be up to us as marketers to figure out which way the parade was going and to get out in front of it. It was up to us to determine what the audience wanted and to give it to them. That was then; times have changed.

When Marshall McLuhan said "The audience is the content," he was focusing on what happens inside your head when you watch a play, see a movie, or read a book. The story is different for each of us because we bring a unique lifetime of experience to it.

The old woman walked into the gray house.

That sentence creates a picture in your mind. But the woman and the house you see are different from what I envision. We're different. McLuhan was right about that. Today, the Internet makes his words literally true.

Your marketing materials are no longer the same for all comers. No longer can you measure response based on gross numbers. No longer can you look out at a sea of faces and think of them as a mass market. They are a sea of individuals, and each of them, based on his or her individual interests and needs, will create his or her own content out of the components you offer on your Web site.

Understanding the significance of "the audience is the content" will make the best of all possible Web sites.

Remember that the Internet culture is acclimatized to a gift culture. All the other players on the Net are giving. Now it's your turn to be a better benefactor than the next guy. Assuming that you are selling stuff and not eyeballs—assuming that you are not in the business of paying people frequent flier miles, points, or discounts just to surf your site—you can make your Web pay people for their time in three ways:

- You can make your Web site fun.
- You can make it interesting.
- You can make it useful.

Each of these requires identifying your prospects or customers very well. Something that's fun to a teenager is not fun to her father. Something that's useful to an engineer is not useful to an accountant.

Make Your Site Fun

This is tough. Way back when, it used to be easier. A list of knock-knock jokes was fun, and having an interactive game was considered the height of fashion.

Now, you can offer fun and games, but you face two challenges: content match and merit. The first asks whether the "fun" is related to your product. If you're in the software business you might be able to come up with a handful of jokes to entertain your customers. This proves that you are a fun company:

Q. How many software people does it take to screw in a light bulb?

A. None. It's a hardware problem.

Q. How many systems analysts does it take to change a light bulb?

A. The light bulb works fine in *my* office.

Q. How many Microsoft vice presidents does it take to change a light bulb?

A. Five: one to work the bulb and four to make sure Microsoft gets $1 for every light bulb ever changed anywhere in the world.

In 1998, Cellular One (www.cellularone.com) thought it would provide entertainment for its customers and potential customers. It created the puzzle game and promoted it on the home page (see Figure 7.1).

Figure 7.1   Cellular One has the right question: Are you game?

The puzzle pieces are scattered throughout the site; when you find one, you click. A brief message comes up congratulating you on finding another piece, telling you how many remain to be found, and giving you a link back to the page you were on. My very first question is this: What's the prize?

I'm invited to play, and it says I can win a prize. But the flow construct just isn't working for me because the game is so boring and the reward is unknown. I'm sorry, Cellular One, but this falls under the category of "Hey kids, let's put on a show!" You can see the marketing people (with little Web experience) huddled with the creative Web people (with little business experience) as they hash it out over lunch.

"We looked over the logs, and people are going only to the product description pages. We created all this other great content, and nobody is looking at it. How do we make them?"

"Oh! Oh! I have an idea!" Then he stops to wipe a bit of blood-orange salad from his chin. "How about a game? It's so cool that you can do interactive stuff on the Web, and Web surfers *love* to play interactive games, and we could give away prizes and stuff!"

"Good idea. That's very good. Just make sure it's tasteful."

Fast forward to 2001. Cellular One still feels having fun is a good idea. That's why it offers a Fun link from its home page and invites you to play (see Figure 7.2).

Some people never learn.

The second challenge you face when trying for fun on your Web site is the question of merit. What the heck is it for? Why bother?

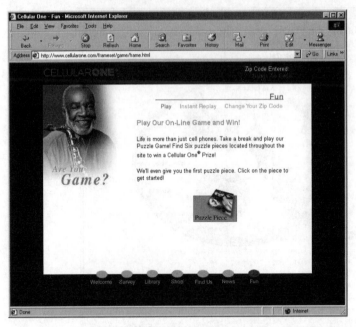

Figure 7.2 Cellular One is playing the very same game and *still* not telling you what the prizes are—three years later.

If you want to accomplish some of the standard advertising goals of awareness building and brand image construction, you could follow some of the big advertisers who are playing serious games.

Coca-Cola knows its audience. A healthy portion of them are young and technically savvy. Rather than trying to lure them to www.coke.com, Coke goes where the customers are. In this case, to the ShockRave site (www.shockrave.com). ShockRave is a site put up by Macromedia (www.macromedia.com) to promote its interactive, animated tool set and browser plug-in called Shockwave. Coke has decided to host a game at the ShockRave site.

We pause for a moment to make this abundantly clear. Macromedia has a software product called Shockwave. To promote it, it set up a Web site called ShockRave where it can show off the software's wonders. Coke is sponsoring a game on the ShockRave site to promote its soft drink. See? This Web stuff is simple once you get the hang of it.

The game is ice hockey, and you're the man with the puck. Now, this game isn't just sponsored by Coke with an ad banner at the top; Coke takes center stage (see Figure 7.3), or is that center rink?

That's some serious fun and games. If your market is the consumer, packaged-goods, youth-oriented, fun-seeking, time-to-kill crowd, take note.

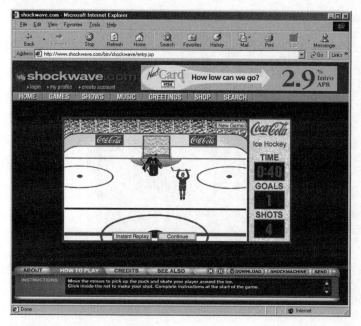

Figure 7.3 Coke wants its logo branded on your eyeball as you shoot goals.

If you work for Warner Brothers or Looney Tunes, take note. If you work for Disney, you've already decided games are an essential part of your brand. The 102 Dalmatians site (www.102dalmatians.com) is a prime example (see Figure 7.4).

You wanna play? Disney figured you did:

Puppy Jumble
Trying to escape from Cruella, a few of the puppies were caught and sent to Le Pelt's Factory! They've gotten the cage open, but they need your help getting to the conveyor belts and safety. Use your mouse to carry each puppy over to its matching outline. Hurry, the clock is ticking!

Ms. De Vil's Dinner Party
Uh-oh, Ms. De Vil's having a dinner party. Quick—click on the silver platters to match all the meals on Cruella's menu before the guests arrive!

Le Pelt's Bakery Game
Le Pelt has chased the puppies into the bakery! It's your job to help the puppies escape. Drag the correct items from the left side of the screen onto different parts of the baking machine. But be careful—some things may actually make Le Pelt go faster!

If you are in the business of fun, get to work! But if you're selling hand-rolled cigars (www.galaxymall.com/product/premiumcigars), hand-stitched, 18th-century hunting pouches (www.firelocks.com/page15.html), or handmade kilts (www.celticclothing .co.uk), maybe you're better off finding value in other ways.

Figure 7.4   102 Dalmatians has information for moviegoers, but it's more about interactivity than anything else.

Make Your Site Interesting

What do you know? It's a serious question. What do you know more about than most people and that prospective customers would find interesting? If you sell antique clocks, you might know that the world's oldest clock has struck the hours for about 1,615 years and has been calculated to have ticked more than 500 million times.

If you sell wrist watches, you might actually want to describe the factory when asked for the time.

If you're Sears, you may want people to know that in "1886 Richard Sears starts selling watches to supplement his income as station agent at North Redwood, Minnesota." And now we're back to the content match and merit challenges again. Is it interesting to your customers or just to you?

AT&T thinks it has lots of different kinds of customers, so it has lots of different kinds of interesting things. There are interesting (yet very topical) games at the AT&T Brainspin page (www.att.com/technology/forfun/brainspin). You can try to find a way to stop the world from running out of phone numbers, learn how Alexander Graham Bell taught his dog to talk, and try to improve bandwidth on the Internet.

I was caught up for several minutes in the Train of Thought Chronological Tour (www.research.att.com/history/train.html):

1924: The First Fax	1951: Direct-Dial Service
1925: High-Fidelity Recording	1954: The Solar Battery
1926: Sound Motion Pictures	1960: The Laser
1927: Wave Nature of Matter	1960: Communication Satellites
1927: First TV Transmission	1964: Touch-Tone Phones
1929: The Artificial Larynx	1965: The Big Bang Discovered
1929: Transatlantic Radiotelephone	1970: The Picturephone
1933: Radio Astronomy	1976: Epitaxy Microchips
1933: LP & Stereo Records	1977: Optical Fiber Communication
1936: Synthetic Speech	1985: The Smart Card
1939: The First Computer	1989: The Speech-Driven Robot
1939: High-Frequency Radar	1989: HDTV
1942: The Horn Antenna	1992: Instant Language Translator
1947: The Transistor	1993: The Computer Video
1948: Information Theory	

I was caught for more than a few minutes on the AT&T Try This! page (www.att.com/ technology/trythis). The AT&T text-to-speech converter is pretty good. It's not HAL 9000 yet, but give AT&T a minute or two and it will figure it out.

Now back to our two challenges. Did AT&T find something to distract even me? You betcha. Does this content have value? Depends on your measuring stick. Did AT&T get me to buy anything? No. Was it trying to? No. Did it leave me with a new and better brand image of AT&T than I had before? Yes. Did it have some content that was compelling enough that I told a few thousand of my closest friends? Absolutely. Was it money well spent? I'd say yes.

If you have the budget and the manpower that AT&T does, you should look into this sort of thing. If you suffer from limited resources, maybe you should skip the find-the-hidden-puzzle-pieces approach.

Make Your Site Useful

Companies are finding the biggest return on their Web investment by making their sites useful. Some people look at the Internet as entertainment. Lots of people look at the Internet as a form of communication (e-mail, chat, newsgroups). But *everybody* looks at the Internet as a resource. They go there to find information, and they go there to get stuff done.

If your site contains information of value to your audience, they can make use of it as a reference. Every site should, at least, have a list of other Web sites of interest—not of general interest, like Yahoo! or Netscape's Netcenter, but sites that contain information about your industry.

Your site can be useful if it offers the latest news on your market segment. You don't want to be an online news agency? Strike a deal with a company like Individual.com (www.individual.com) that can collect the information for you.

Reveal Your Best Knowledge

Think like a publisher for the moment. This is where you go beyond putting papers online because they're interesting. You put information online because it's useful.

InterCorr-CLI International (www.clihouston.com) is an independent research and corrosion testing company. InterCorr-CLI provides test services, corrosion test equipment, and a suite of materials selection software applications. It also publishes an online newsletter, *Corrosioneering*.

> Corrosioneering is InterCorr-CLI's online newsletter. We will periodically post short technical articles that may be of interest to the materials community. This month's topics are:
>
> Emerging Microbial Control Issues in Cooling Water Systems
>
> "Reprinted by permission from HYDROCARBON PROCESSING, May 1998, copyright 1998, by Gulf Publishing Co., all rights reserved"
>
> FAILURE ANALYSIS of Wire Rope
>
> "Reprinted by permission from ADVANCED MATERIALS & PROCESSES, May 2000, copyright 2000, by ASM International, all rights reserved"
>
> High Performance Stainless Steels and Microbiologically Influenced Corrosion
>
> "Reprinted by permission from AVESTA SHEFFIELD, acom 1-1997, all rights reserved"

Industrial metallurgists may find these articles as fascinating as I find AT&T's history of technology. They may be as glued to these documents as I was to the text-to-speech converter. But chances are that they find these articles useful, so they keep coming back.

Make Their Life Easier

To what sort of information would your customers like to have finger-tip access? What sort of an online database could you create for the benefit of your customers?

Glaxo Wellcome makes prescription drugs. It sells these drugs to doctors, who prescribe them to their patients. How do you get more doctors to know and love your drugs? It's a difficult question because doctors are very busy.

When I went to my doctor for a cocktail of vaccinations before one of my more exotic public speaking tours, I found myself in the waiting room along with others who were there for reasons I'd rather not know. Among them was a man in a suit and tie who, like me, looked too healthy to be waiting in a doctor's office. Then I realized he was a pharmaceutical sales representative. The prospect of his having to sit and wait for the doctor to finish with me made my wait infinitely easier. It also made me glad I was not a pharmaceutical sales rep.

Knowing that doctors seldom even have time to log on to the Internet, Glaxo thought about what it could offer that would be easier for doctors to access online than offline. The answer: continuing education. Medical professionals are required, just like lawyers

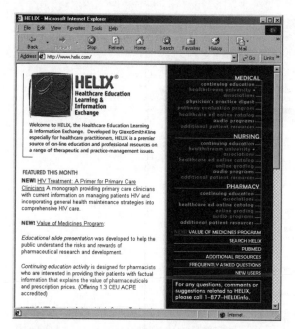

Figure 7.5 Glaxo Wellcome lets medical professionals electronically catch up on their required classroom hours.

and CPAs, to take a certain number of hours of accredited instruction every year. What if they could do it online? That's how HELIX was born (see Figure 7.5).

HELIX instructors are not just the local medicos who were willing to spend some time teaching a class. These are top-notch professionals who can come to town only prerecorded.

> HELIX is a premier source of on-line education and professional resources on a range of therapeutic and practice-management issues. Offering on-line CE courses, links to audio lectures by world-renowned experts, medical databases, associations, and more, HELIX is a convenient and comprehensive resource center to help physicians, pharmacists, nurses and allied health professionals sharpen their skills and stay current with medical trends.

Do you suppose Bristol-Myers Squibb knows anything about migraines? Given that it is the manufacturer of Excedrin, it stands to reason that it might. The company knows people have questions about these debilitating headaches, so it created the Managing Migraines area inside its Headache Resource Center (see Figure 7.6).

> What migraines are and what triggers them
> What you can do to help prevent your migraines
> What may work for your migraines when they strike
> A closer look at migraine sufferers who are "suffering in silence"
> Some surprising statistics about migraine and migraine sufferers
> Some of the most frequently asked questions about migraines

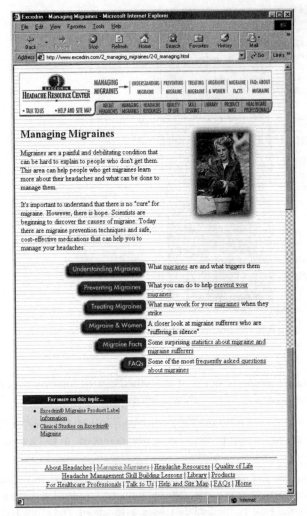

Figure 7.6 Bristol-Myers Squibb addresses the major areas of interest to migraine sufferers to make its Web site useful.

Finding Your Firm's Added Value

How do you determine what value your firm can provide to your customers and to the Internet? Ask them.

Ask your customers. It is not a marketer's job to know what customers want. It is the marketer's job to *ask* the customers what they want. Things change so fast that you must ascertain the needs and desires of your target marketplace again and again. Ask them what sort of service they're getting from other vendors (not just competitors) and what they would hope to find on your Web site. Get them involved with the creation and growth of your Web site.

Ask the Internet. Find an appropriate newsgroup and pose the question, "Has anybody seen a Web site that does *this*? If we offered that on our Web site would it be worthwhile? What else should we add?" This is a great way of getting a large number of opinions and doing some prerelease advertising at the same time.

Ask your business partners. Your vendors, your distributors, and your cooperative marketing partners will all have ideas, questions, and resources that will help make your site a better place. Listen to them, give them their own section on your site, and link to their sites. This will make your site a more valuable place for your customers and prospects.

Ask your sales and customer service departments. Above all, ask your own people. Your customer service department knows the frequently asked questions. Your sales department knows how people look for information about your products. They also know what else people need in order to consider, justify, purchase, and use your products.

The Web Is a Personal Place

At first, we all gathered around the fire and listened to the storyteller regale us with bits of our own history mixed with legend and fantasy. Then we went to the theater, the concert hall, and the movies. Then television and radio brought the communal experience down to the family level. If you're a baby boomer or older, you remember nights with the rest of the clan, gathered around the glowing black-and-white box watching "The Ed Sullivan Show" and "Laugh-In" and talking about them in school the next day. It was a close-knit experience, shared by all your peers.

Then came portable TVs, Watchmans, VCRs, and two things happened at once. We stopped watching TV together, and we stopped watching the same things. Now that "Seinfeld" has been relegated to the limbo of syndication, we've lost the last show that almost everybody watched this side of the Olympics.

Computers were never in that category. They were never a group event; they have always been personal.

A Fine and Private Place

How do you feel when you're watching TV and somebody else walks into the room? OK, so maybe you quickly switch back to the PBS special on cholesterol from the Home Shopping Network Sports-A-Bilia special, but you don't mind if they sit and watch you surf. Somebody looking over my shoulder as I type is enough to freeze my fingers. I can work at a pretty good clip until there's another person there who says "Uhh" as soon as I mistype something.

When you sit down at a computer, it's usually *your* computer (at least it's your session). That means you can change the settings of the browser and the color of the background, and nobody can stop you. You can size the windows the way you want. You can set the margins and change the font size and just make it your own environment.

The worst thing about watching somebody else TV channel surf is that he or she zips right past the good stuff, the serious things of real interest, and then gets bogged down in incomprehensible garbage. Now apply that experience to the Web.

"Don't click there! Click on the Free Stuff button! No, no, not *there*. Hit the Back button. Oh, for crying out loud, you'd think you'd never surfed before—gimme the mouse."

"MoooOOOOooommm! Tell him to quit it!"

And, of course, when it comes to e-mail, we move from personal to private. When I carry on an e-mail conversation with my brother, I don't necessarily want my wife to listen in. And I *certainly* don't want my brother reading the messages of undying devotion I send through cupid's electronic telegraph. It's private.

A Place of Personal Interest

I have a friend who thought the World Wide Web was, well, OK. Even though I had clearly extolled its virtues on numerous occasions, he just couldn't seem to get interested. Not, that is, until I showed him that he could trade his dearly beloved baseball cards online. Within the week he upgraded his PC, got a modem, downloaded Netscape, and became a cybercowboy.

His wife was overwhelmed by all the choices—they scared her: "How do I know what to look at? How do I know where to go?" I asked her where she went first when she walked into a bookstore with so many choices. She got it. Problem solved.

In his article "America at Mid-Decade" (*American Demographics*, February 1995), Peter Francese made this statement:

> No American is typical anymore. There is no average family, no ordinary worker, and no middle class as we knew it. The State of the Union can no longer be summarized in one sentence because the body politic has become a motley crowd.

In this day of "you can have any color you want," you must continue to hold out the undeliverable promise to the public. You must still make them understand that your product will make them irresistible, will allow them to win and hold the ones they love, and will help them rise to the top of their business or social circle. The difference is that you now have a tool to do it for each prospect, one by one.

Don't run away from the responsibility to treat each user as an individual. Change your focus from gaining share of market to gaining share of customer. Measure each customer not as a transaction but as a long-term business partner.

The Web is a personal place full of information of interest to each individual. Unless you are engaged in a battle of joystick skill against another game player, being at a computer is a solitary affair. It's personal. It's work. It's *your* spreadsheet, *your* drawing, *your* document. When you're on the Web, it's *your* surf time.

Make Your Web Site Interactive

We've already seen one way to personalize the experience on your site: have enough information up there that anybody can find something that interests him or her. Users can click to their hearts' content to get that one bit they were after. Alternatively, you can give them something that they can *use* on your site. Something like a software application that gives them answers tailored to their needs.

A Calculated Move

You know there are tons of calculators out there. You can calculate everything you wanted to know about buying a house at FinanCenter (www.FinanCenter.com) including the following:

How much can I borrow?

How much will my payments be?

How much will adjustable rate payments be?

Which is better: fixed or adjustable?

Should I pay points to lower the rate?

Which is better: 15 or 30 year term?

How much should I put down?

How much can I save in taxes?

What will my closing costs be?

Am I better off renting?

Am I better off refinancing?

What will my refinancing costs be?

How can I reduce mortgage insurance costs?

Which lender has the better loan?

Which loan is better?

How advantageous are extra payments?

What home can I afford?

Then you can hop over to Home Energy Saver (www.homeenergysaver.lbl.gov) and find out how to save money heating and cooling your house (see Figure 7.7).

Amerimax Home Products (www.amerimax-inc.com) will help you calculate the materials you'll need for your gutters and downspouts. Icorp (www.icorp.net) will help you figure out how far your new home is from your old one. Charles Schwab (www.schwab.com) will help you calculate your charitable tax deduction if you donate that old home to charity.

At Home Depot (www.homedepot.com) you can do the following:

Estimate the number of yards of carpet you'll need to cover any floor in your home.

Calculate the number of ceramic surface and border tiles needed to cover any surface.

Get fast answers on how much drywall you need for your next project.

Tell us the size of your lawn and we'll estimate the amount of grass seed you need.

Calculate how much insulation you need for your home, plus the best R-Value to buy.

Accurately estimate the amount of paint you need to cover your walls and trim.

Determine the number of rolls you'll need to cover any or all of the walls in your room.

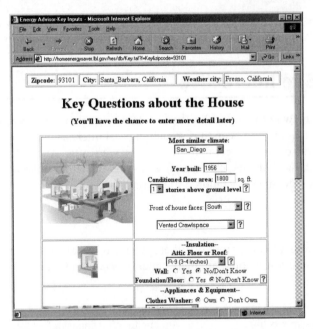

Figure 7.7 Tell Home Energy Saver about your house and find out how much you'll pay for energy and about suggested upgrades.

Take a ride over to the New York State Thruway site (www.thruway.state.ny.us) and calculate how much it's going to cost you to commute to work and back every day. Finally, you can ask Dr. Koop (www.drkoop.com) if your new mortgage is just too stressful (see Figure 7.8).

With all the possibilities, the question reverts to the one you asked yourself when you started this process: What do your customers want? How about tools to help them get their work done?

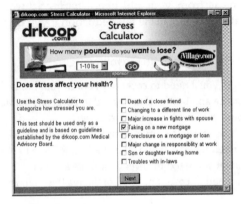

Figure 7.8 Dr. Koop will tell you if you're stressed, or just stressed about being stressed.

Application Service Provider

From *Customer Service on the Internet* by Jim Sterne
(John Wiley & Sons, 2000)

The fundamental question was, How can National Semiconductor sell more stuff? The answer was to get more design engineers to the National Semiconductor Web site. So what could they offer design engineers? Their customers already had a steady diet of Dilbert cartoons. That wasn't going to help.

We're talking about a Web site that half of the design engineers in the world visit at least once a month. They download 400,000 datasheets per month. There are 220,000 registered users. National sends out 48,000 biweekly newsletters, and processes 21,000 orders per month. They had to go one better.

So they asked a question that should be engraved on your plastic terminal casing with a hot soldering gun where you can look at it every day and have to explain it to the various facilities management people and fire marshals who roam your building:

What do our customers do, how do they do it, and how can we make it easier for them to get it done?

In the case of National Semi, they saw that a lot of their customers were spending a lot of time using various slow and annoying simulation systems to design power supplies so they could tell what components they wanted to buy from National Semi. The fastest of these simulation software packages National could find was from a company called Transim (www.transim.com). Here's how Transim described their product:

The Simplis family of simulators are powerful tools developed specifically to deal with the issues inherent in switched mode power supply (SMPS) design: rapidly slewing signals, disparate time constants, and a periodic rather than a DC operating point. The Simplis simulators are based on unique algorithms; they are not Spice derivatives. Instead, they take advantage of the repetitive nature of switching power supplies by "learning" the switching behavior of the circuit being simulated and storing that information for later reuse. Simplis typically simulates a SMPS circuit more than forty times faster than other analog simulation engines. That speed advantage, plus fewer convergence problems, makes Simplis the preferred simulator for SMPS design.

I don't claim to be able to recognize a rapidly slewing signal from rabbit stew, but I do know a brilliant Internet move when I see one. National licensed the Transim software for use by many. And I do mean many. National Semi customers can go to the National site and simulate power supplies to their heart's content (see Figure 7.9).

Instead of getting their companies to evaluate and approve the software, buying the software, installing the software, and supporting the software, National's customers pay from $5 to $10 to run it on the National site. After five or six

continues

Application Service Provider *(Continued)*

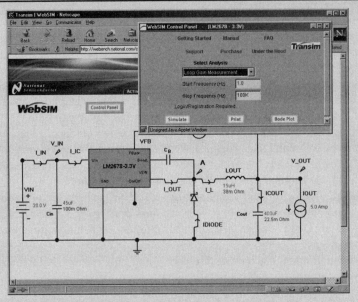

Figure 7.9 National Semiconductor makes simulation software available to its customers for a modest fee.

simulations, the customer knows if the design is going to meet the need. Then comes the good part.

The simulator identifies the generic components you need to turn the inputs you have into the outputs you want. The National Web site then displays the specific National Semi parts you might choose from to build what you have just simulated (see Figure 7.10).

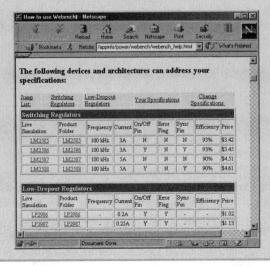

Figure 7.10 After the simulation comes the order form. You know it'll work; all that's left is to buy some parts and build the prototype.

> *This is Web magic. Forget thinking outside the box, this is getting all the way out of town. So ask yourself: What do your customers do, how do they do it, and how can you make it easier for them to get it done?*
>
> *You don't even have to have a gazillion dollar budget to make something that's useful to your customer and a cut above the rest.*

Offline as Well as On

I travel a lot. OK, I travel a *lot*. My family sends me e-mail asking where I am and one month I simply created a cut-and-paste check list that included Brazil, New Zealand, Dubai, Orlando, Boston, New York, Washington D.C., Atlanta, San Francisco, and London, and that was just for the month.

So I was pleased a few years back when United Airlines made available the ability to check flight schedules online. But I was really pleased when it created a flight-schedule application you can download in order to find out when they're flying where without having to browse, e-mail, WAP, call, or carry around a 400-page book. Hey, you can even use it on your laptop when you're in flight. Nice.

Clicks and Bricks

It's a compelling offering: Buy it online, pick it up at the store. No shipping charges. No waiting. No walking through the whole physical store to find the one or two things you want. Click, buy, go get it. That's the way Circuit City decided to play it (see Figure 7.11).

Circuit City CEO Alan McCollough is delighted that over 50 percent of the Web shoppers go for the pick-up option. People want their new digital cameras right now. "We believe it's our obligation to sell however our customers want to buy," McCollough told Darwin Magazine (www.darwinmag.com). Hear, hear.

Sumerset Custom Houseboats (www.sumerset.com) (see Figure 7.12) took top honors in the Inc. Magazine, Inc. Web Awards 2000 because it gave the customers what they wanted: a look at how their boat was shaping up.

Tom Neckel, President and CEO, recognized that a Web site is not for the company, but for the customer. "Our customers' greatest asset is time, and we have used technology and the Internet to help them better manage their time and have fun with the houseboat building process." Inc. Web Awards 2000 judge and author Evan Schwartz even went as far as to dub Sumerset Custom Houseboats "the Dell Computer of the houseboat business."

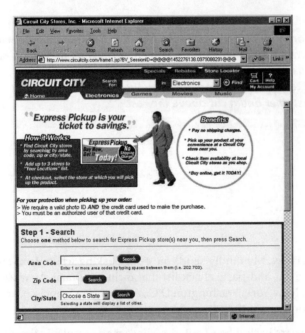

Figure 7.11 Circuit City lets you check your local stores for availability before you decide.

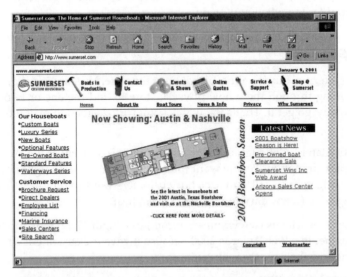

Figure 7.12 Sumerset Custom Houseboats publishes daily photos of the progress of each boat under construction.

Keep thinking about ways you can help your customers get on with business and the business of living. They will thank you.

Personalization—
Getting to Know You

We've come full circle. From interpersonal relationships, to mass communication, to meta-personal relationships. We used to know our customers up close and personal, and the value to the customer was not just having another friend in the community. Personal knowledge of individuals gave customers better service. You knew what they wanted and had it ready for them when they walked in.

As mass communication and mass distribution came in, we lost all contact with our customers. There was one ad on the radio, on television, and in the papers, and everybody heard it, saw it, and read it. Then we got into market segmentation. Knowing a little bit about our customers based on their Zip code or their income bracket helped us tailor our messages.

When database marketing came along, we could provide significantly more value to each customer by cross-categorizing him or her. We could now mail out different messages to 20-something-year-olds in the Northwest who liked the great outdoors and read investment magazines from those we would send to 20-something-year-olds in the Northwest who liked gardening and watching cooking shows.

But then came the Web.

If people will tell you what products they're interested in and what they'll use them for, it's easy to present those products in different ways. Even calculators mean different things to different people. Are you a high school student? A college student? A financial professional? An engineer/scientist? (See Figure 8.1.)

Figure 8.1 HP will tell you slightly different stories about its calculators depending on which market segment you're from.

With a database firmly attached at the back end, a Web site can cater to each individual on an individual basis. This, coupled with the fact that the Web lets you accomplish tasks at any time of the day or night, is what sets the Web apart from all previous forms of communication. It is unique. It is powerful. Customers love it. Heck, they even love it when your site simply welcomes them back by name, as long as you respect their privacy.

We'll look into segmentation, recognition, customization, personalization, and that granddaddy of buzz phrases, Customer Relationship Management, but let's start off easy.

Identification through Segmentation

What's the very first thing you notice about a person? Walking down the street or from across the room? Gender? Race? Clothing? Hygiene? The answer doesn't matter. What does matter is that we use each of these as clues to gain richer understanding. Yes, we pigeonhole people. We classify them and categorize them and try to make them fit into a neat little box so we know how to deal with them. Good, bad, or indifferent, the human mind does this with everything it comes across. Animal, vegetable, or mineral?

It comes as no surprise that Web marketers do the same. What's the first thing you notice about a visitor to your Web site? His or her technical specifications.

Tech Specs

One brief glimpse of your home page and you can already start classifying who's there. The visitor's browser tells you a great deal:

- What kind of computer the visitor has
- What operating system the visitor uses
- What Web browser the visitor uses
- The IP number of the computer or gateway (reverse lookup might pinpoint a geographic area)
- What types of files the browser will accept including the plug-ins the visitor has installed
- Whether the visitor already has a cookie from your server

With a little coding, you can also check to see the speed at which the visitor is connected to the Internet, the resolution of the screen, and a variety of other variables. All told, that's quite a bit for one, single click. Based on that information, you may choose to change the size of the pictures on your home page and the amount of technical wizardry you impose on people (Flash, JavaScript, DHTML).

Demographics

We've been dealing with demographics for a couple of decades now, and we're getting pretty savvy about putting that data to use. If you offered something on your site that I considered valuable, you might get me to fill out a form and learn that I am:

- Male
- 45–50 years old
- Working in 93101
- College educated
- Small Business (<$5 million)
- Professional Marketing Consulting

Psychographics

If you offer some information or membership that is very compelling, I might even divulge some more personal data—information that has more to do with how I feel and what I think, rather than who I am:

- Read marketing, technology, and trade journals
- Read science fiction and detective novels
- Don't watch much television
- Live within three miles of my office

Now you can start categorizing me and serving up information that will interest me. At least, it will be of more interest than the generic content you serve to everybody. But you still don't know who I am. In fact, you don't even know my name—until I tell you.

Recognition—Web Sites That Greet You by Name

In 1996, when I wrote *Customer Service on the Internet* (John Wiley & Sons), Microsoft was just beginning to experiment with personal content (see Figure 8.2). It was brand new.

Now we've gotten used to configuring My Yahoo! (see Figure 8.3) on command. You may choose what you want to see on the Front Page and in what order.

How does Yahoo! know it's me when I click the My Yahoo! button? I didn't log in. I didn't use a password. I'm just another anonymous visitor, but I'm a visitor with a brand on my browser so it knows where I've been *this time*. Yahoo! uses cookies, created by Netscape and now used by all browsers.

In a nut shell, a cookie is a small text file that the Web site can place on your computer. Only the site that placed it there can read it. When you ask for a page, the server looks for a cookie. If you have one, it reads the ID number and finds you in its database. If you don't, it gives you one.

What's the first thing companies use cookies for? To greet you by name: "Hello Chet!" But that's just the beginning. If the database can remember who you are, it can also remember all sorts of things about you.

The choices at Yahoo! are significant enough to be a little daunting:

Keyword Searches	Ski Report (seasonal)
Lottery Results	Sports Scoreboard
Map It	Today's Best Fares
Movies—New Releases	Upgrades and Downgrades
Movies—Upcoming Releases	Vitamins & Herbs
My Bookmarks	Weather
News Clipper	Yahoo! Categories
Quotes/Portfolios	Yahoo! Search
Package Tracker	Zacks Earnings Surprises
Shopping Top Ten	ZDNet Rumor & Comment

Yahoo! puts you in the driver's seat. Not just on your own, personal Front Page, but in all of the sections as well. There are choices like those in the previous list to be made in every section it has:

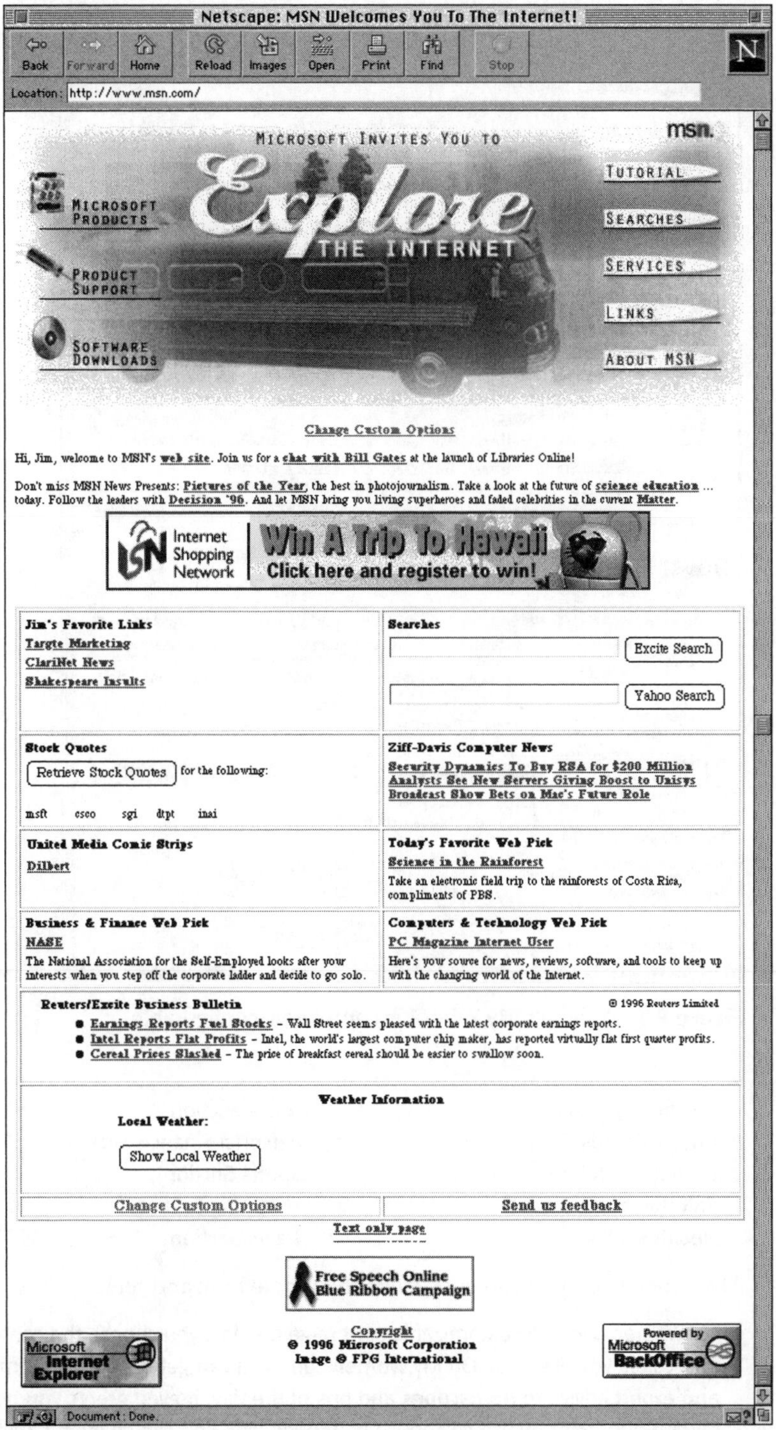

Figure 8.2 Microsoft was one of the first sites to try out personalized content.

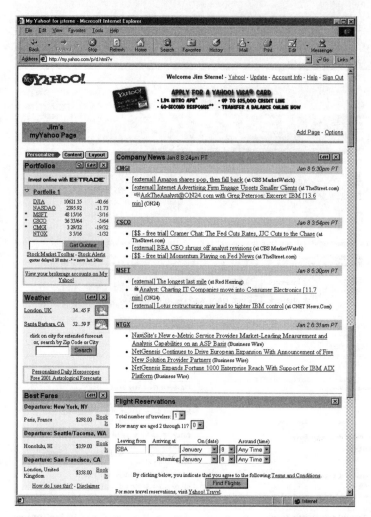

Figure 8.3 Yahoo!'s My Yahoo! is completely configurable.

Business Section	News Section
Chat & Boards Section	Personal Finance Section
Computers & Internet Section	Sports Section
Entertainment Section	Shopping Section
Health Section	Travel Section

At Women.com, you can customize the whole look and feel.

My.Women.com is a customizable start page that lets you choose the content, page layout and colors you like best. On My.Women.com, you can get everything from daily headlines and expert advice to horoscopes and tips of the day; it even greets you personally! It only takes a minute or two to customize your page, and you can change it anytime you want—just click on the "Customize this page" button and follow the links to the content, layout and color-selection pages. If you want to save time by choosing an instant profile created by our editors and designers, just select the one that fits your lifestyle best. (You can always change your mind later.)

My.Women.com is a great way to get all of your favorite Women.com features on one convenient page, as well as links to your other favorite Web sites. Be sure to visit often—some of the features on the page update every 60 seconds! Best of all, it's free: You need only be a member to sign up.

It may seem like a subtle distinction, but sometimes personalization is not about getting more of what you want, but about getting less of what you *don't* want. IBM proved it to itself at its Worldwide BESTeam site (www2.software.ibm.com/partnerweb/bpsoftware.nsf), where it let top-ranking business partners decide how much postal mail they receive.

IBM found that its partners loved to control the amount of junk mail IBM sent them. IBM's not dumb. It knows its all-important, all-significant postal messages build strong partnerships 12 ways. It also knows its partners think most of that mail is junk. The result was more than just happier partners. IBM experienced a significant savings in direct mail costs. A quarter of its partners signed up for mail limitation right away, and it immediately cut 50 percent of outgoing mailings. IBM cut its spending on paper, printing, and postage in half.

Asking Them What They Like

Amazon.com started it all, of course. It came up with the idea of using e-mail to notify you of new books in which you might be interested. How did it know? It asked. At the bottom of every book page, there's a list of the categories in which Amazon.com classified that book. Which classification interests you the most? When you specify a category, or an author, or even a title, Amazon.com will send you e-mail when a new book is published that meets your criterion. It's simple. It's neat. As a consumer, I like it. As a marketer, I love it.

As a consumer, it saves me two hours and a hundred dollars every time I wander into a bookstore. As a reader, I try my best to keep track of my favorite authors. A new Bruce Sterling? How soon can I get it?

But now a new day has dawned. There's a vendor that is willing to scour the shelves, keep track of my favorite authors, and send me e-mail telling me something I really want to know—for free! Amazon sends me an e-mail. I click on the link. I read the review. I buy the book (or not). Amazon.com is simple, fast, elegant, and I always stay up to date on what's being published.

From the seller's perspective, this is akin to the fish jumping into the barrel and handing you a loaded gun. "Sell me!" customers plead. "Here's what I want to buy!" they shout. "I want to give you money!" they insist. Is this a seller's market or what?

There's also nothing like being able to accurately predict demand for your goods. When John Grisham puts out another legal-action-thriller Amazon knows how many people want to hear about it, and it knows how many purchased his last book when it was released. It knows how many copies to buy in advance. That lowers overhead and, we hope, the company passes the savings along.

Customization—Giving Them What They'd Like

You know you're succeeding with personalization when the visitor comes to your site and sees himself or herself. Or, perhaps, visitors see a reasonable facsimile.

The Lands' End Personal Shopper starts out by asking some very personal questions about what you look like. It also uses historical purchasing information to make recommendations, and then you can try things on for size (see Figures 8.4 through 8.6).

You can license this software from Lands' End. That's right, for somewhere between $100,000 and $200,000 a year, your customers can see themselves on your Web site. Alternatively, you can pay Lands' End a cut for every sale made through using the software.

Knowing people's clothing sizes can help them shop, but knowing more about them can help you sell. Here is the message that greets you when you register as a customer at www.designjet.hp.com (see Figure 8.7).

Dear Customer,

HP is interested in knowing about you. The more we know, the better service we will be able to provide you with in the future.

There are more specific reasons why we ask you to complete this registration:

- The information we request below will help us to tailor our offering to your requirements.
- With your approval, HP will mail or e-mail you with information of interest.

Please note that you may change your registration details at any time. Please take a few moments to answer the questions below. All fields are required.

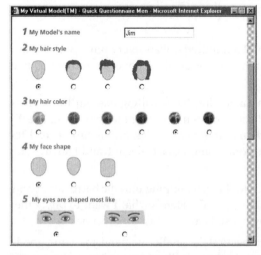

Figure 8.4 Lands' End wants to know your weight, the color of your skin, and the shape of your eyes.

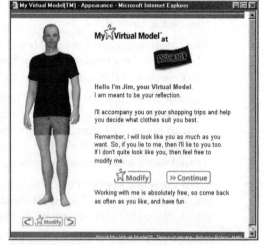

Figure 8.5 Your generic model stands ready to help you try on different styles, day or night.

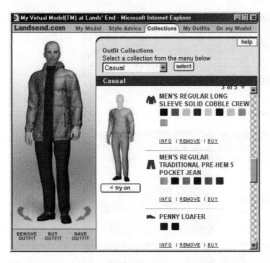

Figure 8.6 Even with the Personal Shopper you can see why I buy clothes only when my wife is with me.

Hewlett-Packard is committed to respecting your privacy. For information on our privacy policy you may read the HP <u>Online Privacy Statement</u>.

Your details and related information will be sent to our business partner in the US responsble (sic) for processing the information on behalf of HP and subject to our security and privacy practices. For information on our security and privacy practices please read the HP <u>Online Privacy Statement</u>.

The page asks for your name, address, and which language you prefer. Choices include English, Français, Italiano, Deutsch, Español, Português, Korean, Taiwanese, Chinese, and Japanese.

Communication Preferences

In order to ensure high-quality service and support and to inform you about HP Designjet products and services that relate to you, Hewlett-Packard may use the information you provided above to contact you. Is this acceptable?

e-mail
postal mail
Telephone

We will not contact you unless you specifically request it.

Then it asks about the printers that you own, and it invites you to tell more.

Choose which kind of information you want to provide to us:

mailing details

If you want HP to send you any information by mail, please fill in these fields.

news preferences

To customize the kind of news that you receive, please tell us what your preferences are.

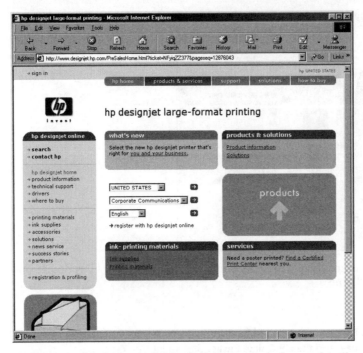

Figure 8.7 This is the HP Designjet home page before registration . . .

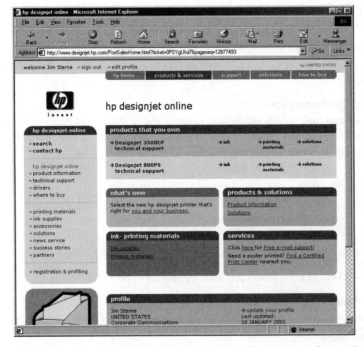

Figure 8.8 . . . and this is the HP Designjet home page after registration.

product details

For enabling your warranty check support and other e-support services, please fill in these fields.

main activity & industry

Increase the customization efficiency.

software applications

Let us know which applications you work with.

preferred resellers

Tell us what is the reseller you prefer to buy from. This will be included in your "how to buy" options.

Once they've got you registered, the Designjet home page looks a little different (see Figure 8.8).

No, you're not going to change the look and feel, as Women.com allows, but you are going to find the navigation a bit easier. You're going to find it infinitely faster to locate the materials and supplies you need. You're also going to find it a lot easier to read—it will be in the language you prefer.

Localization

Going global? If your company has offices around the world, or if you are able to communicate comfortably with international clients in their native tongue, then localization makes sense. After all, the Web is the least expensive way for your overseas clients to get the information they need, so why not deliver it in the most accessible way possible? Because you face a number of trouble spots.

The Internet is nothing if not global. A Web page in Bangor is seen in Bangkok. That means prices for your products in Salt Lake City will be seen in Sri Lanka. Fortunes have been made by matching the proper pricing to specific territories. Now, specific territories hold no meaning.

Do you show a special Web site price? "Buy on the Web for a discount!" If you do, get ready to get nasty calls from your normal distribution chain. You might quote prices after users have filled out a request. What size? What color? What quantity? By the way, where do you live? The price displayed will be based on the answer to the last question.

Pricing isn't the only problem; there is, of course, the language issue. The solution at Case Corporation (www.casecorp.com) is to offer regional pages, starting right from the home page (see Figure 8.9).

Simply choosing Europe as your location isn't enough information to determine what language you wish to read, so Case gives you the choice of English, German, French, and American English (see Figure 8.10).

Figure 8.9   Case sells tractors all over the world and lets you know that right up front.

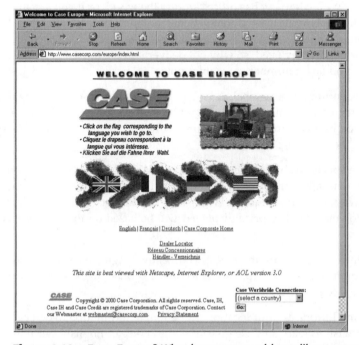

Figure 8.10   From Europe? What language would you like to speak today?

I got involved in a debate at a recognizable, but please-don't-reveal-our-name, multi-national company asking for advice on whether its home page should be English or American.

```
From: <xxx@xxx.com>
To: Jim Sterne <jsterne@targeting.com>
Subject: King's English vs. American English
Date: Tue, 17 Feb 1998 17:42:03 -0600
Hi, Jim: I met you when you were speaking at a conference in San Fran
last year (and I even bought and read your World Wide Web Marketing
book!). I am the Webmaster for xxx—a new TRADEMARK for all the existing
xxx companies around the world which are part of the xxx group of
companies. The Web site I work with represents all of our companies
around the world, although most (90 percent) of our business dealings
are conducted in English either in the UK or the United States.
Questions 1) What is your opinion about consistency of language VERSION
use (King's English vs. American English) within a single Web site? 2)
If English is our chosen language of business, would you recommend we
use King's English, American English, or some combination on our site?
3) Could I HIRE you (immediately!) to write a short summary of your
opinion (King's English vs. American English) backed by some convincing
facts and logical examples?
I'm trying not to reveal my hand in terms of where I stand on this issue,
but it might be all too clear. Please let me hear your thoughts, Jim.
Thanks very much.
```

I was quite intrigued (and flattered) and responded thusly:

```
To: <xxx@xxx.com>
From: Jim Sterne <jsterne@targeting.com>
Subject: Re: King's English vs. American English
>Questions 1) What is your opinion about consistency of language VERSION use
>(King's English vs. American English) within a single Web site? 2) If
>English is our chosen language of business, would you recommend we use
>King's English, American English, or some combination on our site?
Sorry for the delay in getting back to you.
OK, English is the stated language of record. But which one? The first
question is, who is the company? Is it an American company or a UK
company? Or is the HQ elsewhere?
Next, but perhaps the most important question of all: Who are your
customers? The answer is, all of the above.
I recommend to all my international clients that they localize their Web
sites. Here's why. A Web site is not a corporate brochure. It's a single
individual's experience. It's not your publication, it's an electronic
relationship.
Now, if I call the good people at Rolls-Royce Motor Cars Limited and
spoke with somebody with an American accent, I would be appalled! My
whole sense of that firm is exceedingly British and not a whiff of Yank.
All of the years they've put into creating a strong brand would be
dashed to bits in a jiffy.
```

But xxx is truly an international company. That means I expect to be
serviced by a local branch. I want to talk to somebody I can relate to.
If I get a representative who is about my age, went to the same school,
remembers the same popular music—well, that makes the learning easier
and the relationship smoother and I just feel all around better about
it. Provincial? You bet!

If I'm a Frenchman and I go to your site and it's all in English, you
are not making points.

If I'm a Brazilian and there is a portion of your site written in
Portuguese, I'm delighted. Until I realize that it was translated by
somebody in Lisbon. The language is right, but the idioms are all wrong.
You run into the same problem if you hire somebody who graduated from the
University of Mexico to translate pages for Web site visitors from Spain.
I always recommend catering to the people you are selling to. Make the
effort to really *localize*!

So, we now turn to the issue of the King's English or the 'Merican
version. I vote for both. Your products are not the same in both places.
Your pricing is different. Your services vary.

I say you have the King's behind the Union Jack and the U.S. version
behind the Stars and Stripes and maybe even a tip of the hat to our
friends to the North behind the Maple Leaf.

The home page? Tell me—where is HQ?

Surfing the Web is a very personal experience. Anything you can do to
make it easier and more comfortable for your visitors, the more valuable
your site will be to them and the more return you'll reap.

>3) Could I HIRE you (immediately!) to write a short summary of your
opinion (King's
>English vs. American English) backed by some convincing facts and
logical examples?

Jump back, Jack. No way, Jose. Later, Dude. (Now translate those into the
King's English!)

After another message from xxx, I replied once again and settled the issue:

To: <xxx@xxx.com>
From: Jim Sterne <jsterne@targeting.com>
Subject: RE: RE: King's English vs. American English
At 11:37 AM -0600 2/23/98, xxx at xxx wrote:
>To clarify, we have no HQ. We are trying to portray that we are truly
>international. However, if we DID have a HQ and it was London, I'd say we
>should use King's English (honest). But since we are trying to portray
>that we are everywhere, SHOULDN'T THE DEFAULT BE AMERICANIZED ENGLISH?
Yes, sirree, Bob.
>Let's put it this way: I'm guessing that the use of King's English would
>strongly imply that we have a London HQ. However, the use of American
>English would not necessarily imply a U.S. HQ because more people would
>assume we are defaulting to a more commonly accepted form of the
>language.
>IS THIS LOGIC OFF?
Nope. Since the goal is to be international and of-the-Net, then you
need to use the language of record, which is the colonial version.

```
>Perhaps I'm being too arrogant about my homeland by assuming that
>American English is not just the language of choice, but the language
>VERSION of choice.
You're right on.
>In your opinion, am I blissfully ignorant and arrogant?
I hate to get in the middle of an argument between husband and wife. You
two will have to work this one out on your own.
>For the sake of communications consistency (and because I was a
journalism major),
>I STRONGLY resist any attempt to mix English language versions.
Hear, here!
>What would you do?
Punt. (Ooops! Isn't that something you do on the Thames?)
I say American English. (And that's a certified, expert opinion.)
Cheerio!
```

Languages can be tricky, but your problems aren't over yet. The next issue is availability. Case Corporation makes tractors and construction equipment and sells them everywhere. The problem comes when somebody in Asia or Africa wants a tractor that's available only in the United States, or a farmer in London, Ontario wants one that's available only in London, England. Even worse, the customer puts in a stop order on the equipment the customer thought he or she wanted because he or she would rather wait until the X-325 you're shipping to France is available in Germany as well. That's the predicament with internationally available information, and it's a pain in the cash flow.

Give people a choice of countries from which to view your site, and then put the proper information behind those doors. If you get a lot of overseas traffic, those doors can also lead to servers located on the correct continent for faster access.

International Trade Law

The Internet is nothing if not global. As Jeffrey J. Bussgang put it in *Ruling The Net* (Harvard Business School, 1996):

> The fact that the Internet is a truly international network complicates government's role in its development as a commercial environment. In trying to set the rules of the game, governments are realizing that on the Internet, all laws are local—that is, they are enforceable only within a country's physical borders. Even the First Amendment is merely a local ordinance. As such, "local" laws that try to restrict the flow of bits across the network, such as export controls and intellectual property rights protection, are unenforceable.
>
> The Internet as an international network is thus not only a difficult environment for governments to regulate, but it is an environment that is causing governments to effectively lose control over their borders and frontiers. In an environment where intangible goods and services can flow unrestricted to any destination in the world, French media content laws and Singapore's press restrictions become both irrelevant and absurd.

For the most part, we have relied on international letters of credit, trade agreements, and the credit card companies to alleviate the rigors of buying and selling across borders. When the transaction is discrete, from one country to another, the import/export laws are tenable. But the question of who owns cyberspace is one that will be determined in the courts. It will take a long time. If you have a son, daughter, niece, or nephew in law school, advise him or her to consider a career in international trade law.

International Culture

As a general rule of thumb, a crack marketing team on its toes can wrangle the tangled laws holding sway over the sale of goods between one country and another. Just don't go overboard dressing up your products until they resemble snake oil. International culture, on the other hand, is a different kettle of fish. The cultures of different countries must be taken into account when marketing on the Web.

As an example, the previous paragraph is almost incomprehensible to somebody who learned English in school instead of in practice. It should read:

> **Generally, a competent marketing team can cope with the laws governing the sale of goods between one country and another. Just don't make unsubstantiated claims about your products. International culture, however, is a different situation.**

Not as personal. Not as colorful. But not as easy to misunderstand.

Chevrolet's apocryphal marketing faux pas has become famous. Chevy introduced its new Nova back in the 1960s. It marketed the car in Mexico and South America. Nobody seemed to realize that "no va" is Spanish for "won't go."

A hospital was built in Santa Barbara in 1923 at the top of Salsipuedes Street. The founders were pleased with the name of the street and wanted to use it for the hospital. That was until somebody pointed out that the lower end of the street ran through a low part of town. It got its name because of the regular flooding. It was explained that "salsipuedes" is a Spanish term meaning "get out if you can." St. Francis Hospital is still in operation.

An e-mail making the rounds included these other gems:

Coors put its slogan, "Turn it loose," into Spanish, where it was read as "Suffer from diarrhea."

When Gerber started selling baby food in Africa, it used the same packaging as in the United States, with the picture of a beautiful baby on the label. Later the company learned that in Africa, companies routinely put pictures on the label of what's inside because most people can't read English.

The name Coca-Cola in China was first rendered as Ke-kou-ke-la. Unfortunately, the Coke company did not discover until after thousands of signs had been printed that the phrase means "bite the wax tadpole" or "female horse stuffed with wax," depending on the dialect. Coke then researched 40,000 Chinese characters and found a close phonetic equivalent, "ko-kou-ko-le," which can be loosely translated as "happiness in the mouth."

In Taiwan, the translation of the Pepsi slogan "Come alive with the Pepsi Generation" came out as "Pepsi will bring your ancestors back from the dead."

Ford had a similar problem as Chevy in Brazil when the Pinto flopped. The company found out that Pinto was Brazilian slang for "tiny male genitals." Ford pried all the nameplates off and substituted Corcel, which means "horse."

Japan's second-largest tourist agency was mystified when it entered English-speaking markets and began receiving requests for unusual sex tours. Upon finding out why, the owners of Kinki Nippon Tourist Company changed its name.

If you're selling globally, you want to be aware of how your words and images are perceived. A wise old owl in the Western hemisphere is seen as a dull-witted bird in Southeast Asia.

Do's and Taboos Around the World by Roger Axtell (John Wiley & Sons, 1993) has an entire chapter on gestures. It includes some enlightening information about a gesture very common to Westerners:

> **Fingers Circle:** Widely accepted as the American "okay" sign, except in Brazil and Germany where it's considered vulgar or obscene. The gesture is also considered impolite in Greece and Russia, while in Japan, it signifies "money," and in southern France, "zero" or "worthless."

Using color to imply meaning can also backfire. In America a blue ribbon is rewarded for first place. In England, first place gets a red ribbon. In America, black is the color of mourning. In the Orient, white is the color of mourning. Unless you are promoting a regional business to regional customers only, be prepared to think a bit more globally.

During a recent trip to London, I sat next to the human resources manager of a large software company. He was on his way to Paris to review the company's operations and training processes in various European countries.

The conversation meandered hither and yon as it is wont to do on a 10-hour flight, and we got to talking about the difficulties—in fact, the impossibilities—of having a single compensation plan for disparate territories.

The things that motivate a Brit don't really do it for the French. That which would sparkle the eyes of an Italian simply aren't important to a German. Of course, it's not as cut and dried as all that. But when you're balancing income, title, responsibility, time off, desk location, office size, and a dozen other perks, prizes, and payoffs, it gets rather tricky to do it internationally.

If you're selling to an international marketplace, you must take your localization to a deeper level than mere translation. Take a look at TransImage (www.transimage.com) (see Figure 8.11) just to admire all the different ways to say "killing two birds with one stone."

Spanish in Barcelona is not the same as Spanish in Mexico City. Portuguese in Lisbon is not the same as Portuguese in Sao Paulo. English in Liverpool is not the same as English in Los Angeles.

When you localize, let the locals do it.

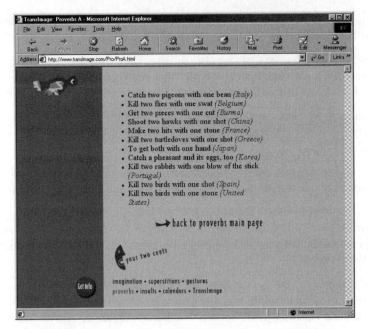

Figure 8.11 Besides killing birds, TransImage also offers up ways to say "tweet, tweet" in 16 different languages.

Personalization—Divining What They Like

This is the area where the Web outshines any other form of communication. You can advertise on the Web, you can do marketing on the Web, you can sell stuff on the Web, and you can provide customer service on the Web. Just like everywhere else. But there's one thing the Web does better than any other medium—it remembers.

When the first edition of this book was published, personalization was still a thing of the imagination. I envisioned some possible scenarios that have come to pass in no time at all:

The Book Store Web Site

Good morning, Mr. Jones. We're glad you're back!

Since your last visit when you picked up Neal Stephenson's *Snow Crash,* he's come out with a *new book.* You may be interested in reading *the first few pages.*

We also have the just-released book on *Marketing Technology* you asked about. Perhaps you'd like to know more about our Thursday *business seminar* series.

One final note: You have 526 Frequent Reader points to your credit. Take a look at the *discounts and specials* you qualify for.

The Local Mechanic Web Site

Welcome back, Ms. Smith. We haven't seen you here at Bay Motors since *July.*

According to our records and your past driving habits, it's about time for your 60,000 mile tune-up. This is a *thorough* maintenance inspection and service, which should cost approximately $475. If you like, we have several slots open and can set the *appointment* right now.

By the way, based on your excellent maintenance records, John Phillips in sales wanted you to know we can offer you a *hefty trade-in* on your 1996 Honda. Last year's models need to go, and this would be a great time to *trade up.*

Gathering the information for this sort of application falls into two camps: explicit and implicit.

Explicit Data

This is the easy stuff, technically. This is the technographics people leave like footprints and the information they tell you—explicitly—while filling out forms.

I'll tell you that I own a particular piece of equipment. I'll click the appropriate boxes that tell you I am a healthy eater, I exercise regularly, and I live a stress-free life-style. I'll fill out a form, or answer a survey, or vote on a daily poll, and you'll remember each and every answer.

The same problems apply here as with all surveys. Only the people who are willing to fill out your forms will do so. People don't always know the answer, but they have to provide one anyway. And, of course, people lie.

Implicit Data

On the other side of the coin is implied information. This is the data you gather by watching what I do, rather than listening to what I say. You'll see that I have a sweet tooth larger than my head and that I attempt to nourish myself half the time with airline food. You'll notice that I have been known to do sit-ups and run with my dog (most) mornings, but that's about it. And you'll see that I tend toward workaholism and plow through computer and marketing magazines while "decompressing" in front of the television set or while on vacation.

Online, you'll collect implicit information by tracking what pages I look at, recording what products I buy, and doing something called collaborative filtering (see the section called *Collaborative Filtering* later in this chapter for further details). You'll follow me around rather than take my word for it.

Implicit data also has its drawbacks. To begin with, the tools for this sort of tracking are expensive. Start with the price of the software, double it for the cost of the consulting you'll need to understand its features, possibilities, and limitations, then add on another 100 percent for implementation services and training. Worth their weight? Certainly— if used well. If you are prepared to spend $100,000 to $250,000 *each* for the various tools that can help you, then you *will* end up with a formidable competitive advantage.

Part of using these tools well is called full disclosure. If you track what I do and you don't tell me about it you can wind up in a world of hurt. RealNetworks (real.com) found that out when it was discovered that it was keeping track of the music you listened to. Microsoft found that out years earlier when Windows 95 interrogated your local area network to find unlicensed, unauthorized software applications in your company. If you're going to watch me, tell me. More on this in the upcoming section, *The Right to Privacy*.

Another patch of quicksand using implicit data gathering tools pertains to how you use the data you gather. You don't want to get too personal too quickly or you'll put people off.

Familiarity Breeds Contempt

Don't you hate it when somebody you've never met comes up to you and says, "Oh, hi! You must be Jim! Your wife has told me *so* much about you!" My first reaction is to be grateful that my wife is discreet and not inclined to babble about my song selections when I sing in the shower. My next reaction is that I don't even know if I'm going to like this person and why is he or she acting like a long-lost friend. They say familiarity breeds contempt; I say overfamiliarity is far worse.

American Express learned this lesson when it started using caller ID. People didn't like it when AmEx seemed to use ESP to recognize them before they even spoke. Answering the phone with "Hello, Mr. Smith, this is Sally at American Express. How can I help you?" was repeatedly met with disdain, distaste, and distrust.

The advent of caller ID did not delight the caller. It was only a matter of time before AmEx allowed callers to identify themselves first. "My name is John Smith, and I have a question about my bill."

"Yes, Mr. Smith, I have your account records in front of me now." That turned out to be quite a coup. Customers got the impression that AmEx's computers were blindingly fast. More importantly, it provided the customer with that all-important feeling of being in control of the conversation. Turns out the correct answer to "Do you know me?" is "Not until you introduce yourself."

We all prefer to shop without being hovered over. Nobody wants to walk into a store where the clerks follow your every move and note each item you glance at. At first, you may just want to be left alone to contemplate the merchandise. Later it's a matter of negotiation dexterity. Frankly, I don't want the car salesperson to know that I've already decided to buy a car and that this afternoon is the only time I have to do so. I want to hold up my end of the illusion of being a savvy, aloof buyer for as long as possible. I don't want the salesperson in the antique store to know that I'm a meerschaum pipe fanatic. That makes bargaining much more difficult when the salesperson knows you're a live one.

A Little Knowledge Is a Dangerous Thing

A wonderful cautionary tale appeared in the *Harvard Business Review* (January–February 1998, page 42). In it, Sandra Fournier, Susan Dobscha, and David Glen Mick suggested ways for "Preventing the Premature Death of Relationship Marketing."

They warned about asking customers for too much. Just how many times do I have to give the guy at Radio Shack my address? I bought something here last week. You really need my address again so I can buy this telephone cable? They warned that too many companies want to bond with an individual and that the resulting flood of "personalized" postal mail is overwhelming. They warned that savvy customers are feeling put out because they are not Gold Club Members or Platinum Card holders.

I was on a United Airlines flight when the captain came back into the cabin to seek me out. When I agreed I was the one he was looking for (while desperately worried that the only reason he'd leave his seat to look for me was to deliver some *extremely* bad news), he handed me his business card and said, "Thanks for flying with us so often." On the back of the card was a handwritten note, signed by the captain. "My crew and I wanted to let you know we really appreciate your 100,000 miles on United. Thanks!"

My first reaction was pleasure at being singled out. I made it into the upper echelon of their database by dint of my brave willingness to be strapped into a thin, metal tube traveling at 500 miles an hour far above an elevation that could support life as we know it. But then I noticed the dirty looks from the guys on either side of me. I felt good; they felt crummy. That's two to one. Those *Harvard Business Review* people were on to something.

As interesting as those cautions were, one tale stuck in my mind. It was from an interview they did with a consumer who had ordered some gifts from a catalog. The catalog company sends annual reminders to their customers, assuming the gifts were usually birthday, anniversary, or holiday related. The company is right. I have purchased gifts from the Harry & David catalog for several years in a row; in November they send me a printout of what I bought last year and allow me to check the ones I want to resend. If you buy lots of fruit baskets for lots of office staff, this approach can be quite handy. Good thinking.

But this gentleman had a problem. He had bought gifts for the physicians and nurses who had taken care of his mother's last days on Earth. It was a very unpleasant time, and now, every year, he gets a cold, calculated reminder of it.

It's easy to make assumptions about people, and it is a dangerous undertaking.

- Al Biland is the CIO at Snap-on Corporation, and he is a seriously into Harley-Davidson motorcycles. He loves to ride his hog on the weekends. I was doing some consulting for Snap-on and used the Harley-Davidson Web site as an example of customer loyalty.

- A woman who used to be my administrative assistant moved to Oklahoma, and I looked up her address on MapQuest to see where she lived.

- After six years of working out of the back bedroom, I finally moved all my papers and computers and executive desk toys to a new office downtown.

- My wife planted roses over the weekend.

- My nephew's birthday was on the horizon, and he was getting interested in the history of heavy metal music.

What do these things have in common? Absolutely nothing, outside of the fact that they caused me to visit some Web sites on the same day:

- www.harleydavidson.com
- mapquest.digitalcity.com/oklahomacity
- www.uhaul.com
- www.dynamiteplantfood.com
- www.geocities.com/SunsetStrip/2308 (The History of Heavy Metal)

Had you been tracking what I actually did, it would be easy to make some bad assumptions about me (see Figure 8.12).

In my files I have a copy of a wonderful ad that Predictive Networks (www .predictivenetworks.com) published in the early part of 2001. There's a full-face photo of a grandmother. You just know she is. Big, baggy eyes, pearls, baby blue twin-set, warm grandmotherly smile. The caption reads:

> College Student
> Trades On-line
> Pacific Northwest
> Active Lifestyle
> Now, What Makes You Think She Goes Rock Climbing?

Use your knowledge wisely.

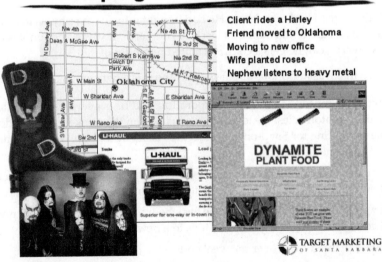

Figure 8.12 How would you classify somebody who looked at this sort of content online?

Pigeonholing Too Tightly

Taking the train from London's Waterloo station to the Gare du Nord in Paris is great. You get there faster, and you don't get seasick. But you also don't get to enjoy the wind in your hair, see the gulls, or smell the sea air. You are sealed in a metal tube that plunges you beneath the English Channel, and you don't see a thing until you pop out on the west coast of France.

When you profile somebody, you can guess what he or she might be interested in next. But you also put that person on a straight and narrow track with blinders on all sides. Adroit retail practice places the staples at the back of the store to force customers to walk past aisles and aisles of impulse items.

Infoseek President and Chief Executive Officer Robin Johnson feels that search engines should keep queries in context. In *Information Week* (October 14, 1996) Johnson said, "If you do a lot of business searches and type in 'chicken stock,' we're not going to direct you to a bunch of gumbo recipes." But what if gumbo recipes were exactly what you had in mind? How can a computer decide that you are either an investor or a chef, but never both?

Sometimes you go to the store as a mother of a sick child, sometimes as a plumber with a leaky faucet. The "milk" you're looking for might be for breakfast, might be baby formula, and might be coconut milk. What if you're trying to find a present for your wife? Will the Sears site not show you the softer side if you spend too much time looking at Craftsman tools?

A Fine Balance

The trick is to be knowledgeable about your guests without being overly familiar. Be attentive without fawning. Be helpful without pigeon-holing people into such small categories that they have to fight your system to find the products or services they want. It's a dance. It's a mutual exchange of data. I don't mind that the woman at the dry cleaner knows my name and phone number. I don't mind that my bank knows my savings balance. I don't mind that Amazon.com knows what kind of books I like to read. But I do mind if that information is used callously.

Drastic Times Call for Drastic Tools

The Internet is different because it is available all the time. The Internet is different because it offers two-way communication. The Internet is different because it can remember everything. But the Internet is also different because your server can do more than serve. It can make decisions about what to serve. It can make decisions about who your customers are and what information might get the best response.

A good number of smart people with smart technology are keeping track of what people like and are using that information to customize their online experience. Rules-based, case-based, neural-net, and fuzzy logic systems are all getting put to use and are all getting surprising results. There are many ways of seeing into the hearts and minds of your visitors. One of them involves seeing into all of their hearts and minds at once.

Collaborative Filtering

Amazon (yes, I know, but it *was* first) realized that it could make recommendations to people based on their history. Not by poring over what they had collected and expending human energies to make recommendations, but by implementing something some folks out of MIT dreamed up and called collaborative filtering.

NetPerceptions (www.netperceptions.com) had a product called GroupLens that Amazon used. GroupLens did more than filter. It compared what you liked against what everybody else in the database liked. It found matches between what you purchased and what the rest of the customers purchase. It could see that you had exactly the same taste as X percent of the others. It looked at what those others had purchased but you had not, and presto! A recommendation.

Foolproof? No. Why? Because sometimes I shop for my family, and sometimes my wife shops for books while using my cookie. That means she doesn't follow the advice, "If you're not Jim Sterne, click here." As a result, some of Amazon's recommendations (but only a very few) go awry. Fortunately, I have the ability to make course corrections (see Figure 8.13).

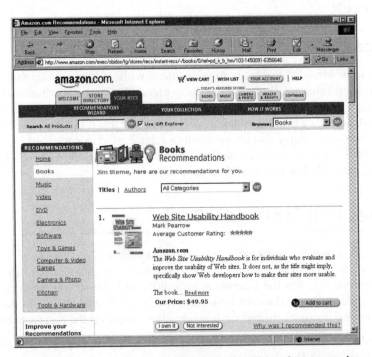

Figure 8.13 At the bottom of the screen, Amazon gives me a chance to tell them I already own the book or that I'm not interested.

Why did Amazon recommend this one in particular? One click and the answer is obvious: because I have previously purchased the following titles:

- *Web Navigation*, Jennifer Fleming, Richard Koman (Editor) (O'Reilly & Associates, 1998)

- *Designing Web Usability*, Jakob Nielsen (New Riders Publishing, 1999)

- *Designing Large-Scale Web Sites*, Darrell Sano (John Wiley & Sons, 1996)

- *Measuring the Impact of Your Web Site*, Robert Buchanan, Charles Lukaszewski (John Wiley & Sons, 1997)

- *Web Site Usability*, Jared M. Spool, et al (Morgan Kaufmann Publishers, 1998)

- *Collaborative Web Development*, Jessica R. Burdman (Addison-Wesley , 1999)

This is one of the strongest reasons that I will continue to buy from Amazon. It has a record of every book I've bought (well, almost) since 1996. The company knows me. I like that. More important, it knows what books to suggest.

Serving Dynamic Content

Macromedia's LikeMinds software (www.macromedia.com) takes the collaborative filtering concept a couple of steps further:

Purchase Engine

Macromedia LikeMinds enables your e-commerce site to leverage valuable purchase history data to make personalized recommendations. For example, it can track which items a visitor buys and when the items were purchased.

Clickstream Engine

LikeMinds builds customer profiles in real time, based on navigational data gathered as customers browse the site. It gauges what pages customers looked at and which items they added to the shopping cart. The system learns by observing behaviors and automatically adapts, in real time, to each customer's changing tastes and needs.

Preference Engine

The Preference Engine leverages explicitly stated preferences to make highly accurate recommendations for products and content that visitors will like. Customers get exposure to items they might otherwise miss. Gift shoppers can also get recommendations based on the gift recipient's shopping preferences.

Product Matching Engine

The Product Matching Engine makes recommendations based on product similarities. This feature enables merchants to immediately recommend new products before customers have seen, rated, or bought them.

Item Affinity Engine

The Item Affinity Engine understands product association and will make cross-sell or up-sell recommendations based on product pairs purchased simultaneously.

Categories

LikeMinds categories allow the site manager to tailor product recommendations to meet business goals and to prioritize recommendations by product category to promote overstocked or on sale items.

There are dozens of tools to slice and dice all of the data you can collect, but the purpose is always the same: Improve the Web experience for your visitor in order to turn more browsers into buyers. Using these tools to personalize the Web experience and to spin the offer of the day requires a firm grasp of the business rules you want to implement.

Building Business Rules

What are business rules? Those are the shoot-from-the hip, gut-reaction, feels-right, intuitive leaps of faith you make that tell you somebody who buys a laptop is just going to *have* to want to see the extra battery packs. These are the assumptions you make about shoppers in general that you then codify into hard and fast rules.

You want to set up the rules of engagement. Visitor A looked at the camping gear on your Web site last week. This week he's back, and he's looking at bicycles. Doesn't it seem obvious to show the bicycle surrounded by things like the camping gear trailer and the oversized poncho? Shouldn't you use the information you have gleaned in order to upsell and cross-sell? Absolutely. Just stay away from the Channel Tunnel problem and you can increase sales.

Spinning the offer of the day is the most subtle way to influence buyers. After classifying them by type of buyer (price, value, status), you can then describe your all-inventory-must-go items accordingly:

- Due to a shortage of warehouse space, we're letting these grimlets go at an incredible discount!
- The quality of these grimlets makes this price a rare find.
- Now you can afford grimlets of your own! Don't be left out.

Business rules can apply to customer service as well. If an individual looks at *this* page of the FAQ, then follows *this* path through the troubleshooting guise, and searches for *this* keyword in the knowledgebase, then it's time to display some fresh content, or pop up a new window, or send the user an e-mail about a new training course he or she should take advantage of.

Hand-Crafted Business Rules

Practitioners of expert systems for the last 30 years will tell you that the hardest part is not the technology. Rather, it's teaching the technology what it should do. Getting a computer to mimic the wisdom of great thinkers isn't really that much of a challenge. It's getting that wisdom into the machine that has people perplexed.

Art Technology Group (www.atg.com) talks about its personalization software in terms of scenarios:

Scenario Elements

Scenarios are robust dialogs between the enterprise and the customer. Scenario elements are the building blocks that allow business managers to develop multi-channel, personalized business interactions. Scenario elements include:

People: target interactions to users or groups based on profile attributes or affiliations

Time: schedule interactions (on a certain day, between certain dates, etc.)

Event: track user behavior (visits a page, views an item, adds to a cart, etc.)

Condition: define conditions under which events can proceed

Action: define actions directed at users (send e-mail, redirect to page, etc.)

Fork: branch different users into sets of interactions within the scenario randomly or by profile data

If, for example, the gardening retailer has an abundance of bare root roses to unload and a repeat customer comes into the site looking for bulbs to plant, the retailer might pop up a banner ad for the roses. You plant both of them at the same time of year, so it might be a good match. If the customer isn't going for it (isn't clicking on it) after, say, three tries, you stop showing that banner ad and show another that says, "Buy 24 Bulbs, Get a Rose Bush for Free." It *that* doesn't work, back off the roses and maybe send that customer an e-mail about roses in a couple of weeks if there are still too many in the warehouse.

The tough part about all of this is that smart people have to spend a great deal of time figuring out what the server should do if the customer comes in looking for bulbs in April. What if the customer's profile shows that he or she never wants to see another rose bush again. Do you offer a discount on daffodils instead?

Your rules should not be too constricting, or they won't work. "Only customers who buy more than $10,000 per week from us should be given this special offer." What if I only buy $9,998.95 from you? Business rules can't be too generic, either. The words all, none, always, never, and their ilk are going to throw a monkey wrench into the gears in a heartbeat. And, while you want your business rule base to be rich and multitalented, you must avoid having too many rules, or they'll conflict through overclassification. Just look at the IRS.

The final straw with business rules comes when you realize that you are trying your best to classify people into narrower and narrower pigeonholes. People are a great deal more diverse than categories that can be assorted, labeled, indexed, and catalogued.

What Are These People Like, Really?

For a taste of just how hard it is to classify Web visitors, here's a sampling of efforts from people who all get A's for effort. First up, a common-sense view of visitors by Melinda Cuthbert in "All Buyers Not Alike" from Business 2.0 Magazine (www .business2.com), December 26, 2000.

What Every Net Retailer Should Know About Who's Browsing the Store

With the holiday season under way, online merchants have readied their Website operations for the predicted onslaught of e-customers.

It's a critical endeavor: Profits from the 2000 holiday shopping season are expected to hit $12 billion, accounting for as much as 50 percent of retailers' annual sales. So the margin for error is dangerously slim.

This year the mood among ebusinesses is not nearly as giddy as it was last year. Holiday optimism is mixed with anxiety, as online retailers labor to avoid the missteps of 1999—when excessive and ineffectual advertising spending, shoddy customer care, and botched fulfillment forced many online retailers to go belly up, and others to take their lumps on Wall Street.

In short, the 2000 season may be the last and best chance for online retailers to finally grow up.

One key element to driving sales in this broadening market is to recognize that not all online shoppers are alike. Retailers that really understand who their consumers are—how they think and how they act—stand to win big during this season's battle to turn browsers into buyers.

We've identified six categories of shoppers, each with unique goals and shopping strategies. Here's a quick guide to who they are and how to win their business:

Newbie Shoppers

Although there are far fewer first-time Internet shoppers this season than last, enough of them still exist to make up a substantial market. These shoppers are somewhat older than the general Internet population. They use the Internet the least and tend to be dissatisfied with the online shopping experience—perhaps because of a general discomfort with technology. When they do buy online, they are likely to start with small purchases in safe categories, such as music and books.

What they need: Newbies require a lot of hand holding. A simple interface, an easy checkout process, and lots of validation get them to buy online. Shopper-to-shopper interaction provides a nonthreatening way for them to learn their way around and affords more confidence in making a purchase.

Reluctant Shoppers

These shoppers are motivated to purchase but nervous about perceived security and privacy issues associated with online shopping. They are wary about giving out credit card numbers and other personal information and are very skeptical of an online retailer's ability to deliver. They are typically female homemakers who use the Web to research purchases and then make their actual purchases offline with established brick-and-mortar retailers.

What they need: They require more information and lots of reassurance to help mitigate anxiety. Access to live customer support can go a long way toward quelling their concerns. Online conversations with other shoppers who had positive experiences can also work to reassure them and lead them to the checkout icon.

Frugal Shoppers

These shoppers turn to the Web in search of the lowest price. They use search and comparison engines extensively and have no brand loyalty. They view the Web as a place to buy, and buy cheap, and they are inclined to be heavy users of group-buying engines. They are likely to be younger, male, and in a higher income bracket. Frugal shoppers are also more likely to comparison shop at retail outlets first and then buy online. They tend to spend on computer hardware, video and computer games, and other electronics.

What they need: With your competitor's best price only a click away, retailers must convince these shoppers that they are getting the best price and don't need to go elsewhere, online or offline, for a better deal. High-quality customer care can be an excellent way to retain customer loyalty once the sale is made. Specially priced items listed on the site or made available through an operator appeal greatly to them.

Strategic Shoppers

These shoppers—typically male and older—know exactly what they want before logging on and are online only long enough to purchase that item. Typically, they know the criteria by which they will base their decision, seek information to match against that criteria and purchase when they are confident they have found exactly the right product.

Strategic shoppers are most interested in saving time and maximizing convenience and are less interested in the recreational or social benefits of shopping. "Get in and get out" is their mantra.

What they need: Comparison engines, product configurators, and archived opinions are essential for strategic shoppers. They also benefit from insights from other shoppers' experiences and real-time answers from knowledgeable customer-service people.

Enthusiastic Shoppers

Shopping is a form of recreation for enthusiastic shoppers. They enjoy the social and experiential aspects more than any other group. The highest percentage are females. In terms of shopping habits, they purchase frequently and on impulse, and tend to be the most satisfied with their shopping experiences, both on and offline.

What they need: They are, as you might guess, a pretty sociable bunch. They like to talk—especially about shopping. So community tools are usually a big hit with them. Fun and engaging tools to view the merchandise and personalized product recommendations will go far to fuel the enthusiastic shopper's passion for using the Web.

Convenience Shoppers

This is the largest shopper group. They are most likely Baby Boomers and have higher incomes than other shoppers. They also tend to make impulse purchases and use both online and traditional retailers. These shoppers buy out of necessity, rather than as a form of recreation. They are grateful for the time-saving aspects of online shopping. Convenience shoppers also develop very sophisticated shopping strategies to find what they need quickly—and it can be difficult to second-guess the needs of this growing group.

What they need: Sites that have great navigation and offer large amounts of information on products—customer experiences, expert opinions, and customer service. They want instant access to information and support and expect highly relevant product recommendations that match their criteria.

Of course, there are some basic guidelines that online retailers can follow that will appeal to all six groups. Effective and knowledgeable customer service agents, sophisticated and accurate search engines, easy site navigation, and shopper-to-shopper interaction will provide a level of support that will increase the likelihood of a purchase—no matter who the customers are or how they shop.

Journalist Daintry Duffy took a more scientific approach in his article called "Know Thy Customer" in the October/November 2000 edition of *Darwin Magazine* (www .darwinmag.com). Daintry classified site visitors into the following categories:

Simplifiers. They're after something specific. They like convenience and solid customer service.

Surfers. They dart around the Web and like cool design and games, and they don't care for dated content.

Bargainers. They'll do anything to avoid paying full price.

Connectors. They like talking to others and interacting, and they don't like complex sites.

Routiners. They read and research online but buy offline and read the news and the stocks.

Sportsters. They are like routiners, but they are deeply into sports and entertainment.

You can try to categorize all of the people who come to your site six ways to Sunday, and you're still going to have a tough time of it. Just what's the exact right content to serve up to a convenience connector shopper after bidding on the Saddam Hussein Puppet at www.disturbingauctions.com?

Oddly enough, the very computers you're trying to teach about business rules could be writing them for you.

Machine-Derived Rules

There's a company in Newburyport, Massachusetts, called Genalytics (www.genalytics .com) that offers some compelling technology. Here's how the company describes it:

> Proprietary and patent-pending evolutionary algorithms are the power behind the Genalytics technology. Evolutionary algorithms allow our applications to automatically generate superior predictive models and provide intelligent e-marketing solutions. Benefits include:
>
> > Real-time customer behavior predictions
> > Scoring and model generation scalability
> > Dynamically adaptive predictive models
> > High volume customer data analyses
> > Online and offline data evaluation
>
> Genalytics utilizes Java and CORBA technology to ensure portability and completely distributed applications. Our applications are compatible with Sun's Java2 ORB and Inprise's VisiBroker for Java, and they run on any Java-enabled platform.

Here's how I describe it: Start with the end result you're after, let's say sales. You want to make more sales online. That's a reasonable goal. Take all of the information you have (and the more the merrier) and drop it all into one happy data set.

You've got technographics, and demographics, and clickstream data, and preferences, and implicit information, and explicit information, and sales data, and then some. You hand all of this data over to Genalytics, and it asks a simple question: Of all the people who did what we wanted them to do (buy something), what traits do they have in common that separate them from the rest of the herd? Now that's a pretty straightforward question, but it's fundamentally important to what Genalytics does next, so let me clarify.

One hundred people walk into the showroom and 25 of them buy a car. (It was a *very* good day.) What do the buyers have in common?

1. They had looked at other cars already.
2. They were preapproved for financing.
3. They've done research for their car online.
4. They came in the morning instead of the afternoon.
5. They came in pairs (couples).
6. They were between 35 and 55 years old.
7. They drove up in a late-model vehicle.
8. They asked for a salesperson rather than waiting for one to notice them.

If you knew this much about the people walking onto your car lot, you'd know right away which ones were the most likely to buy and, therefore, which to spend your time with. But if you ask everybody *all* of these questions, you're not saving any time at all. The trick is to figure out the fewest of the traits listed that are indicative of automobile buyers.

Some of these attributes, although shared by the buyers, were also found in those who came, looked, and split. So we create a statistical model that says that the only information we have about all the people who came in is recorded in numbers 1, 2, and 3. How good an indicator is that of their propensity to buy? Let's say the answer is 6. Is 6 good? Doesn't matter. What matters is that we do it again.

What if all we know about all the people who came in is 1, 2, 4, and 7. How good an indicator is that of their propensity to buy? 4. Hmmm. How about 1, 3, 4, and 7? 12 Ahhhh, now we're getting somewhere. It doesn't matter what the answers are, as long as we can compare them to see which is going to give us the best results. Which attributes best predict the desired outcome?

It might be that number 3 is all you need to know. If they've done their research online before coming into the showroom, then you know there is a sale waiting to be made. The problem is that building these statistical models is a bear. It takes a well-educated mathematician more than a while to put *one* together, much less all of the permutations of eight possible attributes. That's where Genalytics comes in.

When it says evolutionary algorithms, the company means that the software creates statistical models and then mutates them on the fly. So it can "automatically generate superior predictive models." Its software generates something like 200 models every second and compares them all to determine the most clairvoyant attributes.

In a nutshell, Genalytics takes all of your data, crunches it down to the nth degree, and tells you that the people who come to your Web site before lunch, using Internet

Explorer, who click on the Products button and then the Specifications button are statistically more likely to buy your product if you show them the Limited Time Offer banner on the home page.

Nifty.

Three words of caution: (1) it's not all that cheap; (2) it's not easy; and (3) not everybody cares for it.

The Right to Privacy

What seems chummy to some is Orwellian to others. What started as your friendly grocer asking about your health and then remembering your answer the next time you came in has turned into a multinational, overly intrusive, oh-my-god-what-happens-if-it-gets-into-the-wrong-hands, monster-mega-database.

You get that sinking feeling that some insidious individual is watching you for some nefarious purpose. Your innermost thoughts might be sold to other merchants who will flood your mailbox with offers you can't refuse. Or worse—some small, incorrect bit of data is slipped into the stream and suddenly you're pegged as an antique binocular enthusiast or a dental appliance aficionado.

What kind of mail and phone calls would you get if the Christian Coalition should get its hands on your opinions, attitudes, beliefs, and buying preferences? What if the Pacifists for Animal Rights knew every time you looked at www.nra.org? What if your boss signs up with a service that lets him or her know that you went to Career Mosaic three times last week?

Just where, as a card-carrying member of the data-hungry marketing industry, do you stand on the issue of privacy?

We Like Our Privacy

We even pay an additional fee to have our phone number kept out of the book. That's why it was front page news in California when GTE made a little slip-up.

GTE let the cat out of the bag by releasing unlisted numbers and addresses. If GTE had slipped with only a few telephone numbers, it would have been hush-hush. But GTE managed to blab the numbers and addresses of about 50,000 customers. Were they published in the white pages? No. They were published in a database that GTE leases to telemarketers, along with demographic information. GTE could be on the hook for fines of $30,000 per customer, but that's up to the California Public Utilities Commission. At this point, GTE has sent out a letter offering new numbers, free unlisted listings for a year, and a refund. In the fashion of a true phone company, it declined to let me reprint the letter it sent. GTE referred me to its lawyers, instead.

That all happened before DoubleClick (www.doubleclick.com) got a public bruising for buying Abacus Direct. When a banner ad network that can watch where you surf via cookies correlates its data with an aggregator of offline data, fear, uncertainty and doubt are abroad in the land. Rather than just serving up ads that might have something to do with where I'm surfing, they might have been able to send me junk mail for life. Scary.

People don't like it when someone spies on them. People don't like it when you know things about them. More important, people don't like the idea that information floating around out there will come back to haunt them.

The first time I tried to get a car loan I was turned down because I was still a student. I waited one month until graduation and tried again. This time I was refused because I didn't have a job. One month later I had a job but was turned down and the bank couldn't (wouldn't?) tell me why. Finally I opened up an account cosigned by my father, which made me feel about 10 years old again. This time the bank denied the loan because too many people had been checking my credit report in the previous six months. Arrrrgh!

In his column in *NetworkWorld* (January 12, 1998), Scott Brander lamented the data-gathering side of our society. He pointed out that more information is being gathered about us than we suspect.

> The cashier at the airport records your license number as you exit, "for inventory purposes."
>
> Automatic toll-collecting machines keep track of when you pass by so they can provide you with a detailed bill (and someday perhaps a speeding ticket if you take too little time to go from entrance to exit).
>
> Swisscom, the Swiss telephone company, has records detailing every move that a million of its cellular phone users have made over the past six or more months, accurate to within a few hundred meters.
>
> A U.S. luxury car manufacturer advertises that with a call to its 24-hour help desk you can get directions from where you are to where you want to go. The company doesn't happen to mention that the car is using satellites to keep track of where it is and can, upon a request via radio, report its location.
>
> The FCC is requiring all U.S. providers of cellular phone service to be able to accurately report on the location of the origin of any cell phone call to help support 911 emergency call centers.
>
> *Fortune Magazine* reports that NTT in Japan has a prototype system with which the company can report, on request, the location of any cell phone in NTT's system that is turned on, down to the floor of the building the phone is on.
>
> Many U.S. trucking companies use radio tracking systems to monitor the location of their vehicles.
>
> This all is more Orwellian than Orwell ever was.

But it gets much worse. What if you have genetic tests done in preparation for parenthood and that information is released to your insurance company? The fact that one of your genes shows a propensity toward a heart condition could knock your insurance premiums off the chart. And who would want to hire somebody who was genetically challenged?

Remember the movie *Gattica?* (www.spe.sony.com/Pictures/SonyMovies/movies/Gattaca/design_child.htm) (see Figure 8.14).

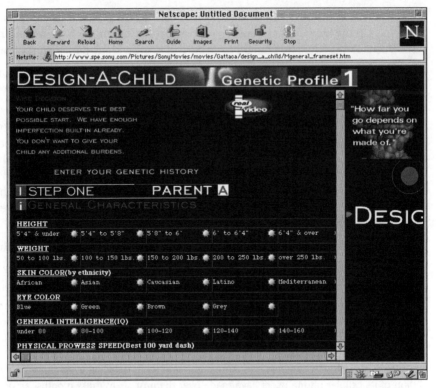

Figure 8.14 The Web site for the movie *Gattica* lets you genetically design your own prodigy.

As a boy, Vincent discovers he is different from his younger brother Anton, a petri dish baby who possesses the perfect genes for success. Where Anton is strong and tall and has perfect eyesight, Vincent is weak and sickly and wears glasses that give away his genetic inferiority. Where Anton earns his parents' constant praise, encouragement, and admiration, Vincent is coddled, pitied, and kept at home. Hey—it could happen.

Jason Catlett runs a company called Junkbusters (www.junkbusters.com) that covers personal privacy and the Web. He e-mailed me the following example of target marketing run amuck:

```
Dear Mr. Jones:

Our research indicates that you have not bought condoms at SpiffyMart
recently. (Your last purchase was eight weeks ago.) Further, you have
stopped buying feminine hygiene products, but you have sharply increased
your frozen pizza and dinners usage in the same time frame.
    It's clear that Ms. Jody Sanders and you are no longer "an item."
(It's probably for the best—she consistently buys inexpensive shampoo,
and it was obvious that the two of you were not economically
compatible.) The Postal Service database confirms that she filed a
change of address form.
```

We at Hotflicks International offer our condolences.

As the number-one vender of hot XXX-rated videos, we want you to know that our products can help you through this difficult period. When you're feeling lonely, check out our unmatched catalog; we guarantee you'll find something that you'll want to purchase!

Order from this catalog, and we'll throw in an extra tape FREE!

Yours Truly,
Hotflicks Marketing Management

Expectations

We have an expectation of privacy. It's a Constitutional right, right? Well, not really.

A quick search of the text page at www.usconstitution.net/const.html indicates the word "privacy" never appears on the page, except for a link to USConstitution.net's own privacy policy.

We've got the Fourth Amendment: "Right of search and seizure regulated."

The right of the people to be secure in their persons, houses, papers, and effects, against unreasonable searches and seizures, shall not be violated, and no warrants shall issue, but upon probable cause, supported by Oath or affirmation, and particularly describing the place to be searched, and the persons or things to be seized.

But that doesn't cover the right to know something about somebody that he or she does not want you to know. For that, we have to follow the trail of the Tenth Amendment: "Rights of States under Constitution."

The powers not delegated to the United States by the Constitution, nor prohibited by it to the States, are reserved to the States respectively, or to the people.

That brings us to the Constitution of the State of *California*, which opens with Article 1, Declaration Of Rights:

SECTION 1. All people are by nature free and independent and have inalienable rights. Among these are enjoying and defending life and liberty, acquiring, possessing, and protecting property, and pursuing and obtaining safety, happiness, and privacy.

Now, we get to argue until the end of time just what privacy means. That is, we get to argue what it means in California.

According to its own Privacy Policy and Data Protection Practices (www.dnb.com/aboutdb/priv_pract.htm), Dun & Bradstreet "collects information on more than 48 million business establishments from 217 countries." Many of those countries have national data protection laws, enacted for the purpose of providing guidelines on the collection, processing, and dissemination of information about individuals.

The European Union Data Protection Directive, which went into effect in October 1998, forces American companies to be a bit more careful than they are used to. One of the rules says that you have to give people access to and the ability to correct their own personal information on data processed in Europe. In addition, you're not allowed to use personal data for anything except the purpose for which it was specifically acquired unless you have explicit consent. In a nutshell, if you sell somebody a teapot, you're not allowed to turn around and try to sell them tea unless they signed a waiver.

This is an ongoing issue that will involve lawyers and diplomats. To keep your eye on the ball, watch the Web. The U.S. Department of Commerce has a report posted, called "Privacy and Self-Regulation in the Information Age," that's worth a look at www.ntia.doc.gov/reports/privacy/privacy_rpt.htm. The Federal Trade Commission has been warming up to the idea that industry self-regulation might not be enough— the FTC may start regulating soon. You can get help from Peter Swire, Associate Professor of Law at the Ohio State University College of Law. He keeps tabs on the issue at www.acs.ohio-state.edu/units/law/swire1/pspriv.htm.

The legal issues are tricky, but the cultural side of the coin is comparatively straightforward. First, you have to consider that some people feel privacy is pretty much dead anyway.

Just Like Real Life

> You have zero privacy anyway. Get over it.
>
> *Scott McNealy, CEO of Sun Microsystems, January 1999*

You think information about you is just between you and the lamppost? Think your financial records, your health records, your shopping habits, your television viewing habits are yours and yours alone? Not quite. Think computers are not already being used to make guesses about how you might act? Think again.

At the Hotel

Credit card fraud detection companies have been at it for years. They use the software that analyzes your purchases as you make them. They want to see if it's really you. Going on a trip to New York? Going to take in a show and stay at a really nice hotel and do some fine dining? You don't usually do that sort of thing. Your credit card company knows that. You present your card at the front desk, and the nice lady asks you to wait and then hands you the phone. "It's for you." It's your credit card company. It detected an attempted purchase outside your normal buying pattern. Is that really you? They'd like your mother's maiden name for verification, please.

At the Airport

The Computer Assisted Passenger Screening System (CAPS) might hold you up the next time you try to get on an airplane. It's a combination of database and transaction watcher that stops people in their tracks, rather than lets them into the friendly skies. If you're in the habit of buying one-way tickets to countries known for terrorism, if you're of Middle Eastern descent, if you like to pay cash for your ticket, you are likely to be questioned, maybe even searched.

The American Civil Liberties Union is concerned about invasion of privacy. Northwest Airlines built and implemented CAPS following a recommendation by the White House after TWA Flight 800 exploded in the summer of 1996. The FAA has handed down the directive that all major air carriers implement such systems by 1999. It's sure to catch some terrorists. After all, the ratio of dumb terrorists in the world equals the ratio of dumb people in the rest of the population.

At the Loan Officer's Desk

You want a bank loan? Your chances of getting a loan are diminished if you have had marriage counseling. Are you buying prescription anti-depressants? Hmmm. Have you been to see a psychiatrist? Tsk, tsk, tsk. Are you going through a divorce. Oooo. Do you frequently buy small amounts of gasoline? Are you using a resume service? All of the above? You, my friend, are not a good risk for a loan.

In fact, you're more likely to file for bankruptcy than most others, and you're going to have a tough time getting a credit card from Sears. In 1997 Sears racked up $1.8 billion in bad debts. It was listed as a creditor in one out of every three bankruptcies filed that year. That kind of pain makes this kind of software seem like a good idea.

On the Web, CyberSource offers a real-time credit check for Web sites that sell. It evaluates how much is being charged, the time of day, the Internet Protocol address the order is coming from, and it cross-references that to standard credit reports—all in the blink of an eye, between clicks of the mouse.

At the Insurance Company

If your credit card shows that you make frequent purchases at Chicago Extreme Adventures (www.mcs.net/~chgxtrem), like to visit www.i-quit-smoking.com, and if you neglected to mention these habits on your application form, thanks anyway.

So how do you, as a plugged-in, top-notch, database-driven marketer, get people to agree to give you information about themselves?

Ask them.

Privacy Solutions

First and foremost, your company has to believe in full disclosure. You must candidly explain what information you are gathering and how you are going to use it. You must include a list of third parties with whom you are going to share this information, and you must give visitors the right to update/correct their personal information. You also have to give them the choice and the ability to delete themselves from your database altogether.

A well-publicized Harris Poll in April 1997 found that 79 percent of people asked to fill out a survey on a Web site declined and that 8 percent gave false information. Of those declining and falsifying, 71 percent said they would have given personal information if they had had a relationship with the company, and 63 percent said they would have divulged information had the site offered specific information on how the information was to be used.

Trust Building

L.L. Bean doesn't use fine print to state its privacy policy (see Figure 8.15). It wants you to feel as comfortable as possible giving the company your name, address, clothing sizes, and credit card number.

Full disclosure means more than saying "We promise to keep your information safe." It means letting people know if information about them is going to be shared and with whom. L.L. Bean tells it like it is, and it covers all the bases:

About the Information We Collect

L.L.Bean has a strong tradition of providing quality goods and excellent customer service. At llbean.com, our goal is not only to carry on this tradition, but also to provide an experience that is unique to the dynamic capabilities of the World Wide Web.

Part of achieving this goal involves working with information that helps us understand what customers want when they visit llbean.com. We do this in two ways. First, we analyze customer information in aggregate—that is, we collect information about thousands of site

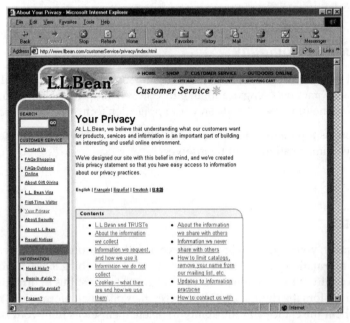

Figure 8.15   L.L. Bean builds trust right up front with full disclosure.

visits and analyze it as a whole. This kind of study involves looking for trends among many visitors to llbean.com, rather than analyzing information about any individual customer. Examples include researching which parts of the site are accessed most frequently, or determining which banner ad generates the best response.

Second, we may use information gathered during your visit to help customize our communications with you. For instance, if you choose to view or buy a pair of hiking boots at llbean.com, we might offer you a link to related products the next time you visit us online, or we might send you our latest Outdoors catalog by mail.

In the end, we hope to tailor our communications with you to fit your needs—so that you receive more of what you want from us and less of what you don't want.

Information We Request, and How We Use It

In several areas of llbean.com, we ask you to provide information by filling out and submitting an online form. Following is a list of the information we request, arranged by site location, and details on how we use this information.

- **Checkout.** We ask for your name, address and contact information so we can send you your order, and so we can contact you if we have a question about your order. We ask for credit card information so we can fulfill your order, and so we can provide this information to the company or companies who process your credit card payment. We may share your name and address with other companies whose products we think you may be interested in. We do not share or sell email addresses.

- **Catalog requests.** We ask for a name and address to complete your request. We may share your name and address with other companies whose products we think you may be interested in.

- **My Account/Address Book.** When you register at llbean.com, we ask for your name, address, phone number, email address, and credit card information (optional). After registering, you have the option of creating a personal Address Book to save shipping addresses. We use the information to fulfill your orders, and we may share your name and address with other companies whose products we think you may be interested in. If you send an L.L.Bean gift to someone in your Address Book, we may contact them by postal mail about our products and services, but we never share their name or address with other companies. We do not share or sell email addresses.

- **L.L.Bean Visa online application.** We ask for name, address and financial information that MBNA, the issuer and administrator of the credit card program, needs to process your application. We do not share this information with anyone other than MBNA.

- **L.L.Bean Live Help and llbean.com email forms.** We ask for your name and email address, and for information to help us answer your question. If you have provided your email address to us only via Live Help or by sending us an email message, we may follow up on your question via email, but we will not send you email for marketing purposes. We do not share questions or comments provided in Live Help with any other company, and we do not share or sell email addresses.

- **LLB-Mail.** We ask you to provide a name, email address and profile information. We use this information only to fulfill your request and, in the case of profile information, to help make sure we're sending you the type of email updates and catalogs you want to receive. We do not share or sell email addresses.

■ **Gift Cards and Gift Messages.** These options allow you to send a personal greeting with your gift order. We make no use of the information contained in these greetings except to complete your order as you have requested.

Information We Do Not Collect

When you visit our site, we do not collect your name, email address or any other personal information unless you provide it to us.

Cookies—What They Are and How We Use Them

Cookies are small bits of text that your Web browser software stores on your computer when you visit some Web sites. L.L.Bean uses a cookie to help make it easier for you to use our site and to help us customize your experience so that we can provide you with the information you need—when and where you need it.

A cookie generated by our site allows you, for example, to retrieve your llbean.com Shopping Cart and address information on a return visit. Cookies do not collect this information, nor is name, address or product information contained within the cookie itself. The cookie simply holds the "key" that, once interpreted by our site, is associated with this information. Because we rely on cookies to make the shopping experience easier and more tailored to your needs, your browser must be set to accept cookies before you can place an order at llbean.com. (You can change the cookie setting in your browser's Preferences, usually found in the Edit menu.)

We also use cookies to help us measure the success of our marketing efforts, so that we can better understand how to reach customers with the information they want about llbean.com.

How We Use Email

After you place an order on our site, you will receive an email confirmation and, in most cases, an email with package tracking information. You will receive these emails only if you have provided your email address during checkout or as part of registering. Recipients of our Electronic Gift Certificate receive an email notifying them of the gift and giving them the information they need to redeem it.

We send LLB-Mail, our email update on sales and products, to subscribers and occasionally to other customers who we think might be interested in learning about sales and special events at our site. Unsubscribe instructions are included in each edition of LLB-Mail.

If you provide your email address only via Live Help or an llbean.com email form, we may send you email to follow up on your inquiry, but we will not use the address for marketing purposes. We do not sell or share email addresses with other companies.

We *do* use email as a means of receiving feedback from our customers, and we encourage you to email us with your questions or comments. We read every email we receive.

Links to Other Sites

Occasionally we provide links to other sites we think you will enjoy. These sites operate independently of L.L.Bean and have established their own privacy and security policies. For the best online experience, we strongly encourage you to review these policies at any site you visit.

About the Information We Share With Others

If you provide us with your name and postal address, we may make it available to other companies who want to tell you about their products. (See below if you prefer that we not share this information.) We may segment the information into groups of customers who have bought similar amounts and types of products, but we never provide details that are specific to a single customer or household.

Information We Do Not Share With Others

L.L.Bean does not share, sell or trade email addresses, information collected as part of a survey or specific details about you or your household. We do not contribute to or participate in shared or cooperative databases, which give other companies access to your personal information. We do not release credit card or financial information for use by other companies (except in the case of financial information included in the online L.L.Bean VISA application, which we provide to MBNA, the issuer and administrator of the program). For privacy purposes, all information relating to our customers is stored on a highly secure server, and all credit card information is stored in an encrypted format. (See About Security for details.)

How to Limit Catalogs, Remove Your Name from Our Mailing List, Etc.

You can write to the address below to:

- Eliminate duplicate catalogs
- Limit the L.L.Bean catalogs you receive
- Remove your name from our catalog mailing list
- Remove your name from lists we rent to other direct mail companies
- Update the name and address information we use when we mail you catalogs. (If you're moving, please indicate when your new address will be in effect.)

Please include a note of instruction and a catalog mailing label and send your request to:

L.L.Bean, Inc.
Dept. CFM
Freeport, ME 04033-0001
USA

Updates to Our Information Practices

From time to time, we make changes to our information practices or alter the functionality of our Web site. We always update this statement accordingly, so we encourage you to periodically review this page for the latest information on privacy practices at llbean.com.

How to Contact Us with Questions or Comments

See Contact Us to choose from several options for reaching us. We're always happy to answer your questions and listen to your comments.

You can count on the fact that only a small percent of L.L. Bean shoppers bother to read all of the above. I'm pretty sure you didn't either. A Business 2.0 poll in January 2001 showed 46 percent never read privacy policies, 31 percent rarely, 15 percent sometimes, and 6 percent *claimed* they always did. But when you need to look over a well-done policy, this is a good one. You may not *like* the idea that L.L. Bean feels free with your home address. Did you catch that part? "We may share your name and address with other companies whose products we think you may be interested in." But at least it is up front and very quick to point out, "We do not share or sell email addresses."

Not so our favorite e-tailer, Amazon.com . . .

Bent Trust

In the first week of September 2000, Amazon sent an e-mail to its faithful customers announcing a change in its privacy policy. It was very clear about it, but if you followed the link, you'd have found this paragraph among the rest:

> As we continue to develop our business, we might sell or buy stores or assets. In such transactions, customer information generally is one of the transferred business assets. Also, in the unlikely event that Amazon.com, Inc., or substantially all of its assets are acquired, customer information will of course be one of the transferred assets.

My take? I wrote the following in September 2000 for *Computerworld*:

Sold for Thirty Pieces of Silver

This week I am lamenting a logical, business-focused, understandable, yet deeply regrettable decision made by someone we thought we could trust. It feels sort of like Moses saying, "Oh, what the Hell," and chipping off the Commandment about having a good old time with his neighbor's wife.

```
Date: Mon, 4 Sep 2000 18:50:31 -0700 (PDT)
From: Amazon.com Legal Notices <legalnotices-b@bounces.amazon.com>
Subject: Update to privacy policy
To: jsterne@targeting.com

Dear Customer,
```

Ooo—how cold and remote. Whatever happened to that great personalization?

```
We have just updated Amazon.com's privacy policy and,
because privacy is important, we wanted to e-mail you
proactively in this case and not just update the policy
on our site, as is the common Web practice.
```

Translation: The information we're collecting about you is valuable and we wanted to be able to say "Hey, we were up front about it!"

```
Thanks for being a customer and allowing us to
continue to earn your trust.
```

Translation: Thank you for allowing us to earn some money on the side off of the information we've collected about you.

```
To read the updated Privacy Notice, visit:
http://www.amazon.com/privacy-notice
```

Translation: No way are we going to publish this heretical manifestation of our brazenness in full view.

```
Please keep in mind that this updated policy applies only
to the amazon.com Web site (and not amazon.co.uk, amazon.de,
or amazon.fr).
```

Translation: What we're going to do to you is *illegal* over there!

```
Thanks again for shopping at Amazon.com.
```

Like lambs to the slaughter.

```
Sincerely,
Amazon.com
PS: We hope you appreciated receiving this message. However,
if you'd rather not receive any future notices of this sort
from Amazon.com, please send an e-mail message to
nolegalnotices@amazon.com.
```

Translation: We'd rather not have to tell you about other devious things we have planned.

```
Please be aware that even if you choose not to receive
these updates, they will still cover your use of Amazon.com.
```

Translation: You have sold your data soul to us and your ASCII is ours!

```
Please note that this message was sent to the following
e-mail address: jsterne@targeting.com
```

Translation: We know where you live.

How could this have happened? Well, a huge database full of nifty customer information excited the heck out of Wall Street. They loved the fact that intimate knowledge about what people like and how they like to buy can be used to sell them more stuff. Right up until they realized the profits still weren't rolling in. Wall Street loved the fact that this data puts Amazon way out in front of the competition. Right up until they realized that it wasn't fungible.

To appease the money-lenders in the temple Internet, Jeff Bezos did a little slight of bookkeeping, turning shopper into swine, and declared his database a corporate asset—something of tangible value, rather than just leverage. His fiduciary advisors warn that a thing only has real value if it can be sold. So Jeff said, "We shall turn yon datawarehouse into a datamart and declare it open for business!"

Blasphemy. Oh Jeff, why hast thou forsaken us?

Trust for Sale

In January 2001, Toysmart.com was going down the tubes. In keeping with its bankruptcy-court settlement agreement, it tried to sell everything that wasn't nailed down and one thing that should have been: its customer database.

The Federal Trade Commission, attorneys general from no less than 50 states, and privacy wonks like Jason Catlett of Junkbusters sued to stop the sale.

Buena Vista Internet Group, a Disney subsidiary and 60 percent owner of Toysmart, offered $50,000 if Toysmart would quell instead of sell. It wouldn't go far to pay off the $18 million-plus Toysmart owed its creditors, but it would keep 250,000 names, addresses, billing information, shopping preferences, and family profiles from getting into the hands of competitors.

Despite having spent the money for the ad in the *Wall Street Journal* to sell the database, Toysmart was pressed into taking the deal by federal regulators.

Mediated Trust

So far we've been looking at the privacy issue from a landlubber's perspective. You collect information on the Web, and you disseminate it (or not) in the usual ways. But what happens if you take a Web perspective? What if all that information can be shared by multiple businesses in real time?

The reason the privacy issue looms so large on the Web is that the cost of gathering personal information is so astonishingly low. Gather up the phone books for the major metropolitan areas? Yes, it can be done. Cross-reference them with credit reports from the major reporting agencies? Sure. Cross-tabulate that with databases of who subscribes to which magazines? Yes, yes, and more. But that's expensive.

What if the phone company published its phone book online? It does. What if you could get a credit report over the Web? You can. How about direct marketing lists? Who do you think invented merge and purge?

In the January-February 1997 issue of the *Harvard Business Review,* John Hagel III and Jeffrey F. Rayport wrote about a new type of organization—the infomediary. As companies move from fighting over raw materials to distribution to brand awareness, they will end up fighting over information about customers.

Hagel and Rayport postulated that the public will demand payment of some kind for personal information. They got it right so far. Then, they say, because consumers won't be able to negotiate on their own behalf, and because those negotiations would be too costly anyway, new companies will be created to do collective bargaining—infomediaries.

The model states that we as individuals will put our faith, our trust, and our information into the hands of these collectives and let them cut the deals for us. They will protect us from the marketers and advertisers we don't want to hear from and will exchange personal information in return for just the sort of goods and services we want at a honey of a price on our behalf.

YesMail.com (www.yesmail.com) (see Figure 8.16) sends you ads based on the profile you create. Over 14 million people have signed up already. CyberGold (www.cybergold.com) and ClickRewards (www.clickrewards.com) are just two of the companies that offer promotions and rewards targeted according to your explicit desires. The infomediaries are out there.

Infomediaries and info gatherers are trying to find a way to team up with each other. That means a marketplace is forming around the data that's gathered. That marketplace will try to operate within the bounds of federal regulation. With a heavy emphasis on personal privacy, the Customer Profile Exchange Network is an organization to keep your eyes on.

Figure 8.16 YesMail.com is proof that people are more than willing to trust a third party with their personal preferences.

CPExchange (www.cpexchange.org) offers a vendor-neutral, open standard for facilitating the privacy-enabled interchange of customer information across disparate enterprise applications and systems.

The CPExchange standard integrates online and offline customer data in an XML (Extensible Markup Language)-based data model for use within various enterprise applications both on and off the Web. The result is a networked, customer-focused environment that allows e-businesses to leverage a unified view of their customers into more compelling e-relationships. More than simply a DTD (Document Type Definition) or XML tag set, CPExchange will include a data model, transport and query definitions, and a framework for enabling privacy safeguards.

Few of today's supply and demand chains share a unified image of the customer, leaving customer support, order management, lead sharing and other primary business functions working independently to grasp a customer's identity, behavior and needs. Customer service capability is severely reduced by this lack of shared information, creating significant and redundant short and long-term IT integration costs.

Businesses will be able to apply CPExchange across a disparate range of back-office applications, front-office applications and Web customer automation applications.

Is privacy important to your customers? You bet it is. Is it important to your company? Just after Thanksgiving 2000, IBM announced the creation of a new position: Chief Privacy Officer.

Getting It Right

So you've convinced the powers that be that tracking people in order to cater to them is valuable and that there is also value in protecting your customers' privacy. That's good. Now it's time to get serious.

Jupiter Communications (www.jup.com) published its take on personalization in one of its Site Operations Reports called "The Personalization Train" (July 19, 2000). In it, Jupiter outlines the five-step, ongoing process, summarized here:

1. *Data Storage.* Consolidating data silos is necessary for an across-the-board personalization effort.

2. *Access.* Putting all of your data in one basket is very difficult and provides no return on investment due to the necessity of proprietary technology for specific functions. The answer then is to cache the data from the individual stores, into a central analysis warehouse.

3. *Mining.* Scheduled and ad hoc analysis paints a picture of market segments and customer classifications.

4. *Tuning.* Determining which customer attributes are meaningful in order to get to:

5. *Targeting.* Creating the specific business rules for sending the right message to the right people at the right time.

Those are the steps, now come the principles.

Bruce Kasanoff has always focused on *how* you actually implement one-to-one business practices. He has been working in the area of one-to-one marketing and CRM longer than anyone except his long-time partners at Peppers and Rogers Group, Don Peppers, Martha Rogers, and Bob Dorf. (They're the one's who coined the term one-to-one.) Bruce runs HowPersonal.com, a portal that helps companies balance personalization, privacy, and profits. Here are his 30 guiding principles that are detailed at www.howpersonal .com, divided into the major three categories of Interact, Invent, and Customize:

Top 10 Ways to Interact

1. Show Relevance First
   Show why your products and services are relevant to the person's needs before you require them to invest time or money.

2. Prove Individual Uniqueness
   Prove to each valuable individual that they have unique needs and information that you are able to accommodate.

3. Individual Controls Information
   Provide every person with the means to specify how, when, and why their information is used.

4. Opt-In Only
   When remembering data about individuals, assume that the answer is no. Require the person to take some action to expressly permit you to remember their information, and enable them to specify in detail how you use their information.

5. Reward Collaboration

Reward individuals—in a relevant and significant manner—every time they give you information.

6. Share Insights

Share insights across your company, as long as doing so doesn't violate your privacy policy and the permission you've received from individuals.

7. Never Rent Relationships

Don't ever rent individual data to other firms. If you can't make more money serving your key stakeholders directly, rather than renting their information to others, something is wrong with your business model.

8. Don't Waste Information

Only collect information that you can use to benefit the individual from whom you collect it.

9. Don't Pretend to Care

Don't pretend to care. You are a company trying to make a reasonable profit, not a trusted and caring friend. Don't get too personal.

10. Link Databases

Provide a standard and intuitive means to link and access information from all the databases present in your company. The simpler and the faster this process works, the better.

Top 10 Ways to Invent

1. Develop Modular Capabilities

Develop modular capabilities, instead of specific products. This will enable you to satisfy individuals without having detailed advance notice of their needs.

2. Constantly Broaden Services

Constantly broaden the range of services you offer to each valuable individual.

3. Leverage Community Knowledge

Leverage the knowledge you have of each individual to make better recommendations to each individual. When opinions matter, more opinions are better.

4. Embrace the Individual's Agenda

Develop services that completely embrace each individual's agenda, instead of your own. The sole purpose of these services should be to profitably meet each individual's needs.

5. Make Loyalty Convenient

Make loyalty more convenient for each individual than disloyalty. There are many ways to do this; the hard part is making this goal central to your business strategy. Loyalty becomes convenient the more you use information about each person to the person's benefit.

6. Don't Automate Old Habits

Decide that no matter what, you will not simply automate existing habits. Instead, look at the technology and ask: what are we trying to accomplish and how big a change does this technology allow us to make? You can do things no one has ever done before; don't settle for less.

7. Use the Simplest System Possible

Always use the simplest system possible, even if this means settling for less function-ality. Once such a system has been implemented and proven, introduce another such system. The more complex a system, the greater its chance of failing.

8. Set System Boundaries

Set limits for each system. Although you want to keep individuals happy, you don't necessarily want to do it at any price. What are the limits of acceptable behavior?

9. Minimize Instructions

To enable a system to adapt, give it as much freedom as is possible. In other words, let the technology come up with the best solution for each visitor; don't let the program-mer(s) specify one approach for everybody.

10. Jury-Rig Tests

Jury-rig a temporary solution to test individual reaction before you increase in ex-panded systems. If necessary, hire temporary workers to do the work that technology would do under expansion circumstances.

Top 10 Ways to Customize

1. Manage People, Not Products

Organize business units around segments of individuals, being sure to provide each segment with a single source for all the services offered by your firm.

2. Save the Person Time

Develop services that save people time. Live by this mantra: never make a person tell us the same thing twice (unless they want to.)

3. Save the Person Money

Offer services that save each individual money, based on information you remember for each individual.

4. Provide Better Information

Offer services that provide each individual with better information, which generally means less information that is more directly focused on what they need to know at exactly this moment.

5. Offer Special Treatment

Look for opportunities to provide individuals with special treatment. This treatment doesn't have to be more costly, as recognition is often more appreciated than expense.

6. Customize Meaningfully

Validate that the type of customization you provide is meaningful to the individuals you are serving. For example, personalized advertising is not nearly as powerful as per-sonalization that addresses directly the most urgent needs of the individual.

7. Separate Modes from Needs

Separate "modes" from needs. Modes require specific functions that are available to everyone (i.e. search functions on your Web site, an easy way to buy a gift, etc.) Needs require you to remember information for each individual; a family with seven kids always needs a way to reduce expenses.

8. Let Individuals Fix Mistakes

Give individuals an easy way to correct your—or their—mistakes. The easier you make this, the better information you will have. The more your personalize, the more often you will assume something about a person that may not be true.

9. Consistent Interface

Keep the user interface consistent. Change the information displayed, but don't change the interface itself.

10. No Secrets

When it comes to managing individual data, keep no secrets from the outside world. If you are worried about how a practice might be perceived by consumers or press, stop that practice immediately. This is the only way to build trust.

The success of your Web site depends on how well you can get into your clients' minds and give them what they want, instead of what you want to give them. Make your Web site their place. Cater to their needs, wants, and desires, remembering that what they want and what they need are different things. I may want whiter clothes, but I need bleach.

They will all need and want different things. They have emotional needs: the need to belong, the need to own, and the need to win. They have informational needs: the need to be made aware, the need to understand, and the need to get the nitty-gritty details. If you cater to them well, they will reward you with their business and with valuable information that will make it easier for you to cater to their needs and wants.

Yes, Jim, but how does this apply in a business setting? It's one thing to cater to individual consumers, but what about building Web pages for client companies?

Those would be called extranets, and they require a chapter of their own.

CHAPTER 9

Professional Personalization— Extranets and Customer Relationship Management

When contact management systems first came out, they helped you keep track of your contacts. That was good. But it was only good if your contacts were individuals. As soon as they needed to be correlated to a specific company, and maybe even a division or department within that company, contact management tools stumbled. And when multiple people inside your company had to coordinate communicating with multiple people in your clients' companies, then the tools simply fell down on the job. Over time, they've made their products more robust, and we've learned the lesson: What works for one does not always work for many.

There are two major areas of interest when talking about communicating with customers online. The first is creating a special place on your Web site for your business clients, and the second is something we've come to call customer relationship management. Let's take these one at a time.

Extranet—Your Own Store

It wasn't until the seventh in the search results for "Internet Glossary" on Yahoo! (skipping the Jane's Internet Defence Glossary—how did *that* get in there?) that I found one that included a definition of extranet. It was the PC & Internet Glossary authored by Stephen Jenkins, located at homepages.enterprise.net/jenko/Glossary/Index.htm. This is Stephen's definition:

> **Extranet**. Very similar to an Intranet with the added feature that the information contained can be accessed externally by business partners.
>
> Be sure to take one of these on your next fishing trip.

The *local area network* (LAN) is what ties your computer to the ones down the hall. The *wide area network* (WAN) is what ties your department to the other departments in your company, even though they're located in far-flung cities. The Internet (network of networks) is the glue that ties the networks from different companies together. The intranet is what you get when you create Web services for use inside your company and you don't let anybody else have access to it. Intranets are for internal use only.

Until someone invented the extranet.

The term "extranet" was coined to describe intranets that talk to each other. If you allow a customer to access your intranet to get information, voila! You have an extranet.

One would imagine that you start with all of the tricks, tools, and techniques described in the previous chapter and surround them with business-to-business tools. But that hasn't happened yet. At the moment, extranets are being created as EDI on steroids. Here's Stephen again:

> **Electronic Data Interchange.** A standard used by businesses to transmit documents to each other electronically such as Invoices & Purchase Orders. The companies using EDI must adhere to controlling standards regarding the information they provide & the format of that information.

The problem with EDI is that you had to write software to communicate between each and every trading partner. Expensive and time-consuming. In today's world of distributed, client/server, object-oriented, peer-to-peer computing, the World Wide Web has become the network architecture and the Web browser the graphical user interface of choice.

Through this medium, the company that opens its electronic doors the widest will walk away with the business. It will provide access to and through the enterprise—not just to customers and prospects, but to employees and vendors as well.

The Internet provides that communication layer, and now all you need to worry about are preconfigured products, special-order products, contract pricing, order placement and status tracking, business rules, workflow, and such niggling questions as these:

- Who is allowed to order?
- How much may they order?
- What is the approval cycle?
- How is a discrepancy resolved?

This is the area that will take today's corporations and turn them inside out. Many companies have spent many dollars creating narrow electronic data interchange systems for their special clients. Now it is time to start creating wide interchange systems for all their clients.

In the first edition of this book in 1995, the passage read:

> The World Wide Web is in its infancy, and it will mutate frequently. But if you look just over the horizon at the competitive world of tomorrow, you'll see it at its logical extreme. You'll see customers demanding instantaneous intelligence about the status of their orders, your

average of stock on hand, and your estimated time of delivery. They'll want to see their current balances and have online options about methods of payment. They'll want to review discussions your other customers have had about the good, the bad, and the ugly. Ubiquitous electronic data interchange and a terminal on every desk. The company with the most freely available information wins.

Customers will expect a feedback screen at every turn so they can speak their minds. They will expect prompt replies. The customers will become part of the process and, through their suggestions, help shape the process. Your whole company will be on display, and your customer will be part of the operations committee as well as the product planning council.

Those wonderful old AT&T "You Will" commercials are as dated as those paragraphs. Replace the future tense with the present tense, and you begin to see the picture.

The National Semiconductor Purchasing Portal

National Semiconductor is all extranet, all the time. In March 1997 it knew the Net was the way to go. By the end of that year, it had customized customer service applications running for different customers. It was able to pass shipment requests of sample chips to the marketing team, so it could keep its finger on the pulse of leading-edge developers.

Phil Gibson, director of interactive marketing, made sure the import of this data was understood. "There's a fairly common pattern in the development of sophisticated electronics. A design engineer orders a sample and hooks it up to a test bed. If it looks like it'll work, he orders a handful for prototyping. If it still looks good, he orders a couple of hundred for a test production run. At this point, our salespeople, and they may be several layers down the distribution channel, are well aware that a large order could pop out of this company the second they decide to go into a test market run. That's when we get real close to the customer so manufacturing can be ready the split second they turn on full-scale production. With the information from our extranet, marketing and sales can track the trends across multiple industries."

Yes, they hosted a wonderful online simulation service for the design engineers who use their products. Design engineers, however, represent only part of their customer base. They are the ones who research, select, test, decide, and green-light the products. But when it comes time to actually make the purchase, the task falls to the purchasing agent. You'll remember the discussion about National's My Private Bill of Materials (see Figure 9.1) from Chapter 1, "Using the World Wide Web for Marketing—What Are You Trying to Accomplish?"

What is My Bill Of Materials? It is a personalized table for National's registered users that allows you to build a personalized website for the parts you specify (containing Part Numbers, Package Type, Part Status, Pricing & Distributor Inventory, Standard Pack Method and list of user selected distributors with on hand available inventory to sell along with hot links into their order forms). You can create multiple projects and select the information that you would care to see. Each project will become an additional link on your private website.

All attributes in this selection criteria are updated daily, so you can get the latest information available for the parts you want, when you want them.

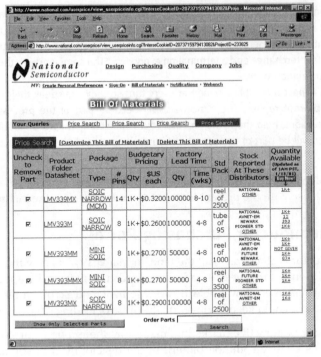

Figure 9.1 My Private Bill of Materials at National Semiconductor.

Then comes the sales order process. Leads are tracked and orders placed. "Everything comes in through the extranet," according to Phil. "We don't pay commissions without the sale being approved on the site."

National understood that the road to success was to figure out what its customers do for a living—as individuals—and make it as easy as possible for those customers to accomplish their goals.

The Dell Extranet

Dell Computer Corporation (www.dell.com) had an advantage over the rest of us. Michael Dell decided from the very start that the company was going to make machines to order. When the Web came along and everybody started tearing their hair out about mass customization, Michael was very well positioned.

Dell was one of the first that allowed not just online ordering, but online configuring of products. Then it realized that its corporate customers needed something more. Business customers wanted to "more efficiently manage all phases of computer ownership: purchasing, asset management and product support." So Dell started adding features to its Premier pages, and it hasn't stopped.

Online Purchasing at Your Price

When you open your Premier catalog and configure your system, the prices you see are the discounted prices your organization has negotiated with Dell. You'll know instantly what the system will cost, and you can place your order online.

Manage Your Standards

Premier Dell.com can help your organization manage its IT standards. When your users open the online catalog, they are offered only the options pre-approved by your organization. You can make your standard choices as broad or as narrow as your organization needs.

E-Quote and Order Management

Manage work flow and the purchase order approval process efficiently with the Premier E-Quote and order management features.

End users can use E-Quote to configure a purchase online, send a copy of the quote to another person in the organization for approval, and save the quote for up to 30 days.

Authorized purchasers receive notification of saved e-quotes via email and may review, approve and place orders online.

Authorized purchasers can select e-quotes from the list and order online.

Paperless Online Purchase Orders

With a Paperless Purchase Order Agreement on file with Dell, your purchase orders can be submitted electronically for instant order acceptance. You save time and paper!

View your purchase order online before placing, then print for your records.

Download your purchase order in text format to use for your internal purchasing system.

Buy a Dell for Home

If your organization qualifies, your Premier Dell.com website will include the Dell Employee Purchase Program store with great deals for your employees who want to purchase a Dell system for home use.

Order Status

Want to know the status of your order? Premier Dell.com will include Multiple and Single Order Status, which allow you to track an order from submission to shipping. (See Figure 9.2.)

Want to know the shipping details? If the carrier for your order has tracking information available on the Internet, the "Shipping Detail" feature automatically takes you to the tracking number and status information for your order.

Register for OrderWatch Service and you'll be alerted by email when your order ships.

Your Account Team

Have a question or need a problem solved? An updated list of the names, roles, email addresses, direct extensions, and fax #'s for your Dell Account Team is posted on Premier Dell.com. No more searching the Rolodex or calling outdated numbers!

Purchase History Reports

Purchase History Reports, updated daily, are available to authorized users on your Premier Dell.com. Need to know how many, what kind, and when they were ordered? Select from 4 different reports with 11 different pieces of information about each transaction. Complete info with a click!

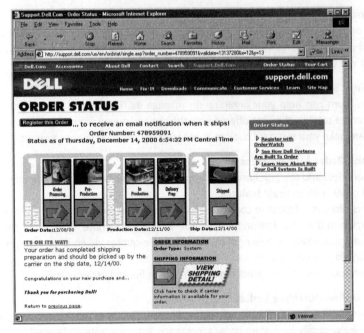

Figure 9.2   Dell shows you exactly where your order is at the moment.

Report Search lets you find information about a particular transaction by entering the PO number, the order number or the customer number.

Order Summary Report shows all invoiced and non-invoiced orders for up to 13 months. Just click on the order number box to view details and status of an individual order.

Invoicing

Premier Invoicing allows you to review your unpaid invoices online, 24x7. Want to find out if a payment has been posted? Want to reconcile your purchase orders and invoices? The information is at your command whenever you want it.

Standard reports let you view all unpaid invoices placed under credit terms.

ImageWatch

Available through Premier Dell.com, ImageWatch service gives you information about technology changes before they impact Dell products, allowing you to better manage and plan for technology changes in your organization. Contact your sales representative to identify whether your organization is eligible for access. (See Figure 9.3.)

HelpTech

HelpTech, available only through Premier Dell.com, gives your help desk access to all the information available to Dell technicians. Enter the Service Tag number to request technical information for a particular system, including Troubleshooting Toolkit, System Specific File Library, Knowledge Base and more!

1. System Specific Information Enter the system service tag # for your Dell product to access as-shipped system configuration information, the call status on any outstand-

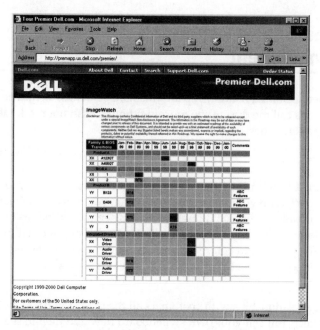

Figure 9.3 Dell lets you keep an eye on new, upcoming technology as well as when your current computers may be given thumbs down.

ing technical service calls, as well as a list of service parts and limited warranty information for your system

2. Multiple Program Simulator (MPS) MPS provides screen captures from the installation routines of common software. It can be used by your help desk staff to quickly find information and guide end users who are installing software on their local machines.

3. Service Call Status lets your technical staff find out the status of all service incidents for your organization.

Service Call Management lets your technical staff find out the status of all service incidents for your organization's customer number.

With Service Call Watch, you'll be notified by email of service call updates and changes.

File Library

The Dell File Library contains updates for drivers, utilities and BIOS that can be downloaded directly to your Dell system from your organization's Premier Dell.com. Register for FileWatch to receive update alerts by email.

Knowledge Base

Dell staff constantly documents information about Dell equipment from the manufacturing department, from end users and from technicians in the field. An extensive FAQ section covers products including CD-ROMs, modems, drives, computers and more!

Now imagine combining all of the above.

Getting Really Personal—Customer Relationship Management

> I'd like to see someone build a relationship antimismanagement system. The system shouldn't let reps call me during the morning (home) rush hour, ask me for credit-card information or pester me for 44 cents overdue.
>
> *Allan Alter, Computerworld Editor*

No Web site is launched fully formed for two important reasons. First, if you waited until everything was perfect on your site before launching, you'd get to the market far too late for your site to have the impact it might otherwise enjoy. Second, technologies and customer expectations are constantly rising. That means your site will never be finished. If you wait for completion before launching, your site will never see the light of Web. The sidebar titled *The Evolution of a Web Site* explains how most of us brought our sites to life.

Of course you manage relationships with customers all the time. You try to make sure your invoices are correct. You call your own switchboard now and then to see what it sounds like when your company answers the phone.

I sat down to a classic rubber chicken lunch at an industry conference, and the man next to me and I started chatting. He was from a company that writes operating system software platforms for wireless handheld devices, something I was interested to know about but didn't have an abiding desire to learn everything I could. Once he had deter-

---

The Evolution of a Web Site

From *Customer Service on the Internet* by Jim Sterne (John Wiley & Sons, 2000)

1. BROCHUREWARE

Also known as shovelware. This is when you wander into the literature room with a snow shovel, scoop up as many brochures as you can, fling them onto the scanner and voila!—a Web site is born. It contains product information, company information, press releases and maybe some investor relations stuff. Yawnsville.

2. CUSTOMER CONSIDERATE

Somebody in customer service realizes they can post information on the Web that might actually be useful to customers. Up go the Frequently Asked Questions pages and the Troubleshooting Guides.

mined that he wanted me in his database, he asked for a business card. As he took it from me and handed me his, he asked me for my birth date. I was a bit surprised—so much so that I told him. As he wrote it on the front of my card, I asked why he was interested. "So we can send you a birthday card," he answered, as if it were the most obvious thing in the world.

I've gotten used to getting birthday cards from my dentist (time for another check-up!), from my insurance carrier (time for another check-up!), and from my financial adviser (time for another check-up!). But come September, I'm going to get a birthday card from a wireless operating system software company, and I'm just going to scratch my head. Customer relationship management is something best done carefully, one step at a time. A relationship is grown, it isn't bought. A relationship is built over time, it's not achieved by collecting 37.5 bits of data about an individual.

But what if? What if your extranet had different features for different visitors based on the following?

- Industry sector
- Job responsibility
- Level of influence
- Size of company
- Degree of training
- Depth of understanding
- Previous purchases

3. E-MAIL OVERLOAD

Once customers realize there are things you could have put up on your site, they start the barrage of questions. Where's my order? Do you have an alternative? Who do I talk to about that? The Webmaster tries to handle it but soon turns it over to the call center. The call center realizes e-mail is a different animal and tries to get the IT department to help out with some automation.

4. EXTRANET

Now fully focused on the customer, the IT department gets into the swing of things. Order processing, order status, business rules.

5. CRM

Customer Relationship Management. The brass ring on the merry-go-round. The Holy Grail. The pot of gold at the end of the rainbow. The Omega to the Web's Alpha. The hope of every marketing and customer service person who's ever tried to make Microsoft Excel work as a database.

- Number of Web site visits
- FAQs reviewed
- White papers downloaded
- Discussion depth with sales rep at industry trade show
- Customer service calls
- Customer service e-mails

Plus every other bit of information you ever collected about your customers.

What if you could consolidate all of the pertinent pieces of information that you collect at every single touchpoint? That's what I see as the Holy Grail. I define true customer relationship management as collecting all of the information about each and every customer at each and every touchpoint and making it available in real time at each and every touchpoint.

Touchpoints

A touchpoint is where the company and the customer come in contact. Some examples of touchpoints include:

- Advertisements
- Direct mail
- Trade shows
- Seminars
- Sales calls
- Retail stores
- Telephone calls
- Faxes
- Letters
- E-mail
- Web site

What does it mean to make this information available? If a customer receives a direct mail piece, it is specifically targeted to that individual.

You'd never again receive a discount coupon good only for first-time buyers if you've purchased the product before.

You'd never get a phone call asking you to subscribe to a magazine you've been reading for years.

You'd never have to sit through another presentation on how the vendor's company was founded because it would be able to see how many years you've been buying from the company.

You'd never be told the fundamentals of local area networks by the tech support people who would see that you are a Cisco Certified Network Professional.

You'd never be asked again about loading dock restrictions by your vendor's shipping department.

You'd never have to explain your problem to a series of people as they pass you from one desk to another.

The CRM Promise

The logic goes like this: If we can remember everything about our customers at the moment of contact, then we'll always be able to say "Yes, I can help you," instead of "Yes, I can transfer you to somebody who might know who might be able to help you."

What's the result? Step one: faster service.

If the customer service rep or the sales rep or the Web site has all the necessary data, then he or she or it can take care of the problem pronto.

Step two? Higher productivity. That's followed by lower costs, which are nice, but the goals are higher customer satisfaction, which leads to increased retention, which engenders increased loyalty, which results in bigger profits.

You want another path to increasing the bottom line? How about bringing this whole discussion back around to marketing? What if you had all that information about all of your customers? Then you could run a Genalytics-styled analysis that would tell you exactly where to find people who are most likely to become your customers and exactly what to tell them that would most likely convince them to do so.

That's the plan. That's the big picture.

It's not too hard to imagine. It's not too much to ask. It's just not really easy to implement.

The CRM Problem

Let's start with the fact that information about your customers is scattered all over the place:

- Marketing database
- Sales contact management systems
- Shipping department data systems
- Customer manufacturing records
- Accounting system data
- Customer support call center system
- Web site interaction logs

All of that data is maintained in different systems by different departments, and bringing it all together in one database is only one-third of the problem. The next third is figuring out how to get it back out to the people on the front lines who need it the split second it's required. The final difficulty is determining just which bits of information are critical to the task at hand.

It's a technical challenge to move data from one place to another inside a company. Calling it a challenge does not mean that it's impossible; it's just going to take some doing. It's a technical challenge to pull out the right data and get it to where it can do the most good. It's going to take some real leaps of technology and business management to figure out which bits of information are the right bits. We don't want to end up with a sales rep picking up the phone and saying, "Sure I can help you, Ms. Smith! Just give me about 20 minutes to read your file . . ."

The biggest problem with CRM, of course, is that there are no hard and fast rules to follow and no return on investment formulas to use as guidelines. There's no end to the time, effort, and dollars you can expend. There's no ultimate "Winner!" square on the CRM game board to aim for. There's just the ever-ratcheting levitation of customer expectations, on the one hand, and the ever-regenerating supply of new tools and services, on the other.

When you get down to the tactical level, the way to assess ROI is downright boring:

1. Measure everything in sight.
2. Implement your new system.
3. Measure everything in sight again.
4. Compare the results from 1 and 3.

Like the Internet itself, customer relationship management systems are obviously a good idea whose time has come. How you implement CRM at your company is a question that will keep you and your consultants employed for years.

Countless Tools

In the second edition of *Customer Service on the Internet*, I included a list of categories of CRM-type tools and some examples. Since then, everybody and his brother who makes any type of data management system has slapped the CRM label on it. You simply cannot tell the players without a program.

Rather than create that program here, let me simply steer you toward ISM (www .ismguide.com) (see Figure 9.4), a consulting firm that has shouldered the responsibility to produce a Manhattan-phone-book-sized catalog.

The Process—What Does It Take?

How do you know you're off on the right foot when undertaking a CRM project? First, there's a little matter of self-evaluation. Barton Goldberg of ISM (www.ismguide.com) has been helping international corporations with CRM software selection for more than 10 years. He also helps them with business process reviews. Just where do you fall on Barton's CRM Process Evolution chart? (See Table 9.1.)

Figure 9.4 The ISM Guide to CRM Automation evaluates and compares the top 30 CRM software packages using 124 business, technical, and user-friendliness criteria.

Table 9.1 CRM Process Evolution

BROKEN	OK	IDEAL
No process ownership	Individual process ownership	Total CRM process ownership
Poorly defined or competing goals	Basic goals for individual process performance	Collaborative goals, including customer and support groups
Below-average performance (declining results)	Adequate perfomance (stable results, stay in business)	Exceptional performance (above industry norm)
Poorly defined, competing or nonexistent metrics	Basic performance metrics for individual processes	Well established metrics for individual and combined CRM process
Process interfaces nonfunctional (extreme silo mentality)	Primary and secondary processes interface "as required" to get the work done	Seamless integration between primary and secondary processes
Operating procedures nonexistent or nonenforceable	Operating procedures generally followed	Well-established CRM operating procedures that cross individual process "boundaries"
Significant individual process variations (cowboy approach)	Individual process variations within reason	High degree of process integrity Variability by design to serve customer and company needs
Out of touch with business direction or emerging strategic vision	In tune with business direction or emerging strategic vision	Actively support or lead business direction or strategic vision

Front Line Solutions ran a survey in 1999 asking companies working on CRM projects for their tips on how to put your best foot forward. In order of importance, the responses came back as follows:

- Get executive sponsorship
- Create a cross-functional team
- Get stakeholder buy-in
- Make the business need drive the IT
- Choose your vendors wisely
- Start with pilot projects
- Phase in as you are able

It has a lot to do with technology, but even more to do with resources, politics, and common sense.

The thing that *I* keep learning as I work with more and more companies is that technology is very good at solving specific problems. If you want to identify the most likely buyers, there's software that can do that. If you want to remember to send me a birthday card, there are systems available. If you want to have dynamic content served to specific people in specific ways based on specific criteria, no problem.

But if you want customers to be loyal and recommend you to their friends and spend more and more of their money with you—if you want to invest in some serious customer relationship management—invest in your people.

Getting Really Personal—Putting People Back into the Mix

Or "How I switched from being a loyal customer of one company to another," wherein our hero loses his faith in a tried and true vendor and regains his convictions of what makes a company great and worthy of his business.

Skin-Deep Beauty

I started getting the MacWarehouse catalog when it first came out in 1987. It was the first time I'd seen personalization from the *company* side of the equation. On the cover, there was a fresh, young, smiling, female face and a text bubble that said something like, "Hi! I'm Keri. I'm here to help you find the products that you're looking for!"

She was so sweet, and so earnest, and that picture graced the cover of their catalog—and then their Web site—for a dozen years. Inside the catalog, every page had another smiling face. "Hi! I'm Ken. I can help you with your networking needs!" and, "Hi! I'm Susan. If you're looking for a new printer, I can help!"

Figure 9.5 Once noted for the personal touch, MicroWarehouse is just another online catalog.

The people who answered the phone were bright, energetic, interested in the products and my needs, and reflected the enthusiasm projected by those eager faces. What great branding. I felt like I was buying from them and not just a company. But, alas, times change and so do companies.

The firm now mails out MicroWarehouse, MacWarehouse, Data Comm Warehouse, and Inmac catalogs. But today, Keri can be found only in a subthumbnail reproduction on the About MicroWarehouse page as part of the company history. The home page (www.warehouse.com) (see Figure 9.5) is devoid of Keri, and it is devoted to selling more stuff, rather than making nice.

I was sad, but took Keri's departure in stride. After all, things change. But I started having trouble with the company as a vendor and even went so far as to write about it, wearing my "Business 2.0 Website Critic" hat:

The Where Oh Warehouse
by Jim Sterne, Business 2.0, February 6, 2001

It was time to buy a new laptop online. I avoided price-shopping in order to avoid taking a chance on quality and headed straight to MicroWarehouse, where the cheerful smile of virtual salesgal Keri reassured me of her company's commitment to service.

I wanted the laptop with extra memory, a spare battery for intercontinental air flights and a bunch of other extras. Sadly, the site was out of stock. I resorted to the telephone where a nice man said, "Oh we have some. We ship out of a different warehouse."

I said, "Yes!" to overnight shipping and waited. The next day, I got the batteries, the external floppy drive, and the port expander. In other words, I got the hay, the oats, and the saddle—but no pony. Back to the phone.

"Oh—a mix up in shipping. Your laptop will be along in 5 to 6 days," said the not-quite-as-nice man. I asked for some consideration for the overnight delivery charges and he told me to call the shipping company. They told me to call back the MicroWarehouse man, who said he'd send me a certificate for $25.

When the laptop finally arrived, the packing slip enclosed indicated that my order for the external CD-RW has been cancelled. Back to the phone, where I heard, "Backordered beyond our time-limit, so we had to cancel."

I calmly explained that I was going to pack up all the stuff and ship it back. Within seconds, a supervisor explained how they had found an alternative unit, cheaper, with the same specifications and would it be OK if they paid the shipping?

Better. Much better.

The following week, I saw a cable adapter and a pack of CD-RW disks I wanted (a good opportunity to use my hard-earned $25 certificate). I placed the order as easy as you please. An e-mail came within moments telling me how I could check the status of my order online. So I went back to the site two or three times a day.

"Verifying CC Info," it said.

"Awaiting CC Auth," it said.

"Processing," it said.

"Pending Shipment," it said.

That sent me clicking to their "Definitions" page—"Your order is shipping direct from our suppliers. I went back to the phone to find out when these items would be shipped. "Backordered beyond our time-limit, so we had to cancel," said the now-grumpy man.

Two things occurred to me. First, expectations of online commerce are so high these days that all systems had better be good-to-go at a site before you dare sell anything. Second, I no longer think Keri's smile is about a commitment to service. How sad.

Sadder still is that I finally found Keri's picture again, the one I remembered so well. Only this time, it was smiling down on me from the top of my order cancellation page (see Figure 9.6).

Several weeks after the above article was published, I received the following:

```
From: YorkJ@MWHSE.com
To: jsterne@targeting.com
Subject: Your Article in the 2-6-01 Edition of Business2.com
Date: Wed, 24 Jan 2001 08:21:06 -0500

Jim, I am CEO of MicroWarehouse, and last night saw the article
referenced above. I want to make certain that we have taken care of your
needs, even though it has clearly been very "messy" for you along the
way for you. Susan Fazelpoor, our head of Customer Service will contact
you promptly if you can quickly email back your telephone number.
Secondly, it is obvious we have some work to do, particularly regarding
the way we handle backorders. I'm going to do a deep dive on this so we
can fix what appears from your experience to be broken. Thanks very much
for bringing this situation to our attention. (The ultimate mad customer
```

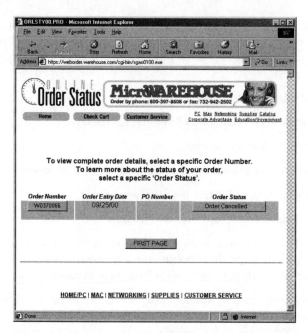

Figure 9.6   Keri seems to be smiling at my cancellation—the last time I'll see her.

```
doesn't let you know what is wrong, in hopes that problems won't get
fixed!) Best regards, Jerry York
```

Jerry did indeed call me and was very pleasant and very reassuring. He told me he considered himself the Chief Customer Satisfaction Officer and that he had already made some changes. Customers would be notified by phone. Additional training would be rolled out.

Then Susan called and was very gracious. "We'll get to the bottom of this" had a nice ring to it, and "We're really sorry" sounded heartfelt. I guess writing articles for magazines makes me something of a target for apologies in the eyes of industry. An honest apology is nice, but will Jerry's efforts have an impact on his organization? Will my next order go flawlessly? Time will tell.

Before that article actually hit the streets and the Web, another company gave me a call.

Personal Personalization

"Mr. Sterne?" asks a fresh, eager, young, female voice.

"Yes?" I reply with that tone of voice that clearly communicates that I know this is a telephone solicitation and I know I'm about to have my time wasted and this had either be a very good or very short call. Isn't the human voice wonderful?

"My name is Jenn Barr from CDW," which I instantly recognize as one of MicroWarehouse's competitors. Had someone at CDW read my article and seen an opportunity for some free ink? Nope. It hadn't been published yet. "We've noticed that you haven't purchased anything from our Web site in quite a while, and I wanted to introduce myself as your account manager and find out if I can set up an extranet for Target Marketing?"

During this enthusiastic introduction, I'm thinking:

It's been at least six months since I purchased anything from CDW.

They're being proactive. Isn't that refreshing?

They're tracking me and actively pursuing my business. Isn't that impressive?

They're willing to set up an extranet for me. Isn't that something?

They're giving me a personal account rep. Isn't that friendly?

Maybe I'm getting ahead of myself and reading too much into this. Maybe she's just a telemarketer along the lines of trade show booth window dressing who smile nicely but couldn't regale you with product knowledge if lives were at stake.

How can they afford to spend this sort of telephone time on a business that has only four computers and a fax machine?

So I say, "Sure."

And so begins my tour of the CDW site and the reaffirmation of my belief that as cool as technology gets, it's still humans that make the world go 'round. CDW has a little of both.

CDW Pushes the Right Buttons

Jenn Barr asks me to log into my very own extranet. I type in the user name and password she's given me and see that my company name is already on the page—the logo would come later (see Figure 9.7).

Jenn can see that I've logged in successfully. In fact, she can see my whole account history. She can tell when I last visited my CDW pages and how often I've been there. I, of course, can review any open orders I have. I can look at my account history. I can search and compare products at will and add them to my shopping cart.

But the thing that keeps surprising me is how human-oriented the features are. When I customize my account information, it's much more than just shipping and billing information. First of all I can, "Create Your List of Target Marketing Solutions."

> If you're Target Marketing's administrator, you'll be able to create a list of product standards which will be shown on this page. All of the extranet users will be able to see your list of preferred products, brands, and solution bundles.

So I can say that we're going to be using Brand X computers and Brand Y printers from now on and "all the other extranet users" can see and abide by my preferences (see Figure 9.8). I can create a 'bundle' for a new hire, and a different one for a new executive. While I can set up a list of my own preferences, CDW did not fall prey to the trap of creating a contact management system for one person—this is for my whole company.

Figure 9.7 CDW makes it very clear that this is the Target Marketing extranet. I already feel special.

I can set up an Employee Purchase Program so employees can get the same volume pricing discounts for their personal purchases that the company does. I can authorize specific employees to make purchase, or I can assign that responsibility to somebody else.

I can also authorize employees, or groups of employees to make company purchases. What are they allowed to buy? That's up to me.

Type of purchasing rules:

People Restricted

– Cannot checkout

– Or can make purchases with approval

Price Restricted

– Can purchase up to a specific dollar amount and no more

– Or can purchase up to a specific dollar amount and no more unless approved

Once I'd set up a group and set the rules for that group, I got an instant e-mail:

```
Jim Sterne, your CDW extranet administrator, has appointed you as an
authorizer for the CDW Purchase Authorization System. As an Authorizer,
you will receive e-mail if an employee exceeds their CDW spending limit.
    When you receive an e-mail, you will need to log on to CDW.com with
the user name and password below in order to approve or disapprove the
employee's order.
```

Figure 9.8　The company-wide preference list lets me standardize my company's technology.

The thing that really stood out on this site was that they brought Keri back. Well, not Keri herself, and not in that phony, "Hi There!" kind of way. Instead, they brought me Jenn, Adrian, Katie, Scott, and Louis (see Figure 9.9).

Jenn is my Account Manager and my Primary Contact.

> In addition to placing your order, call your Account Managers when you have questions or are seeking product advice. Their knowledge of your systems and your past purchase history allows them to make the best possible product recommendations for you and your company.

Adrian Steinke is my Sales Manager. I can get help and advice from him and place orders if I'd rather talk to a human than work the Web site.

Next comes Customer Service. Katie Prochnow is my Sales Support Manager. She is my:

> . . . contact for general CDW questions and concerns. If you can't reach your Account Managers, your Customer Service team can point you in the right direction.

Figure 9.9 My personal account managers and support people are just waiting for me to get in touch.

Next up are Scott, who is the Technical Support Manager, and Louis, who is the Technical Support Supervisor:

> With 24-hour, 7-day a week post-sales support, this team of troubleshooters has more certifications than we have room. Lead *(sic)* by Scott and Louis, they will help configure your system, walk you through general or specific technical questions, answer any Microsoft Windows and NT issues, and much more. If they don't know the answer, they will find out. Just call or e-mail.

CDW has the order desk phones manned 24/7. Its tech support desk is manned 24/7. Pick up the phone, buy products, solve problems—you name it. You're sure to get *some*body. But these people are *my* people. If I have a technical problem that isn't a quick fix, I may want to talk only to Scott because he knows what happened yesterday. I don't have to repeat myself.

I can call, I can send an e-mail, or I can chat. But if I want to be sure I get to the right person, I can wait until they are at their desks, logged onto the Web site, and ready to talk. How can I tell? It's right next to each of their pictures. It's either going to show "In" or "Out," and the choice to wait or talk to somebody else is mine.

My hopes are high at this point, so I decide to put Jenn to the test. "I want an external USB disk drive, Jenn." She walks me through the process of searching through thousands of hard disk products. I'm getting a lesson in how to use the site, as well as some insight into what Jenn meant when she told me she had three months' worth of training before CDW let her on the phones.

Good Help Is Hard to Automate

"Like having a personal wardrobe consultant!" That's what it says when you head over to the Lands' End Personal Shopper.

My Personal Shopper lets you access an expert shopper who suggests products that best suit your unique taste, style and preferences.

Create a personal profile.

It only takes a few minutes to create your own profile so that your Personal Shopper can suggest items and outfits to suit your style. Just provide us with some basic information about your clothing preferences so that your Personal Shopper is able to tailor recommendations just for you.

What size do you normally wear?

For which occasion would you like to create a profile?

Now you'll be guided through a series of image choices. Select the image that you feel best expresses your personal taste and dressing style.

Lands' End leads you through a series of choices. Do you prefer what the mannequin on the left or the right is wearing (see Figure 9.10)?

Many people have special likes and dislikes when it comes to fabrics, colors and styles. Please mark the items below which you would like to EXCLUDE from consideration. A marked box means you will not be shown clothing with that characteristic. Feel free to exclude as many characteristics as you like (see Figure 9.11).

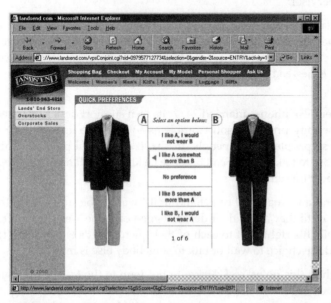

Figure 9.10　Do I prefer A over B? Well . . . I like the darker pants, but the pink shirt on the right just isn't me.

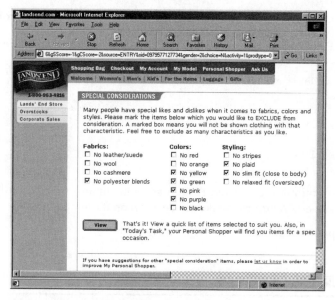

Figure 9.11 I really don't look good in green. Trust me.

Thank you for providing us with your preferences. Based on your profile, your Personal Shopper has selected for you the following items in a sample of recommended colors. To learn more about an item, click on its image (see Figure 9.12).

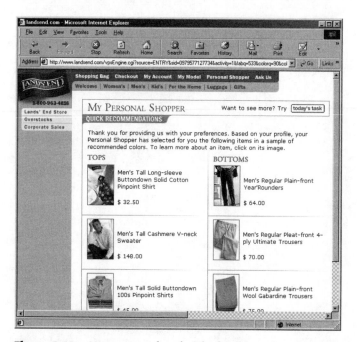

Figure 9.12 Here are my hand-picked fashions, but there's no way to tell them I cannot wear plain-front pants.

Yes, my Lands' End Personal Shopper is always there for me, but not very flexible.

On a Thursday evening at 6:30 California time I sent Jenn Barr at CDW an e-mail:

```
Jenn,
I'm trying to understand the difference between:
the HP JetDirect 170X
and
the HP JetDirect 170X OfficeConnect
besides $1.46.
What can you tell me?
Thanks
```

She writes back six minutes later even though she's in Illinois, in succinct English rather than tech-spec-eese, and I can make my decision on the spot.

That's the sort of personal personalization that matters.

Personalizing What Matters

The Internet is a communication tool. So is TV. You can tell lots of people lots of things. But the Internet is much more like a telephone because it is a two-way street. How should you use the Internet for personalization? Use it to connect your people with your customers and/or your customers' people.

Use the Internet to create, grow, and nurture relationships rather than manage them.

CHAPTER 10

Partner Relationship Management

T he first time I heard the acronym PRM, I was sitting in Kevin Nix's office in Redwood Shores at one of the most successful software companies south of Redmond, Washington. No, Kevin doesn't work for Larry Ellison. Siebel Systems (www.siebel.com) (see Figure 10.1) did well as a sales automation software company. Then it did very well as a call center software company. But when it turned its attention to customer relationship management, things really heated up. "Succeed with a new perspective . . . your customers!" has been the rallying cry of all CRM aficionados.

One would not expect a company like this to rest on its laurels. Kevin, the director of product marketing at Siebel, was telling me about a new slant on the customer angle.

"Customers live all up and down the supply chain," he told me, "and the buck starts at the end user. That's the person who drives the car, or eats the sandwich, or uses the computer. But there was a long line of vendor/customer relationships before that, and they're all business partners. So 'partner relationship management' seemed like a natural." The resulting product was Siebel Channel Applications.

> Siebel Channel Applications . . . supports the entire process of managing of partners over the Web. Siebel Channel Applications automate the business processes between organizations and their partners by enabling them to work collaboratively to market to, sell to, service, and retain customers.

Channel conflict has been the name of the game since it became apparent that manufacturers, which had always been dependent on their channel partners, could now sell direct online. But how do you sell direct on the Web and through other channels at the same time? Good old-fashioned channel conflict just took center stage.

Figure 10.1   Siebel's customer focus has made it a mainstay of customer-centric systems.

Let's get one thing cleared up right away. This is a marketing book. We're not here to discuss supply chain management, which is designed to manage the flow of goods and materials between raw materials excavators and smelters, manufacturers and assemblers, wholesalers and distributors, and finally retailers. We're here to talk about managing the flow of leads and sales from the raw materials clan through everybody who might get a piece of the action by trying to get end users to purchase.

Direct Sales Becomes Possible

Manufacturers were confused. They had the goods. They had the brand. But they didn't have the distribution network.

"Oh, that's OK, because FedEx and UPS will be happy to set up complete, tactical logistics systems for us."

They didn't have the relationship with the customer.

"Oh, that's OK, because the customer is going to do everything online now."

Didn't work out that way. The alternative was equally as faulty.

"We'll just direct the customer from our site to our distributor's site and let them take the sale as per normal."

That would be fine if there were a logical and fair way to divvy up the leads.

Some tried to sell products that weren't readily available through the channel, but that just frustrated the customers who wanted to buy regular, brand-name products. Some manufacturers tried selling under a different name as a competing retail outlet. Lead balloon. Some tried selling the same products with a new brand on them and found they were competing only against themselves.

It was clear that customers wanted to buy as easily and as quickly as possible. It was also clear that they wanted all the vertical market expertise, multiple product integration, consulting skills, semi-independent product choices, geographic proximity, and the other things that channel partners have provided for lo, these many years.

> Do you sell direct online?
> Wrong question.

> Do you let customers buy direct online?
> Yes—they were drawn to the brand
> Yes—they took the time and trouble to find you
> Yes—they want to buy from *you*
> Yes—they are ready, willing, able
> Yes—every additional click lowers their likelihood of buying

Customers don't care how the products get delivered as long as the order is placed, the products show up, and somebody can show up to help them set it up and fix it if it breaks. So what do you tell your channel partners? You tell them you're there to help them succeed, and you start rolling out Web-based features to prove it.

Give Them the Information

One of the biggest problems in working with channels is getting them the information they need to sell your products. From the other side of the fence, the hard part is getting the information they need to sell your products.

Now that we are all connected 24 x 7 and on all continents, a prospective customer can go to your Web site just as easily as to your reseller's site. That means the prospect is pretty well informed these days. If that customer calls on your reseller and that reseller doesn't even know as much as you have posted on your public site, it doesn't bode well for a sale.

Your PRM pages have to have more information, more specifications, more hints, tricks, and tips, and more customer service than your public pages or your customer pages. Unless, of course, you have in-house accounts—then *they* need to be treated like royalty.

When it comes to product information, these guys need to be able to read the manual, see the exploded diagrams, study the delivery schedules, and read the problem reports, just like the product managers inside your company. They need to know how long a given product is going to be sold and how long it's going to be supported.

Yes, I can hear the gnashing of teeth from here. I understand that you don't quite trust your channel partners with the keys to the data cabinet, but you're going to have to get used to it. The fact that this sort of information *can* be made available to them means that it *will* be made available to them. If it *will* be available then they are more likely to want to sell products from the companies that *do* make it available. Shouldn't that be you?

Give Them the Marketing Materials

It happens all the time. The gals and guys on the front line want to run a little local promotion. Maybe they're hosting a seminar. Maybe they're trying to hit their end-of-quarter numbers. They whip up a little ad for the newspaper or for their trade journal, and they stick your products in the ad.

They sort of look like your products. That sort of looks like your logo. That's sort of the description that has been professionally prepared, reviewed, edited, approved, and sanitized by the legal department. But it's not. In fact, some of it is flat wrong. How did this happen?

All they had to do was call you on the phone or send you an e-mail with photo-ready layout and typeset copy and you'd have run it up the flag pole, around the approval bend, and through the committee meetings in no time at all. A couple of weeks. What's a couple of weeks? Everything when you're trying to hit your numbers.

So those partners of yours aren't waiting. They're out selling.

What if they could log on, download, and be good to go? What if you had done all the heavy lifting in advance and laid it all at their fingertips? They would be more inclined to use your materials simply because it would be easier than dishing up something on their own.

This is where the idea of taking the extra step that we've covered for customers comes into play for your partners. The extra step, in this case, would be going to your partners, getting *their* logo art work, and creating a print-shop-friendly or magazine-friendly ad with matching right-reading-emulsion-side-up negatives and two sets of matchprints ready to ship at the touch of a button. If you want to maintain control over your image, provide the image.

Here's another step: Prepare the proposal. The boilerplate, the color laser printer images, the ROI spreadsheets, the corporate backgrounder all need to be reproduced every time. Why not do it in advance? Hand it to them on a silver platter, and they'll sell more of your stuff than your competitors' stuff.

Give Them the Leads

What are your partners forever complaining about? Lack of good leads.

Like any sales person, if they didn't' complain about a shortage of good leads, they wouldn't be good salespeople.

The problem is: How do you divide them up? Who gets the leads? There are several methods of handing out leads, and the best approach is to duplicate online whatever you are dong offline. One of these should work for you.

Territory

Who owns the turf the prospective customer inhabits? Get the site visitor to sign in by Zip code, and you're all set. Not that simple? You say your resellers sell into more than just one set of cities and they overlap? You say they've set up sites of their own and you can't control them?

The first place to look for an answer is in your agreements with your resellers. Yes, you must be nice to them no matter what or they'll start selling the competing brand, but what did they actually agree to in the first place?

Product Line

Barring a clean geographical division of labor, there's always the product mix approach. Some resellers are allowed to sell and service certain products, and some are not. This works well in the suburbs and the backwoods, but in the bright lights of the big city, you're going to have a battle on your hands. Your largest channel partners are going to be able to support your whole product line, and they're going to want some assurances that you're giving them leads just as good as you're giving the next guy.

Sale Size

Like controlling the dissemination of leads by product line, there is sheer size of sale to consider. Some resellers cannot deal with giant contracts for your products. But also like controlling by product line, this doesn't hold true for your most sensitive accounts: the big guys.

Round Robin

Some manufacturers have tried the simple round-robin approach. Line up the partners alphabetically, and when a lead comes in, it goes out to the next in line. Not a good plan. Never works.

Percent of Offline Sales

The only logical way to control leads on an equitable basis and maintain the goodwill of your partners is to combine these approaches and to give to each according to his or her ability.

If you have 150 resellers and one of them make 45 percent of your sales, then that reseller should get 45 percent of your leads. Appropriate to the reseller's location and expertise, of course, but in keeping with his or her offline sales volume. This motivates them to sell more offline.

Give Them the Tools

What if you made it easier to be a partner? What if you gave partners all the information they need about doing business with you, right at their fingertips? That brings us right back to the conversation I had with Kevin Nix at Siebel Systems. The product Kevin was describing is called eChannel. On their Web site, Siebel Systems described it this way:

> Siebel Partner Portal is a partner-facing application that enables a vendor organization to deploy a highly effective Web site for attracting and managing partners and for streamlining business processes related to partnerships. In turn, the partner portal gives partners access to critical information and the tools necessary to transact business with the vendor and its customers.
>
> Using the partner portal, partners can access functionality offered by Siebel eChannel. For example, users can search for opportunities, conduct eCommerce, manage service requests, manage market development funds (MDF), look up relevant literature and more (see Figure 10.2). In addition, the partner portal offers targeted and personalized news briefs and communications to partner users when logging into the portal.
>
> Siebel Partner Manager is a full-featured application that enables partner managers within a brand owner or vendor organization to manage the entire partner lifecycle process—recruitment, registration, profiling, certification, joint planning, execution, measurement and analysis.

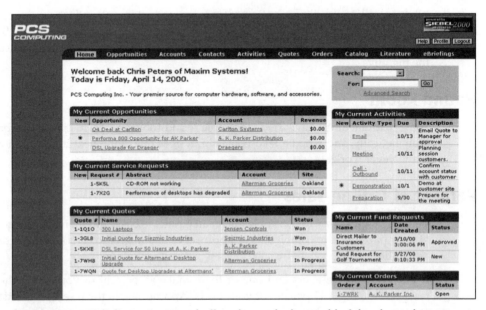

Figure 10.2 Siebel's Partner Portal offers the workaday world of the channel partner at a glance.

Let them sign up for their certification training online. Heck—let them *get* their certification training online. Let them take their tests online to maintain their good standing as certified expert solution providers.

Do you keep track of partners' sales in order to dole out the annual awards, trips, cars, and boats? Let them see their comparative scores online. Their competitive flame can be fanned to reach for a few more sales per quarter.

Then, of course, there are the online tools that you've been creating that you can hand over to your partners. Can somebody configure your products over the Web on your site? Then why not on your reseller's site?

Here's where an understanding of the basic functions of the Web come to the fore. If you have created a product configuration module, it's easy to lend that functionality to your resellers. The page that the end customer sees may look like your partner's site, as if it's coming from the partner's servers. In fact, it can be hosted on your servers in full or in part.

This concept comes in very handy when it's time to make the sale.

Give Them the Sale

One solution some manufacturers are using as a stopgap measure is to list their distributors on the site. They convince users to buy and then show them where the goods can be acquired. The drawback here is *procurus interruptus*.

The customer wants to buy. The customer is looking at the product he or she wants. Just when the customer is being told how your products are superior, just when the customer is learning about your excellent service, just when the customer decides to acquire your stuff, he or she can't.

If you make people take another step to order your products (call an 800 number, go to a local store, print out and send in a coupon) you stand a good chance of losing the sale. Steven Klebe from CyberSource has seen it over and over again. "In all the stores we've put online, the numbers come back proving it. For every additional click you force a user to make, you lose sales."

You might consider closing the sale by taking the order on your Web site and passing it along to the dealer or distributor nearest the customer. You might even set up a hierarchy of dealers who enjoy various levels of partnership based on sales volumes, co-op advertising expenditures, in-store displays, and so on. Top-flight distributors might even earn a page on your Web site promoting the other products they carry.

Polaroid Gets the Picture

Polaroid.com/play is for fun stuff. Household stuff. Kid stuff. If you want to buy a PhotoMAX MP3 camera you can click the "Where to Buy" tab and get a dealer locator. Then, if you live in Santa Barbara as I do, you'll have to drive at least 64 miles to buy one (see Figure 10.3). This is not a great solution.

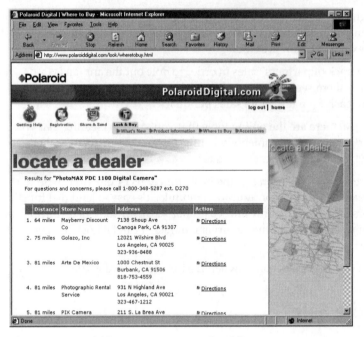

Figure 10.3 Whither e-commerce, Polaroid?

Polaroid isn't ready to run afoul of its retail channel partners. When there's a camera store every 10 minutes in the big cities, Polaroid wants to be nice to all of them. The article in the June 8, 1999 edition of *USA Today* said, "Polaroid.com last week began selling its $199 ColorShot and PhotoMax digital photo printers and likely will add scanners and digital cameras in coming weeks."

But the weeks have come and gone. Maybe by the time you read this, Polaroid will have figured out a way to sell consumer items direct. Maybe it will have picked up a few lessons learned from the business-to-business side of the house.

The business side of Polaroid takes shape at www.polaroidwork.com. There you can find Solutions Organized by Profession. You will see that the C-211 Zoom will offer digital still camera capture with a built-in photo printer, creating a new imaging category, *"digital printing cameras."* And you can click the "Buy Online" button to get your hands on one without getting in the car. The choices may be limited to Amazon and CDW, but the interplay between these Web sites is worth your attention (see Figures 10.4 through 10.6).

My wife and I were in Chinatown in San Francisco looking for a Mah Jong set. We'd been in a lot of different stores that all sported the $29.95 cardboard box with the plastic tiles made by the same factory. After the fifth stop, my lack of a shopping gene got the better of me and I asked the woman behind the counter if they had something a little nicer. She asked, "Bone and bamboo?" I nodded.

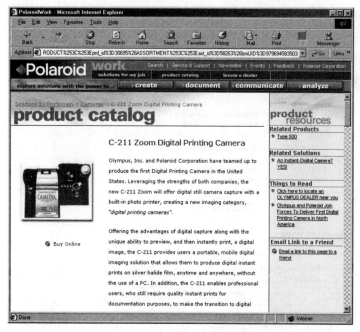

Figure 10.4   Polaroid offers to sell you this digital printing camera online . . .

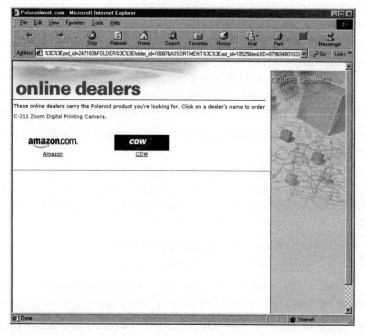

Figure 10.5   . . . and the partner choices are slim . . .

Figure 10.6 . . . but the results are most satisfying.

This eighty-something-year-old shopkeeper, in the middle of a bustling city, walked from behind her counter without so much as locking the cash register, said, "Follow," and headed out into the street.

My wife and I looked at each other and scrambled out of the store trying to keep pace with this grandmother. She scampered past three stores and into another, turned right past the first display, and stopped halfway down the aisle. "This one," she said. "Very good," she said. "Not antique, but bone and bamboo. Good touch." She smiled at us and scampered back to her own store. We were nonplused.

After buying that very set, we went back to her shop for a tea set, a dozen chopsticks, a silk robe, and six rice bowls.

Polaroid didn't leave me with a map to a retail outlet. It didn't even leave me standing at the home page of a partner's Web site. It recognized my desire to buy, took me by the hand, and led me to the very page on its partner's site where I could simply click on the "ADD TO CART" button and be on my way.

Even better, the handoff was so smooth that CDW welcomed me as an old friend. Notice the "Log Off" link in the upper right corner.

And what of Amazon? Oh yes, I got the very same special treatment, recognized as I came in and even offered my choice of 1-Click shipping destinations (see Figure 10.7).

For those who are concerned that anybody could go from Polaroid to Amazon or CDW as Jim Sterne and make a purchase, rest assured that it's all within my control. I had

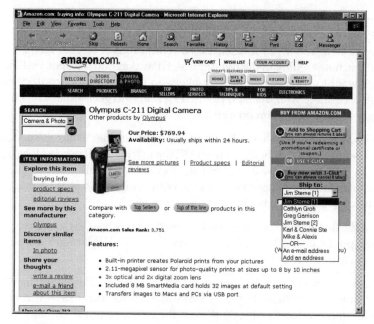

Figure 10.7 Amazon welcomed me with open arms as well. Aren't cookies wonderful?

previously logged into CDW and turned the 1-Click feature on at Amazon. It's quite simple for me to reverse both of those settings at any time. For added safety, both of these features have timers. Don't do anything on the site for a certain period of time? They'll log you off for you.

But what if your partners aren't as sophisticated as Amazon or CDW? What if you have a couple of hundred resellers who are good at what they do but are not so hot online? That's the problem that Hewlett-Packard's large-format printing department faced in the beginning of 2000.

HP Goes the Extra Mile

I started by consulting with the Hewlett-Packard's Inkjet Commercial Division in Barcelona at the start of 2000. That division is responsible for the large-format printers that have become well and truly wonderful in their power and capability. Its offices are lined with five-foot-by-seven-foot "posters" that look like photographs. The staff likes to hand their visitors a jeweler's loupe for closer inspection.

The Barcelona group understood a very important distinction when it comes to creating a personalized Web site. Rather than looking at the marketplace from the top down (from market segment to regional district to vertical market to product application to individual customer), they decided to collect all the data possible in order to build a picture of their marketplace from the ground up—one customer at a time. More about this approach in the next chapter.

In the summer of 2000, I was contacted by Rudy Herrera, who is responsible for marketing programs for the HP Designjet Sales Center in San Diego. Rudy asked me to help flesh out a new initiative for resellers. With hundreds of resellers selling and servicing these machines selling in the five-figures, HP was agonizing about selling direct. But it didn't want to compete with its resellers—a classic channel conflict situation. How do you encourage your dealers/partners/resellers to get online? The HP answer was, finally, you hand it to them on a silver platter.

Step 1: HP declared online sales to be as good as offline sales as far as services were concerned. If somebody bought direct from HP, the machine still needed local support. HP makes the sale (see Figure 10.8), and the local reseller still gets the installation, training, maintenance, and supplies business. With competition putting margins on a never-ending diet, the service business is the profitable side.

Step 2: The Affiliate Program on Steroids. HP created a full-boat, e-commerce site filled with all their products and handed it to its resellers. But HP thought it through one more step—it created one online store for *each* of its resellers.

If you're shopping on a reseller Web site and want to buy an HP product, there's a link to what HP calls the HP AisleOnline. It looks like the reseller's site—it acts like the reseller's site—the products arrive as if from the reseller—but it all happens on HP servers and is fulfilled by an HP contractor (see Figures 10.9 through 10.11).

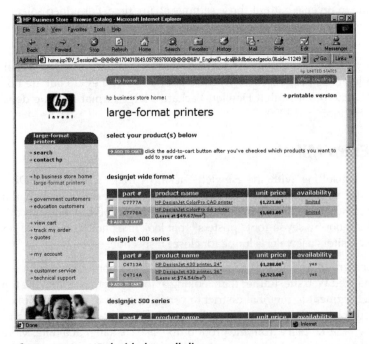

Figure 10.8 HP decided to sell direct . . .

Figure 10.9 . . . as well as create an online HP "aisle" . . .

Figure 10.10 . . . for the Web sites run by its many resellers.

Figure 10.11   Resellers need only point to "their" online catalog and HP does the rest.

The reseller does nothing but supply the necessary logo.gif to make the e-commerce site its own and plug in its own pricing (with the ability for the reseller to put in contract pricing for specific customers).

Oh, and one more thing—it's free. A gift from HP to its partners. Co-op marketing was never like this.

OK, yeah, sure, fine, Jim, but what if you're a retail store chain? Sell direct?

Ace Hardware Aces It

The right question is: Do you let your customers buy direct? The answer must be, Yes.

Ace Hardware partnered with OurHouse.com to offer 220,000 products online (see Figure 10.12). Unlike Polaroid, it was not paranoid. But like HP, it didn't want to hurt its channel stores: its life blood. So Ace *does* sell direct, but it also drives store traffic. It publishes in-store promotions on the site. It encourages people to go to the store and talk to that "friendly hardware man."

Like, HP, Ace set up independent store Web sites for free. Do you want to shop at the big Ace Hardware store in the sky? Fine. Would you rather click over to your neighborhood store? Great. Online sales are made by OurHouse.com/Ace, and revenue is

Figure 10.12   Ace Hardware customers demanded to buy online.

shared with the stores. Ace also pushes people into the stores from the Web site (see Figure 10.13).

But Ace didn't stop there. It did exactly the same thing—in mirror image. If you go to the store and you can't find what you want or the item is out of stock, no problem. Just wander over to that Ace kiosk over there, look it up, and click to buy.

The obvious question is about return on investment. The obvious answer is that if you are dependent on your channel partners for local services then they *are* your customers and the same rules apply: You must be dedicated to making them successful.

The not-so-obvious answer is that you may gain much more than sales.

Get the Customer Intelligence in Return

One of the benefits to turning the supply chain into an information chain is that information can run uphill as well. A manufacturer wants to know everything there is to know about its twice-removed customers. Now it can find out—if it can convince its partners to participate.

If knowledge is power—if knowledge is an asset—then sharing with outsiders must be wrong. Think about this from the ground up:

Figure 10.13 Ace Hardware (via OurHouse.com) *wants* you to go to the store.

- The customer doesn't want the salesperson to know all of his or her buying plans.
- The sales rep doesn't tell the dealer everything about the customer.
- The dealer gives information to the wholesaler only on a need-to-know basis.
- The wholesaler doesn't trust the manufacturer, who might sell around him or her.

The whole point here is to get information flowing in both directions in order to help all sides. The more the middlemen know about their market, the better they can service it. But how do you get them to give up information freely? Education is the answer. The question is: What's in it for me?

Replace Inventory with Information

This is where we dip down into supply chain management, or material handling, or whatever you want to call it. The sharing of information up and down the partner chain means lowering the amount of stuff (material/goods/atoms) in the system.

If the manufacturer knows what the wholesalers' forecasts look like, if the wholesalers can get their hands on the distributors' projections, if the distributors can take a look at the proposals flowing out of the value-added reseller's shop, then everybody can tighten his or her just-in-time deliveries and save a few thousand dollars.

Everybody ends up stocking and replenishing using a real perspective of real customer desires based on real information from actual customers.

Replace Random Leads with Solid Prospects

Even those hardest to convince, salespeople in the field, will come to understand the value back to them, if they are willing to share some of that hard-earned customer information. They've spent many years in the trenches learning children's names and golf handicaps, and that will never change. That sort of personal information really does make a difference when two people are sitting opposite each other and building a personal relationship of understanding and trust.

But all the other information (stock levels, growth trends, market shifts, etc.) can mean a great deal if it is harvested in the field, brought back to the threshing house for milling, and ground into nourishment for the field workers.

Take the data collected by the salespeople and send it up the chain to the manufacturer. It can run 16 kinds of analyses and come up with some aggregate information that can make the difference between a sale and a loss.

The manufacturer can start sending reports back to the field, indicating how to handle the 150 leads that came in for this territory:

- These 6 have the highest likelihood of buying within the next 20 days.
- These 12 are 40 days out.
- These 50 need to be called within 5 days to follow up.
- These 25 should be sent the nice brochure.
- The rest should be sent the cheap flier.

If that type of reporting is based on the information gathered at both ends *and* on feedback from the field about the follow-on interactions with those contacts, it will become more and more accurate over time. The phrase "You sent me crummy leads" will be a statement of fact instead of mere grousing.

PRM Best Practices

Like most things on the Internet (aside from answering your e-mail within 24 hours), PRM requires some thought. Every bit of information you collect is going to cost you something to collect it, store it, retrieve it, and make decisions based on it. That means you can't just jump in with both feet.

In May 2000, Bob Thompson of Front Line Solutions (www.frontlinehq.com) released a report called ePartner2000 Best Practices. Based on interviews with 35 companies, Bob identified what it takes to get partner relationship management done right. If this list sounds like the rules for getting CRM done right, then you've just realized how hard it can be to implement a major software system.

Business Executive Sponsorship

Business executive formally sponsors the project, provides direction on the specific business goals to be accomplished, and resolves critical issues.

Requirements Analysis and Planning

Project team performs a thorough analysis of short- and long-term requirements, soliciting input from all key stakeholders, but especially channel partners.

Right Solution Partners

Project team selects solution partner(s) based on the strength of the technology and commitment to services and support.

Project Team Staffing

Project manager staffs the team with competent and committed professionals, with expertise in all critical functional and technological areas.

Phased Implementation

Project team implements a pilot or prototype first, then rolls out applications and user groups in phases.

How well do you get along with your channel partners? How much can you do to make them more successful? The answers are different for every company. But if you make it your business to give them the best tools possible, they will make more sales for you.

And yes, I know, even after you do *all* of these things, your resellers are going to come back to you with one question: Got any more leads?

That brings up an important question: What are you doing to bring more people to your site?

CHAPTER 11

Attracting Attention

Posted by the author to inet-marketing@einet.net, Tuesday, April 18, 1995, in response to the question: Is simply setting up a Web page enough? How do you let people know about it?

> Shout it from the roof tops. Write it in the sky.
> Promote until your budget pops, until they all surf by.
> Announce in proper newsgroups. Mail directly through the post.
> Fire up the sales troops. Televise the most.
> A 1-800 number won't get you any calls.
> Unless you advertise it and paint it on the walls.
> Put it on your letterhead. Put it on your cards.
> A Web site will be left for dead unless it's known on Mars.
> Your Web site can be funny, pretty, useful, crisp, and clean,
> But if you don't promote it, its message won't be seen.

Each day we are hit with thousands and thousands of commercial messages. The newspaper and the morning shows during breakfast, the billboards and the delivery trucks on the road, the signs on the sides of the buses and buildings we pass along the way, all blend together in a blur of commercial broadcasting.

Every day we see new ways of delivering advertising messages. I was surprised when I first saw ads for the movie *Titanic* on large bags of popcorn at the local movie theater. I didn't expect to see advertising on the little plastic dividers between my purchases and

Figure 11.1   Green freeway advertising is cheaper than a billboard and environmentally correct.

those of the person in front of me at the grocery store. As you drive along California highways, you'll see that they have been "adopted" by local companies (see Figure 11.1). It made me wonder where all of it was going to stop (see Figure 11.2).

With technology changing so fast, will it surprise anybody when we see a press release like the one shown in the sidebar titled *Your Name in (Northern) Lights New Marketing Medium Announced*?

The people you are trying to attract to your Web site are looking for something of value. Something that is entertaining can be considered valuable. Something that improves their chances of gaining stature is valuable. Something that helps them achieve their goals is definitely valuable. You might offer the most helpful, useful, important, captivating Web site ever written, but if you don't let people know it's there, it will remain a secret.

You can let wired people know you are open for business on the Internet in several ways. You must, however, be very certain that everything is in its place and works before you let the cat out of the bag.

Figure 11.2   We can only hope that it never comes to this.

Your Name in (Northern) Lights
New Marketing Medium Announced

COMPANY SLOGANS IN THE SKIES BEFORE THE END OF THE YEAR

SANTA BARBARA, CALIFORNIA 4/1/01—Scientists have announced a new method of using the Northern Lights as a display for advertising. This latest development on the marketing front has large companies scrambling to be the first to sign up with a new service being offered by Target Marketing of Santa Barbara (www.targeting.com).

"It's essentially a breakthrough in ionospheric and magnetospheric physics," says Jim Sterne of Target Marketing. "Years ago, original studies had been focused on the use of low-frequency signals to communicate with space probes across vast distances, and now the Internet gives us a large enough platform to control the Northern Lights."

Computer models generated back in the early 1980s indicated that a blanket of loosely woven copper wire spread over a huge area could generate controlled pulses. The intent was communication with spacecraft that had left the solar system. Low-frequency communication has long been used to communicate with submarines far out at sea. It was deemed impractical at the time, however, to construct such a system due to its enormous cost. Today the Internet backbone provides the platform, and the characteristics of modern routers and switches provide the controls.

The clock rates of modern computers and the use of interference pattern techniques can generate signals between 400 and 500 GHz. These signals interact with the ionosphere and can be tuned to cause alterations in Northern Lights contours. Target Marketing plans to display the first commercial messages in Northern Lights one year from the date of this announcement. This announcement has started a bidding war among several corporations.

In individual press releases, Scott McNealy announced a new virtual machine called Javlcicles, Microsoft announced Windows NL, and AT&T and Earthlink have petitioned the FCC for new frequency auctions. Bill Gates was overheard wondering how many programmers it would take to make the Northern Lights appear over the lower latitudes.

Wait Until You're Ready

There are a million details to consider when you launch a new product. Timing the press release, the brochures, the advertising, the direct mail, and the trade shows is nerve-wracking at best. If the brochures show up a week late the leads may pile up, but there's no real harm done. If you announce a new Web site or an additional service on your site and the site's not ready, the harm may be irreversible. People are going to look at your new site within seconds of an announcement—literally. Think about your reaction if the site you want to visit isn't ready.

While you are working away on your computer, a small beep or some other alert indicates a new e-mail message. It's from the SCUBA diving list you subscribe to. You've recently posted a question about diving in the Cayman Islands, and you are hoping for an answer. Instead, it's an announcement about a new Web site dedicated to Caribbean diving. You're interested; maybe there's information there about a hotel you're considering.

You click on the link, and it pops up your browser. Half a minute goes by, and you are greeted with a large "Under Construction" sign. "We'll be up and running soon!" Thinking to check it out later, you add it to your bookmarks and hold a grudge against the fools who announced something that wasn't there.

Two days later, in a normal review of your bookmarks, you come across this dive site address and try it again. Again, you find the site is still not available yet. You delete it from your bookmarks. There are so many resources out there, so many Web sites to see, and so many varied entries in your bookmarks, it's overwhelming. You gave the site a shot—two, in fact—and it blew it. Never again. Plan your announcements carefully.

Public Relations

The days are gone when you could make a big noise and garner editorial attention just for being on the Internet. At first, editors were pleased to write, "A Flower Shop in Cyberspace," "Digital Equipment Corp. Offers Online Test Drive," and "B of A First Bank on the World Wide Web." Just being on the Web is no longer cause for this type of consideration.

If you are the first one in your niche to go online or if your Web site offers something unique, you can still get some attention in the trade press in your industry. This sort of mention lets the rest of the world know your firm is a cutting-edge organization with a crack team of advanced thinkers on board. This is a distinctive measure of successful Web marketing.

A well-positioned Web site may harvest ink in your industry trade journals for being technically fashionable. It is also a great place to communicate with the press. A "What's New" section is a standard selection on most corporate Web sites. This is the area that shows off new products, your latest announcements, seminar schedules, and news. News and announcements lead to press coverage.

Letting Them Know

Mass e-mailing press releases directly to editors and writers has been a bad idea ever since it was possible. In February 1995, Kim LaSalle, then of LaSalle Communications in Indianapolis, posed the question to a number of journalism discussion groups. The results were mixed. The majority of those responding didn't care to have their e-mailboxes filled with unsolicited releases that didn't pertain to their specific focus. The same can be said about their fax machines and in-boxes. If it's a well-targeted item, within their area of expertise, they want to know. They all agree, however, that electronic mass mailing is more bane than boon.

E-mail systems are getting smarter these days, and editors are learning how to set up filters to keep from being drowned in electronic press releases. So how do you get your message to the right reporter at the right time? If your product or service revolves around the Internet, try Eric Ward (www.netpost.com).

Eric has been in the online world of public relations since the start of the commercial Web. At first, he focused on helping large companies figure out how to get links on other Web sites to point to their home pages. He soon found himself competing with Web sites offering automagic services. Those sites let you type in a description that is blasted out to hundreds of other sites, letting them know you have something of interest on your site.

Eric is more of a relationship manager than a technologist, and when he expanded into the press release business, he kept it that way. Here's how he describes what he does:

> In a nutshell, my mission for my clients is to build *inbound links* to their sites from any number of places on the Internet. My approach to building awareness and *link popularity* is based on several techniques, including but not limited to:
>
> - Announcement strategy based on your site's content
> - Submitting far beyond just search engines and directories
> - Submitting to appropriate online media contacts included
> - Holistic submissions based on a site's features
> - Every submission done individually, by hand
> - Thousands of reviewed and cataloged submission outlets covering hundreds of topics
> - Online and printed campaign report provided
>
> My NetPOST service begins with me looking through your Web site and then, based on the content, features, and intended audience, I search and identify the very best and *most appropriate* outlets to submit your site information to. These submission sites include the very best search engines and directories, and far, far more. A NetPOST campaign will also include submissions to human reviewed directories and site collections, site reviewers, Web news filtering services, On-line Web zines and Email-zines that announce and review Web sites and Web events, Web announcement mailing lists, print magazines that focus on the Internet industry, newsletters, E-digests, Web-digests, print Web directories, online service directories, Book/CD link combinations, etc.
>
> I also identify and submit to industry specific reviewers and submission sites. Every step of the campaign is carried out by me, not a machine or unknown account executive.
>
> The above technique is proven to work. It is exponentially more effective than just submitting to every search engine and directory you may find. The directories and search engines should only be one component of your awareness plan, or you are wasting your time.

Eric Ward made a name for himself because he focused on the Internet industry. Whatever industry you're in, you should be able to find a PR company that knows the editors and knows whether they like paper, fax, or electronic press releases.

Filling Them In

Once notified that something is worth looking into, editors can check your Web site and read all about your latest endeavors. They can also copy your text and paste it directly into their articles. This is a wonderful time-saver for them. It might also increase the likelihood of your message's duplication, rather than its interpretation.

As more and more companies set up Web sites, more and more journalists are visiting for the latest news. Journalists also find your site useful for background information. Your description of the company history, your presentation of the corporate mission, your gallery of the senior executives, and your electronic links to other Web sites of interest can all contribute to any given editorial mention.

If press relations is one of your goals, consider the types of publishers who would access your site. Provide them with the appropriate electronic components—text, images, sound bites, and video clips. The easier you make it for editors to put together a story, the more often you'll appear in print. One look at the Intuit Just For Editors page (see Figure 11.3) will show you how to do the job right, all the way down to screen shots ready for downloading and printing.

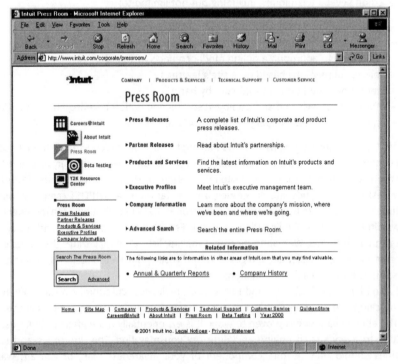

Figure 11.3   Intuit knows how to cater to the press at its site.

Keeping Them Interested

Announcing a new site is one thing, but what do you do for an encore? How do you keep new surfers coming? This is where your people with experience in event marketing come into the picture.

The most fun part of creating a Web site is the tremendous number of creative ideas it engenders. The most aggravating part of creating a Web site is the tremendous number of creative ideas it engenders. You are going to end up with dozens of interesting, useful, and exciting things you could do on your Web site. You won't have the budget or the time, so you will need to keep track of the best ideas for rolling out later.

A Web site is always a work in progress. You don't just create it and it's done, like a brochure. Think in terms of a newsletter, a TV show, or a monthly seminar. Each item you create can live forever on your server. When an item grows old and stale, it needs to be replaced. That's why I grind my teeth whenever I see an "Under Construction" sign. Of course it's under construction!

New features can offer an opportunity to make another announcement if the new content or service you are offering is noteworthy; this is Public Relations 101. If you have a compelling story that editors will be interested in, they will be interested because their readers will be interested. If their readers are interested, then they'll tell others. The nifty part about the Internet is that you can go directly to those readers and they can tell others at the speed of light.

Announcing in Newsgroups

Used carefully, newsgroups can be a great place to launch a Web site due to the tremendous word of mouth they engender. The key word here is "carefully." Electronic word of mouth is unlike anything you've experienced before. As Ron Richards of ResultsLab (www.resultslab.com) puts it:

> Discussion-group word of mouth is capable of causing product and service appraisals to be distributed with amazing speed and breadth. Sellers must have an interactive Internet presence to compete, and once they have it they are operating in a fish bowl. I've seen products soar, or be destroyed, in just months from it.

If you post to rec.bicycles.racing that your new Web site lists all of your bicycle products, you are sure to incite flames. If you're putting up a Web site that lists bicycle races around the world, you will have no problems whatsoever announcing it in rec.bicycles.racing. However, you are sure to incite flames by posting this announcement to rec.bicycles.tech.

Stay on Topic

People in rec.bicycles.tech may retaliate, and the results can be unpleasant. Consider a real-world allegory. A man runs into a room and shouts at the top of his lungs, "We won the Super Bowl!" If the room is a sports bar, this newsbringer will be greeted with cheers and invited to join other celebrants. If the room is a quilting session of octogenarians, this interloper will be sized for a white jacket that fastens at the back. Be sure to announce where the news will be well received. How can you tell? There are two ways to get a clue: the FAQ file and reconnaissance.

Almost all newsgroups have a frequently asked questions (FAQ) document that is posted regularly. This digest will include the answer to "Is it OK to advertise?" Almost all newsgroups answer this question with a simple "No." Others will provide qualifications. Ignore these rules at your peril. Posting an aberrant message reveals that you have not read the FAQ or, worse, hold it in contempt. The unpleasant response can be damaging to your reputation, your Internet access, and your person.

Reconnaissance will go a long way toward helping you understand the microculture of the newsgroup where you want to place your announcement. Read the newsgroup for a few weeks. See what others are posting, and assess how the group responds.

The Penalty for Misbehavior

The tale of Laurence Canter and Martha Siegel has become legend in cyberspace. Known as the Green Card Lawyers, they were the first to abuse the ability to post to thousands of newsgroups with the push of a button. The wrath they incurred and the price they paid are lessons to all of us. They were warned, they were cautioned, and still they ridiculed Internet customs. In their book, *How to Make a Fortune on the Information Superhighway,* Canter and Siegel describe how they advertised their services for helping noncitizens fill out applications for the Green Card Lottery.

Canter and Siegel started off on the right foot by participating in the alt.visa.us newsgroup. People had specific questions, and they knew the answers. They were willing to share their knowledge, and the result was great. "Within a day or so our electronic mailbox overflowed with individual immigration inquiries. People we had never met wanted to hire us as lawyers."

Then they tried an experiment. They posted an ad for their services in about a hundred alt.culture.(country) groups. In their own words:

> Hundreds of requests for additional information poured in. . . . We also received our first "flames." . . . A few individuals did not like the fact that we had posted our notices to a number of newsgroups. We were informed that when you post to newsgroups, you must post only on the topic of the group. "What," someone wanted to know, "does the Green Card Lottery have to do with alt.culture.japan?" Others advised us to look into "Netiquette," the informal code of behavior certain people believe must be observed when you operate in Cyberspace. Still others were not so polite.

Undeterred by this negative response, Canter and Siegel widened their operations. They posted to 1,000 newsgroups and then to 6,000. Each time they were met with flames and ill will. Each time they ignored the signals and shrugged them off. You'd almost expect these people to walk gladly through a Japanese home in their hiking boots, raise their voices when their host could not understand them, and insist vehemently that their host bring them a knife and fork for their dinner—even after having been told that these are contrary to local customs and good manners.

It doesn't matter if you think your actions are proper; it matters what your clients think. You must respect the culture of whatever country you're in, even if it's that newly founded realm called cyberspace. The result of their continued breach of Netiquette harmed them and others around them.

> Call after call came complaining about what we had done . . . . The amount of (electronic) mail was particularly staggering because a number of protesters decided to do more than just apply bad language to the situation. Instead, they sent mailbombs, huge electronic files of junk designed to clog up our computer by their sheer size.

This clogging shut down the computers at Canter and Siegel's Internet provider. When data overflows a disk drive, the computer objects and goes into a coma. After the system operators rebooted the system, thousands of additional flames were waiting. This actually happened several times. The access provider terminated Canter and Siegel's account. Canter and Siegel went elsewhere and experienced the same situation. The sad part is that many others were using those access providers as well and had their service interrupted for days on end. Thousands of people were said to have requested information just to make Canter and Siegel spend money on brochures and postage. It was rumored that a program was written to dial Canter's pager every 20 minutes between the hours of 1:00 A.M. and 5:00 A.M.

The stories of revenge enacted by indignant Netizens range from the simple to the unbelievable. Net lore is often spurious, but it is also indicative. In a population this large, there are sure to be those with an equal but opposite sense of right and wrong. They may also possess the ability and desire to carry out such acts of revenge.

The lesson for the unsophisticated marketer is that unconsidered postings can cause direct personal harm. The lesson for the rest of us is that unconsidered postings can destroy any good will you have tried to foster in the Internet community. Do everything in your power to stay off the Blacklist of Internet Advertisers (see Figure 11.4) (http://math-www.uni-paderborn.de/~axel/BL/).

Newsgroup Participation and Signatures

Canter and Siegel started off on the right foot. They answered specific questions. They were helpful. They received serious leads this way. That was before they learned to spam the newsgroups with their ads.

Let's say you make espresso machines. You read the alt.coffee newsgroup. When somebody posts a complaint about the difficulties of frothing milk when making latte, you are helpful. You offer a few tips on the fine art of holding the wand just below the surface so that the steam pulls in air as very fine bubbles. Then you mention that your company's Web site has complete frothing instructions in a variety of formats from line drawings (they load quickly) to ShockWave animations (they're more explicit) to video clips of Orin Smith, CEO of Starbucks, personally showing you how it's done. This is offering specific help for a specific problem. You are a participant, not an advertiser.

Wait for a question you can answer. If somebody asks about an upcoming regional bike race, you can write to the group with the answer and add a short "By the way, we have a Web site where you can find all sorts of biking information."

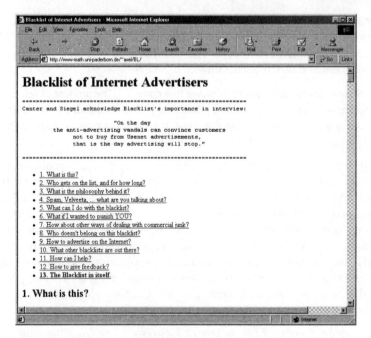

Figure 11.4 This is a good place to learn from others' mistakes.

The best approach to newsgroups is to become a frequent poster. Through your participation in newsgroups, people will recognize you as a voice of reason. They will read your postings because they are always well thought out, considerate of others, and helpful to the group. Spend a few months sharing helpful insights and advice, even asking a few interesting questions. In time, people will equate your wisdom with your company and your products. This name recognition is achieved through the use of a signature.

Every e-mail or posting you send can include a prewritten, several-line chunk of information. Your signature is like your letterhead or business card. It may contain your company name, phone number, e-mail address, and personal quote, along with your corporate slogan. It may also contain "Come see the latest at our exciting new Web site at http://www.xyz.com."

It's best to keep your signature as short as possible. Mine is borderline:

```
Jim Sterne            Target Marketing of Santa Barbara
jsterne@targeting.com        http://www.targeting.com
Author, Speaker, Consultant          +1 805-965-3184
Internet Marketing & Customer Service Strategy Consulting
Subscribe today to the mostly monthly "Full Sterne Ahead"
```

Above all, remember the public relations aspect of posting to newsgroups. Select the individuals who will represent your company in newsgroups as carefully as you would select those who would be interviewed on television. Public written announcements, statements, and comments need to be clean and to the point. They need to be proofread to ensure that every http and : and // are correct. Should you have enough of a following, you might consider creating your own newsgroup.

Announcing on Lists

An e-mail list acts just like a newsgroup. The only difference is that your message goes directly to the participants. Instead of their having to go to the newsgroup, your message is delivered directly to those who subscribe to the list. At first this sounds like the direct marketer's dream come true: Self-selecting people with a common interest have all expressed a desire to talk about things that relate specifically to your industry. Posting to lists, however, requires as much restraint as posting to newsgroups, sometimes more.

A list subscriber doesn't look at postings during a free moment as the newsgroup reader does. The subscriber is barraged with messages all day long. People in large organizations who belong to two or three lists will routinely receive more than 100 e-mail messages per day. Your announcement comes right to their screen. It had better be on topic.

Yes, Liszt at www.liszt.com *is* the right place to go to find lists (see Figure 11.5). The "advanced search" at Yahoo! is a good place for newsgroup searches.

Search Engines

How are people really going to find you on the Web? Four ways are possible; a fifth is probable. They might type in your domain name (www.your-company.com) because they saw it in one of your regular marketing media. They might hear about it from a friend or on a list. They might click on a link from another Web site that points to your

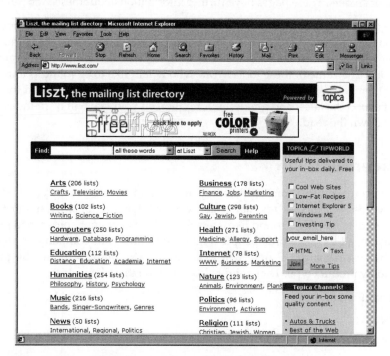

Figure 11.5   Liszt is a great place to find, well, lists.

site. They might see a banner ad you have placed on other Web sites. But chances are very good that they will hunt you up in a search engine.

IMT Strategies (www.imtstrategies.com) surveyed 360 Web users in the United States over 18 years old and asked, "What is the primary way you discover new Web sites?" Almost half said search engines (45.8 percent). The next largest group was word of mouth at 20.3 percent, which was pretty close to random surfing at 19.9 percent. Magazines came in at 4 percent, and with 2.1 percent, "by accident" beat out newspapers, television, e-mail, banner ads, other, don't know, and radio at the bottom with 0.4 percent.

Seems like the search engines are worth some of your time.

It Wouldn't Be a Web without Spiders

It has often been noted that the worst thing about the Internet is that you can't find anything. Seek and ye shall . . . become confused, become lost, become frustrated. It's like having access to the entire Library of Congress with no card catalog. It's like having all the information in all the Yellow Pages at your fingertips but no index. If you're out for a spin, it's fun; if you're looking for something in particular, it's not.

Because this is a known problem, skilled minds have been at work building solutions. That is how the World Wide Web has attracted spiders. According to the Web Robots Pages (http://info.webcrawler.com/mak/projects/robots/robots.html), web robots are programs that traverse the Web automatically. Some people call them Web wanderers, crawlers, or spiders. These pages have further information about these Web Robots.

What are they doing out there? Collecting information. Their goal is to provide some sort of indexing for a chaotic Internet. These automata visit Web sites, study them, and bring the results back to their databases. The value of these tools to the searcher is tremendous. The value of these tools to one who would like to be found is immeasurable. But there are so many Web sites that these engines are always behind the times. You can't expect the latest and greatest information on your site will be re-indexed 6 to 10 weeks down the road.

Creating Spider Food

Obviously, you want to attract spiders to your site and have them list you first when somebody goes out to look for that which you sell. Laying out tasty spider food is much easier than making a sound like a female spider. Begin your spider food production by listing all the keywords people might use to find your company or products. Do you make keyboards? People will look you up by company name, by product name, and by product type. They might also search on these keywords:

- Keyboard
- Keyboards
- Peripherals

- Input devices
- Keypad
- Touch screen

Oh, and don't forget key board, keybaord, keybroad, and keeboord.

You might also want them to find you if they search on *computer services* or *installation* or *repair*. Give it some thought, and create as long a list as possible. At that point, you can start hiding the keywords in plain site around your Web site. Different spiders work in different ways, but some basics prevail.

Home Page Title. Your home page is a document. That document has a title. That title is what appears in the very top of your browser window, in the actual browser header bar. The title is not the first words on your home page, but the words that are HTML coded as

```
<title>These Are The Most Important Words To A Search Engine! </title>.
```

Make sure the title of your home page, and every other page on your site, is the best combination of words you think people will search for.

Meta Tags. The next HTML code you can make use of is the meta tag. These words will not be visible to the human surfing your site, but spiders will pay attention. Don't forget to add a <description> on your page. This won't be rendered by the browser either, but it will show up as the description of your site on the search engines.

First Paragraph. Spiders look at the first paragraph on your page as the most significant. They assume that if you really have something important to say, you'll say it right up front. The tricky part is making this paragraph meaningful to humans while peppering it with spider food.

Proximity. Do you sell tennis shoes? Then a home page that talks about tennis shoe styles and tennis shoe sizes and tennis shoe brands will get listed higher by the search engines than people who sell "shoes specifically designed for tennis." The proximity of the words "tennis" and "shoe" makes all the difference. The repetition doesn't hurt either.

Variations. Shoes, foot coverings, sandals, boots, you name it. Search engines are getting smarter by the day.

Search engines are getting more and more sophisticated, and you have to keep up with the changing times. One of the more progressive means of getting your site to the top of the stack is with cash.

If you want to be the first one listed at GoTo.com when somebody searches for a "home loan," you're going to have to cough up more than Ameriquest Mortgage (www .ameriquestmortgage.com) is willing to pay (see Figure 11.6).

Amazon has started doing the same (see Figure 11.7).

A search on Amazon for "internet marketing" brings up books in the center column based on an unpublished algorithm that might be based on how popular the book is,

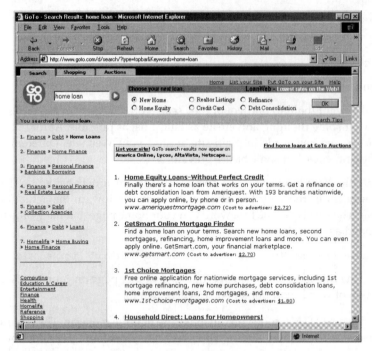

Figure 11.6 Every time somebody clicks from GoTo.com to Ameriquest Mortgage, it costs the mortgage company another $2.72.

Figure 11.7 How much is it worth to have your book appear when somebody does a search?

how big the profits are from its sale, and how much the publisher paid. But the books on the left are displayed according to a very published algorithm: cash on the barrel head.

If you'd like to dock my Amazon account my three and a half cents, just search for books on Internet marketing. I have no idea if this placement is making a difference in sales; I only know that "internet marketing" is a popular enough topic on Amazon that my 100,000 points, for which I paid $100, will last about two weeks.

When it comes to paying for search engine listings, the answer is easy: It depends on how much you pay. But with search engines that rank sites based on inconsistent algorithms, the question still remains: How do you rate?

How Do You Rate?

STACKING THE DECK, by Jim Sterne
From *CIO Magazine*, December 1997

The content is cool, the GIFs are animated, and the back-end applications are tightly bound to the server. And yet, in spite of the time you've invested, you seem to have created a stealth Web site. All that wonderful functionality is going to waste because nobody can find you.

It's not that nobody knows you exist: Your brand name is widely recognized. But when people use Internet search engines to find you, they come up with 126,023 links to other sites that mention your company, your products or services, or your subject matter. The actual link to your site is number 126,021.

What's a Web site owner to do?

Stuff the ballot box, of course!

Search engines are highly pragmatic. They don't all work the same way but are, by nature, very programmatic. They look at HTML document titles, meta tags, text, links, referrals—the works—and they pigeonhole what they find. In so doing, the search engines actually evaluate your site for the prospective customer on the other side of the mouse.

It's not hard to finagle the search-engine rankings to get a better slot at or near the top of the page. But that raises an interesting problem, which occurs right where three distinct needs converge.

First comes the need for Web site publishers to make their Web sites visible. After all, you're doing those searchers a service by helping them find you. Right?

Next, there's the need for search engines to provide the most balanced possible view of the Web. Why is that important? Income. Survival. To understand this one, you also have to understand the third piece of the convergence: what searchers want.

Typically, searchers need only one thing. Actually, that's the problem: they need one thing, and they end up with 126,023. So they hope that AltaVista, Excite, Infoseek, Lycos, WebCrawler and other search engines will be beacons in

continues

How Do You Rate? *(Continued)*

the dark, lighting up that one-in-a-million page with the single bit of information they want. They depend on the engines to rank their findings according to a strict meritocracy.

If searchers cannot find what they want at a particular engine, they will stop going there. If they stop going there, the engines can no longer sell advertising. If search engines can't sell advertising, they greatly diminish their prospects of ever making a major initial public offering.

So let's tally the score: Search engines and searchers need the purest databases possible. But pity the poor Web site that nobody can find. Isn't there a middle ground? Isn't there something you can do to shine more light on the site in which you've invested so much?

To start, you can take some simple, virtually foolproof measures. Title your home page something other than the ubiquitous Home Page. Use meta tags— HTML coding that, among other things, describes a Web page's content—to provide a description of your site that search engines can display. And keyword tags, which let you identify words searchers are most likely to use to find you, can incorporate those important phrases that don't quite fit in the description or on the home page. A men's footwear retailer, for example, might include the following terms in the keyword tag: shoe, shoes, wingtip, brogan, dress shoe.

There are also some things you should not do. Don't overstack the deck. If you use the same phrase too frequently in your keyword tag, the search engines will simply kick your entries to the end of the list. And don't use trademarks registered to others; several lawsuits have already been filed over such infringement.

What's the right formula? Depends on whom you ask. If you've been on the Web more than 10 minutes, you've already gotten spammed with bulk e-mail from people promising to help put your site in the top slot in all the search engines. If you prefer professional help, consider turning to resources like Web-Ignite (www.web-ignite.com).

Anybody can use keywords to steer site traffic. Simply fill the meta tags with sexually related idioms or a few celebrity names and the words "Microsoft bug," and the hits will keep coming. But if you want to attract people who are genuinely interested in your products, then you need to track what happens after they hit the home page. Web-Ignite will concentrate on keyword phrases that attract the people who dig down deep rather than those who just hit and run.

You come up with a technique that puts you at the top of the list today, and you're going to have to check back tomorrow to see whether you're still king of the hill. If not, it's time to create a new technique. You could spend your life doing that. Or you could outsource it to a company like Web-Ignite. But is it the right thing to do?

Unsolicited e-mail is wrong. Yes, it is commercially viable. Yes, a small investment for a bulk electronic mailing can yield a large return. But it's wrong to sad-

dle users with paying access fees and phone charges to download huge packets of junk mail.

When it comes to helping people find your site, I'm not on such solid moral ground. If you can create a better Web site, you'll be more successful. If, like Amazon.com Inc., you can afford humorous radio ads that draw more people to your site, more power to you. If you can build a better banner and place it on the exact spot on the Web to draw searchers to you, well done! If you have bright minds working for you who know how to target direct (postal) mail to drive traffic, then I want to hear from you. So why not offer kudos to those who know the ropes when it comes to keywords?

Because deep down, I want my Web search experience to be pure. I want to find only those pages that really meet my needs, not those that just want to grab my attention.

But the real world now includes ads on public television and interstitial pages in content Web sites. (Those are the ads that pop up between the time you click and the time the page you wanted finally shows up.) So I guess I'll get used to the idea that the first few pages of my search results will be spattered with the efforts of those who know how to manipulate the system, hoping they're also among those who best meet my needs.

Where Do They Search?

Media Metrix (www.mediametrix.com) likes to keep track of the most popular Web sites. According to its survey in March 2000, Yahoo! gets twice the traffic as Lycos, which gets 25 percent more traffic than Go.com, which beats out (in descending order), Excite, Alta Vista, Snap.com, Ask Jeeves, LookSmart, Goto.com, and Iwon.com. But don't forget about Google.com. It's an up-and-coming search engine.

Also don't forget that there are people out there creating industry-specific search engines. Talk to your largest industry associations. If they don't have such a thing on their own sites, they probably know who does.

Make Them Show You the Money

In May 1997 Viaweb (www.viaweb.com) released a study comparing the amount of money spent by online shoppers coming from different search engines. Per-capita spending varied surprisingly between search engines, differing by as much as a factor of 3.

The study examined more than a million visitors arriving at 132 sites made with Viaweb software during a 120-day period from mid-December 1996 to mid-April 1997. Viaweb's tracking tools showed that traffic from search engines generated an average of 17 cents per visitor in online sales, with individual search engines ranging from 10 cents to 31 cents (see Table 11.1).

Table 11.1   Search Engine Value

SOURCE	VISITORS	SALES	SALES/VISITOR
Excite	226,321	$26,478	$.12
Infoseek	217,448	$26,170	$.12
Webcrawler	179,551	$17,943	$.10
Yahoo!	170,522	$53,553	$.31
Alta Vista	164,369	$37,067	$.23
Lycos	24,895	$5,302	$.21
HotBot	16,917	$2,513	$.15
Total	1,000,023		
Average		$169,026	$.17

All search engine traffic is not created equal. Clicks from each are not worth a constant amount. It's nice to get lots of traffic, but it's great to know the value of that traffic.

Links from Others' Sites

Another way to attract people to your Web site is by literally sprinkling the World Wide Web with links to your home page. People looking at travel tips for Hawaii might find a link to your surf shop in Maui. They might find your coffee shop by visiting the Caffeine Archive (www.caffeinearchive.com) or come across a link to your shoe store while looking at the Tap Dance home page (www.tapdance.org).

Beg a Link

The first way to get a link on somebody else's page is to ask for one. Simply ask. Often, Web builders just want to create a resource for their constituents. If your site offers something of value, it's in their interest to point to it as a service. If another site builder is not willing to create a link to your home page, then perhaps he or she will create a link to some piece of information on your site. A computer repair organization might think it's a grand idea to link to your discourse on how diskettes are manufactured.

Borrow a Link

. . . and pay it back in kind.

If you have a Web site of interest to a cooperative marketing partner, you might ask about creating a reciprocal link. A vendor or supplier will quickly see the benefit of this kind of a deal. "Our products are made from some of the best <u>stuff</u> on earth," would link to the company that supplies some of your components. Conversely, your page could boast, "Our parts are used in some of the <u>best products</u> on earth." We all like to talk about our success stories and show examples of our products in use. Host a link to microbreweries in exchange for corresponding links to your beer stein factory. Perhaps a chiropractor will include a link to your vitamin shop.

These links may be even further removed from the day-to-day. Have a contest and give away somebody else's product as a premium. Create a reciprocal link to that vendor's site. Discuss a topic that's important to your company but not central to it, perhaps the environment, and point to sites associated with that topic.

Hired Help

It doesn't take a huge company to pay attention to selected newsgroups, post announcements, register your Web site in directories, and send press releases to the right editors. You'll remember Eric Ward (www.netpost.com). He describes his services this way:

> My primary activity is conducting personalized, content-specific awareness campaigns for significant Web launches, Web-based events, and Web-based promotions. My method to accomplish this is a combination of carefully researched and selected URL submissions, along with matching your Web launch/event news to *exactly* the right Internet media contacts, editors, writers, reporters, site reviewers, news outlets, news headline services, etc., that are appropriate for your particular news. As a columnist myself for *Ad Age* magazine, and a 40-hour-a-week Web user, I have an experienced sense of how Web sites and their intended audiences find each other.
>
> You cannot short-cut or automate this process and succeed. The quality comes by looking at the specific content of your site, and then taking the time to research, locate, and submit to outlets that are a perfect match for it, based on its subject, content, and features. This is time-consuming to do, and I thrive on the challenge of it. No two campaigns I have ever done were identical, or could they ever be. The submission campaign I did for Amazon.com Books was far different than the one I did for Rodney Dangerfield's Rodney.com.
>
> My focus is on targeted, content-specific launch submission campaigns to the exact outlets that
>
> a) make sense for your site
> b) seek submissions, and
> c) represent a legitimate chance for coverage, review, or inclusion
>
> These include:
>
> General search engines
> Search engine special guides (Lycos AtoZ, Excite Channels, etc.)
> General directories
> General announce sites
> General announce mailing lists or newsgroups as appropriate
> Search engines specific to your site's industry and content
> Directories specific to your site's industry and content
> Announce sites specific to your site's industry and content
> Announce mailing lists or newsgroups specific to your site's industry and content
> Human-reviewed Web indexes and guides, both general and in your industry
> E-zines
> Web-zines

E-digests
Print Internet magazines
Print Internet guides
Internet News Sites
New syndicates
Web Filtering Services
Web filtering agents
Popularity Trackers
Content Ratings Services
Content Recommendation Agents
Topical Web forums sites
Internet TV and radio shows (at shows like CNet Radio, TechTalk, NetTalk, and others,
    my clients are featured regularly)
Print yellow page Web directories

OK, so I'm obsessive about it. I am constantly seeking and evaluating the best of MANY DIFFERENT possible submission sources. And while I do include search engines and directories, these are only a small part of a legitimate awareness-building campaign, and sadly, search engines and directories are all that most folks submit to. This is such a shame, because the majority of the best opportunities for awareness come from sources that *aren't* search engines. I actually do a custom search for outlets for my client's campaigns based on the site content; thus no two campaigns I do are ever the same.

I choose not to get involved in reciprocal linking pursuits, nor paid listings, nor submissions with other strings attached. If you need these, we should talk by phone about my consulting services where I can help you learn how to pursue these more knowledgeably on your own so you don't get taken.

I have clients and references in seven countries.

I take on limited clients, and you don't see my banners slapped all over the Internet in search of business because I have plenty, solely via word-of-mouth and referrals. Rather than attracting everyone to me, I prefer to attract people to my clients and their sites. I will candidly tell you right up front that there are no silver bullets for Web site promotion. Every site has different needs. This is the fundamental failure of any type of auto-submitting services. Your site needs to be evaluated and campaigned for based on its content and merits.

To me, the act of building awareness of a Web site is a process, and an art.

I provide this excerpt not to promote Eric's services, but his ideas. He's been at this since 1994, which, you'll recall, was when the National Science Foundation first dropped out of the picture and removed the Acceptable Use Policy stating there shall be no commercial traffic on the Internet. In other words, Eric was the first. He's also right on the money. Just look at that list of places he researches for postings.

Do It Yourself

If budget, time, scope, or just plain orneriness is keeping you from seeking professional help, there's a Web site you should know about. Danny Sullivan has been covering search engines since late 1995. He did some research, posted some of it to the Web, kept adding to it, and Search Engine Watch was born (www.searchenginewatch.com) (see Figure 11.8).

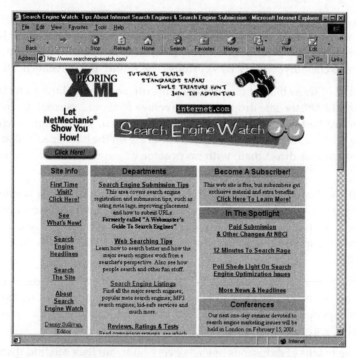

Figure 11.8 Search Engine Watch tells you how all the major search engines work and how to post to them.

Buy a Link—Banner Ads

You see banner ads wherever you go. Any site that has sufficient traffic is selling (or trying to sell) banner ad space. The way sites sell that space varies, and some interesting models have emerged. Where you place your ads will have a significant impact on the response you get, and there's already some interesting technology out there to help. Finally, there are some tried and true ways to increase your response that have been discovered by going out there and giving it a try.

But before we dive into the different ways you can pay for an ad banner, we'd better talk about whether banner ads are a good idea at all.

Nobody Clicks on Banner Ads Anymore

Just because something doesn't do what you planned it to do doesn't mean it's useless.

Thomas Alva Edison

Actually, people *are* still clicking on banner ads—just not as much as they did in the beginning. The beginning, to hear some tell it, was that first banner ad that showed up on the Hotwired site for AT&T. "Have you ever clicked here? You Will."

Of course, the ad was an instant winner. The Web, back in October 1995, was all about exploration, and the several hundred people who had Web sites were always checking out what others had done to see if there were new ideas in displaying information or enticing people to click. Everybody was curious. The result? 100 percent clickthrough.

People soon tired of these blatant attempts to sell stuff, and the clickthrough rates fell. Between 1996 and 1998, the rate dropped to an average of about 2 percent. By that time, corporate America had cottoned to the fact that there were lots of highly educated, higher-income folks out there, and they started pouring on the banner ad dollars. With rates about the same as direct mail, with no postage or paper costs, this online thing looked great.

Still, the clickthrough rates continued to slide. If you have to show your banner ad to 400 or 500 people to get a single click, then it no longer looked like the cool new idea that was going to reshape advertising as we knew it. But that's only if you compare today's banner ad response rate to the glory days of gray backgrounds and less that 100,000 Web sites.

How many people drive by your billboard on the highway every day? How many people hear your ad on the radio? Do you even *remember* seeing an ad in this morning's newspaper? Still, people are buying this advertising space and for significant amounts of money. Why? Because ads work.

They don't bring in tens of thousands of leads every hour, but they can find themselves in front of the right people, at the right time, with the right message. They also create brand recognition, given enough repetition.

It's understandable, then, that the number of banners is increasing. An AdRelevance (www.adrelevance.com) survey reported a record 65 billion ads served in December 2000, up 21 percent over November of the same year. Amazon is said to be the winner in the ad placement and expenditure game. When you spend $61.8 million in one month (December 2000), you deserve a tip of the hat. Heck, Barnesandnoble.com only spent $23.8 million, and it was second.

Don't despair of banner ads. They work. Just make sure that you don't expect them to carry more weight that they can.

Before we reveal how you can make a better banner, let's look at the different ways you can buy them.

The Four Basic Business Models

There are four basic ways ad space is sold, and they differ significantly. You can buy based on the number of times your ad is shown, the number of times somebody clicks on your ad, the number of qualified leads resulting from those clicks, or a commission on sales. Your choice.

Impressions

A freeway billboard is sold based on impressions. Television ads are the same way. You pay on a CPM (cost per thousand) basis.

But the Web is different in one important way. With all the others, the more impressions, the more you pay. On the Web, the better identified the audience, the more expensive the impression. If you want to show your banner to a thousand people, it can cost anywhere from $5 to $50, maybe even $100. Why? Because the $5 crowd just happens to be there—they are the random crowd. Imagine there's a billboard on the highway and a thousand people go by. Five dollars, please.

Let's say that you sell golf carts, and the only people who drive down that highway are the purchasing agents, buyers, managers, and owners of golf courses. As Ron Popiel would ask, "Now how much would you pay?" Don't answer yet! Because we can slice and dice that audience up even finer. Where are they from? What time of day do they drive? The more selections you make from a magazine subscribers' list, the more it costs. Web sites that specialize in a particular type of visitor can charge more to put your banner in their face.

For some, that's just not good enough. Procter & Gamble started it when it told Yahoo! that it was going to pay only when somebody actually clicked.

Clickthroughs

You saw my ad? So what? You clicked on my banner and came to my Web site? Now we're talking!

There are two major flaws and one great benefit with this approach. The first flaw is that it allows for free branding. When somebody sees your logo, it makes an impression. Whether that person picks up the phone, or drives to your store, or clicks on your banner at that very moment is beside the point. Branding is about building trust over time. Many studies have shown that Web site ad banners create, build, and secure branding. The clickthrough model disregards the value of branding by not asking for payment on delivering an impression.

Ali Partovi, the vice president for business development at LinkExchange (since acquired by Microsoft), has a strong grasp of the value. He says that in tests for The Internet Antique Shop, it put up a banner that said, "Collectibles. Click Here." It scored ever so slightly higher on the clickthrough rate than another banner that said, "Collectibles.net. Click Here." The obvious choice was to go with the latter because it included a branding message.

People who see the first banner may not be interested in looking at antiques right now. But if they might be interested later, there's no way for them to find that banner again and click on it. Had they seen the second banner, they had a good chance of remembering what Web site to visit. I know I did—three months after the fact.

The second major flaw with clickthroughs is that the seller of the banner space has no control over the creative. You could design and test a banner that got as few clickthroughs as possible. Then the site owner would have to let you run your banner for years until it fulfilled the requisite number of clicks. All the while, your company and/or product name is there for all to see.

The one great benefit, of course, is for the buyer. If you're buying, ask for clickthroughs. Just make certain the numbers reported are audited and correspond to the numbers you get in your server logs. Paying for artificial clicks does not make for good advertising.

Leads

So you don't want impressions and you don't want clicks? How about leads? A lead is counted when somebody clicks on a banner, goes to your site, and fills out the form. Name, address, buying habits, time-to-purchase—all the information that tells us this is a qualified buyer. Can it work? Yes. Can it be profitable? Ask Sherri Neasham.

Sherri runs FinanCenter (www.financenter.com) (see Figure 11.9). After you spend time configuring the loan that's just right for you, you can apply for that loan online. When you do, FinanCenter sends your application to a mortgage lender, who pays Sherri a nice little bounty for bringing you in.

Actually, it's not so little. Consider the cost of finding somebody who wants to borrow money. You advertise, you do direct mail, you hang cardboard fliers on door knobs. What does that cost? How many people does it bring in? Divide the former by the latter, and there's your cost per lead. In the mortgage industry, the answer turns out to be in the hundreds of dollars. To the mortgage company, Sherri Neasham offers one of the least expensive ways around to find potential customers.

The people at CyberGold (www.cybergold.com) are banking on the same concept (see Figure 11.10). Let's say it costs you $25 worth of marketing to get the name and address

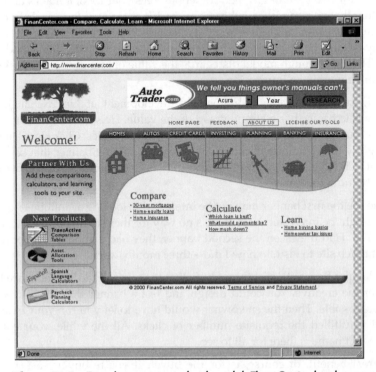

Figure 11.9 Based on a pay-per-lead model, FinanCenter has been profitable since 1995.

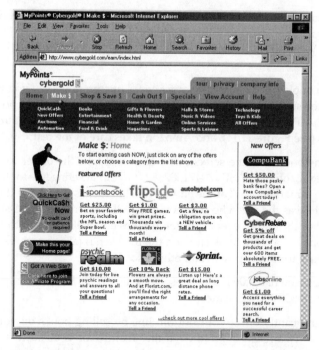

Figure 11.10 CyberGold pays you in cash to read ads.

of one person interested enough in your services to read your brochure. Would you be willing to spend $2 instead? Sure you would.

Paying people to read ads sounds completely backward. Aren't ads the things we put up with so we can get our content for free? This thought pattern caused George Gilder to say, "That proves they're not ads. They're minuses!" As an advertiser, you simply pay CyberGold (now part of MyPoints.com) for every person who is willing to read your ad, visit your site, fill out the form, enter the contest, or whatever it is you want them to do. In their own words:

> Your attention is valuable, and you deserve to be paid for it.
>
> MyPoints Cybergold is working to create "win - win" exchanges between consumers and marketers. We are making it possible to literally pay for attention.
>
> MyPoints Cybergold is your "attention broker". We find advertisers that want to pay you for your attention. As with any trusted broker, participation is completely voluntary and privacy is protected absolutely. You can opt out at any time, and no advertiser will ever get your name or email address.
>
> The site you see today is only the beginning. MyPoints Cybergold technology will also match ads and other online information to your personal interests and demographics. We envision a world in which "every ad is a wanted ad".

Sales

You can forget about impressions, clicks, and leads and go for the gusto: sales. It works on the Web just as well as it works in the physical world. The first example was

Amazon.com's Associates Program that debuted in the summer of 1996. The concept is so simple as to be laughable, and the implementation has been brilliant. You want to sell books from your Web site? Become a retail storefront to the Amazon.com back-end delivery system.

Let's say you wrote a book called *Customer Service on the Internet.* Let's say you wanted to sell it from your Web site, but you didn't want to have to take orders, box books, and open an account with UPS. The Amazon Associates Program awaits. Just put up a link to its site from yours (see Figure 11.11), and Amazon takes care of the rest.

Notice the URL at the bottom of the screen. One click will take the buyer to http://www.amazon.com/exec/obidos/ASIN/0471382582/targetmarketingA/ to buy the book. Notice the "targetmarketingA" at the end there. That means if you buy the book, Amazon.com can tell I was the one who sent you and will send me a commission of 5 percent to 15 percent at the end of every quarter. It takes about 10 minutes to sign up and start earning money as a retail book store on the Internet. It takes a serious out-of-box thinking experience to come up with something so elegant.

By the end of 1996, Amazon had 4,000 associates. In January 2000, *Fortune* reported that Amazon had more than 350,000 associates.

Are you going to significantly affect your bottom line by selling books on your Web site? No. Why bother? Two reasons. First, it's a nice feature for your customers and prospects. We're all looking for recommendations. More important, however, is that it will give you a clue about putting the shoe on the other foot.

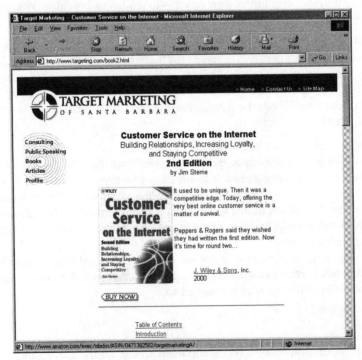

Figure 11.11 Buying a book from Target Marketing is just a click away.

Who might benefit from selling your products on their site? If they make fertilizer, they may want to sell your seeds—to encourage the purchase of their fertilizer. The company that sells batteries might want to promote your remote controlled submarine that requires eight of them.

If dreaming up these types of connections and contacting each of them seems like a daunting task, there's help at hand in the form of Commission Junction (www.cj.com) (see Figure 11.12).

Affiliate Marketing with Commission Junction lets you:

- Quickly join and set up a program with our Web-based application
- Work with an experienced and professional customer service team
- Work with an experienced and professional customer service team
- Partner with hundreds of thousands of Web sites worldwide
- Manage all of these marketing relationships seamlessly online
- Receive payments in your currency in one monthly check
- Rely on a trusted third-party tracking and reporting system
- Access our advanced ASP technology with one password and i.d.
- Find answers to all of your affiliate marketing questions online
- Focus on your core business while we provide the tools to manage your affiliate program
- Start increasing your online profits today

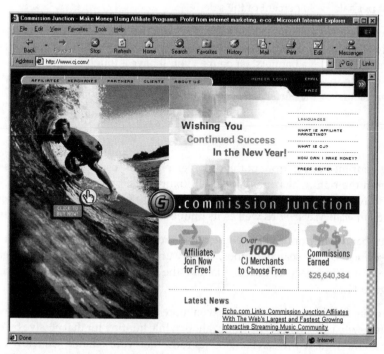

Figure 11.12 Commission Junction will broadcast your affiliate program offer to thousands of order takers.

In other words, it does all the behind-the-scenes work for you. It even helps your affiliates sell more stuff. This approach works whether you are selling a single pair of bamboo sunglasses that will be the perfect addition to a South Seas online catalog or if you are the A&E Television Network with more than 3,500 product links across 5,549 affiliates, enjoying a 1.5 percent clickthrough rate while paying out only a 10 percent commission.

Who else out there might benefit by selling your goods and services on their site?

The Tariff

Here are some general prices at the moment, and to steal a line from Omar Ahmad of Netscape, VWPYMMVPDCCAWYH (void where prohibited, your mileage may vary, professional driver on a closed course, always wear your helmet).

- Search engines, general rotation: $5–30 CPM (cost per thousand)
- Search engines, specific pages: $30–50 CPM (see the upcoming section, *Targeting*, for more details)
- Search engines, keyword buys: $50–70 CPM (see the upcoming section, *Targeting*, for more details)
- Small topic-specific sites: $50–80 CPM
- Clickthroughs: $.25–1.25 CPC (cost per click)
- Cost per lead: $1–$200 CPL
- Cost per sale: 5–30 percent of the sale

It will cost you somewhere from $500 to $1,000 to have an animated banner created, $1,000 to $2,000 for a banner that can handle data entry (a form in the banner), and the sky's the limit for Java banners. Of course, you'll have a tough time finding a site that will be willing to serve a Java banner. They're just too big and bulky, and they tend to cause problems for the surfer.

Targeting

Getting your message in front of the right person can be as straightforward as placing your ad in the right magazine. If you sell luxury cars, you need to promote them in *Time* and *Newsweek* and *The New Yorker*. If you sell fishing gear, you might consider *Florida Sportsman Magazine* as well as its online version (www.floridasportsman.com).

Put your banner in front of the people most likely to want your products. That's not rocket science. On the search engines, you'll want to buy the Shopping and Services > Outdoors >Fishing page at Yahoo!, just like the good folks at www.sasktourism.com (see Figure 11.13).

On the other hand, if you want to get even more specific, you could buy a keyword. A keyword is what a searcher types into Yahoo! while hunting for that elusive bit of information on the Web. If you sell bamboo fly rods, then your banner will show up every time a fly fisherman does a search on "bamboo fly rods."

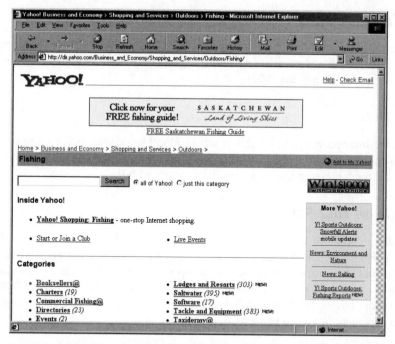

Figure 11.13   Every time somebody goes to the "Shopping and Services > Outdoors > Fishing" at Yahoo!, the Saskatchewan Tourism Authority is there to lure them.

But to really get matched up with the people most likely to like what you're selling, consider the Dart service from DoubleClick (www.DoubleClick.com). This is the same technology described in Chapter 7, "Value-Added Marketing—It's Personal," only this time it's used to figure out what banner you are most likely to click.

First, Dart tracks what you do—your behavior. This software is used across Double-Click's ad banner network, and it can get to know you pretty well. DoubleClick serves ad banners to lots of different sites as a service. You give it your ad and tell it you want your ad to be shown to people with certain interests or in certain geographies or at certain times of day, and it takes care of the rest. When a surfer shows up at one of those sites, Dart starts paying attention to what that surfer clicks. Did you spend more time on this page than that? Did you click on this banner and not that one? Eventually, the software has enough data points to create a profile of you that it can update on the fly.

As soon as you click, your profile changes. As soon as your profile changes, Dart compares it to those of other people with a similar profile, sees what banner ads *they* clicked on, and serves the banner they clicked on the most, to you. Response (clickthrough) rates tend to go up dramatically with this sort of system in place. That *is* rocket science.

If you're trying to figure out where to advertise on the Web, the real world has caught up. The Standard Rate and Data Service, known better to the industry and librarians everywhere as SRDS (www.srds.com), has come out with its *Interactive Advertising Source Book*. As it was for print, it will be the bible of buying ad space online.

Random Creative Tips

Here are a few broad hints about what works with banner ads. If this is your main line of business, note that I go into a lot more detail in my book *What Makes People Click, Advertising on the Web* (Que, 1997).

Click Here

This is the Internet version of a call to action. Don't leave your home page without it. Yes, it sounds trite and even a little obvious, but banners with "Click Here" or "Click Now" do much better in the click race than those without.

Time Is on Your Side

There are a couple of ways your ad can stay up longer than usual. When it does, its chances of getting clicked go up. Maybe the site you advertise on offers a framed space for ads. That would mean your ad shows up in one portion of the screen and stays there as the surfer navigates around in the other window inside the browser. You might also consider having the banner follow a surfer from page to page on a Web site, making it a persistent image on the screen.

Beware Banner Burn Out

Studies indicate that if users haven't clicked on a banner the first three times they see it, they simply aren't going to. Don't let your banner get overexposed to the same surfer.

The Seven-Word Limit

The standard banner size is 468 pixels wide by 60 pixels high. That's not very big. Getting your point across in a small space that is likely to be scrolled off the screen in the blink of an eye is a challenge. Given the small amount of time and the small amount of space (think font size), seven words is a good limit.

Keep It Small

Vegas.com allows only banner ads that are 8K or less. Motorcycle City will go as high as 12K. Some sites will let you serve Java banners with streaming video. No matter what they allow, consider the poor surfer. Waiting for ads to download is worse than waiting for the dentist. At least at the dentist's office you can find the hidden pictures in the seven-year-old copies of *Highlights Magazine*. You want your banner to load ASAP, giving it more exposure time.

Bright Colors Attract the Eye

Cliff Kurtzman from Tenagra (www.tenagra.com) had just done a major beautification upgrade of his Tennis Server site (www.tennisserver.com) when he noticed a huge drop in the number of clickthroughs his clients' banner ads were getting. His conclusion and advice to others? Put your banner on ugly sites so they're the most interesting thing on the page.

Use bright colors to attract attention. Be aware of the color schemes of the sites where you want your banners so you can be sure to contrast without clashing.

Always Use Your <Alt>

While waiting for pictures to download, the surfer is faced with the textual place-holders for those banners. Most of them say "<alt>", which indicates no text was placed in the HTML identifying the graphic.

The majority of the rest say "Click Here" or, even worse, "Support Our Sponsors." For heaven's sake, put in a few words for branding and attention grabbing. It doesn't cost any more.

Click Here

I wouldn't have believed it, but the results are overwhelming. The words "Click Here" work. Are we all lemmings who do as we're told? No, but we do like crisp, clear instructions.

Animation Is Unavoidable

The eye is drawn to things that move—it's part of being an animal. So make your banner move. Annoying? You bet. Effective? Yes, indeed. Does it hurt branding? It can. If your banner jumps and bounces and flashes and gives people headaches, you're not doing your brand any favors. But if it quietly draws attention to itself, no harm done and more clicks per impression.

Interact

Banners can include data entry boxes, voting buttons, and more. Give people something to do on your banner. Some banners can even take the order for whatever you're selling without taking the surfer away from the page he or she is on.

One of the better implementations of this approach was a banner for a Web Marketing conference put on by Thunder Lizard Productions and created by e/y/e/s/c/r/e/a/m interactive (hey, that's how they spell it). It was a combination banner that invited you to enter your e-mail address to get an e-mail sent to you immediately with all the conference details and a button that invited you to Click Here. You could either get the information sent and continue surfing or go to the site and find out more.

Streaming Media

Would you like your banner ads to be five times more effective?

A study by Millward Brown (www.mbinteractive.com) in November 2000 showed that when you stream audio and video at people, they can't help but watch and remember—and sometimes click. "The interactive nature of the Web, coupled with the strong ability of streaming ad copy to actively involve viewers, means that streaming ads have the potential to outperform Television advertising," according to Susan Blank and Nigel Hollis, researchers at Millward Brown.

Test, Test, Test

In direct mail, the A-B split is what you do to find out which envelope got opened most, which list had the best prospects, and which offer got the most responses. On the Web, you can make splits from A to Z without licking a stamp. So test everything, but do it in a controlled fashion.

Start with the offer. Do more people click for Buy One, Get One Free or for Buy Now and Get 20% Off? Test it and see. When the offer is nailed, try out different language— Click Here versus Click Now versus CLICK! NOW!!! Try a few things and see which gets people to do as commanded. You've got the right offer and the right words; what about color and layout? Test multiple designs to see which work best.

When you have the best banner you can make, try it out in different places. Different Web sites draw different types of people, who may click on different sorts of banners.

Just keep trying. Make sure the deal you sign with the content sites where you will place your ads allows you to publish multiple banners over time. It would be a shame to be stuck with one banner and not be able to try out alternatives.

Beyond the Banner

Banners aren't the only way to get people to your site. There are many other types of ads online. Once you get visitors beyond the clickthrough, you'd better give them a bridge to cross from the site your ad was on to the site you own. First, a few banner alternatives.

Interstitials

Interstitials show up between the page you're on and the page you wanted to go to. Some show up as whole new browser windows. This type usually times out after a little while. The thought is that you'll see it, read it, and click on it. If you ignore it, it'll go away.

I always wonder about the creative types who think this is a good idea. It's intrusive.

So what? So are the ads on television.

It keeps me from seeing what I really want to see.

But the ad might have something in it you want to see even more.

The extra window might crash my machine if I already have windows open.

You need more memory.

Most of the time, they time out before the message even downloads. Dumb.

Our ads are aimed at those with higher bandwidth.

Sorry—I'm not buying it.

But, in case your customers are, take a look at some examples at Unicast (www .unicast.com) (see Figures 11.14 through 11.16).

Shape Shifters

New ways to get attention include new shapes and placements of your message. In the winter of 2001, CNET (www.cnet.com) came up with new "Interactive Advertising" that got rid of the banners and brought in what looks more like newspaper display ads (see Figure 11.17).

But more than just a change of shape and location, these ads can pack a punch: animation and significant content available in the display, rather than making you click away (see Figures 11.18 and 11.19).

Pay Per View

More than just clicking on ads, Spedia Network will pay you to surf. Why? Because you use its browser (see Figure 11.20).

The SpediaBar is a free software application that lets you earn money while you surf the Internet. It's a small bar that docks next to your browser (Netscape Navigator or Internet Explorer) and displays advertising. You earn one point for each minute you have your SpediaBar open and you actively browse the Internet with normal surfing behavior. This amounts to $0.70 per hour if you are a Premier member.

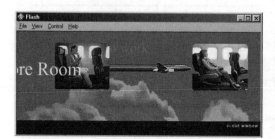

Figure 11.14 American Airlines feels . . .

Figure 11.15 . . . you might sit still for . . .

Figure 11.16 . . . its interruptive shill.

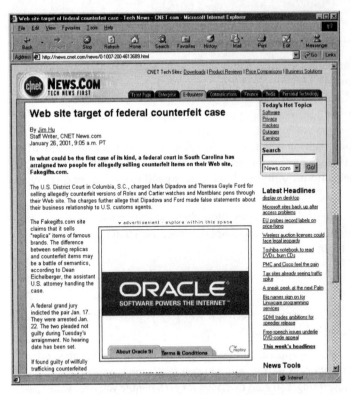

Figure 11.17 CNET cleaned up its act considerably by removing the banners and adding the display.

Figure 11.18 The Oracle ad includes tabs at the bottom for multiple screens . . .

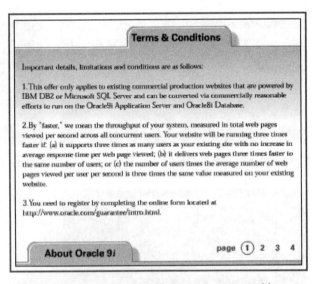

Figure 11.19 . . . and multiple pages accessed by page number . . . as well as links to click through to the Oracle site.

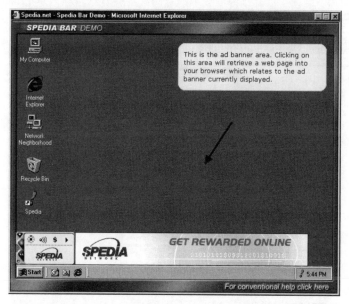

Figure 11.20 Spedia has more than 1.5 million people signed up to use its navigation bar and more than 1,000 advertisers.

Why is that appealing to advertisers? Because Spedia keeps track of what surfers are looking at and can use that to target your ads to the right surfers. Because people have to register to use it (they do want to get paid, so they will fill out those forms), Spedia can target geographically, demographically, psychographically, and then some.

Preemptive Advertising

ValueSpeed (www.valuespeed.com) calls it eCRM. I call it customer stealing.

If you sign up with ValueSpeed and your prospects sign up with you, they are added to a buddy-list of sorts that knows when they wander onto a competitors' site. And just when they go to click on the buy button—wham! They get a better offer (see Figure 11.21).

> ValueSpeed's *Shopping Wizard* alerts your users to a range of possibly better deals, drawing from your site's data or our own in-house shopping robot capability.
> The *Shopping Wizard* offers you:
>
> - a value-added deal-finding service for users;
>
> - incremental revenue to your site from referral commissions; and
>
> - an additional means of drawing traffic into your site.
>
> The tool can currently compare offers across the entire Web on popular categories including books, videos, CDs, auctions, airline tickets, electronics, and software. Our highly developed workflow tools allow us to add rapidly new products and merchants to suit your needs.

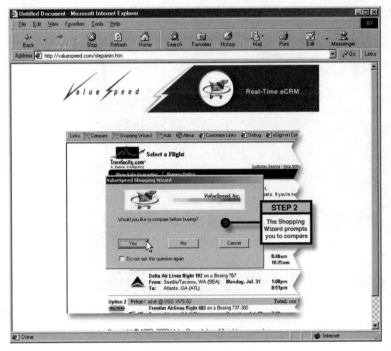

Figure 11.21 ValueSpeed makes sure you know about its clients' offers before you go with the competition.

New technologies come down the pike every time you turn around. What's interesting is when old techniques work wonders.

Brought to You By . . .

The first efforts on the Internet were to build branded Web sites. They all were supposed to be billboards on the information superhighway, but the traffic on this highway wasn't driving near the Web site created to show off a new product or an old favorite. Traffic was going places where things were happening.

It became clear that you had to make some noise about your site on others' sites. Sponsorship was born. It started out the same way it did on television, and some examples of sponsored sites still exist today.

The Playbill site (www.playbill.com) (see Figure 11.22) has everything you want to know about live theater, including a method to buy tickets. Knowing that people looking for a good show to see will wander over to the Playbill site, the creators of BroadwayNewYork.com purchased an ad banner at the top of the page.

Knowing that theater-goers tend to be more upscale, and knowing that the preferred method for buying tickets is credit cards, American Express decided to sponsor the site. You'll notice that "Presented by American Express" is an integrated design ele-

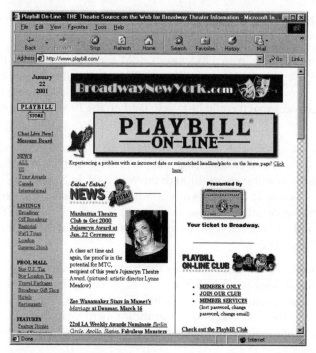

Figure 11.22 Playbill is sponsored by American Express and sells advertising to BroadwayNewYork.com.

ment, whereas the BroadwayNewYork.com banner is in the classic, ephemeral ad location at the top of the page.

If you want to go whole-hog with a sponsorship, you can follow Sun Microsystem's lead—IBM did.

Sun (www.sun.com) invented Web event sponsorship quite by accident at the end of 1994. A Webmaster at Oslonett in Lillehammer, Norway, was taking snapshots of the Olympic games by day and scanning them onto his Web site by night. Sun had set up a link from its home page to this unique reporting effort to show off a creative use of technology and the glory of the human spirit. Then Sun got the phone call.

Oslonett was flooded. Word had gotten out, and the hits came in, but there was simply not enough horsepower in its server to serve the world. Oslonett appreciated the link and the traffic, but it was getting buried. Could Sun do anything to help? Sun seized the opportunity and shipped a hefty number cruncher to Norway overnight. Within 24 hours, it became apparent that even more power was needed, but even with more computer power, the phone lines couldn't handle the traffic. The only solution was to mirror the Lillehammer data on another computer at Sun headquarters in Mountain View, California.

Twenty-four hours later, tens of thousands of daily users were getting scores, pictures, and front-line reporting. Forty-eight hours later, lawyers from IBM, the official Olympic games sponsor (with no Web site), were on the phone with Sun Microsystems' lawyers.

By the time they finished talking about it, the Olympics were over. A rollicking success for the "information wants to be free" Internet!

While Sun was out finding new events to sponsor, IBM was out sewing up the Web site rights for the 1996 Centennial Olympic Games. IBM became the Official Internet Information Systems Provider for The Atlanta Committee for the Olympic Games. IBM didn't take any chances that it could be overlooked on the 1996 Web site (see Figure 11.23).

In 1993, IBM signed an agreement with the International Olympic Committee to become a Worldwide Partner to the Games, agreeing to provide and integrate full, end-to-end technology solutions and systems through the year 2000. In Nagano, it cost IBM a cool $100,000,000 (see Figure 11.24). That's one hundred million dollars in people and equipment to make the reporting and networking systems run and support the Web site. That's a healthy budget. IBM felt it got its money's worth because it did it again in Sydney in 2000 (see Figure 11.25).

But something didn't add up for Big Blue after the turn of the millennium. After 38 years of sponsoring technology for the Olympics, IBM threw up its hands and said, "Enough!" Actually what it said was, "Too much!" IBM spokeswoman Debbie Gottheimer put it this way, "The IOC asked for a significant increase in our sponsorship commitment. We felt that was not commensurate with the marketing benefits we would receive in return."

In August 2000, LogicTier (www.logictier.com) was named Internet sponsor of the 2002 Winter Olympics in Salt Lake City along with NBC and Quokka Sports, displaying a much smaller presence than IBM had at first (see Figure 11.26). But given how relatively unknown LogicTier is compared to IBM, that little logo can mean a lot.

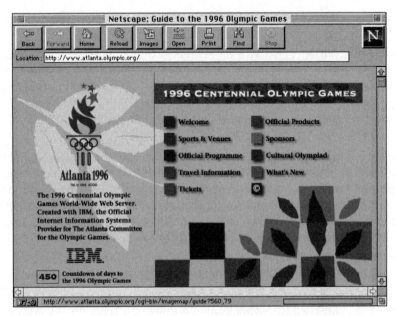

Figure 11.23   IBM made sure it owned the 1996 Olympic Web site.

Figure 11.24 Not to be left in the lurch again, IBM signed up to be the official provider for 1998 in Nagano . . .

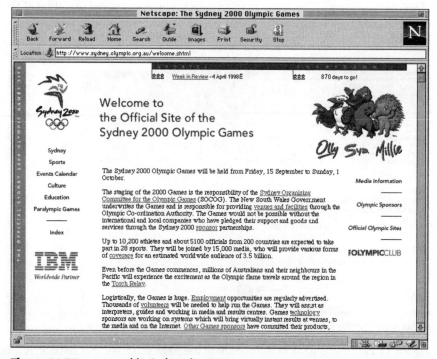

Figure 11.25 . . . and in Sydney in 2000.

Figure 11.26 LogicTier gets to show its logo to millions in return for more millions.

Don't think you have to limit yourself to commercially supported endeavors to find a place for your logo. The folks at HP figured they'd get some attention if HP's logo could be seen by the millions of shoppers who wander around at Amazon (see Figure 11.27).

Figure 11.27 If you scroll to the bottom of the page you'll see that Amazon is "powered with HP".

What does that cost? An undisclosed number of high-end HP 9000 V-Class enterprise servers. Don't have a couple of those handy? Don't want to support an entire Web site? Head over to iVillage.com and see how Charles Schwab is sponsoring articles there on investing.

E-Mail Marketing

E-mail is everywhere. Web sites may have been the first wonder of the Internet. Banner advertising may have astonished marketing mavens around the world. Streaming media might someday give us the video phones we were promised at the New York World's Fair in 1964. But e-mail will bring people to your site and keep them coming back for more.

IDG List Services (www.idglist.com) provides a succinct list of the "10 Benefits of Emailing" in the media kit for renting *The Industry Standard* e-mail list:

Quick lead generation. Email has quick output and quick response for lead generation.

Selectivity. Email offers the same list selectivity as traditional list rental.

Media reinforcement. Email can be an adjunct to any media to quickly reinforce a message, product announcement, seminar date, or trade show.

Cost effectiveness. Email is extremely cost effective on a cost-per-contact basis for customer acquisition.

Higher response. Overall responses may be higher, as only relevant materials will be sent, which assures a more receptive audience for the offer.

Lower costs. There are no production, paper, or postage costs—only the cost of the email server companies.

Privacy issues. Subscribers choose to receive email solicitation through a negative option given upon subscribing. Subscribers are also aware of the source of their name and are always given the choice to opt out. This addresses the privacy issue directly and again assures a responsive audience.

Customer dialogue. As an interactive medium, email establishes a dialogue with new and present customers. Repeated messages can create an effective brand awareness or a continued response from and conversation with the customer.

Trackability. Email is also a trackable medium, as you can direct responders to answer through many types of response vehicles.

No postal undeliverables. Undeliverables are quickly identified and an effort is made to correct them and resend.

There is one guiding principal to e-mail that you must adhere to or else. Spam: Don't.

Permission Marketing: Opt-out versus Opt-in

What's that? You say you haven't read Seth Godin's book, *Permission Marketing* (Simon & Schuster, 1999)? It's worth a look—a serious look.

Tony Priore and I wrote the following in *E-Mail Marketing* (John Wiley & Sons, 2000):

> A sharp line divides real e-mail marketing and spam. Spam is unsolicited. That means the recipient never asked for it.
>
> Once you start haggling over *how* a recipient asks, that sharp line starts to blur. There is a difference between opt-in and opt-out. There is a difference between requesting a white paper and agreeing to a lifetime supply of monthly newsletters. There is a difference between sending messages that are well received and messages that spell harassment.
>
> The modern marketer takes acceptable practices on the Internet very seriously. While the differences between spam, opt-in, and opt-out sound like a quarrel over shades of gray and splitting hairs, it's really a question of brand management and customer respect. We'll be up front. We believe in a well-defined, hard line that says opt-in is where it's at. Anything less is asking for trouble.

Seth Godin outlined the rules, the tests, and the levels of permission marketing. Here are the four rules:

The Four Rules of Permission Marketing

1. **Permission must be granted—it can't be presumed.** Buying addresses and sending direct mail are not permission—it's spam, and it's likely to be ignored. Consumers don't want to be bought and sold and then marketed to.

2. **Permission is selfish.** People grant their permission only when they see that there's something in it for them. And you've got about two seconds to communicate that something.

3. **Permission can be revoked as easily as it's granted.** It can also deepen over time. The depth of permission depends on the quality of interaction between you and your customers.

4. **Permission can't be transferred.** It's a lot like dating. You can't give a friend the authority to go out on a date in your place.

The Four Tests of Permission Marketing

1. Does every single marketing effort you create encourage a learning relationship with your customers?

2. Does it invite customers to "raise their hands" and start communicating?

3. Do you have a permissions database? Do you track the number of people who have given you permission to communicate with them?

4. If consumers gave you permission to talk to them, would you have anything to say? Have you developed a marketing curriculum to teach people about your products? Once someone becomes a customer, do you work to deepen your permission to communicate with that person?

The Six Levels of Permission Marketing (in Descending Order of Impact)

1. **Intravenous treatment.** The doctor treating you in the emergency room doesn't have to sell you very hard on administering a drug.

2. **Green stamps.** Executives suffer through long layovers to gain frequent-flyer miles. Here, the company rewards customers in a currency they care about.

3. **Personal relationships.** The corner dry cleaner enjoys implicit permission to act in your best interest. A favorite retailer can "upscale" you (recommend something more expensive) without offending you.

4. **Branding.** Given a choice between the known and the unknown, most people choose the known.

5. **Situational selling.** If you're in a store and you're about to make a purchase, you often welcome unsolicited marketing advice.

6. **Spam.** Where most marketers live most of the time: calling a stranger—at home, during dinner, without permission. You wouldn't do it in personal life; why do it to potential customers?

If you want to find fresh prospects, head over to an e-mail list management company like yesmail.com., described earlier in Chapter 8, "Personalization—Getting to Know You." Yesmail.com has over 15 million people signed up to receive e-mail about subjects as diverse and distinct as desktop video, cooking Mexican food, retirement investments, and helping kids with homework. It also has 1,621 people interested in your special offers for ferrets, 1,524 interested in gerbils, and 1,661 who care about lizards.

These people signed up and are interested right now. This is not a six-month-old list. It's a dynamic list that yesmail.com protects feverishly. These subscribers are its bread and butter. If it sends messages its subscribers don't want, they will unsubscribe. We can't have that, so yesmail.com is very careful about what goes to whom. As a result, your message will go only to people who care, and *that's* why response rates average between 5 and 35 percent.

A good list is half the battle Then all it takes is killer creative.

Quick Tips on E-Mail Masterpiece Making

I'll point you again to my book *E-Mail Marketing* (John Wiley & Sons, 2000) for the full story. Here, for those of us who want it now, are the bare bones details:

- The subject line is critical: It's like getting them to open the envelope.
- Grab their attention in your opening sentence and then keep them reading.
- Deliver value or they'll stop wanting to hear from you.
- Take care with layout and design to make it (a) readable and (b) professional.
- Personalize to whatever degree you can afford.
- Provide a clickthrough as the response mechanism.
- Carefully tailor the landing page (the page they hit after clicking).
- Test and measure, test and measure, test and measure as a life style.

Direct response e-mail marketing (if you are very careful to avoid looking like anything that could be construed as spam) is a powerful way to get people to your site. E-mail, however, is even better at getting them *back* to your site.

E-Newsletters

Get people to sign up for a newsletter. Do *not* send them an e-mail inviting them to sign up for your e-mail newsletter. If you're not sure why that's a bad idea, I have two words for you:

Spam: Don't

Then create a weekly or monthly newsletter that they'll find valuable. How will you know if they like it or not? They'll tell their friends to subscribe if they like it, and they'll unsubscribe if they don't.

You provide value, and at the same time you pump up the name recognition. And, of course, they've given you permission to try to sell them something. If you try too hard and are too ham-fisted about it, they will unsubscribe. It's a wonderful, closed-loop feedback system. Besides, if you sell to them well, people really *like* knowing about the latest discount special.

I invite you to sign up for my mostly monthly musings at www.targeting.com for an example. And when I finally get the archives of *Full Sterne Ahead* up on my site, I hope to have as nice an archive format as Boldfish (www.boldfish.com) (see Figure 11.28).

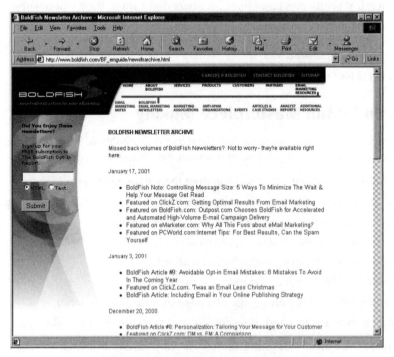

Figure 11.28 Boldfish shows the subjects of its newsletters in its archive by date, plus a handy place to sign up *on every single page* on its site.

Notice the option for the HTML or the plain-text version in Figure 11.28. You'll want to be sure you send the HTML version only to people with e-mail clients that can read HTML. If you're not careful, you could end up with egg on your face, like the folks at Coach, the luxury leather store.

I signed up months and months before receiving my first Coach e-mail message. I don't recall whether it asked which format I preferred. I'd have told them. I'm a text-only kind of guy. It's a conscious choice I make by altering a setting in my e-mail client. As a result, when I got the first one, they offered to let me unsubscribe. That's nice, actually. In fact, it's critical. Even if I *ask* for a newsletter, if there's no obvious way to sign off, then the next one is spam. The problem I had with the Coach invitation to unsubscribe was that was *all* they sent me (see Figure 11.29).

In pale blue lettering over an overly complex URL was the barely legible sentence, "If you wish to unsubscribe from one or more categories, click below." That was it. That was its entire marketing message to a hard-won newsletter subscriber. Oops.

Had I turned that little feature on, I would have been presented with a graphic that offered me nothing but a vague reason to head back to the site (see Figure 11.30).

How big is the sale? What's on sale? Is it a limited time offer? All Coach leather may be selected for its tactile quality, strength, character, and grain, but this promotion left the company holding the bag. Lesson: Deliver value, don't promise it.

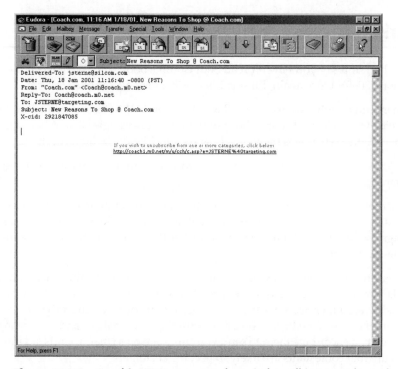

Figure 11.29   Coach's HTML message doesn't do well in text-only mode.

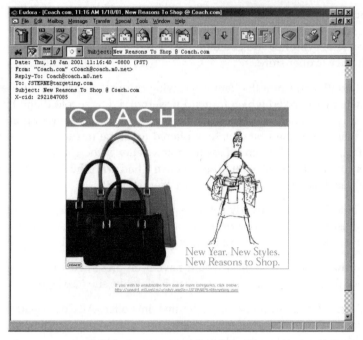

Figure 11.30   Coach does not score well in the motivational department.

Viral Marketing

What's that? You say you haven't read Seth Godin's book *Unleashing the Ideavirus* (Do You Zoom, 2000)? Once again, I'll say: It's worth a look—a serious look.

Viral marketing is what we used to call word of mouth. What's changed? The ability to tell 23,496 of your closest friends about something with a single click. When free e-mail accounts hit the Web, it was big news. Friends told friends. Millions of them.

You just have to be very good at coming up with something people are really going to get behind.

Viral marketing, when defined as a concerted effort to get people talking about your products or your company, is more magic than mastery. Planning a viral marketing campaign is like planning on the success of Pet Rocks, Beanie Babies, or some other over-the-top-hot-popular product.

If there is a real reason to visit your site, if you are offering real value, then you can get referrals. Jupiter Communications reports that 57 percent of online customers would go to a site recommended by a friend. Just give that friend an incentive. If your customers are the type to be turned on by sweepstakes and contests and pass-along marketing, you can encourage them to send your message on to their friends, ad infinitum. Just be sure that contestants are likely to become customers.

That's great for drawing a crowd, but true viral marketing is when you go over "the tipping point" and your meme, your message takes on a life of its own. What is it that captures the imaginations of tens of thousands so that they would forward your idea or promotion to friends, who send it to friends, etc.? There are an infinite number of variables in the mix that are beyond the control of mere marketers. But then, Seth Godin is no mere marketer.

In January 2001, Jupiter Research (www.jup.com) reported its expectations that advertisers will send 268 billion e-mail messages in 2005. Ouch. Nua (www.nua.com) thinks that as of November 2000, there were 407.1 million people online. Let's say that number doubles in four years. That's roughly 320 e-mails per person. Why is it that I feel as if I get that many every day?

Bottom line? There better be something *very* compelling about your message to make it stand out above the crowd.

Offline Marketing

I remember the day, lo these many years ago, my father came home and showed us that his new business cards included the telephone area code. Direct dial was in; operators were out. Several years later, his card included a telex number. Then it acquired a Zip code for his postal address. Later, his fax number replaced the telex, and then an additional four digits of the Zip code appeared. Now, of course, your e-mail and URL better be visible.

My personal favorite for driving traffic to a business-to-business Web site is direct mail. We have years and years of experience finding just the right people in just the right-sized companies in just the right positions to target with just the right message. Like your e-mail, make the offer as clear as possible. Why should they come to your Web site? Why should they sign up for your newsletter? What's in it for them?

Don't forget your traditional promotional methods. Put your Web address in your print ads, in your direct mail pieces, in your television spots, on your letterhead, and on the marketing specialties you hand out at trade shows. The Web is now the most popular way to learn about goods and services. Make it as easy as possible to find you.

You've seen plenty of offline ways to get people to Web sites. The Web advertising frenzy of 1998 saw cars wrapped with slogans, cardboard sleeves around double-latte cups with URLs, stickers on fruit with online offers, boats in the harbor with sales on their sails, and restroom walls plastered with, well, reading material.

Maybe you were one of those who received a catalog from Amazon. Amazon? A paper catalog? Yep—it has decided to stop toeing the Internet line and start going for sales. But then, again, there are some tried and true media that are going the other way.

Radio Star

From *Full Sterne Ahead*
September 2000 (www.targeting.com)

I'm driving along and hear a song I like, or a commercial I'm interested in. What to do? Whip out a scrap of paper and a pen and jot it down—and then wave sheepishly to the lady in the next lane who was leaning on her horn trying to avoid the need for a new paint job.

It's still going to be that way for a little while. The iTag was a very cool little bauble for your key ring that came pre-set to your favorite radio station. You like what you hear? You push the button. (It only had one.)

You could plug it into your serial port, upload your "tags" and see a list of what was on the air at the time. How did it know? It was just a clock!

iTag was a cool little gadget meant to be portable and suitable for impressing your friends. The sad part arrived on the 18th of this month (September, 2000):

```
> From: "Xenote" <kc.22423.268.0@kc.xenote.com>
> To: jsterne@targeting.com
> Subject: IMPORTANT: Xenote regrets operations will cease 9/22
> Date: Mon, 18 Sep 2000
>
> Dear Jim,
>
> We regret to announce that we must discontinue the
> Xenote.com service for the Xenote iTag.
>
> XENOTE.COM WEBSITE WILL SHUT DOWN THIS FRIDAY, 9/22/00
>
> The Xenote.com web site and all user accounts will be
> disabled on or before Friday, September 22nd.  Current
> economic conditions are such that we have been unable
> to secure funding and must therefore cease operations.
```

But to prove that good ideas still have a shot, there's the $19.99 programmable relative to the iTag; the Sony eMarker (www.emarker.com). It's just not as cool as the late, single-button original (www.itag.com).

Cat Scan

Like millions of other subscribers to *Wired* and *Forbes*, I got my hands on a :Cue:Cat slimline scanner thingy (www.digitalconvergence.com) (see Figure 11.31).

With a :CueCat device developed by Digital:Convergence, you will swipe a cue, which looks like this: (picture) and be taken directly to a specific Web page . . . giving you the

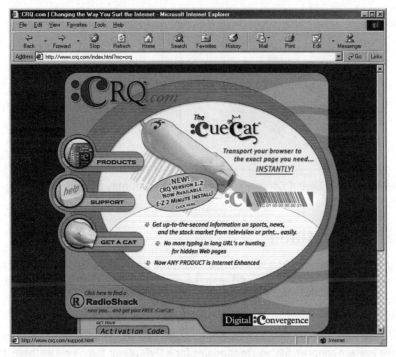

Figure 11.31 :Cue:Cat—cute idea, bad implementation.

information you want instantly. No more wading through dozens of Web pages or typing in long URLs. Just the information you want with a single swipe.

You can only use it while plugged into your computer.

David Parrett (dparrett@ProSavvy.com) wrote to tell me about his experience with the :Clueless:Cat scanner:

```
> I recently received a :Cue:Cat from a contact at Forbes
> In the package was a Radio Shack brochure which allowed
> the reader to scan various barcodes to reach the
> corresponding product pages on their website. It could
> have been a terrific promotion, had the scanned links
> targeted the right location!  Instead, I was sent to a
> Radio Shack page which told me that I had either entered
> the url incorrectly or the information had been moved.
```

I'd say the Radio Shack Web development team was running low on batteries.

Will your company ever put barcodes in your print ads? Maybe. Because Digital Convergence teamed up with Cross Pens to create the Cross :Convergence, which is the same concept, but now is wireless, is pen-sized, and fits in your pocket (see Figure 11.32). There may be something to this in the long run.

The Pens

Cross
:Convergence™

Figure 11.32 The Digital Convergence/Cross Pen team may be onto something—a human form factor.

Mall to Mall Competition

What if you took the wireless scanning idea on the road? What if you made it not only wireless but mobile? What if it could scan the product on the shelf and it would tell you where better deals could be found online? Then you'd have something called a Bar-Point (www.barpoint.com):

> Confused? Here's an example of how BarPoint.com's patent-pending technology empowers the average shopper. Say you're shopping for a DVD player (aren't we all these days?). You're at the local electronics store or department store and a particular unit catches your attention. You tinker a bit with the display model, and soon a salesperson comes over and asks you if you need any "help." Of course, you do.
>
> But the salesperson won't be able to give you the answers you need. Answers to questions like, "Has this DVD player gotten great reviews?" or "Is this the lowest price on this model?" BarPoint.com has those answers and delivers them to your wireless device in a matter of seconds. Bye-bye, salesguy.

If you're selling online what can be bought in a retail store, it's time to make sure your products are in the BarPoint database.

Exchange, Vortex, E-Marketplace, Group Buying, e-Procurement, Trading Hub, Reverse Auction

It doesn't matter what you call it, and there are dozens of business models to play with. On any given day there's another article in the business press about how these sites are going to take over the world, fall like a house of cards, threaten the free market, create perfect markets, or be shut down by the Federal Trade Commission.

What you *do* need to understand is that the Internet gives some pretty interesting tools to the procurement officers of the world. The procurement officers of the world are pleased as punch.

The ability to post a request for bids on the Internet and wait while vendors trip over each other to offer the lowest price is a dream come true. If you are responsible for the sale of your goods, you owe it to your bottom line to select the right exchanges in which to participate. You can't chase them all, but you can align yourself with those that are offering the best services and attract the most attractive buyers. If that's where the buyers are headed, you need to be represented.

As exciting as all this whiz-bang technology may be, there is one thing that we learned about Internet marketing over the past seven or eight years: We learned that nothing happens in a vacuum.

Integrated Marketing

You want people to remember your name? You want people to take the time to come to your Web site? You want them to sign up for your newsletter? You'd better be prepared to approach them from all angles.

The brand that's advertised through only one channel is going to have a tough time up against the big budgets that can afford to be on TV, in the paper, in the magazine, online, and in half a dozen other venues. Remember:

- You have to get people to recognize your name.
- You have to get people to be familiar with your name.
- You have to get people to trust your name.
- You have to get people to think of your name when they want to buy.

One banner ad or e-mail marketing effort will not make it.

A Bird's Eye View of Advertising on the Internet

Clickthroughs may be artificial
Branding can be beneficial
Pushing ads is superficial
Pop up ads are interstitial
E-mail spam is sacrificial
E-mail spam's a blasted bore

Direct response can bring in cash
Animation adds some flash
Privacy and cookies clash
Java makes my browser crash
E-mail spam brings naught but trash
E-mail spam just makes me sore

continues

A Bird's Eye View of Advertising on the Internet (Continued)

Banners spawn in mass profusion
Making money's an illusion
IPOs spell cash infusion
Legislation brings confusion
E-mail spam is an intrusion
E-mail spam just makes me roar

Banner selling's one tough story
Due to so much inventory
Tightly targeting your quarry
Is the road to clickthrough glory
E-mail spam revenge is gory
E-mail spam means legal war

This industry is young and learning
Each investor daily yearning
Many trying, many hurting
While we with fame and flame are flirting
E-mail spam just leaves me burning
E-mail spam strikes to the core

So, that's the take from my perception
If you think you take exception
Feeling that I need correction
E-mail it to my attention
But PLEASE don't spam me anymore
To e-mail spam say, "Nevermore"

Take a deep breath. Relax. Clear your head. You'll need a clear head because I have a question to ask. After all this catering to customers, answering their questions before they ask, worrying about the perfect navigational design, creating Web-based services and tools for your customers, listening to their feedback, personalizing their Web experience, creating workflow-driven, business-rule-managed extranets, catering to your channel partners and doing everything under the sun to get people to come to your site . . . how do you know you're doing a good job?

CHAPTER 12

Measure for Measure

Heaven doth with us as we with torches do,
Not light them for themselves; for if our virtues
Did not go forth of us, 'twere all alike
As if we had them not.

MEASURE FOR MEASURE, ACT I, SCENE I

I t's wonderful to count and calculate and tabulate—but if you don't do anything with the numbers, it's as if you had them not.

The bloom is off the rose when it comes to the Internet, and knowing what works and what doesn't is a necessity. We're no longer looking at hits as a viable indicator of our Web marketing prowess. Pageviews have given us the most consistent, yet deeply unsatisfying, look at our success.

With so many options, there has to be a way to focus on what provides you with the best return on your investment. Unfortunately, there are as many ways to measure things as there are things to be measured, multiplied by the business goals of those doing the measuring.

In May 2000, Matt Cutler of NetGenesis (www.netgen.com) and I published a white paper called "E-Metrics, Business Metrics for the New Economy." We interviewed 20 leading Web managers from sites you'd recognize including Barnes & Noble, BBC Online, Charles Schwab, iVillage.com, Microsoft—you get the picture—in order to find out what they were measuring and how they were measuring and what they were doing with the results they got.

When we took the E-Metrics white paper on the road and performed an around-the-world series of seminars, we started out with the same questions you'll have to ask yourself when you want to start recording a baseline against which to test your progress: What are you trying to accomplish? What challenges do you face? What are you trying to learn? Why do you need to know? How will that help you in your business? What are your most important business goals at the moment?

The answers we got were many and varied. Take a quick look at these, and see if you can spot a few that are worth a tick-mark for your organization:

Increase repeat visits
Understand user behavior
Identify E-Metrics focused on VC/investor interest
Integrated view of customers
Identify key metrics appropriate to business
How do we establish a baseline to work from?
How much impact is traditional marketing having on the site?
ROI—where to spend on promotion and infrastructure
How to continuously learn from ongoing data
How can an offline business measure effectiveness on the Web/branding?
How do we optimize banner rotation?
Compare E-Metrics with industry/competition
Measure the value of personalization for e-mail marketing
Do we have effective customer segmentation?
How do we define unique users and move to personalization?
How do we identify real people versus unique users?
How do we get to details about users?
How do we understand shopping cart abandonment?
How do we measure traffic flow?
Understand how customers navigate to deliver the best user experience
Conduct clickstream analysis
Understand content freshness
Understand where customers are coming from
Understand reach
Metrics for customer intelligence relevant to our business model
Understand loyalty of users
Define patterns for loyal customers, understand lifetime value
Identify action for insight gained about users' behavior
Understand and optimize acquisition of customers
Understand how to track conversions
Measure customer satisfaction
Predict future purchases
Get buy-in and have senior management understand the importance of E-Metrics
Identify measurement standards
Process for establishing objectives for measurement
Get everyone on the same page, fix communication breakdown
Cost justify investment for measurement software/services
Get agreement on what to measure between staff and upper management
Process for developing custom reports for individual users within organization
Integrate multichannel offline data

Correlate e-mail data to Web-derived data
Using consistent methods for measurement across business
Data accuracy–get consistent, accurate numbers
Identify correct tools and methods for measurement effort
Track Flash and media content applications
Track data collected from mobile-commerce
Get real-/near-real- time data
Understand sampling as an option
How do we deal with privacy/security?

If you're feeling a little woozy right now, it's OK. Most people get a little lightheaded at these altitudes—it's perfectly normal. Just sit down, put your head between your knees, and breathe into this paper bag. Good. The room will stop spinning in just a moment.

The best approach is to take this a step at a time:

1. Somebody comes to your Web site.

2. Your Web site responds.

3. The visitor wanders your site looking for things.

4. The visitor leaves or buys something and then leaves.

5. The visitor leaves footprints all over the place for your analysis.

6. The visitor comes back or not.

7. You try to determine if the visitor thinks you're doing a good job.

8. You try to determine if the public/industry thinks you're doing a good job.

9. You try to determine the visitor's lifetime value to the company.

It'll take some doing. Where do you start? Here's where I prove that I'm a consultant . . . It depends.

Getting Them There in the First Place

Let's start at the beginning: Somebody comes to your site. Before the visitor actually shows up, the first question is this: How much did it cost you to get him or her there?

Reach

Your first problem is figuring out if you are reaching a healthy percent of the potential buyers out there. The term "reach" has long been used in broadcast to gauge how many households out there in television land had the opportunity to see your message. In our white paper, "E-Metrics, Business Metrics for the New Economy" (www.netgen .com/emetrics), Matt Cutler and I made the following point:

If you are trying to attract the attention of the 5 million buyers of 3-D rendering software tools for architects, you might place a banner ad on an architectural portal Web site. If that site draws 1 million distinct people a month who fit the description of a potential buyer, your reach on that site is 20 percent of the total universe of 5 million buyers.

Another aspect of reach is *total site reach*. Assume you decide to promote your software on the Expedia travel site. If Expedia attracts 25 million unique users per month and your ad was shown to 5 million unique users, then your reach to Expedia users was 20 percent for the month.

Some companies do not measure their reach until the potential buyer has clicked on the banner. They do not consider that prospect as "reached" until the message has been delivered, read, and acted on. Others call this step acquisition.

So you can count how many households or humans you reach, but do you know if they are even noticing? Are they responding to your invitation?

Acquisition Cost

Ameriquest Mortgage (www.ameriquestmortgage.com) knows exactly how much it costs to get a pair of eyeballs to its site from Goto.com (see Figure 11.6). It willingly paid $2.72 for each visitor. It now has a baseline. What would it cost to run a direct mail campaign to drive traffic to its site? If Ameriquest Mortgage sends 100,000 postcards, each costing 10¢ for paper and printing and 20¢ for postage, it would have to get an 11 percent response rate to get the same value.

On average, if you take the total cost of advertising in the home mortgage industry and divide it by the number of loan applications the mortgage companies receive for their trouble, it costs about $250 per application. Or, the companies could cut a deal with Sherri Neasham at FinanCenter.com for an order of magnitude less than that. You want a loan application sent to you electronically? That'll be $25, please.

The cost of acquisition has nothing to do with branding. We are not measuring whether people feel better about your company because of your animated banner ads and interstitial interruptions or if they feel worse. Cost of acquisition has nothing to do with sales—we'll get to that later. We are measuring only the number of people who show up at your Web site. It is the cost of acquiring somebody's attention, the acquisition of their eyeballs.

You could stand on a street corner with fliers that say, "Come to our store and we'll hand you $5." What would happen? People would walk in, they'd get their $5, and some would spend it there. The next day, you hand out fliers that offer $2. The next day, $4. In time, you get a clear idea of what it costs to get people to show up. If you're good at tracking, you get an idea of how much it costs to get them to show up, look around, buy something—and come back and spend more another time.

If your only task—your only responsibility—is to get people to come to a specific landing page, then your company's conceptual grasp of "integrated marketing" is woefully short of the mark. As Matt Cutler points out, "It doesn't matter that 20 million 14-year-old girls came to your Web site because of your Ricky Martin/Britney Spears banner ad—they're *still* not going to buy your BMWs" (see Figure 12.1).

What matters then is not how many people show up, but how many of the right people show up. Are they qualified leads? Are they serious potential buyers? Are they *actual* buyers? The sure-fire way to Web success is to track from that very first click all the way through to the sale and beyond. All in good time. Let's not get ahead of ourselves.

At the moment, you know that you've spent $X and got Y people to show up. At least you think you know. The site you buy banner ad space from says you got 2,082 click-throughs yesterday. Your referrer logs show that you got only 1,765. What's wrong with this picture? Nothing—it's quite possible that both are correct. You banner *was* clicked 2,082 times, but only 1,765 made it all the way to your landing page; 317 people clicked by mistake or waited too long for your page to load and hit the Back button. Happens all the time. Nothing you can do about those who are mouse-click-challenged, but as for those whose patience ran out, it's on your shoulders to do something. You are responsible for making your site as fast as possible and for knowing just how fast that is.

Figure 12.1 A banner ad we're unlikely to see—it would simply attract the wrong crowd.

Web Site Performance—The Need for Speed

Your server spits out files as fast as it can. One HTML (text) file and a dozen graphics files make up your home page. The server slings them out in the blink of an eye. Unless, of course, 50 others have asked for the home page, 4 are watching streaming videos, 6 are downloading your whitepaper.pdf, and yet another is running search after search on your database.

Is it time to have multiple servers or even serving services push pages for you? Yes. How do you know? Because you use an electronic stopwatch to see how fast things are going. How would you know those third parties are serving your videos quickly enough? Same way.

Keynote Systems (www.keynote.com) was one of the first to offer performance monitoring services. On its site, it shows off the speeds of the faster well-known sites on the Web (see Figure 12.2).

Keynote measures your Web site from afar to make sure it's working to your liking. It will test your home page, your log-in pages, your e-mail servers, your pagers, and then some. It will test all of the above from up to 50 locations around the world. Keynote has a number of ways of looking at your site:

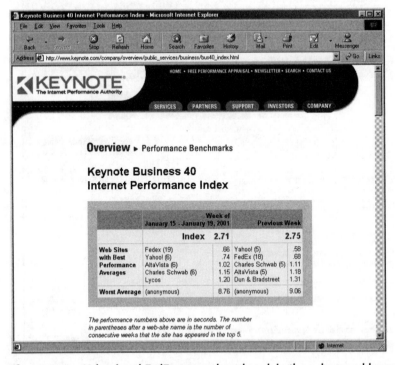

Figure 12.2 Yahoo! and FedEx are neck and neck in the subsecond home page response race, according to Keynote Systems.

Perspective: Measure the time it takes to access and download a single object or the entire contents of a Web page.

Transaction Perspective: Identify and compare how long it takes to execute a multi-page, interactive transaction.

Streaming Perspective: Streaming Perspective is the industry's first performance measurement service for monitoring the quality of streaming content.

Consumer Perspective: Measure the time it takes to access and download the sum data elements of a Web page over a 56 Kb modem, DSL or cable connection.

If there's a problem, Keynote will e-mail you a notification or page you. But, of course, it offers more than just throwing a red flag in your face. If you've got problems, it has consultants who can even help if the problem isn't on your server. In the e-mail Keynote sends when you first sign up, it assures you that you're not always to blame:

```
Please note that over 75% of all instances of site inaccessibility
detected by Keynote Red Alert are NOT due to problems with the server,
software, LAN, or ISP connection (though Keynote Red Alert detects these
problems also). The vast majority of instances of site inaccessibility
are due to problems with your "extended global connectivity", that is,
problems with the Internet backbones to which you connect, their peering
with other backbones, and the routes that are broadcast to direct
traffic to your site.

Expect to be surprised about problems you did not know existed. Also,
understand that there IS something you can do about it, and that our
staff can assist you in working with your bandwidth providers to zero in
on and resolve these problems. Our customers include the world's largest
ISPs and Internet backbone providers, because they know that monitoring
your site from within its own network simply WILL NOT detect "extended
connectivity" problems, which are THREE TIMES more prevalent than LAN
and server problems.
```

BMC Software (www.bmc.com) goes one step further. It allows you to create a click-stream scenario that its SiteAngel service remembers. SiteAngel records your mouse clicks, your passwords, and even your credit card number for testing an online purchase process from home page to final checkout.

Like Keynote, SiteAngel will test your site as often as you wish for as long as you wish and will e-mail or page you if there are problems. It can verify that specified text was or was not found on the returned page as well as how long it took. Taken all together, you get graphs with high-level summaries of how all your critical paths compare to the operational goals you have set (see Figure 12.3).

Now that you know that your server is serving pages, it's time to determine if the pages are serving your customers. Speed is important, but it turns out that lucidity is critical.

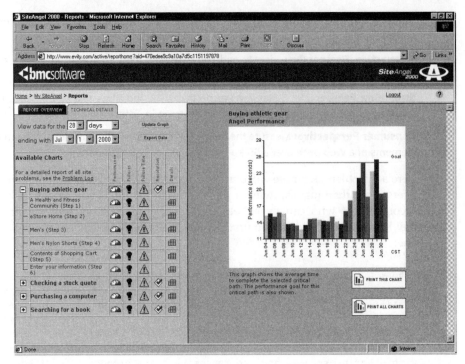

Figure 12.3 SiteAngel from BMC replays a recorded session to see how long it takes to click through your site.

Clarity Counts

Just how easily understood is your Web site? You are not the right one to answer that question. You wrote it! Should you take the time to find somebody who can review your site for lucidity? Just look at these results from a NetRaker press release:

> Results of a nationwide study (by NetRaker Corporation (www.netraker.com)) released today (September 7, 2000) reveal the factors that cause people to stay or return and interact with a company's web site in real numbers. The study indicates that clarity and navigation are more significant measurements than performance, and that if a company improves even a little bit on these things, there is a direct impact to increasing bottom line.
>
> Using accepted measurements of a site's actual physical performance through SiteRaker, one of the applications in the NetRaker Suite, AOL's speed was gauged almost twice as fast as the other two sites. Yet, as illustrated in the previous finding, "site effectiveness and efficiency"—the most important measure to-date by other measurement companies—was unable to compensate for poor design and functionality in meeting a user's expectations.

Speed alone does not make for a happy surfer. There are other qualities that are more important. As described in Chapter 3, "The Usable Web—Be Kind to Your Users," Webcriteria (www.webcriteria.com) does something similar, but it calculates more

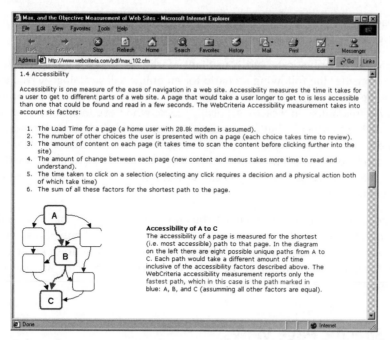

Figure 12.4 Max from Webcriteria worries about how long it would take for a human to plow through your site.

than the amount of time your server takes to respond. Its product, Max, calculates how long it would take a human to read your pages, understand the choices, and make a decision (see Figure 12.4).

All of these tools are going to tell you something very important: How fast is your Web site? How fast it serves pages is one thing, but how fast is it at reading a cookie, identifying the owner, choosing the right dynamic content for that visitor based on previous pages viewed, previous visits, and previous purchases, finding that content, and serving it up after concluding that the items you wish to show are in stock, ready to ship, and the owner of that cookie has not been placed on credit hold recently? And how fast is it comprehended by the visitor?

And to think that we once measured our success by counting hits. How quaint.

Navigation Fascination

As users select links to traverse, the log dutifully records their actions. The home page has five or six choices. Which do they pick the most? Each of those second-tier pages has five or six choices. Where do they go from there? Print ad professionals and retail shelf-space marketers pay close attention to where the eye travels on a magazine page and in a grocery store. You'll want to be just as diligent on your Web site.

Internetworking sophisticate and consultant Mark Gibbs (www.gibbs.com) asks his clients to consider the following scenario for an online sales catalog: A Web site user begins at the home page, looks at the index, finds a particular product page, and then looks at the guarantee. In 9 cases out of 10, people who have looked at the guarantee do not buy the product. What's wrong with the guarantee? You need to address the basic question of the quality of your marketing materials. Despite the technical wizardry at hand, your presentation must still be compelling. If you can measure the paths taken by the majority of visitors, you can test different vocabulary, different layouts, and different offers.

Anonymous hits on your server can tell you only so much. It's sort of like counting the number of times the front door to your store opens. You don't know if it's one person coming back four times or two people coming in together. You don't know if people came in the side door. But if you recognize them when they come in, you have the opportunity to collect a wealth of information.

Measuring Specific Page Views

Knowing how many times people requested specific pages within your site can at least let you know what interests the great unwashed out there. You can get a feel for what information is most important to the masses. You can see which products are more popular and which are being ignored. You'll get a feel for which areas can be put on hold for another day and which need immediate attention. You'll be able to tweak your navigational systems to help people get around. But the numbers aren't as discernible as they seem.

Personal Cache Confusion

Page caching is one problem that will cause your traffic to be *under*counted. Two kinds of caching problems haunt us: personal and institutional. Each individual's browser caches pages, and whole corporate sites can cache pages.

When an HTML page is downloaded, it is copied into a cache file on the local client computer. This allows the user to revisit that page without reaching across the Internet again. This design helps keep extraneous traffic off the Net and makes it much faster to look at a previously viewed page.

When measuring visits to your Web site, there is no simple way to know how many times one individual looked at a specific page. He or she may have looked at the cached version over and over, without grabbing a fresh copy or recording a footprint in your log. Printing your pages can have the same effect. Do you use some sort of percentage calculation for pass-around or photocopy readership when you analyze your collateral? You may want to do the same for caching and printing. What should those figures be? Good question. Ask your site visitors.

Institutional Cache Confusion

Let's say your organization sells IBM equipment. Lots of your employees use the IBM Web site from their desks. You have a firewall. All of this traffic goes through one port in the firewall.

As a good Net citizen, you have the ability (and some would say the duty) to store a copy of the IBM home page on your local (proxy) server. That way, whenever employees want to look at something at IBM, they make a local call to your server. When they click on something on that cached page, they make the long distance call to IBM. Every page that's viewed gets cached until the allotted cache file space runs out, then your proxy server starts deleting the oldest pages. How can IBM record the number of times its home page was read from a foreign server? It can't. Factor that into your measurements as well.

How Interested Were They?

The logs show the time each file fetch was made. On average, visitors looked at *this* page for only a few seconds, but they spent three minutes on *that* page. This gives you terrific insight into their level of interest, right? Wrong. If they stop to answer the phone, talk to their office mate, feed their goldfish, or work on a spreadsheet while perusing your site, the logs won't tell you. You know only when they asked for the files that weren't cached.

Look at your pageview numbers as a good internal comparative diagnostic. You may not be able to tell what really happened, and you can't use your numbers to compare your site to another, but you can use them as a sort of canary in a coal mine to compare changes from day to day.

How Interested Were They, Really?

If you want to really, *really* know what people are looking at, watch them. "Eyetools, Inc. (www.eyetools.com) (see Figure 12.5) uses innovative patented eyetracking technology developed at Stanford University to produce dramatic improvements in web site design."

That's right. Eyetools looks for site design flaws and dead zones based on eye movement. The founder, Greg Edwards, has two patents in the field of inferring mental state from patterns of eye movement and got his start at Stanford with the groundbreaking Stanford-Poynter Eyetrack study (http://eyetracking.stanford.edu). If you're serious about site navigation, this is the way to measure it.

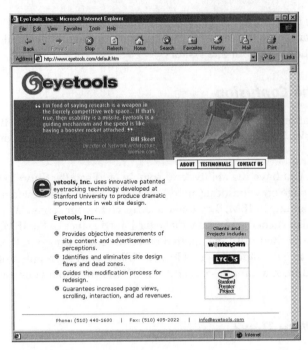

Figure 12.5 The fancy headgear keeps track of precisely where on the screen the surfer is looking.

From Clickstream to Life Cycle

Do you have a lot of people come to your home page and then leave? Maybe you have a very slow Web site that frustrates people into leaving before they've seen the goods. Maybe your promotions are drawing the wrong crowd. Perhaps your home page is simply plug ugly.

Do people get confused on your home page? If you watch your traffic patterns, you can tell. Do they click something on the home page and then exercise the Back button after every click? They don't know where to look because everything looks like a possible link. Do they go right for the search box? They don't see an obvious link to their heart's desire.

Do site visitors get caught in endless loops? Do they get confused by your offers? Do they seem to be interested but then wander off?

Do your would-be customers get all the way to the finish line—the Submit button on the order page—and then abandon their full shopping carts?

If you keep track of where people go and what they look at, you can build a mathematical model of how your visitors act on your site, and it will point you directly toward any problem areas.

One of my favorite diagrams from the E-Metrics white paper is Figure 18, The Customer Life Cycle Funnel (see Figure 12.6).

Does your customer life cycle funnel resemble a martini glass? Then you're attracting a lot of people to your site, but they're the wrong people. Fourteen-year-old girls and BMWs do not mix. They come to the home page and leave upon arrival. It's time to check your advertising and see why you're not pulling in serious leads.

Does your funnel look like a margarita glass? You have the right people showing up, but they lose interest. You're having a navigational or persuasion problem. They're interested, they're here—they came, they saw, and they got confused or bored, and they bolted.

Does your funnel resemble a wine glass? You've got the right people and they like what they see, but they just don't seem to be able to seal the deal at the end of the process. People are abandoning their shopping carts. Time to review your sales-order process and make it easier to use. Show the shipping charges up front. Let them find out how much the tax is *before* they have to enter their life story.

You say your funnel looks like a shot glass? Congratulations! You've got the right people, they're interested, they've followed the optimal site path you've designed, and they end up making a purchase. Well done.

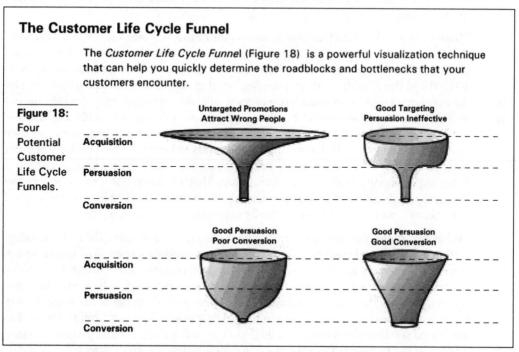

Figure 12.6 The funnel diagram helps determine the roadblocks and bottlenecks that your customers encounter.

For this sort of measurement, staring at server log files is simply not going to cut it. You need professional help.

Log Analysis Is Only the Beginning

Matt Cutler had been responsible for IT support at an insurance company in Connecticut while still in high school, and Eric Richard had worked at IBM's Almaden Research Center. The two met at the Massachusetts Institute of Technology and founded NetGenesis (www.netgen.com) in 1995 before they graduated. Consulting soon gave way to software, and NetGenesis rolled out the means to acquire, store, and analyze the data gushing from your Web site.

"Back in 1994, '95, and '96, you had a browser that talked to a Web server that was serving HTML files out of a single directory," says Matt. "As we all know, modern Web applications are much more complex today. There are many different specialized software systems that, together, have to interact and interrelate to create a seamless end-user experience. The modern infrastructure has a lot of complexity associated with it, and the idea is to collect data from each one of those components so you can understand the actual user experience and figure out what worked and what didn't."

To help larger companies get a handle on the customer base, Matt recommends the tried-and-true audience measurement system called quintile analysis, used for decades in broadcast.

"Basically you take a set of users who have come onto a Web site, say 100,000, and order them according to a quality metric. The metric could be average number of page views per user or how long someone typically stays on the site. You order them from one to 100,000 and then divide them in quintiles, equal groups of 20,000 each. Then you plot the average success factor in each one of these quintiles. So in your top quintile, users 1 to 20,000 might have an average number of page views per user of roughly five whereas your bottom quintile, the 80,000 to 100,000, is maybe less than one page view per user. Then you plot a graph. If the line that corresponds to how your best customers differ from your worst customers shows a steep slope in the middle, it says your top group is behaving differently from your bottom group. That's healthy. But if this is a very flat line, it means there's very little difference in behavior between your best customers and your worst customers and no one is really expressing preferences on the site."

"What this allows you to do is segment your customers, determine the differentiating factors between good customers and bad customers, and determine how you can push your bad customers to behave more like your good customers. For instance, if you've found that people who come in through the home page tend to be pretty bad customers, perhaps the real interesting content is not linked on the home page. If they have to click two to three levels down to find it, it would be pretty straightforward to say 'based on this information, let's increase the number of links that people are interested in at the home page so we can drive people to the effective content.'"

The NetGensesis software consists of a group of accumulators or adapters to interface with the various servers on a site (be they HTML servers, Flash servers, database servers, etc.), a datamart for storage, slicing and dicing tools for reports and analytical data drilling (see Figure 12.7), and a set of activators that can take action based on triggers from the data.

If you recognize a specific pattern that recognizes the pattern of a serious prospect, the trigger can send out just the right e-mail to just the right sales rep or just the right direct mail piece to the prospect. If you don't have contact information, the trigger can cause just the right dynamic content to appear on the next page, suited especially to that visitor.

Now that you have the tools that let you measure discrete data elements, how are you going to turn those measurements into meaningful metrics, so that you'll know what actions to take based on the results? We've already covered reach and cost of acquisition; now let's see what the yardsticks, stopwatches, and depth gauges are telling us.

Abandonment

A man spends 15 to 20 minutes wandering through the aisles of a large grocery store filling a shopping cart with various and sundry. At some point, the man stops, looks into his cart with a quizzical look on his face, turns around, and walks out of the store, leaving the full shopping cart behind.

A rarity? Happens all the time online.

We'd like to think that people are coming to our sites to buy things. Why then are so many full shopping carts left in the middle of the check-out line? The Boston Consultancy Group (www.bcg.com) determined that 65 percent of people who started to fill up a cart abandoned it before checking out. BizRate.com says that number is more like 78 percent. The biggest problem reported in any study you care to read is that buying on the Web is difficult.

Customer service falls into two broad areas: before and after. After the sale, the customer needs questions answered and problems solved. Before the sale, the customer needs help deciding which products to buy and help with the purchasing process itself. Web sites are getting better and better at helping people choose the right golf club (www.rangergolf.com), choose the right PC (www.hp.com/desktops/helpmechoose), and choose the right satellite phone model in Australia (enterprise.powerup.com.au/~satelite/helpme.htm).

But sadly, helping potential customers figure out how to buy something online is an area rife with hazards and ripe for improvement. Poor navigation, insufficient information, and interminable wait times are more the rule than the exception. These are the places to spend your time and effort if you want more people spending more money at your site.

Navigation (Again)

So, "Make It Easier To Buy" is a good motto and one that Amazon took to the extreme with its patented 1-Click buying button. But the art of measurement and metrics is all

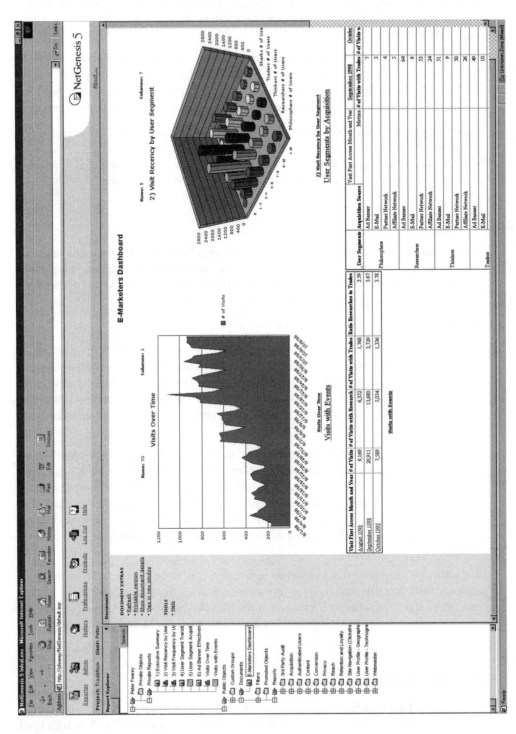

Figure 12.7 The NetGenesis 5 Dashboard offers a digest of who's doing what on your site, for how long, and how often.

about knowing *how* to make it easier. That means getting a baseline on your site of how many people are leaving in medias res, making some changes, and then watching to see whether your changes had a positive impact.

In his book *Designing Web Usability* (New Riders, 1999), Jakob Nielsen extols the virtues of the standard format. It doesn't matter what that format actually is, as long as it is prevalent. The point is that your shopping cart should act just like all the other carts your customers have seen in their surfing travels. Do not make your customers have to learn something new.

Information

Before you buy something, you want to know how much it costs. Not the price, but the price, plus the shipping, plus the handling, plus the packaging, plus the tax, plus whatever other convoluted surcharge can be tacked onto "the price." Often, you have to put the item into the shopping cart, take it all the way through the check-out process until just before the final purchase button in order to find out that the $53 necktie is going to cost $92 to get it into your hands. No sale.

I recently purchased a laptop carrying case online from the laptop manufacturer. It was designed for the model I owned, so I knew it was the right size. But there was only one photo of it so I couldn't quite tell if it had enough pockets for the file folders I need to carry while on the road. What's the Internet philosophy when buying from a reputable firm? Buy it! And then return it later if it's not what you had in mind.

Sure enough, the case did not have the features I was hoping for, and back it went. The lesson? For the cost of one more photo, one more paragraph, one more bullet item in the list of features, that company might not have had to shell out for the shipping and restocking charges, or (heaven forbid) charge me for shipping and handling, obliterating the chances of my buying from them in the future.

In an ideal world, you can post enough information on your site so that anybody who goes there will find all the information he or she needs to make a buying decision. In a dream world, all that information will be available within three clicks from the home page. Yes, you will have to compromise. So take a long, hard look at the e-mail questions you receive. Analyze the server logs regarding your Frequently Asked Questions pages to see which are the *most* frequently asked. If you can't publish everything, at least you can publish what people are most anxious to learn.

It Simply Doesn't Work

Even the best sites are subject to technical faults. We've all learned to live with the occasional 404 message. We've gotten used to having to hit the Reload button every now and then. When those problems crop up during a search for information, we shrug them off and keep moving, keep searching, keep learning. But when a technical fault occurs during the execution of a purchase, we are taken aback.

It's very disconcerting when an automatic teller machine fails while you are trying to withdraw the grocery money. There are no witnesses. Your word against theirs. The feeling is the same on a Web site.

You intended to make the purchase. You tried to make the purchase. But you were rewarded with some cryptic message. The server is too busy. The transaction timed out. The information you provided was insufficient. The total came out $100 more than it should. The Web site simply did not respond. What do you do? Where do you turn?

If you're running a Web site with a shopping cart on it, make sure it works and make sure it works every day. Testing is not something you do once and decide it's done. Hire a mystery shopping firm to periodically buy something from your site. Engage a Web server performance testing firm to test the speed of your servers. Buy a link-checking software package to make sure those 404s are not found on your site.

Measure Twice, Cut Once

You'll learn a great deal more if you take the time to measure what's happening on your site. You cannot manage what you do not measure.

In our interviews with Web managers, people from NetGenesis and I found that the information online stores are collecting includes the following:

- The ratio of abandoned carts to completed purchases per day
- Number of items per abandoned cart versus completed transactions
- Profile of items abandoned versus purchased
- Profile of shopper versus buyer

When a shopper with the profile resembling an abandoner begins placing items in a cart, and the list of items is very similar to those in other carts abandoned in the past, a dynamic Web site can take action by offering special incentives or displaying messages regarding the ease of completing a purchase. The point is to turn more shoppers into buyers. Watching shopping behavior for signs of trouble can prove very powerful.

Don't wonder at the behavior of your customers who abandon their shopping carts without paying; question the behavior of your cart. In our white paper, "E-Metrics, Business Metrics for the New Economy" (www.netgen.com/emetrics), Matt Cutler and I made the following point:

> Suppose that shoppers at a business telephony Web site tend to buy two or three items at a time. When a shopping cart begins to fill with ten or twelve items, the activity might set off a trigger to include persuasive content on the next screen. The site might offer to open a business account for the shopper, or offer a chat session with an online service representative to discuss the shopper's needs.
>
> Abandonment does not apply strictly to electronic shopping carts in online stores selling packaged goods. Any multi-step buying process may suffer from abandonment. An online brokerage wants to make sure that its users do not merely trade, but also add more funds to their portfolios. If a steadily trading client makes no deposits over a given period

of time, the site might offer specialized consulting, education, or access to additional investment research.

Between clicking on a banner ad and making a purchase, there are many points where a prospective customer may fall out of the life cycle. The overall abandonment rate is the number of people who commence but do not complete the buying process.

If the reason is a lack of qualification, you will need to adjust the mechanisms that attract people to your site. If the problem is poor site navigation, a new site design may be in order.

If all else fails, you could ask your site visitors why they're leaving. That's what SurveySite does for a living (www.surveysite.com). "SurveySite's Shopping Cart Analysis program captures the attitudes and opinions of online shoppers immediately after they have made the decision not to purchase. We do this by programming our 'pop-up survey' software to display a small survey invitation window to randomly selected respondents as they leave the purchase page or Web site. Our software is specially programmed to only choose those individuals who do not make a purchase. We can capture people who leave the purchase page by selecting a bookmark, closing the browser window or exiting the page/Web site in any other way."

So what's it going to take? Better explanation of your pricing? More up-front description of your return policy? Bigger pictures of your product? Measure, test, measure again.

Attrition

It's one thing when a customer abandons a shopping cart. It's quite another when they never come back. Here's how Matt Cutler and I described this undesirable phenomenon it in our E-Metrics white paper:

> Once a customer, always a customer? Not so. The *attrition* rate is the percentage of existing, converted customers who have ceased buying from you and have gone elsewhere during a specific period of time. As reported widely in the media, when Delta Airlines added a $2 surcharge to fares not booked over the Internet, the marketplace protested that the fees were unfair. The number of people who had previously purchased on a regular basis, but stopped coming back, appeared to grow alarmingly. Had Delta offered a discount for buying online or an additional 1,000 frequent flier miles, like their competitors United Airlines and American Airlines, Delta likely would have avoided this infamous marketing episode.
>
> Attrition is different from abandonment. If you switch your telephone service from Bell Atlantic to MCI, then Bell Atlantic considers you to have "attrited"—a sure sign of a lack of loyalty. If you call up Bell Atlantic, start to switch over, but then balk at a certain contract term and hang up, then you have abandoned the conversion process.
>
> Attrition is the flip side of retention and carries with it the same considerations regarding time scales. If a customer does not buy a new car from you for three, four, or five years, it could mean that she is now purchasing from your competitor, or it may simply be that she likes her current model. If a music lover who buys CDs from your site on a weekly basis does not come by for a month, some sort of recovery action is in order.

Conversion

One would assume that a major goal of your Web site is to sell stuff. Are you selling stuff? Revenue from your Web site should be the simplest thing to measure of all. Standard accounting practices should capture that information. But what about the cost of conversion?

This is the same issue as the cost of acquisition, but we're tracking customers all the way from the banner ad to the Submit button on the order form. If they are buying, it would be very valuable to know which method of acquisition and which mode of persuasion are bringing in the best sales—not the most sales, the *best* sales. "I'll make it up in volume" doesn't work if you sell below cost. We're accustomed to measuring our most profitable products; now we have to measure our most profitable methods. So what's your cost?

Another metric for conversion is how the Web affects your offline sales.

A salesperson can spend a lot of time explaining a product to a prospect. The theory, the history, the references, the warranty, and more may need to be imparted before the prospect turns into a customer. If you have a product or service that falls into the long-lead-time category, you should look to your sales force as a measure of your success. Do your salespeople notice that their prospects are better educated? Asking more sophisticated questions? Making purchase decisions faster? If so, salespeople can do more prospecting and close more deals.

Tracking attrition, conversion, and navigation in general helps identify what people are looking at, but it also reveals how they are looking. With that knowledge, you can implement automated persuasion techniques to improve their chances of buying.

In the E-Metrics white paper, Matt Cutler and I came up with a whole host of additional things you could measure based on the activity on your site, including the following:

- Churn
- Recency
- Frequency
- Monetary value
- Duration
- Yield
- Net yield
- Connect rate
- Stickiness
- Slipperiness
- Focus
- Velocity

Optimal Site Path

From *Customer Service on the Internet* by Jim Sterne
(John Wiley & Sons, 2000)

In March, 1999, eMarketer (a Web site well worth watching) interviewed J. G. Sandom, head of Ogilvy Interactive (http://www.ogilvy.com/o_interactive). In that interview (http://www.emarketer.com/enews/enews_sandom.html), Sandom described the power of forecasting what somebody might need on a Web site and how to make the most of it:

If we're trying to reach women between the ages of 35 and 45 with x income level, we go back and look at their pattern through the site. You can actually go and say, "Hmm, it looks as though there are about six or so OSP's (Optimal Site Paths) that really worked for this particular target segment, for this particular objective."

Having done that, our next job is determining how we drive these individuals through the correct OSP's.

We use any number of techniques, but I'll give you three of them.

One is we use outbound e-mail. For example, I'll use my generic example again, you go to the home page, go to the car configurator, finance configurator, dealer locator, and then you go to the e-mail center and tell the dealer you want to buy. But what if a user goes to the home page, goes to the car configurator, but she never goes and figures out the financing terms? We can do an outbound e-mail. And the e-mail says, "Ford Credit is doing a special this month." There would be a link in that e-mail where, if she clicks on that link, it takes her automatically into the financing configurator. So now we've got her to step three.

Using the outbound e-mail we've persuaded them that there was an offer, and made it compelling enough so that they clicked and went to the next step of the OSP. Outbound e-mail is one great technique.

Another technique would be personalization, that's the ability for the end user to create a personalized home page. That personalized home page may have any number of things on it.

It's not about layout—it's about what is on that home page. It may include things like user defined best picks. I've gone in as an end user and said of all the thousands of possible links in the site, these are the six sections I go to all the time. I select them with radio buttons. Boom! They now appear on my home page. We also do what we call ECRM-defined best pick, CRM being customer relationship management. So, as I said before, we track user behavior. So even if someone says I want to have these six links on my home page, we know that he goes to these two other sections all the time. And we have business rules behind our site which say if we track this guy's behavior and he

continues

Optimal Site Path *(Continued)*

goes to these other things that are not on his personalized home page to find, you know, through his form, and he goes there more than x times during this period of time, then automatically post those other sections to his personal home page.

Another thing that a personalized home page might include is an archive of personal searches. If you're like me I never remember what searches I did. So it's nice to have all the searches you've done of a site.

The last thing, and the most important thing—the reason I brought this stupid thing up in the first place—is we always make sure that we auto-rotate on people's personalized home pages the next step on the OSP.

If a guy comes in and he goes to the home page, he goes to the car configuration, maybe now he's even gone to the financing configurator—but he hasn't gone to the dealer locator, we would rotate OSP's on his personal home page, including, of course, a link to the new groovy little dealer locator that we've got now. And guess what? There's a little editorial comment on that link that says, "If you go in now and check out our new dealer locator you get a coupon for $20 off your next oil change at the dealer nearest you." We give them an incentive to go there.

Another way of driving them along the OSP is to pop open a daughter window—it's got a little messaging, a little promotional information, to move them to the next step.

Yes, the example is from the marketing perspective. But it only takes a small turn of your head to get the customer service viewpoint.

What if you could tell that people who complained about delayed shipments also seemed to have problems assembling the bicycle they ordered? What if your site had a deep enough database to make the connection between people who always complained about getting the wrong products shipped to them and the speed with which they were placing their online orders?

What could you do about it? You could get proactive. Send them an e-mail. Personalize their version of the standard newsletter. Add a button to your home page that only they can see.

- Seducible moments
- Personalization index
- Freshness factor

While parts of the white paper have been reproduced here, I encourage you to download that paper from www.netgen.com/emetrics for the description of each of these measurements. There were some other areas, though, that we did not touch on—mostly due to a lack of space. A 60-page white paper seemed long enough.

The Softer Side of Assessment

Some measurements that don't come right out of your server logs can influence whether you think your Web site is "successful" and may prove valuable during the next performance review with your boss.

Measuring Searches

In an article in *Fast Company* (February 2001), Alissa Kozuh talks about her role as the editor of Nordstrom.com—and she talks about reading people's minds. She reviews 1,500 daily searches on the Nordstrom site, or 45,000 each month.

"People in the fashion industry can call a trend anything they want," Kozuh says. "But what the customer decides to call it is ultimately what matters most to us."

It is Alissa's job to tweak the Nordstrom database thesaurus so that people get relevant responses. In August 2000, Nordstrom relaunched its juniors department, "Brass Plum." That was the top of the list for popular search terms, but none of Nordstrom's products or manufacturers used that term, and very little was found in the way of search results. Alissa worked her magic, and now the younger surfers can find what they're after, including the .5 carat Cubic Zirconia Navel Ring (see Figure 12.8).

Now, shoppers searching for "prom" or "party dress" get considered pointers rather than database matches. Do Alissa's efforts pay off? According to *Fast Company*, "By poring over the statistics each day, Kozuh can suggest tweaks that will give shoppers a better hit rate. Nordstrom.com won't disclose what percentage of its shoppers abandon the site empty-handed. But the company does say that after it introduced the new search engine, along with the overall site redesign, sales jumped 32 percent during the next three months compared with the six-month period before the relaunch."

So get out your tape measure and track the trends on your site. What people type into your search field can give you some interesting insights:

- Is your advertising having an impact on the types of people coming to your site?
- Are people searching for terms your competition uses?
- Did that mention on "Oprah" have an effect on your site traffic?
- Is there a new buzzword that you should include in your site map?
- Are people still looking for discontinued products?
- Must people resort to your search engine because your navigation is not up to par?

One other interesting aspect of the work that Alissa does at Nordstrom—it was worth mentioning in the press. Are you measuring *that*?

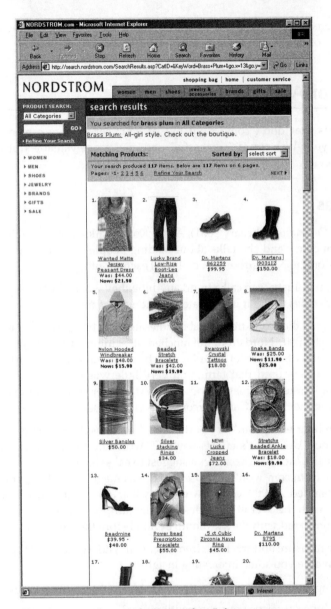

Figure 12.8 The words "Brass Plum" do not appear on any of pages featuring these items. But these are the items sought when searching on those words.

Measuring Editorial Exposure

Did you create an industry stir at the introduction of your Web site? Did the trade press lavish praise on your bold, forward thinking? Did you garner more ink than you would have had you spent the resources elsewhere? Don't forget this important gauge of marketing success.

Alicia Rockmore, brand manager at Van den Bergh Foods, was very pleased with the attention Ragu garnered for being the first packaged goods product on the Web (www.eat.com). Its story was picked up by the computer press as well as the food industry journals.

Granted, Ragu was the first, and those days are gone. It's too late to be the first in your field to get on the Web and enjoy the spotlight. But you can be the first in your industry to offer interactive, personalized services that the competition hasn't even thought of yet. And as Alissa Kozuh discovered, you can be the first to use information about your site visitors in an interesting, newsworthy way.

Go out and get yourself some ink.

Customer Satisfaction

The final measure of success will be the vote of confidence you get from your clients. When you do ask people questions about your products, your company, and your site, what is the ratio of casual users to active responders? What is the quality of the information you gather from your visitors? Do they take the time to give you some insight into their likes and dislikes about your products? Do they offer suggestions for new product features and propose new ways to conduct business? Do they express delight at your new, superior customer service?

This area is important enough to rate its own chapter. If you skipped Chapter 6, "Feedback," now would be a good time to check it out. But here's a bit of advice: Don't depend on the Web for your Web site feedback. Get out into the world and talk to customers face to face. Or get somebody to do it for you.

Derrith Lambka isn't an industry gadfly. She's a woman who has been there, done that, and understands what it takes to get it done again. She founded Insights for Action (www.insightsforaction.com) (see Figure 12.9) in order to collaborate with clients to create great online customer experiences.

Insights for Action becomes the voice of the customer. Derrith is very enthusiastic about her work. "Customers are great at identifying problems. We are great at generating new and innovative ideas to solve those problems. We become 'investigative reporters' about customers. We uncover what they hate, what they see as a minimum requirement, a nice to have and something you could do that would really 'wow' them."

"We put the learning from research into actionable design plans. So many times in my career, I've seen researchers who knew a lot about customers but after they'd presented their information and written their report, the binder sat on a shelf and wasn't acted on. What was missing was putting the insights from the research into a practical application for the customer."

One-on-one customer interviews with a video camera bring faceless customers to life. It's part Q&A, part empathy, and part usability testing. If you're not hearing your customers speak for themselves, you should talk to Derrith.

While you're worrying about what customers say about you as individuals, you should also be aware of what the world thinks of you in general. What used to belong

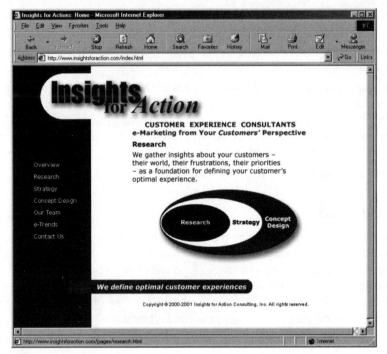

Figure 12.9 Insights for Action goes to where your customers live and work to find out how they think and feel.

exclusively to the folks in public relations has spilled onto the marketing manager's desk and successfully splashed the Web manager as well.

Reputation Management

Remember all those "sucks" sites in the *Web Ridicule as a Business* section of Chapter 2, "Customer Service First"? Well, they're not all you need to worry about. What do you do if you come across a site that's out to get you? You call on your lawyers, who call on the powers of trademark violation, and you cross your fingers and watch your checkbook wither.

But what do you do if ordinary people join in an ordinary online discussion and talk about how much ordinary trouble they've had with your company? That's not actionable. That's just ordinary.

On the other hand, if they're more than cranky, they could be breaking the law.

Just Because You're Paranoid Doesn't Mean They're Not Out to Get You

In August 2000, 23-year-old Mark Simeon Jakob, a community college student, forged a press release from a company called Emulex that said the company had a loss that quarter of 15 cents per share instead of the 25 cent profit it really had. It also said the CEO had resigned.

The "news" sent Emulex shares down by 62 percent in one day. Jakob had shorted 3,000 shares of Emulex the day before and earned $54,000. Then, he bought 3,500 shares at the depressed price and pulled in another $186,000. Yes, the stock came right back up, and yes, Jakob was hauled off for his fraud, but the people who lost money on the stock because they believed the "news" and had sold while it was crashing are out of luck.

Reputation management can mean looking out for the bad guys. Usually, however, the phrase is used to see how the public at large feels about you.

Aggregate Attitude

According to Jakob Nielsen, reputation management, ". . . is an independent service that keeps track of the rated quality, credibility, or some other desirable metric. The things being rated will typically be Web sites, companies, products, or people, but in theory anything can have a reputation that users may want to look up before taking action or doing business."

If you don't like this book, you can say so on Amazon.com. Can I control what you say? Nope. All I can do is try to make this book the best I can in the time I have. Can I influence what happens in the reviews on Amazon? I've seen several attempts.

People have asked me to write reviews of their yet-to-be-published books on Amazon. People have asked me to help them get more reviews for their book on Amazon than their "competitor's" book. People have asked me to give a bad review to other books in order to make theirs look better.

This is *not* the sort of reputation management I had in mind, but we're in the same ball park. I'm more interested in sites like Deja.com and Epinions.com and BizRate.com, where the public is invited to present their opinion and review the aggregate results.

How does BizRate get people to express fresh opinions? At the source. If you're brave, like CDW, you hook up with BizRate, which offers a chance to win $100 if you'll answer a survey. The offer appears at the end of a purchase on the order confirmation page, so they're catching people right at the moment the service has been rendered (see Figure 12.10), and the questions are many and varied (see Figure 12.11).

How satisfied are you with each of the following aspects of this online purchase?

How satisfied are you overall with this purchase experience at CDW Computer Centers' site?

How likely are you to purchase from CDW Computer Centers the next time you are in the market to buy this type of product?

Including this order, how frequently have you purchased the following online in the last six months?

How much did you spend on this purchase? (Including shipping, handling and taxes)

How much were the shipping and handling charges?

Does your company have a corporate contract with CDW Computer Centers?

How frequently have you purchased the following offline in the last six months?

What types of products did you just purchase from CDW Computer Centers?

Which of the following most influenced your decision to visit CDW Computer Centers' site today?

Which of the following, if any, influenced your decision to purchase from CDW Computer Centers today? When do you expect all of the items in your order to be delivered?

Figure 12.10 BizRate collects customer satisfaction information at the point of sale.

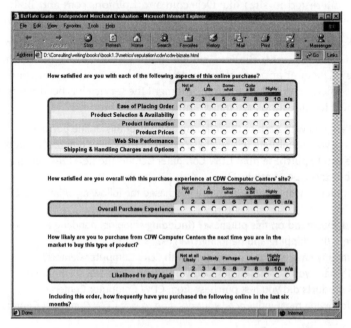

Figure 12.11 BizRate wants to know a great deal about how you feel.

And that's only the half of it. When BizRate says, "Please take a moment" to answer some questions, it has a pretty hefty moment in mind.

The interesting part is that the vendor (CDW) can participate for free—as long as it doesn't mind the results being published (see Figure 12.12).

But it doesn't stop there. BizRate follows up with an e-mail and asks *more* questions. Did the products you ordered arrive in the time you expected? Did the merchant offer order status information, and how pleased with it were you? How likely are you to buy from CDW again? If not, why not? What could CDW do to increase the likelihood that you'd buy again?

How does BizRate make money? It will sell detailed information back to the merchant for tens of thousands of dollars a year, including the comments shoppers have been encouraged to type in while taking the survey. Merchants who care about their customers find that it's a pretty good deal.

Other sites, however, are not working hand in hand with the merchants, and you might end up in the sights of sites like these:

- www.complaint.com
- www.EllensPoisonPen.com
- www.BitchAboutIt.com

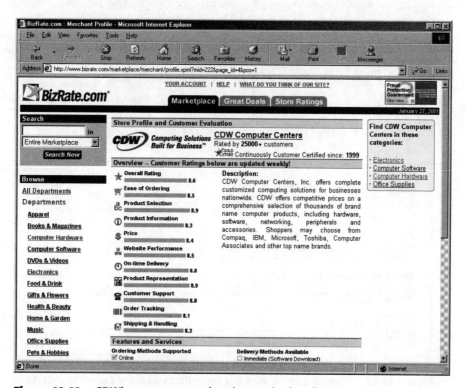

Figure 12.12 CDW's scores are on the BizRate site for all to see.

- www.thecomplainet.com
- www.fightback.com
- www.planetfeedback.com

Somebody in your company has to monitor these public outpourings of anguish, or your firm may end up in the company of The Horrible Pain of the Internal Nose Zit on www.hissyfit.com (see Figure 12.13).

Oh—and before you think your online reconnoitering is limited to unhappy customers, don't forget to look out for those unhappy employees. My personal favorite is the Blockbuster Customers Suck!! page at http://members.nbci.com/bbsucks/site.htm:

> Welcome to my page! If you are a Blockbuster or any video store employee, you should enjoy it. If you are a customer of a video store, you may want to leave now. I think it is pretty obvious what this page is about so if you don't think you will find it funny, why not leave now instead of reading it and then sending me nasty emails which I will post on this page.

If that gets too depressing, switch from the telescope to the microscope and look back at your own customers. Are they buying from you?

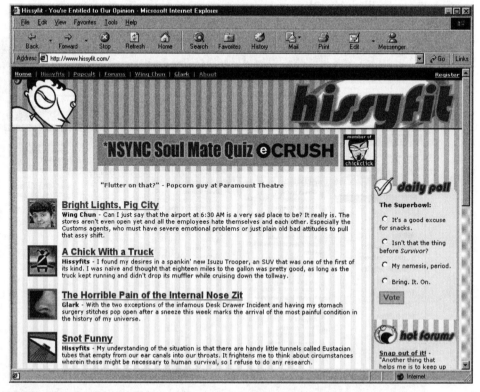

Figure 12.13   There are some sites out there that you do *not* want to include a reference to your company.

The Bottom Line

You can measure pages and downloads and even sucks sites, but when push comes to shove, it's the money that matters. Finally (and the most difficult question for many companies doing business on the World Wide Web), are you making significant sales you wouldn't have made otherwise?

When I send in my two proof-of-purchase labels for my Ragu Net Surfing Team T-shirt, the folks at Van den Bergh Foods can be pretty sure I bought two jars of Ragu Sauce because of its Web site efforts. Colorado Boomerangs (www.pd.net/colorado) might be able to tell if it has increased its sales of the Kilimanjaro Hook by counting its Web transactions. But it'll have to factor in how many sales were lost from other channels. Everybody who used to buy the Kilimanjaro Hook from in-flight magazine ads might be buying it on the Web now.

Are sales made on a Web site actually new sales? Don't discount the novelty element. Good customers might want to shop your Web site just for fun. They might be shopping there because it's convenient. This is where a good survey can help you collect the

Loyalty

From "Customer Loyalty Online," *eMarketing* **Magazine
March 2001**

What makes a customer loyal to a vendor? What makes a surfer loyal to a Web site?
It starts with awareness that builds into confidence. I'd never driven a Lincoln Town Car, but they've been around for ages and I'd heard of them, so they must be OK. Then confidence builds to trust. They've been around so long that when I'm upgraded into one for free by the rental agency I figure, sure, why not? Then trust becomes habit. I want to rent the same car, or buy the same cake mix, or click over to the same search engine because of familiarity.
If you can afford to buy public awareness, and then can gain confidence to become a habit, you've started online life off to a good start. But you'd better be on the ball, because your competitors are going to be out to get you. They're going to raise the stakes. You're going to have to raise the barrier to switching.
How hard was it to switch from one long-distance calling service to another? They *paid* you to do it! How hard is it to start buying books from one Web site versus another? Not very. Why then, do I continue to buy my books from Amazon.com when there are dozens of sites that have lower prices? It's not just that I know the Amazon site so well that it's habit, it's because Amazon knows me so well that it's simple. Brutally simple. One-click buying is the height of ease of use. A friend e-mails me about a book. I click. I buy. I'm done.

continues

Loyalty *(Continued)*

It boils down to remembering enough about me to make my life easier. I don't want to go to another book store because I'll have to type in all that credit card information and all that shipping and billing information and I've been there and done that.

So what can you remember about your customers? Don Peppers and Martha Rogers, who coined the term one-to-one marketing (www.1to1.com), want to know why a drug store can't help customers remember when to take their pills, which over the counter products they're allergic to, and when they should refill their prescriptions and replace their hearing aid batteries.

Loyalty then, is based on value. How much do your customers value your service? Whatever the answer, it will give you a clue about how to price your products. How much do they value you over and above your competitors? That will give you an indication about how loyal they might be. But the value proposition is a two-way street.

How much do you value your customers? That will tell you how much you should be investing in them. It's your responsibility to gauge the profitability of each customer to see which are truly valuable and which are a drain on your resources.

qualitative information you need to complement the sales statistics you'll compile as a matter of course.

Track this information long enough, and you can get a feel for the loyalty factor.

Understanding loyalty and putting numbers on it are two different things. Here's how Matt Cutler and I approached it in our E-Metrics white paper:

> When determining the valuation of a Web-enabled company, it would be useful to have a standard, cross-industry e-metric indicating the loyalty of its customers. But loyalty is simply too industry-specific and even site-specific and involves an enormous number of variables.
>
> If you have an email account at Yahoo! and you check it every day, you should earn a high loyalty rating from Yahoo!. However, if you also have an email account at Hotmail and check that daily as well, then you are not really as loyal as Yahoo! might imagine. If you check your stock portfolio at Schwab every weekday, but you check your mutual funds at Fidelity, are you still considered loyal?
>
> Measuring the loyalty of a Web site user means creating an index you can use daily to see how the changes you make affect your customers. The Bain & Company study indicated that the average Amazon.com customer must remain loyal for approximately 2.5 years to become profitable.
>
> Each site must create a loyalty ranking system of its own depending on its goals and its experience. Here are our three scenarios again, involving the retailer, the considered purchase, and the business-to-business relationship, with different approaches to loyalty as an e-metric.

The Retail Experience

Customer loyalty here is measured in purchases. How much do they buy? How often do they buy? Are they a profitable customer? The formula for loyalty will include the following variables:

Visit Frequency: Scored based on number of visits per month.

Visit Duration: Scored based on number of minutes per visit.

Visit Depth: Scored based on number of page views per visit.

Purchases per Visit

Number of Items Purchased per Visit

Total Revenue of Purchases per Visit

Profitability of Purchases per Month

If additional marketing programs are implemented, the customer might be evaluated on factors such as:

Number of Referrals per month: Did the customer refer others?

Value of Referrals per month: Did those referrals buy? How much?

Questionnaire Propensity: How willing is the customer to answer survey questions?

Contest Participation: How willing is the customer to participate in contests?

Reward Points Program: How willing is the customer to participate in affinity programs?

The Considered Purchase

Loyalty can be measured on a short-term basis to try to clinch the sale. It can also be measured on a much longer-term time scale. If the customer is buying a refrigerator, chances are excellent that she will not need another one for years. You can keep her in your database for those years while waiting for the right opportunity to remind her of your quality and value. Insurance companies keep information on newborns in their database for decades in order to offer additional auto insurance in fifteen and a half years.

Most loyalty calculations will revolve around how the user browses your site. Here we begin with the same variables as above in the Retail Experience, but with a twist:

Visit Frequency: This is scored based on visits per decision period and mapped to a decision-making curve. Buyers of one type of product will visit a certain number of times in the first period, a certain amount in the middle of the process, and signal that a buying decision is actively being made when they increase (or decrease) to a different number of visits in a set time span.

Visit Duration: Scored per session. This is another indication of how close to a decision the user may be.

Visit Depth: Page views per visit are as revealing as frequency and duration. To this list, we add the important analysis of how the user traverses the site:

Site Path: How well is the user following an optimal site path?

Contact: How often does the user send email, engage in a chat session, or fill in a form on the site? What sort of questions does the user ask?

Product Configurator: How many times does the user run the configurator and which features are selected?

The Business-to-Business Bond

The metrics change again when it comes to extranets. In the business-to-business environment, the emphasis on selling is replaced with a focus on service. Taking orders and solving problems are paramount, while a less aggressive eye is kept open for up-selling and cross-selling. Loyalty comes in many shapes and sizes, and hence loyalty metrics naturally tend to differ greatly between different sites with different business models.

Visit Frequency: In this environment, the watchword is consistency. Is the user coming to the site at set intervals and doing what is expected?

Visit Duration: Are there any changes in the amount of time it takes the user to place the order?

Visit Depth: Is the user looking at products above and beyond his or her norm?

Visit Tenure: Time elapsed since first visit.

Purchase Tenure: Time elapsed since first purchase.

Purchase Frequency: Number of purchases per quarter (or month).

Total Lifetime Spending: Total spending since first visit.

Visit Recency: Time elapsed since most recent visit.

Purchase Recency: Time elapsed since most recent purchase.

Required Clicks to First Purchase: Minimum number of clicks required to complete the first purchase in a visit. The first purchase may require more clicks than repeat purchases.

Required Clicks to Repeat Purchase: Minimum number of clicks required to make a repeat purchase.

Actual Clicks to First Purchase: Actual number of clicks until the first purchase was made.

Actual Clicks to Purchase: Number of clicks until a repeat purchase.

Customer Loyalty Futures is a UK-based think tank of executives from large, multinational corporations. Its mission is to explore the process of customer loyalty management, while considering leading-edge theory, best practice, and innovation regarding the design and application of customer loyalty improvement strategies. Customer Loyalty Futures was founded by Bill George in 1995, and it is now owned by ThinkService in the United States (www.thinkservice.com).

In his white paper, "Customer Loyalty, What Does It Mean to You," Bill describes loyalty this way:

> The delivery of Service, under-pinned by the performance and commitment of employees and intermediaries, is much more influential in determining customer attitudes and behaviour; and that the benefits of recognition as a powerful motivator both internally and externally, are poorly understood and practiced.

Just as importantly, I experienced at first hand, that without boardroom level understanding of the concept of Customer Loyalty and Customer value (£), strategies aimed at improving Customer retention and loyalty requiring total internal commitment in order to optimise and sustain the external effect, and often requiring significant investment—ran the risk of being viewed as tactical, marketing led, initiatives at best.

As a result Loyalty is currently viewed as a marketing issue by the majority of companies and because of this imbalance few attempts have been made to formulate and implement fully integrated business strategies aimed at consciously building internal loyalty in order to support and drive external loyalty and profitability over time.

In order to build sustainable Customer allegiance it is necessary to understand the psychology of Loyalty and the key principles of the process of what I call Customer Loyalty Management. Think of these as a providing a framework within which you can consider the task of Customer Loyalty Management:

Everyone should be viewed as a customer (employee /intermediary /consumer /client /shareholder etc.) with needs and values which must be satisfied or reinforced before they will behave / perform consistently in the way that marketeers and managers want them to do so.

Customer Loyalty Management is a multi-faceted process embracing all elements of the marketing and managerial mix.

The role of senior management is to provide leadership in this context and to promote a culture within which customers, both internal and external, feel truly valued and are fully empowered.

The job of marketeers and managers is to understand the needs and values of their individual customers and target segments, with the goal of converting a higher prportion of their "uncommitted" customers to "advocates" (and particularly those most valuable) through the effective application of a mix of best possible strategies.

Measurement and tracking of performance data against the key indicators of loyalty, both internally and externally, are essential to evaluate the effectiveness of strategies employed and to manage the development process.

Measuring the Effect—The Indicators of Loyalty

To measure the effect of strategies (inputs) employed, we need to understand the indicators (outputs) of loyalty, of which there are several.

These can be considered as part of a continuum, or on a hierarchical basis, with satisfaction the most widely used but least reliable indicator, through commitment to advocacy and delight as the ultimate indicators of goodwill both internally and externally.

For those who can track it, Retention is a powerful indicator of loyalty. Conversely, defections say a lot about the erosion of goodwill to a supplier or employer, which is why the current focus on customer complaints handling and recovery is so crucial to understanding in this area.

How do you measure loyalty? Keep in mind that I *am* a consultant: It depends.

The next question is whether you are improving the loyalty of the customers you *wish* to be more loyal.

Lifetime Value

We know how to tell if a product is profitable. We're learning how to determine if an acquisition and persuasion method is profitable. Now the question is whether our customers are profitable.

Lifetime Value is a common offline metric used to determine the financial viability of each customer. Now that we have another tool for communicating with and serving our customers, this tool has to become part of that measurement mix.

It's time to add on to the cost of acquisition and persuasion with the cost of customer care. If your FAQs can trim the cost of phone calls, if your software update downloads can defray the cost of buying, recording, and shipping a tape, if personalization engines can keep track of each customer's level of education in order to deliver just the right just-in-time training, then you can tally more and more customers on the profitable side of the ledger sheet.

Competitive Benchmarking

How well do you stand up to your competitors? What are they serving up on their site?

Somebody needs to be assigned the periodic task of surfing the competitive sites to keep an eye on the horizon and an ear to the ground. You can do it on the cheap, or you can take it seriously, as long as you do it.

When I say seriously, I mean the way National Semiconductor does it. Once per quarter, it has an independent research company interview a panel of dozens of design engineers and purchasing types. The customers are asked to perform specific tasks—find a specification, identify a part, and so on. Some are familiar with the site and blast right through. Others are not so fortunate. The neat trick is that they are asked to do these things on the competitors' sites as well, and they don't know that they are doing this on behalf of National Semi.

They are then asked what they like and don't like, what they would like to see in the future, and how the sites could be made easier to use. They are also queried on what new features might be added.

The cheap approach is to add this task to your intern's growing list of responsibilities. Once a month, have the intern take a fresh look at your top rivals, comparing how fast the sites load, whether the information is fresh or dated, whether they're offering personalization, if they have extranet capabilities, and so on.

Want to be alerted to changes on competitive sites? NetMind can help (www.netmind.com) with its URL-Minder service. Tell it the page you want to watch—like the "What's New" page, or the Press Releases page maybe?—and it will notify you when there's a change.

Look to companies like MediaMetrix (www.mediametrix.com) to see who's getting the most traffic or NetRatings (www.netratings.com) for what sort of people go to those sites. Sometimes you can find that sort of information online because people like to brag.

Here's the braggadocio from a company called Vicinity:

The Result

The geographic data-enabled HP Small Business site is attracting the attention of customers. The site receives about eight times the number of hits it previously did. During one month alone, the site received 21,000 page views.

That's useful information to Sun Microsystems, IBM, Dell, and Compaq, among others. And this showed up in the *Denver Post*:

Microsoft Corp. plans to open its online software store in August, a move that is making some resellers nervous. "The reason behind it was we get 120 million hits per day, or 1.5 million visitors, to microsoft.com," said Neil Farnsworth, general manager for business development with Microsoft's end user customer unit. "We're providing visitors a way to get involved in the buying process."

Thanks, guys.

Let's say you sell hydraulic hoses. Isn't it nice that you can wander over to the Microsoft Network (www.msn.com) at any time and get the Top Ten Most Popular Sites for "Hydraulic Hoses"? (see Figure 12.14).

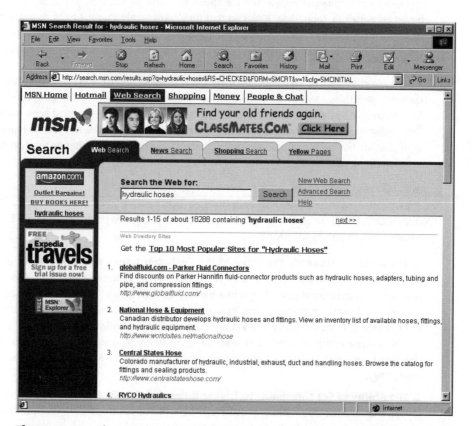

Figure 12.14 The search engines, like this one at MSN.com, are a wealth of competitive information.

A whole host of companies has come forth to lend you aid in this, your hour of need. If it's worth $100,000 or more to you, RivalWatch.com will keep an eagle eye on your competitor's prices. The folks at FatBrain.com are *very* interested in how Amazon, Barnes & Noble, and Borders price their goods. After all, they're exactly the same goods. That sort of due diligence must have impressed Barnes & Noble. On November 16, 2000 it acquired FatBrain.com.

Action Adventure

Having reams of numbers at your fingertips is great. Pie charts and bar graphs and trend lines look very handsome on your wall, what with color printers being so inexpensive these days. But they don't do a bit of good unless you act on them. Knowledge may be power, but if you don't use that power to improve your relationship with your customers, what's the point?

As Matt Cutler and I pointed out in our E-Metrics white paper (www.netgen.com/emetrics):

> The e-business managers with whom we spoke are certainly not strangers to taking action based on e-metrics. More than 70% said that they consistently alter their site design, while nearly as many modify their ad campaigns. This is not surprising, as site and ad changes are tactical in nature and can be made quickly. Fewer reported that they make more strategic changes in promotions, partnering, or product mix based on e-metrics results.
>
> The site changes that Web executives are ready to make revolve around serving specific content, advertising, and promotions to specific users based on ever-changing user profiles. As people's interests and behavioral profiles change, the Web site must keep pace or face losing its user audience. In time, our interviewees hope to see not just changes to their content, but more strategic corporate changes—like dynamically altering their product merchandising mix—as well.

Lynne Harvey, senior consultant/analyst from the Patricia Seybold Group (www.psgroup.com), wrote an article called "The Future Use of Analytic Applications" (November 2, 2000). In it, she nails the three key capabilities provided by CRM and CI (customer intelligence) solutions:

1. The Ability to Quantify the Value of the Customer Interaction. The analytic applications' reporting solutions help quantify the value of the customer interaction. The metrics tracked and reported can help guide e-businesses with their CI and CRM strategies. For example, call center managers, sales managers, and marketing managers can determine the number of customers that interact and purchase at particular touchpoints. They can also determine which touchpoint is best suited for doing business with customers (e.g., whether John Smith responds better to an e-mail campaign or Mary Jones prefers telemarketing).

2. The Ability to Set Thresholds to Trigger Rules and Events. The results of the calculations that analytic applications provide can be used to set thresholds that can trigger business rules and events, which in turn automate the delivery of specific content (such as personalized offers and product recommendations). The analytic application can then be used as the "brain" to help facilitate real-time interaction and personalization. For example, I spent $500 buying books on line at books.com one week, and the site's analytic application calculates the average order size on a weekly basis. The analytic application could then compare my purchases against the average purchase rate metric and, if it's greater than the average, could trigger a special discount or coupon for future use.

3. The Ability to Help Qualify Customer Information. Analytic applications can also be used in tandem with CI and CRM solutions to help sort out and qualify customer information, thereby enriching a company's customer intelligence data-gathering activities. When James Weston calls the customer service department to find out when the video that he purchased online will arrive at his house, the customer service department can then ask him what kind of delivery service he typically prefers. The information about the call can be entered into a CRM system and analytic applications can help determine how Jim's delivery preferences affect the company's current delivery services model. In this example, analytic applications could help the company determine if Jim's delivery service preference is profitable for the company.

Each of these capabilities fits into the gather, analyze, strategize, and act framework for delivering customer intelligence and ultimately fostering the development of a deeper mutually beneficial relationship between the customer and the company. This is, after all, the main goal of CRM.

By now you *must* have figured out that this book is about the relationship between the customer and the company. That relationship does not improve until you take action. That action doesn't have to mean starting up whole new product lines or closing plants. It can mean many things. Table 12.1 lists some actions you might take in response to customer behavior on your site.

Table 12.1 Business Rules Examples

TYPE	EVENT	ACTION
A	Customer arrives via "low cost" banner and navigates to bicycles	Show best-value bicycles first
	Customer then looks at camping gear	Show best-value camping gear mixed with camping-related bicycle equipment
	Customer requests e-mail notification	Send Spring sale e-mail in April and May showing best-buys
	Customer requests postal mail notification	Send Spring sale postcard in March and April showing best-buys
	Customer visits bicycles 10 times within 1 month	Send notification of "special" sale on best-buy bikes

continues

Table 12.1 Business Rules Examples (*Continued*)

TYPE	EVENT	ACTION
B	Customer arrives via "status" banner and navigates to bicycles	Show name-brand bicycles first
	Customer then looks at camping gear	Show name-brand camping gear mixed with camping-related bicycle equipment
	Customer requests e-mail notification	Send Spring sale e-mail in April and May showing name-brands
	Customer requests postal mail notification	Send Spring sale postcard in March and April showing name-brands
	Customer visits bicycles 10 times within 1 month	Send notification of "special" sale on brand-name bikes

You cannot manage what you do not measure, so start measuring. You cannot manage if you do not have an understanding of how a Web site should go together and how to make it work—from a business perspective. That's what Chapter 13, "Managing Your Site and Your Sanity," is all about.

Metric Meter

One single click makes the whole thing tick
When a visitor comes to your site
It's a finger flick that does the trick
But the data keeps you up at night

Do you measure the click? The landing? The hit?
The page? The session? The sale?
There's got to be more to keeping Web score
How do you know you've prevailed?

E-Metrics begin to measure the wins
And the loses, the trip ups, and flaws
To point out those sins that cause us chagrin
And give site visitors pause

It can be a short tale from the click to the sale
In a blink from the link to the bank
Or it can take weeks while curiosity peaks
For a sale to be made, let's be frank

Memberships can be tallied and gauged
And leads are a good thing to track
But conversion and loyalty
Are the E-Metric royalty
These need a new measuring tack

We have been lacking the knack to be tracking
What alters the shape of your funnel
And changes those leads into e-commerce deeds
That light at the end of the tunnel

E-Metrics are new, now it's all up to you
To get these e-yardsticks extended
Then you can tell if you've done something well
Something better, or done something splendid

CHAPTER 13

Managing Your Site and Your Sanity

C ongratulations. You, who were once responsible for brochures, and trade shows, and direct mail, and product positioning, and public relations, and all that jazz, are now thrust into the limelight. You, who have single-handedly kept the leads rolling in, the literature rolling out, and the competition off guard, are now responsible for making sure your Web site looks the right way, says the right thing, and does the right stuff. All eyes are on you. It's time to shine.

Taking the bull by the horns, you happily dive in, ready for a new challenge, excited by the prospect of learning something new. You know marketing backward and forward, and it's time to apply it to this newfangled gizmo called the Internet.

Only one little problem. It's a quagmire of technology.

You can lose teeth arguing whether it's easier to teach marketing to an engineer or technology to a marketer, so let's just leave it at this: You're each going to need to learn something of the other's art in order to make your Web site a competitive edge and not a corporate embarrassment.

If you turned to this page looking for advice on how to put together a great Web server, you're out of luck. If you were hoping to get the technical lowdown on load balancing and the intricacies of transaction integration, I'm afraid you've come to the wrong book.

On the other hand, if you are wondering about managing your Web site from a business perspective, I can offer a few insights that might keep you from the depths of despair while dealing with diverse departments in your organization.

Most of the battles you are going to fight are political. No, I take that back. They're *all* political. How much money are you going to spend on a given feature? How much space will you allocate to a given button on the home page? How much effort should go into a given partnership? These are daily battlefield encounters. Here are a few rules of engagement.

Your first step, whether you are firing up a new site for the first time, firing a Web development company for the last time, or firing up the troops to re-create your site (Once more unto the breach, dear friends, once more!), is to identify who's responsible for what. Without that, it's every man for himself.

What happens when your industry's biggest trade journal "forgets" the embargo date and publishes your new product announcement a week early? Marketing goes to IS and says, "This *has* to go up tonight! We're getting pounded on the phones by people looking for content on our site!"

"But," sputters the IS representative, "you told us we had another week to double-check the content, verify all the links, test the CGI scripts, and stress-test the database. We haven't done any of that yet."

"So how long will it take?" asks marketing.

"It would only take two days, but we have this payroll problem that has all our attention right now, and our biggest customer is coming in tomorrow to inspect our extranet compliance," counters IS.

"So today's Wednesday. That means we could have it up over the weekend, right?"

"Only if it's OK with you that nobody gets a paycheck on Friday."

The problem escalates when each side realizes the other will not budge, and neither has the power to call the shots. Soon, the head of IS and the head of marketing are avoiding each others' voice mails. Yes, there are unsupervised minors at all levels of corporate America.

In today's world, the only one who can solve a dispute between IS and marketing is the CEO and that's the problem. No offense to the business leaders of the world, but the Web is just too complex an animal for CEOs to have to micro-manage.

IS handles the care, feeding, currying, and veterinary concerns of the beast, while marketing focuses on its training, socialization, and psychological well-being. That represents a huge amount of knowledge, and the CEO needs to stay on top of running the whole darn zoo.

So what's the solution?

Some companies have taken to creating a new position at the highest level—the Chief Web Officer. This is the person who can set the standards and make the decisions that affect multiple departments. Call it the Web Strategy Manager or Head Web Head, I don't care. Just put somebody in charge.

At the end of a worrisome meeting of senior executives at a multibillion dollar client of mine, the CIO pleaded for the immediate establishment of a committee to take control of Web development efforts that had been dispersed, disorganized, and indiscriminate. At the top end of the table, the CEO snorted and said, "How about we just pick two people and empower them to take control of this mess and make some decisions!"

I stood up from my chair and applauded.

You're going to have to get the top brass to sign on and get them to work together. That is *not* going to be as easy as it sounds, and it doesn't sound very easy, does it?

Customer Interface: Building Bridges

By Jim Sterne
From *CIO WebBusiness Magazine*, June 1998

In the beginning, the information technology people discovered the Internet. They found it was easy to create a Web site . . . and they did. Six months later, the marketing people discovered the World Wide Web and were shocked and appalled that the IT people had been representing the company to the world. They responded by snatching control of the Web site and loudly proclaiming ownership.

Soon, however, the marketing people learned that a decent Web site is more than just an online brochure. Marketing needed the help of technology people to turn the Web into an interactive medium. At most companies, this launched a new era.

The IS department has typically reported up the chain through operations or finance. Marketing has typically reported to the president or CEO. The two departments used to cross paths only at the annual company picnic.

Now, thanks to the Web, marketing and IS must work together. They have to make their needs known and create the foundations of a working relationship. It won't be easy. But it starts with common goals and a willingness for each group to imagine themselves in the other's shoes.

M E M O
To: Vice President of Marketing
From: CIO
Re: Our External Web Site

We've learned a lot in the three years we've had a Web site up and running. But if we are to take advantage of the Web and work closely together, the marketing team needs to understand a few things about the technology and the process of Web site development.

A Web site is frighteningly easy to create. A little HTML goes a long way, and everybody who has a teenager at home knows that a Web site can be created in a couple of hours. But get the least bit fancy and the magic fades because the basics behind a sound Web site go hand in hand with the basics of software programming.

continues

Customer Interface: Building Bridges (Continued)

If you want the site to be bulletproof, to collect information properly and to dynamically serve personalized pages, we can deliver. But we need help from you.

Think of the IS department as the builders of your home. We have architects, we have supervisors, and we have people who are good at concrete, framing, electrical, plumbing and wallboarding. You have an idea of how many rooms you want and where you want them, and you want to take care of the interior design.

The coordination between all involved in construction takes good timing and strong communication skills. If the concrete gets poured before the plumbing is installed, there will be problems. The same goes for the Web. We have established specific procedures for how new content gets hosted on the server to ensure we don't finish the walls before the electrical conduit has been installed.

Adherence to these procedures is paramount to the timely success of each project.

That's why we require functional specifications documentation.

Like builders, we need to create architectural drawings from which to work. If we don't have an accurate survey of the land, the resulting structure will not be built to code, and you won't be happy living there. To help make our working relationship better, I pledge that we will:

- *Keep you informed as to all changes in our completion estimates.*
- *Ask sufficient questions so that we can go about our work without interrupting you.*
- *Explain to you that what you are asking for is either easy, hard or beyond our reach.*
- *Stay educated about the best tools and techniques for getting the job done.*
- *Make it as easy as possible for your people to maintain their own content.*
- *Create standards and procedures that work best for all members of the Web team.*

Together we can create a trustworthy Web site that is both a testament to good, solid software engineering techniques and a communication tool we can count on.

MEMO
To: CIO
From: Vice President of Marketing
Re: Our Web Efforts

Thank you for today's memo. I, too, want to work together with IS and get the most out of our Web efforts. For that to happen, it would help if the IS department had a clearer idea of what marketing has to deal with on a day-to-day basis.

To use your construction analogy, we are building multiple houses for multiple types of customers. It is our job to find out what sort of house each customer wants to live in and then create a description of that house that's so compelling the customer will fall in love with it.

Like you, we move from project to project with changing requirements and tight deadlines. We also work in an arena where the competition is actively out to make our houses fall down. As such, we sometimes have to respond in very short order.

If the marketing team discovers a new marketplace metric or suddenly faces a new competitive product, the response must be swift and sure. A new brochure can be designed, printed and delivered into the hands of tens of thousands of prospective customers within a few weeks. But the moment we issue a press release announcing our new strategy or product, prospective customers will come knocking on our Web site. We have to be ready for them.

To remain competitive in this electronic world, we must find better and faster ways to communicate with the public. We also have to educate our front-line staff and publish critical information at a moment's notice. I'm trusting that the IS department will come up with the ways and means to empower the rest of the organization to use the Web effectively.

In addition, we need the Web to deliver things that traditional marketing techniques can't. We need precise numbers: the hits, the page views, the sessions, the clickthroughs, the travel paths, the logons—all of which tell us whether we're doing a good job. We need them daily, and we need to be able to drill down and slice and dice them every which way we want.

To help the company use the Web as a competitive tool, I pledge that the marketing department will:

- *Maintain structure by adhering to regularly scheduled updates.*
- *Use the given tools to make content changes without interrupting the IS department.*
- *Refrain from dabbling in experimental technologies.*
- *Outsource only those tasks that will not compromise the integrity of our data center.*
- *Avoid promising new features to customers before they can be delivered.*

Together we can create a vibrant Web site to foster building electronic relationships with our customers.

M E M O
To: CEO
From: CIO and Vice President of Marketing
Re: Our Web Efforts

The Web represents new possibilities for reaching new markets, servicing our current customers and conducting business in whole new ways. Marketing and IS are finding ways to use the Web for furthering the stated goals of the company. But the more we study the Web phenomenon, the more we realize that the Web offers an opportunity to transform the company into a new type of organization.

continues

Customer Interface: Building Bridges *(Continued)*

At the same time, the Web represents a real threat that our competitors (and others we don't think of as competition) are enabled to change and adapt before we do.

The Internet can dramatically change the dynamics of our industry. Along with the ability to conduct commerce at the speed of light comes the ability to establish new strategic alliances, deliver new services and create new value chains.

The majority of our efforts to date have been off the books and off the clock. As the time comes to implement our new ideas, we require two things from you: a clearly defined statement of corporate direction for the Web and a formal commitment in terms of budget and organizational structure.

Your job, should you decide to accept it, is to make those promises come true. To do that, you're going to have to work out who owns what.

Format Ownership

Take a look at the following four pages from General Electric (www.ge.com), starting with the corporate home page (see Figure 13.1). They don't seem to match.

The stage may be set, but the brand is all over the map. GE may bring good things to life, but this looks more like an NBC Television site. Jack Welsh is on the Board of Directors, as is Gary Reiner, GE's Senior VP and CIO, but did you know that NBC is "NBC, a subsidiary of General Electric Company"? Is this the place to find out?

Just one click away from the home page, and you're in another world (see Figure 13.2) of pastel colors, vertical menus, and an absence of navigational tabs.

Meanwhile, GE Appliances goes for the more traditional text-on-the-left, the nontraditional photos, and something that looks like a banner ad at the top right (see Figure 13.3).

GE Plastics takes on a completely different look and feel (see Figure 13.4) leaving one to wonder how many design companies are cashing General Electric checks.

But, Jim, these are all different marketplaces. People buying polymers aren't out shopping for refrigerators.

Different marketplaces? Yes. Different brands? No. You want different brands, you look at the Bristol-Myers Squibb home page (www.bms.com) and compare it to www.excedrin.com and www.clairol.com. Bristol-Myers Squibb makes both Excedrin headache medicine and Clairol hair care products, but they can all look different because they are different brands.

Figure 13.1 The GE home page sets the stage.

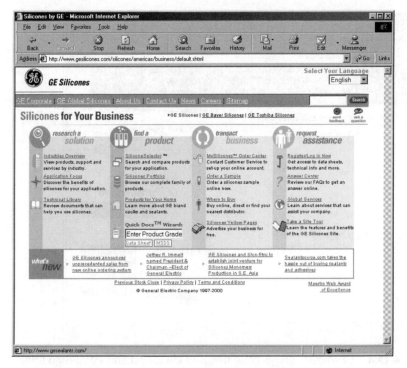

Figure 13.2 GE Silicones uses pastels rather than GE.com's deeper tones.

Figure 13.3 GE Appliances does, indeed, look homier, but it does not look like the corporate home page.

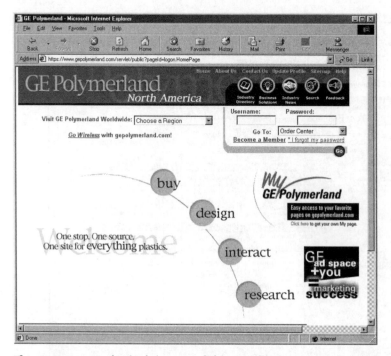

Figure 13.4 GE Plastics brings good things to life for yet another design firm.

Now go take a look at IBM's Web site. Doesn't matter what page. You can tell at a glance that you're on the IBM Web site because once you've seen one IBM page, you've seen them all.

You want your brand to be cohesive. Yes, it's nice to have autonomy. It's nice to call your own shots, out from under the thumb of the marketing communications fascists who carry 12-pound binders describing in gruesome detail how you may use the logo. But you're not helping your customers by being independent.

Having each department design its own top-level navigation and color schemes results in the customer having to relearn how to get around on your Web site every time he or she trips over an invisible corporate boundary that's meaningless to anybody outside the influence of your infernal, internal organizational structure.

Once Web visitors have finally figured out what to expect at the bottom of every page, don't pull the rug out from under them by allowing different divisions to create their own toolbars. Establish a standard set of buttons or a standard implementation of a frame for the index, and apply it across the board.

Do you really think people who buy polymers only eat fruits and nuts or live in Reykjavík and have no need for in-home refrigeration? No, I'm not for giving MarCom indiscriminate, omnipotent control over the every aspect of your company site.

Opening voice over for 1960s television show, "The Outer Limits"

There is nothing wrong with your television set.
Do not attempt to adjust the picture.
We are controlling transmission.
If we wish to make it louder,
we will bring up the volume.
If we wish to make it softer,
we will tune it to a whisper.

We will control the horizontal.
We will control the vertical.
We can roll the image, make it flutter.
We can change the focus to a soft blur
or sharpen it to crystal clarity.

For the next hour sit quietly
and we will control all that you see and hear.
We repeat: there is nothing wrong with your television set.
You are about to participate in a great adventure.
You are about to experience the awe and mystery
which reaches from the inner mind to . . . THE OUTER LIMITS

I simply want your customers to feel as at home on the home page as they do deep in the heart of your datasheets and order forms regardless of which department or division they've stumbled into. If you work for a large firm, pity us poor surfers trying with all our might to find something worth buying and standardize your look and feel across the board.

Those responsible for the navigation bars, and the logo placement, and the background colors, and the general layout are apt to make a mistake or two along the way. They might require a frame set or insist that chartreuse really is this year's "in" color. But in the long run, they will save you the expense of having those things designed for you, and they will save you the time you need to focus on more important matters, such as how are you going to describe your product so that it sells better?

Just because there are people at corporate headquarters telling you how large your product shots can be doesn't mean that they're going to write copy for you. They may lay out the design of your product home page, specification page, tutorial page, testimonial page, ad infinitum, but you are still going to have to decide how many of those elements to use, what you're going to tell people, and how the product is going to look. You, my friend, are in charge of the content.

Content Ownership

If, as I have assumed in the previous section, you are responsible for the success of your product, then you should have control over how it looks and what is said about it. Also, as mentioned, that jurisdiction does not extend to the stage your product is placed on or the frame that goes around it. But if you have been tasked with making sure this product line sells well, then you should have control over how it appears inside those predetermined corporate confines.

Does your product sell better door to door than online? Put the majority of your money there. Do your customers *always* walk into your stores for help with your products? Then you don't need to offer as many FAQ pages as the other guy. If live, online presentations boost sales, then that's a better use for your limited funds than an e-mail contest.

As content owner, you're responsible for tone, style, spelling, grammar, quantity, and quality of your product's portrayal. Then you're going to trust the look-and-feel people to make sure it is displayed in the best possible light, on the poshest stage, surrounded by the most impressive proscenium. Provided, of course, that the technical team is able to lift the curtain, turn on the lights, and swing in the scenery at the right time.

Technology Ownership

You may be one of those souls for whom all of the above *and* all of the below is your fault, I mean responsibility. If so, you have my heartfelt condolences. You are a one-man-band, and everybody else in the company is your director, all tapping out different beats and rewriting the music as you go.

Should you be lucky enough to work in a larger company, then you will be supported by a technical staff, or your supervisor has seen the wisdom of outsourcing. In that case, the worry and bother of running a server, managing a network, managing an ISP vendor, and tweaking applications servers, mail servers, and streaming media servers is out of your hands and on the shoulders of the engineers. Just don't expect them to speak your language.

Because this is the first time the VP of Marketing and the CIO have been in the same Zip code outside of a golf course for the annual company picnic (and they were on opposing teams then), it will do you no end of good to bone up on some of the computerized wizardry that your opposite number works with on a daily basis for self-protection.

When the head of the IS department or the project leader at your Web development company says, "We can't process that many output streams because the backbone accumulator can't support that many actuated plug-ins in portal mode," the correct response is not, "How many plug-ins *can* it support?" The proper response is, "You have absolutely no idea what you're talking about, do you?"

On the other hand, if they tell you that the Unix config files need to be updated to account for your home page missing if the surfer forgets to type the trailing forward slash, the correct answer would be, "Why on earth wasn't that done in the first place?" See? It pays to know a little.

Needless to say, if you outsource and have the choice, work with people you trust. How do you find them? The same way you find a surgeon, a dentist, a lawyer, or a plumber. You rely on recommendations. But this isn't about simply recognizing when somebody is out of his or her depth. This is about understanding the possibilities.

It pays to understand how XML is going to change how you work with your trading partners. It's important to know just enough about how online auctions work to imagine how they might change in the future. It's critical that you have a feel for where things might be going so you can help them get there.

In the meantime, you have to make the best of the tools and people you have and implement logical, repeatable processes.

Process Ownership

Process is everything and even more so on the Web. Once again, building and maintaining a Web site requires cooperation from two very different quarters. The more you think about process ahead of time, the less time you'll spend arguing about proper procedures down the line.

Content will need to be analyzed for format, technical accuracy, spelling, and feasibility. What are the steps of approval? Who are the gatekeepers? What committees must sanction the content prior to submission for server staging? No need for Machiavellian constraints. Just a nice, logical flow to ensure that others have checked the i's for dots and the t's for crosses.

As a result, the IS department can stand firm as printer to marketing's publisher. A printer's job is to faithfully reproduce whatever the client desires. A publisher is responsible for content from concept and format to spelling and grammar.

Brush up on your flow-charting techniques in order to communicate better. Figure out the paths of least resistance so that the most content can be hosted in the shortest time. Identify what constitutes success for any given project.

Creating the Next Site

Who are the Web site stakeholders at the company?

Which departments/divisions/product lines/services might be represented on your Web site?

Which of these should be represented on the Web site in Phase I, Phase II, etc.?

Who are the customers for each product line?

What might the customers want from a Web site?

What services might be put on the Web to meet those needs?
> This is "green hat" or go-wild brainstorming—there are no bad ideas, just ideas that won't get implemented yet.

What does the company want from the customers?

Given what the customers and the company want from the Web site, what are the stated and prioritized goals of this site?
> What objectives can be identified that will help reach those goals?
> What metrics can be used to measure the success of those objectives?

When does this site need to be operational?

What are the available resources for making this Web site happen?
> How many people are interested in spending how much time?
> How much money is available to buy outside services?
>> Web design services
>> Web coding services
>> Web housing services
>> Consulting

What is the process for getting material approved and on the Web?

What are the criteria for prioritizing specific Web content?

Which of the great ideas for Web services should be implemented in Phase I given the criteria previously listed?

How will an outside agency be selected to provide services?

Who has final go/no-go approval?

What will it take to get that person to say "go"?

Proposal for Publishing on the World Wide Web

The proposal will be used to evaluate the project to be included in the company World Wide Web site. Please furnish as much information as possible to speed the approval process.

THE PROJECT

Project Name
What does the proposing group call this project?
Project Identification
Assigned by the review committee for future reference/reporting.
Project Description
What will this addition to the Web site do?
How will it look?
Provide a diagram of the page calling tree.
What are the expected results?
How will those results be measured?
What is the life expectancy of this project?
The Audience
Who is this project for?
How large is this segment?
How is this project directed toward them?
Response Mechanism
How will response to this project be managed?
Competitive Analysis
Who is doing anything similar?
How successful are their efforts?
Why is this project better?
Promotion
How will this addition be publicized?

THE PLAYERS

Business Unit
Identifies the chain of command
Project Manager
Primary stakeholder
Response Manager
Responds to incoming data
Design Manager
Lays out the interface
Content Developer(s)
Writes, draws, paints

continues

Proposal for Publishing on the World Wide Web (*Continued*)

    Processing Manager
       Designs the back-end processing

THE TOOLS

    What text, graphics, and HTML tools will be used for authoring?
    What tools will be required on the server?
    What new software will be required?
    What tools will be used to manage response?
    What training will be required to use these tools?

THE TECHNICAL DIMENSIONS

    How many pages, graphics, and MB of data will be added to the server?
    How much data will be collected?
    How many visitors are expected over time?
    How many pages will they view per session?
    How much data will they download per session?
    How often will pages be updated?
    How much material will be changed per update?
    How will the project be tested prior to going live?

GUIDELINE DEVIATIONS

    How will this project vary from the Guidelines?
    What is the expected benefit of these deviations?
    Does this call for a waiver or an alteration to the Guidelines?

THE COST

    Define the funds required for:
       Training
       Design
       Copywriting
       Graphics creation
       Back-end development
       Integration
       Testing
       Fixes
       Documentation

      Promotion
      Updates
    Where will the funds come from?

THE TIMELINE

    Define the time required for:
      Training
      Design
      Copywriting
      Graphics creation
      Back-end development
      Integration
      Testing
      Fixes
      Documentation
      Promotion
      Updates
      Success determination

POTENTIAL RISKS

    Define the risks associated with this project.
    How can these risks be minimized?
    How will potential problems be dealt with?

THE ALTERNATIVES

    How else might this project's objectives be met?
    Why is this approach the best alternative?

THE LOST OPPORTUNITY COST

    What is the risk of not producing this project?

MEASURING SUCCESS

    How do we define "success" for this project?
    Which metrics will tell us if this project was worthwhile?
    How will we capture that data?
    When will we know?
    How and when will a no-go decision be made?

Don't Bite Off More than You Can Chew

Jim Shanks is the CIO at CDW. I wanted to find out what the manager of such a successful site had to say about getting the job done well. His first bit of advice was to make changes a little at a time.

"We're always adding features and sometimes changing the look and feel. But we don't save it all up for one big push. There're too many things to test and too much that can go wrong unless you roll things out bit by bit."

But how do you prioritize? "You ask the customers what they want. And they come up with some pretty good stuff. One customer said they bought so much from us that we know what he has better than he does. We asked him if he'd like us to show him a screen with all of his purchases including model numbers, serial numbers, purchase dates, that sort of thing. He said he'd love it—especially if we could add a few fields for him like what the item was in or which budget it had come out of. When we were done, we started using it ourselves. So now we have this asset tracking system that gets new features because we want them and new features because our customers want them and everybody's happy."

Best Practices

We're all pretty new at this. Even if you've been building Web sites since 1994 you haven't been building them with today's tools, today's techniques, and today's tensions. We all need all the help we can get. So let's create a formal place where help can be found—on the intranet.

People need to know what's expected of them. If you have a corporate template for layout and design and it's not available on your intranet to whoever is in need, you are not practicing what you preach. But take it a step further. Create a library of success stories and watch it fill with offerings from those who have come up with a better way. Create another for mistakes made and lessons learned, and you'll need to offer incentives to get people to boast of their blunders. The result is that others will be able to learn without having to make the same mistakes.

A list of best practices puts a human face on formal, dictated procedures. "This is why doing it that way worked out so well for me" is an excellent persuasion device. But you'll need more than that to get people to see that giving up their autonomy is a good thing. For that, you need a thought leader.

Vision Ownership

Somebody needs to be the lighting rod of innovation. Somebody needs to hold the visionary torch to encourage senior executives to lead, middle managers to take risks, and front-line Web managers to buy into the value of a centralized organization. Somebody has to convince the CEO to spend more time, more attention, and, of course, more money.

Just before an all-IBM-manager meeting in 1994, John Patrick and several of his team members showed a demonstration of the World Wide Web to Chairman Lou Gerstner. They had mocked up an IBM home page with Gerstner's photo prominently displayed (see Figure 13.5).

Under the photo were the words:

Hello, I'm Lou Gerstner, chairman of IBM. On behalf of all of us at IBM, I'd like to welcome you to our World-Wide Web server.

Through our server, we'll try to make it easy for you to learn about our technology and some of the things we're doing at IBM—and also make it easier for you to share your ideas with us.

We'll update our information on a regular basis and do our best to keep it interesting and informative. We're committed to the Internet, and we're excited about providing information to the Internet community. I hope you'll check back here often.

Figure 13.5 The shot seen, and the audio heard, around IBM.

Gerstner was as impressed as we all were the first time we saw the Web in action. He was surprised that it could handle audio as well, and he agreed to record the introductory message.

The demo was shown again to several hundred IBM managers at the meeting, complete with IBM's commitment to the Internet in the chairman's own voice. After that, it wasn't very hard to get the different divisions to cooperate. Gerstner looked like a leader instead of a soothsayer.

That original page (see Figure 13.5) stayed up on its site for historical reasons for several years. It has since been replaced by a more confident description of the power of the Web (see Figure 13.6).

The visionary takes the heat off the CEO by saying all the things that are just a little too far fetched.

In 1994, they were the ones saying, "Someday, planet-wide access to e-mail will be a given!"

In 1995 they said, "Someday, shopping online will be commonplace!"

Figure 13.6 These days Gerstner looks very pleased with the real value the Web has delivered.

In 1996 they said, "Someday business-to-business buying will be an everyday occurrence!"

In 1997 they said, "Someday wireless commerce will be routine!"

In 1998 they said, "XML communications between corporate databases will be the order of the day!"

In 1999 they said, "Broadband videophones will be conventional!"

In 2000 they said, "Dynamically personalized Web sites will be the norm!"

In 2001 they said, "The Internet will be everywhere and anywhere you are—like electricity!"

Those sorts of wild-eyed pronouncements made people smile and kept the pressure off the CEO. The CEO could say mealy mouthed things like, "The Internet is very powerful, and we will take every advantage of its abilities in the future." Yawn.

Meanwhile, the visionary garners the admiration of the free thinkers who hang on every word uttered by this paragon of prescience, and that's where you want them when it's time to bring the hammer down. When this highly regarded, gray-haired, golden-robed enthusiast looks upon his flock and says, "Economy of scale is your friend," people trek back to their corporate clans and spread the word.

It's not quite that dramatic at CDW, but Jim Shanks knows that a bit of spin-doctoring is required to get people on board. "When new salespeople come in, we put them through a lot of training. I get in front of them and ask if they'd like an administrative assistant who wouldn't forget anybody, would know the current price of everything we sell, and would answer prospect and client questions 24 by 7, and when they get all excited about it, I tell them that's what CDW@Work is about. They love it."

"If I just told them, 'We have an extranet and it's really cool,' they wouldn't understand the value. You've got to explain it so they understand the value to *them*. You've got to sell it to them."

Ownership Ownership

Finally, you'll have to decide who's going to be responsible. At the top of this chapter, I proposed a Chief Web Officer. Your company might need that. But in the long run, the answer really is the CEO.

The buck stops there.

Just because the head of your company is an older gent who has his secretary print out his e-mails and drop them into his in-basket does not let him off the hook for knowing about how this technology is changing his world.

Somebody has to realize that the Web is not something for the marketing department to play with, but that it has become an integral part of our ability to communicate with prospects, customers, and trading partners. The question must always be on everybody's lips: How might we use the power of the Internet to make this process or transaction easier, better, cheaper, faster?

Customer Experience Ownership

There must also be somebody with an even *higher* authority. Your brand—the image that people have of your company—comes from every touchpoint. Who in your firm is the customer advocate? Who stands for the customer at meetings? Who looks at your company through customer-colored glasses?

Once a quarter, CDW brings in more than 100 customers for a technical seminar. It trains them on the products it sells, and it runs focus groups about Web site features

---

A Brand Is Not a Name

From *What Makes People Click: Advertising on the Web* by Jim Sterne (Que, 1997)

A brand is not a name. A brand is not a positioning statement. It is not a marketing message. It is a promise made by a company to its customers and supported by that company.

If not, it would be enough just to change the name of San Francisco's Candlestick Park to 3Com Park. As Jamie Graham put it in Creativity Magazine (Jan/Feb 1997), "It won't be long before we're vacationing in Pearl Drops (formerly Yellowstone) Park, admiring 2000 Flushes (Niagara) Falls, and the Pontiac Grand Am Canyon."

A brand is something that lives apart from what the company plans, because it is the culmination of all of the interactions a marketplace has with the firm.

> *A person sees an ad and has an impression.*
> *She looks up information on the Web, she has an impression.*
> *She calls the firm and talks to the receptionist and the impression changes.*
> *She is put on hold and hears the music and "Your call is important to us."*
> *She talks to a sales rep.*
> *She waits for the materials to arrive.*
> *She reads the materials.*
> *She talks to her colleagues about the product.*
> *She reads about the firm in the financial pages.*
> *She reads product reviews.*
> *She makes the purchase.*
> *She sees and feels the product packing.*
> *She tries to use the product.*

and usability tests on the new site designs it is planning to roll out. Jim Shanks is assessing eye movement tests like those offered by Eyetools to make sure the customer stays tightly integrated into the Web development process.

What people think of your company as a whole, and of your products and services by extension, will depend more and more on how they are treated online.

Your Web site is the window to the soul of your company. Prospects and customers will be able to see straight into that window and tell if your corporate culture is thriving and nurturing or hiding behind layers of management with only "CYA!" as the common rallying cry.

Make sure that the care and feeding of your Web site is not overlooked by those who have risen to power during the days when production was everything and customers were an afterthought.

She calls customer service.
She talks to her friends about her experience.

If you take the sum total of how she feels and thinks about all of her interactions with the company and how well they met her expectations and lived up to the promise . . . and you multiply that by the thousands or millions of people who have also read about, talked about and interfaced with the company and the product . . . you have a brand. You want that brand to be a positive sentiment.

You want the public to know, deep in their heart of hearts, that your company stands for confidence, your logo implies trust and your products mean dependability. Or, you want them to think of you as young, hip and fun-loving. Either way, you want them to think of you in these terms for all of the days of their lives.

In an essay in Understanding Brands by 10 People Who Do (Kogan Pge Ltd., 1996), Wendy Gordon, chairman of The Research Business Group, stresses congruency between all of the different levels of human communication. These Neuro-Linguistic Programming levels are:

1. *Vision (I promise), e.g., 'I have a dream' (Martin Luther King).*
2. *Identity (I am), e.g., I am a caring, giving person.*
3. *Belief (I believe), e.g., I believe in state education.*
4. *Capability (I can), e.g., I play tennis and cook Japanese food.*
5. *Behavior (I do), e.g., I work full time.*
6. *Environment (where), e.g., I live in London.*

Gordon suggests that strong branding requires all of these levels of communication to agree with each other. If you can identify the message to be conveyed on each of these levels and then see to it that every interaction with the firm and its products confirms those messages, your brand will be as strong as possible.

CHAPTER 14

Looking toward the Future

When will there be a billion people on the Internet?
What time is it?

Tomorrow will bring new methods of communication, new competitive challenges, and new demands from your customers. Keep a very open mind. As Robert Hamilton of FedEx puts it:

> In my opinion, the prospect of near-universal connectivity, most visibly illustrated today by the Internet, redefines at least three of the four P's of Marketing immediately, and probably the fourth shortly thereafterward.
>
> If the majority of customers exhibit any predictable behavior regarding their networks, the "Place" of the business transaction becomes a logical one, no longer just a real one.
>
> "Promotion" must acknowledge this behavior and at least add a new dimension, which will turn advertising on its head since the best 'Net presence is a content-rich and user-selected one. "Product" will evolve in ways that emphasize the network-based features, whether this be distribution of software to enable remote-control access over distant processes, or service/product extensions into Netspace.
>
> In short order, as these developments attract more people to Netspace, "Price" will be set based on an entirely new set of variables. So, at the root, the discipline will be grounded in the same four basic aspects as ever; those aspects, however, will be totally redefined over time.

There are more scientists and engineers alive today than have ever died. More technology allows us to make more technology faster. The more things change, the more things change. The enormous potential for capitalistic gain, coupled with the ability to produce technology at blinding speeds, means that keeping track of the changes around us is more important than ever.

The big, giant, capital H *Hope* is that we'll use all this nifty technology to communicate better with our customers. But just how we communicate is subject to change without notice.

Predictions

I had to laugh when I reread this chapter about the future from the 1995 edition. The anticipated technologies all seemed so remote then and so routine today.

We were going to get animated pictures that could actually move. You'd be able to enjoy a text-chat with a friend and even see his or her photo every time he or she added to the conversation. Then you could click on a link and take your friend to the next Web site with you. Virtual Modeling Language would let you "fly" through 3D landscapes instead of just clicking on flat pages.

Sun Microsystems was playing with something called Java that would revolutionize distributed programming. Sun was so excited that it posted a list of astonishing applet examples, including these:

- An animated "Under Construction" sign (with audio)
- Scrolling images
- Speaking clock
- Wave form
- Tumbling duke
- A simple 3D model viewer
- Some animated titles
- A simple spreadsheet
- Dynamically generated color bullets
- Live feedback image map
- Fractal figures
- A simple bar chart applet
- A multilingual word match game

Breakthrough stuff in 1995.

What will the Web look like in 2005?

Wild-Eyed Scenarios

I was lucky enough to attend a lecture by Arthur C. Clarke, delivered at Foothill College in Los Altos Hills, California, in the late 1960s. That was before the moniker Silicon Valley had been assigned, before Steven Jobs had long hair, and before *Star Wars* was a movie or a government program. Clarke was asked about his vision for the future of education. He related the following story:

A young boy at the beach scampers between tide pools. He reaches down into one and pulls out a small shell with tiny claw legs sticking out. Curious, he holds his find near his wristwatch and asks, "What is it?"

The wristwatch analyzes the specimen and replies, "It's a hermit crab. It lives in tide pools all over the world. This is a young one. It will grow to be twice that size and find protection from predators by living with anemones."

"What happens when it gets too big for its shell?"

"It leaves its shell and finds another."

"Can I take it home?"

"No, it would die. But you can find an empty one and take it home."

The child carefully places the crab back in the water, continues his search, and pockets an empty crab shell. The interaction has been coded as an educational experience and recorded in the school database via satellite.

At the end of the week, a question about turtles will appear on a test to see if the child understands the difference between animals that live in borrowed shells and those that grow their own.

Here are a few scenarios for tomorrow. See if you can imagine your company involved in some way.

Online Real-Time Datastream Control

From *What Makes People Click, Advertising on the Web* by Jim Sterne
(Que, 1997)

Looking through an eyeglass-weight display, barking out instructions and waving data-glove encased hands, tomorrow's ad maestro manipulates the reach, the frequency and the message delivered to millions of surfers in real time.

Our maestro sits at the virtual command center located anywhere a phone cell can hear her. The display shows levels of response across multiple sites to multiple banners from multiple profile types. With a push of a virtual button, a literal blink of an eye, the promotion balance is adjusted.

The image of the control panel resembles the angled table of an old analog recording studio. Dozens of knobs line up across a field of vertical slots, waiting for a touch to send them higher or lower. But these do not control the amplitude of the signal coming in. They control the types of people the message is going out to.

Each has a label floating over it that grows in brightness the higher the knob is set. The labels include auto, business, college, computer, education, entertainment, health, home, and more.

In the background, where musicians would have played and sang, hovers a mathematical grid, a rubber sheet, waiting to be pulled and stretched by generated results. It is black and at rest.

continues

Online Real-Time Datastream Control (Continued)

The product for this session is WebSim business gaming software. It simulates a Web site and puts the player in the webmaster hot seat. Can you make your navigation easy enough? Can you keep it updated frequently enough to keep return visitors returning on the stingy budget you had to spread over servers, artists, net connectivity and Java programmers?

The maestro reaches for the sliders. As she sets each knob, a chart on the far side of the rubber sheet duplicates her choices with vertical, colored bars indicating the selected profile. She sets Computers to 80, Internet to 100, and Business to 40. Then she reaches for Entertainment and slides the knob up to the 60 mark, watching the blue bar on the far wall follow her movement exactly.

She selects from a quiver of banners; a cross-segment marketing message aimed at everybody—the baseline. She tosses the banner toward the rubber sheet and nods as it rises and comes to rest up above, hanging motionless (see Figure 14.1).

Above and to the left, linger three gray zeros—the banners to be displayed yet, the clickthroughs received, and the response rate as a percent of exposures. To the right, she dials in a gray 10,000; the number of images to be shown in this first test run. At the lower right the session budget of $82,800 challenges her to deliver.

At the bottom left are the figures that show the degree to which the average clicker follows the banner's path to the final goal of downloading the software.

She is set. It is time.

She runs through the numbers one more time and decides she really needs to net $5,000 for this session. It would only take a day, but all the prep time she put into it, the banner artwork she envisioned and paid for, and the fact that the non-complete penalty was going to come out of her pocket, meant she was at risk. She deserved the reward, but it wouldn't come easy.

Why had she said she could double the response they got through direct mail? She had still been glowing after her big win with the bond-fund company. She had read the Wall Street Journal cover to cover for three weeks and just knew Alan Greenspan was going to make a move. She had that one wired. She walked away with a big smile on her face and hefty commission.

This one didn't have that kind of background to it. It was just another new software package in a sea of new software packages. Their mailing numbers were pretty good and that made them harder to beat.

They had sent out 90,000 pieces over three runs at a cost of $69,300. They got a 3% response rate and followed up by sending a package costing $5 to each of the 2,700 responders. The data entry, the diskette, the quick-start guide, the

WEBSIM   YOU'RE THE WEBMASTER   CLICK
COMPETE FOR PRIZES   THE PERFECT LEARNING ENVIRONMENT   HERE!

Figure 14.1 The first ad goes up as a test.

postage. It added up. All told, they spent $82,800 at a cost of $31.66 each. Not bad as far as the cost of leads goes.

"I'll take the same budget and return twice the response. You make your software and documentation available on your Web site and I'll get people to download it. I'll create all the promotional materials, and personally place the banners. And my fee will be included."

They took her up on her offer.

The maestro gives one last look at the budget counter and prays for a break. She is set. It is time.

A handle to her left resembles the brake lever on a San Francisco cable car. She moves it forward without hesitation and watches the impressions counter ratchet down to zero. On the ad banner network she's using 10,000 impressions are the work of a moment.

The results of her efforts gleam from the meters.

Impressions   10,000
Clicks   200
Downloads   1

Only a half a percent who clicked bothered to get the software!? She had successfully ignored the knot in the pit of her stomach up until now. Then she spots the telling number. Average level of depth: 1. It take three clicks to download.

She snaps her fingers and the entire display is gone, replaced by the bridge page on the client's Web site; the page a clickthrough takes you to. It looks fine. It's not the problem.

She flips the goggles up onto her head and looks into her own, physical monitor on her desk. She types in the URL for the bridge page and waits. The wait stretches.

She clicks on a picture of her client and settles herself while she waits again, this time for him to answer the call.

"Well, if it isn't the bionic woman! Nice hat. When are you going to start the banners rolling?"

"I thought I had. When are you going to free up the load on your server?"

"What are you talking about? Our server's fine."

"Wrong. Check it out on an outside line and see what the rest of the world is seeing."

"OK, OK, give me . . . a . . . second . . . to . . . switch . . . to. Oh, my."

"Oh, your."

"Hang on. OK, I killed it. It was a backup!"

"At two in the afternoon? What's the matter, can't you tell your AM and your PM?"

"That's very strange. Why would somebody be messing with the time of day?"

"The same people who said they fixed your Millennium Bug?"

continues

Online Real-Time Datastream Control (Continued)

"Damn!"

"Please, there's a lady telepresent."

She flips the goggles back down and waves her colleague adieu. Another snap of the fingers reconstitutes the controls. With a quick glance at the interest levels of clickers, she makes a small adjustment to the sliders and gives the lever another full throttle shove.

This time she listens more carefully to the telltale pitch. The clickrate pitch is a tad higher, that's good, but in the several minutes it takes to run through another 10,000 impressions, she only hears that sweet little bell ding three times. The numbers tell the story. Three percent clickthrough, of which only one percent downloaded.

She gives herself one more test run before opening the floodgates. A little work is needed. The bridge page loads fine. The license agreement page loads fine. The download page loads fine. But you have to scroll two clicks down to the download button. Why hadn't she caught that before?

She grabs at the helpful, friendly, warm and charming top paragraph and shoves it to below the precious download buttons. She smiles and runs the third round. The software retrieval rate goes up to one and a half percent. She smiles. The clickthrough rate is still at 3%. She frowns.

A quick calculation. She has used up a half of one percent of her budget and realized a tenth of a percent of her target. This is not good. The knot makes itself known. She studies the surfer interest profiles with all of her attention.

The rubber sheet is now distended into a shape like the Matterhorn after too many martinis. There are two of them. She has a large enough sample to spot the problem. Those interested in computers responded nicely. Those interested in the Internet responded very well. Those with a thing for business were abysmally indifferent and the entertainment crowd was stretched up to where the black sheet had gone through all of the other colors and reached a white snowy peak at the top.

It is time to adjust, and to let out the throttle a little. She sets the interest sliders accordingly and re-dials the impressions to 200,000. She rummages through her quiver of banners (see Figure 14.2).

She eases the trolley car lever forward. She wants to feel the response levels.

It takes longer to run through these banners. She listens as the response rate resonance turns melodious and the sweet download bell sounds more like a telephone than a tentative patron at an empty bakery. When it's over, she starts to relax a bit. A four percent clickthrough with a two percent download.

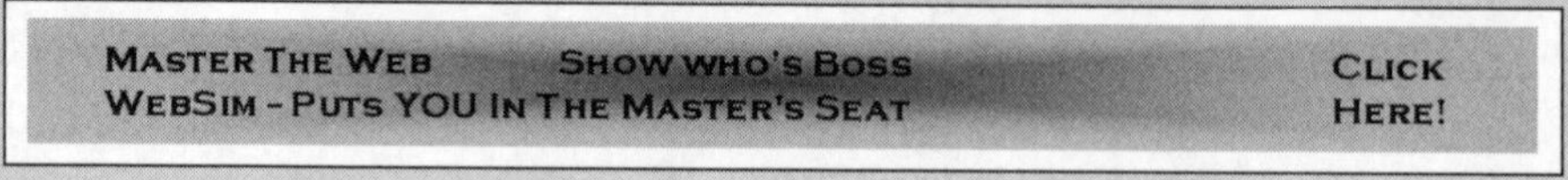

MASTER THE WEB   SHOW WHO'S BOSS   CLICK

WEBSIM – PUTS YOU IN THE MASTER'S SEAT   HERE!

Figure 14.2   The second ad drops the prizes and leans on the ego.

She realizes she didn't trust her gut. They told her this game was for older folk. Business people looking for a tutorial. They said the gaming crowd as defined by most banner networks were kids. Teeny boppers who wanted to play shoot 'em up, blast 'em and watch 'em bleed games.

She knew better. Kids are savvy. Now is the time to prove it. She reaches in her quiver and grabs a bright orange, animated, in your face ad and tosses it into position (see Figure 14.3).

Time for the big guns. She steadies herself, dials the impressions to one-point-five million and eases the lever into play. A smile dances cautiously across her face. The timbre rises. The sweet bells of the telephone ringing settle into a steady tone. The sound like the emergency broadcast network on the radio signals all is well.

The noise finally quiets and the results are good. She's burned through 42% of her cash and only brought in 36% of the downloads, but she has a secret weapon on her side: frequency.

She dials up two million banners. She hits the full repeat button for full frequency and knows she's got the numbers she needs, even before she starts. At the 5,400 download mark a small light blinks and the music halts. There's no need to buy any more banner space. She met the contract. The rest goes into her pocket.

The next morning she doesn't need to report to her client, they'll know when they look at their server logs. She need only e-mail the invoice.

There was even enough left over to fix up her own Web site a little. She could hire some outside help. Maybe she'd wait until the WebSim contest was over and make the winner an offer.

Figure 14.3   The third banner was designed to appeal to players.

The Interior Designer

If you think like a science fiction writer, it's not hard to imagine the following:

The workstation beeps, announcing an incoming call.

"Hi, Connie, this is Allen. Hope I'm not interrupting."

"Hiya, Allen. Not at all, I'm delighted for the excuse to ignore this billing for a while. What's up?"

On Connie's screen a small video window pops up, showing Allen in his architectural studio. "You know that new house Michael has been talking about on Maui?"

"Off again?"

"On again. Full steam. I've finished the preliminary drawings, and he said he wanted to see it decorated. You wanna take a quick look and see what you think?"

"Sure!" says Connie, clicking on the small Receive button next to Allen's image. "I've been waiting for him to move on this. Oh, Allen, it's beautiful!" She swings around the side of the house to view it from the water. "Two docks? His and hers?" The words Resident and Guest appear and hover over their respective landings. "Ahh. And what about inside? Did he mention anything in particular?"

"You know Michael," says Allen with a grin. "He says 'Just let Connie do it,' and then starts suggesting the living room should be marble, the main fireplace should be slate, and the front hall should be sandstone . . ."

"Sounds like our boy. That was all? Didn't he mention wall treatments, bedspreads, or throw pillows?"

"Nope. Just that he wanted to see what you thought it should have."

"Marble, slate, and sandstone. Let's see . . . floor" she says, holding down the Alt key, "marble, Seravezza, midnight gray."

"That looks nice," says Allen as the floor of the model on his screen fills with color, "and the veins match the rocks along the lagoon. How did you know about this one?"

"I saw it at Peter and Kathy's new office, very nice, by the way. They have some Santa Barbara Stone I can't wait to put someplace, but this one seems to be the right fit here. Now, then, fireplace, Welsh slate, cadet blue."

"That looks more green than blue."

"So does the lagoon. Front hall, floor, Vermont slate, Seashell 4."

"Looks like you're on a roll," Allen laughs, "Have fun with it. I think you'll like the upstairs."

"Oh, I think so, too. I always love your stuff. Oh, but wait a second, Allen." Connie hits a couple of keys. The model Allen transferred came complete with dimensions. Connie's database of materials, colors, and textures includes manufacturers. After automatically sending update requests, a spreadsheet appears on both screens showing material quantities needed, suppliers' bids, and lead times required. "Looks like that Welsh slate delivery will kill us. If he's all ready to start, I don't want to be the one holding things up. Let's see." Pressing the Alt key again, Connie adds, "We need cadet blue slate for the fireplace from any vendor with delivery in less than four weeks."

The spreadsheets update with new dealers and delivery dates. The color in the drawing changes to a muddy aquamarine. "No, no, no. Give me some time to try a few more things. Besides, the wall treatment will help."

"Copy me when you send it to Michael, OK?"

"Will do. See you later, Allen."

Android Customer Support

"If you've rebooted and the same error came up *before* you ran the totals, then, well, I'm stumped," says Bertie, the cartoon-like character in a small video window on Bob's screen. "So, I've logged your problem and have routed it to somebody who can help." Another window appears. "This is Nathalie. She's just taking a quick look at our conversation and will be able to ask a few more intelligent questions than I can."

"It looks," says Nathalie, reading intently and pausing to finish, "like the problem might be insufficient memory." She looks into the camera at the customer. "Did you upgrade to version 3.6?"

Sensing the head movement, Bertie remains quiet to let the customer answer.

"Uhmm, I think that was the first thing we tried. Right, Bertie?"

"Downloaded first thing, Bob. You're right. Nathalie, is there another way to improve the memory without a hardware upgrade?"

"Let's try resizing the cache," she says and sends a small diagnostic tool down the line. Once everybody is happy that the fix works, Nathalie adds it to the Bertie customer service database for future reference.

Are We There Yet?

It's going to take us some time before we wake up in a world where the software knows what we want before we do, but there are a lot of interesting things going on today.

Here are a few quick hits on several items that have made their way to the front lines, a few that have shown up on the radar screen, and a few that are still over the horizon.

Every Computer Will Talk to Every Computer

The problem with electronic data interchange (EDI) is that you had to write the software to convert your data into a standard lingo that could be translated into data that could be read by your trading partner. You had to do that each and every time with each and every new trading partner. XML (extensible markup language) provides the potential for a single data dictionary so that you have to write the translation only once and be done with it.

Think Euro. Rather than calculating the exchange rate for each currency in each country, you need only to turn your Florins (Aruba) into Euros and let the other guy worry about turning them from Euros into Kroon (Estonia), New Kwanza (Angola), or Karbovanets (Ukraine).

The upshot is that if you publish information on your site, it can be understood (not just read) by your trading partners, so that they can mirror that data on their site with continuously up-to-date data. They might also suck that information into their decision-making process for the automatic selection of machined parts to fit their design.

In every business sector, there are consortia building a common data dictionary so that everybody can talk. You say tomato and I say tomahto, but by the time it goes through XML translation central, we're making beautiful salads together.

Let's bring this into the world of marketing and advertising. The adXML.org is an international, open standard organization that is trying to write the dictionary to "describe the way advertising data is formatted and exchanged between agencies, advertisers, publishers and other value-added advertising specific products and services over the Internet." So if you send me a file containing an audio clip, another one with a video clip, and another one with descriptive information, you describe it however you wish. If your description is adXML compliant, then I can translate on the fly and take action. I can turn your hodge-podge of files into the award-winning, prospect-attracting rich media ad that you intended.

Everything Will Talk to Everything

It's not just software that's talking. The handheld gadgets, gizmos, and electronic thingamabobs are everywhere. There's also the Internet connected refrigerator (www.electrolux.com/screenfridge) (see Figure 14.4), the handheld scanner/faxer/e-mailer (www.capshare.hp.com) (see Figure 14.5), and the wired picture frame (www.kodak.com/US/en/digital/accessories/smartFrame) (see Figure 14.6).

The result of all this interconnectedness was brought home by Don Tapscott, who tells the tale of the midnight snack. "The refrigerator doesn't want you to have the chocolate cake, but you persuade it to say nothing to your wife about it. Of course, the fridge is good friends with the microwave, which can't resist telling the blender, and well, you *know* what a blabbermouth the blender is!"

Don't be surprised to get an extra quarter of a percent interest off your home loan if you're willing to accept the free toaster—the free toaster that just happens to burn the bank's message of the day into your toast every morning.

Everybody Will Talk to You via E-Mail

"You'll find the photo-realistic, human-like faces within this software to be astonishing. And, we've only just begun. Soon you will be able to actually use your own voice or the voice of a loved one in your Facemail application. Imagine being able to deliver a joke to your friends in your own voice. Or grandparents having their e-mails read to them by their favorite granddaughter."

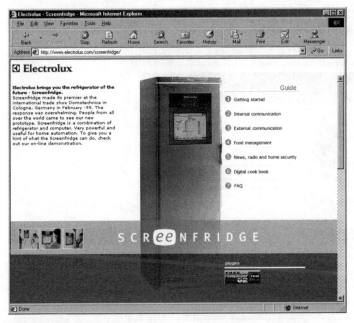

Figure 14.4 Electrolux feels the ScreenFridge is "very powerful and useful for home automation."

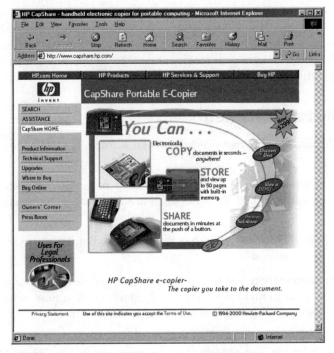

Figure 14.5 HP lets you scan something and e-mail it.

Figure 14.6 Kodak lets you download photos instead of printing them.

So far, the folks at www.facemail.com have only AnnaNova-like talking heads (see Figure 14.7), but they can smile, wink, look disgusted, and register surprise—all while reading your e-mail to you in annoyingly computerized voices. But their vision of you using your own likeness to deliver your message might be an interesting interim solution until the bandwidth improves—and it will.

Broadband Broadly Implemented

Yes, we'll all get T1 speeds to our wrist watches, and Dick Tracey is a reality. Next question?

The next question is whether voice activation will keep pace. Moving pictures are great, but the need for controls on devices too small to accommodate human fingers is overwhelming.

"Freeze! Go back. Show me that car again. No, the one James Bond was driving. Make it blue. How much does that cost?"

High-speed Internet connectivity has so much value that people are working 'round the clock 'round the globe to make it so. Plan on it. Start deciding now what sort of high-bandwidth content you're going to create for your customers.

You can already create live, talking head, animated PowerPoint presentations. Dial-up is already fast enough for the likes of Mshow (www.mshow.com) (see Figure 14.8).

Of course, all of these will be available wirelessly.

Figure 14.7 Facemail—for when you're too tired to read your e-mail by yourself.

Everything Is Wireless

Who needs wires? All we need anymore is really good batteries. Even today, my laptop lasts longer than I do on intercontinental flights, and my mobile phone lasts several days without recharging.

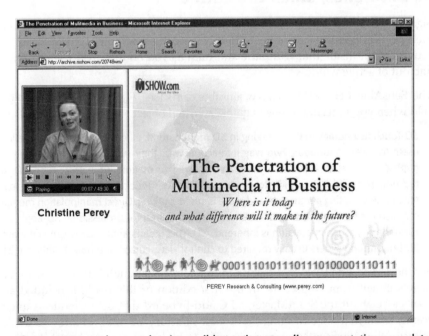

Figure 14.8 Mshow makes it possible to give an online presentation complete with synchronized IP audio/video streaming, telephony, and animated graphics.

Expect your customers to want access via digital phone, personal digital assistant, wristwatch, and eyeglasses. What's that? Your data is available only via Internet Explorer 8? I'll be buying from your competitor who beeps my pager whenever there's a change in status of my order. They'll interrupt my car radio to tell me that my FedEx package has left the building in Memphis, and they'll have a digital butler call my shipping department the minute the signature is dry on the receiving papers to tell them to deliver that box to me at once.

Everybody Will Partner with Everybody

Do you want fries with that? Watch for cross-selling and upselling to get cross-channel and cross-category. You're buying a car. Do you want insurance, a three-year maintenance agreement, two years of car washes, a discount on a gasoline futures contract, and a parking space locator service with that?

Wouldn't Sun Microsystems like to know what Cisco Systems knows about you? Wouldn't a systems integrator like ICL like to know how much training ITC Learning Corporation has delivered in the past six months? Wouldn't Mobil Oil like to know your forklift maintenance records? Watch for large alliances of large companies to start trading information about you. Partnership potential is huge, given the ease with which information can be shared.

Feel the Difference, Smell the Coffee

Sight and sound just aren't enough anymore. If you want to feel your way around the Web, you can get the iFeel mouse from Logitech (www.logitech.com). It has a small, active weight inside that will rattle and hum as you bounce over buttons and slip in and out of active windows.

The SensAble PHANTOM (www.sensable.com) (see Figure 14.9) stops your finger cold when you're trying to push against a virtual object.

> 3D Touch technology makes working in 3D more natural, efficient and intuitive by allowing users to have continuous, two-way interaction with their work. Touch is the only "fully duplex" sense, enabling users to send and receive information at the same time. 3D Touch technology provides the ability to directly manipulate models and data, which means less time is spent setting parameters and more is spent working. Direct manipulation metaphors can also considerably reduce the learning curve required for professional 3D applications. Furthermore, touch interaction is inherently 3D. This means applications can eliminate the 2D buttons and sliders usually required to control view, cursor, and object editing in 3D.

For those who don't feel that feeling things conveys enough information about them, there's iSmell from Digiscents. In the first edition of this book, I included an April Fool's joke about the ScentMaster, a PC add-in board that uses chemicals to generate scents, from Idaho Computing. "The first olfactory or 'olaf' board," said the press release, "the $199 ScentMaster consists of a 16-bit board, three external chemical vials,

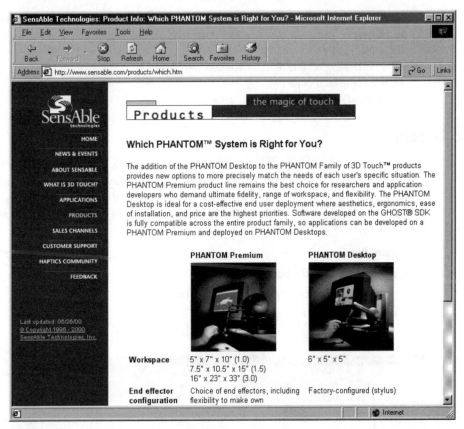

Figure 14.9   The PHANTOM lets you push, prod, poke, and press on things that aren't really there.

and a small spray-emitter module. The chemicals last up to six months and refills are $5.99 each."

"The scent board functions much like a sound card, interpreting files with an OLF extension. Instead of playing sounds, however, the ScentMaster mixes three chemicals (primary scents) to produce the desired effect."

Several years later, I find myself reading about the iSmell device.

How does it work?

The iSmell is a speaker-sized computer peripheral device that attaches to the serial or USB port of your personal computer and plugs into a standard electrical outlet. The iSmell emits naturally-based vapors into the user's personal space. The device is triggered either by user activation (like a mouse click) or a timed response (as is the case with a DVD ScentTrack). See the iSmell designs.

Why would I want digital scent technology?

Many reasons. To send and receive scented e-mail. To enjoy more lifelike and immersive interactive games and online entertainment. To enjoy your personal aromatherapy track while using your computer. To sample groceries, cosmetics, and home care products before purchasing on line. And for scented web sites.

Is this some kind of joke?

Well, it may be funny, but it's not a joke.

Body Scan

You may not be old enough to remember Jimmy Durante, but he used to say "Everybody wants to get into the act," and it's no different today. The only difference is the extent you want your body in the act. Not happy with the Land's End's My Virtual Model, you might feel that you have more in common with your Image Twin (www.imagetwin.com) (see Figure 14.10):

Apparel Retailers

- Direct customers to proper size of ready-to-wear apparel
- Reduce store and catalog returns due to incorrect size
- Increase customer loyalty

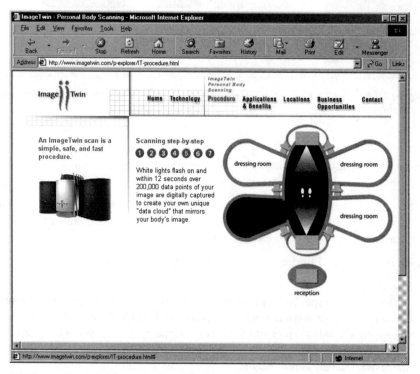

Figure 14.10 Walk into the booth, get scanned, and your data is shared on the Web.

- Reduce time for try-on
- Improve size inventory management
- Increase online shopping
- Improve consumer's confidence of receiving correct size

Apparel Manufacturers

- Produce better fitting clothes using improved measurement data
- Enhance pattern development
- Increase access to extensive database
- Create opportunity for mass customization

And what's in it for the consumer?

Apparel Consumers

- Select better fitting garments
- Order on line or via catalog with more confidence
- Save time from trying on
- Customize clothing
- Reduce hassles related to returns

For those of you who spotted the second benefit there, go to the head of the class.

Automated Comparison Shopping

Of course, when all of your likes, dislikes, shapes, and sizes are in one neat data package, your profile can be spread around the Web (under your control if the CPExchange has anything to say about it) (www.cpexchange.org).

So why should you have to shop for yourself at all? Cary Rosenzweig, Vice President of Marketing at mySimon (www.mysimon.com), will be happy to tell you about how the five stages of shopping (awareness, research, comparison shop, purchase, post-purchase services) can be managed by a software assistant named, that's right, mySimon.

"The first-generation shopping bots failed to give the buyer or the seller the value they were looking for. Those bots assumed the buyer was buying on price alone, and the seller didn't want to play the 'I'm cheaper than you' game so they set their servers to block the bots."

"mySimon understands brand value, and the retailers' brand messages become integral to the purchase decision. The *next* generation of shopping bots is going to extend beyond the research and comparison phase into awareness on the one side and negotiating and managing services on the other."

The Web is going to get to know you so well, you won't even need to be there.

Thought Control—With the Shoe on the Other Foot

Lest you worry that your life will be taken over by a Net Gone Mad, be assured that you can stop the wholesale abuse of your personal information and your wallet with a mere thought. Voice recognition? Who needs it? Log ins and passwords? A waste of time. You want to control the Web?

If you think you can, you can. And if you think you can't, you're right.

Mary Kay Ash

Melody Moore thinks you can—or at least, will be able to. Her paper called "A Research Agenda for Brain Computer Interfaces" (http://www.acm.org/sigs/conferences/assets00/assets00schedule.html) says controlling your computer with your mind is not science fiction any more (see Figure 14.11).

The way Melody tells it, it's quite believable. "A neurotrophic electrode—a tiny hollow glass cone fitted with gold wires—is inserted into the brain. The tip is coated with a substance that encourages brain cell growth. The brain cells (neurites—microscopic tentacles of neurons) grow up inside the cone and out the tip, holding the electrode in

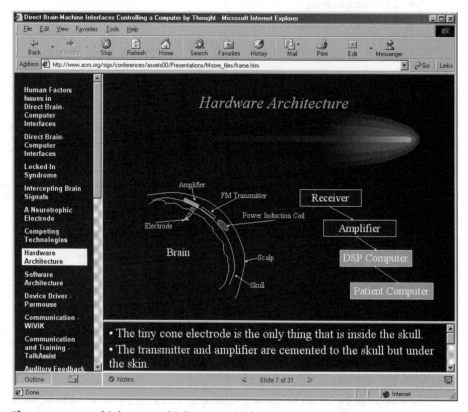

Figure 14.11   I think I can, I think I can, I think I can . . . move the mouse.

place. This gives it long-term stability which has been a big problem with other techniques. The signals are generated during imagined movements and translated into mouse movements on the computer screen."

A no-brainer.

And don't even get me started on bio-tech and nano-tech.

The World Wide Web is *still* in its infancy, but it is now showing signs of the adult it will come to be. Look just over the horizon at the competitive world of tomorrow and you'll see it at its logical extreme. You'll see customers demanding instantaneous intelligence about the status of their orders, your average of stock on hand, and your estimated time of delivery. They'll want to see their current balances and have online options about methods of payment. They'll want to review discussions your other customers have had about the good, the bad, and the ugly. Ubiquitous electronic data interchange and a terminal on every desk. The company with the most freely available information wins.

Customers will expect a feedback screen at every turn so they can speak their minds. They will expect prompt replies. The customers will become part of the process and, through their suggestions, help shape the process. Your whole company will be on display, and your customer will be part of the operations committee as well as the product planning council.

Make Your Mistakes Today

Pushing your Web site to the edge and a little beyond will help you and your company learn the intricacies of dealing with your public one-on-one. New procedures, new staffing, and new responses to old questions will all be a part of the learning process.

Make sure your best and brightest are at the heart of your experimentation. They will be leading the company into a new way of communicating with customers. They will be finding out what your customers want.

So, go surf the Web some more. Reassemble a team. Read some more books. Get some more tools. Rewrite your site style guide. Go upstairs and demand a larger budget so you can go make all the mistakes you need in order to be one of the survivors.

Above all, listen to what your customers want. All things considered, they're pretty smart.

WARNER MEMORIAL LIBRARY
EASTERN UNIVERSITY
ST. DAVIDS, 19087-3696